A Time to Heal

GS 1378

A Time to Heal

A Report for the House of Bishops
on the Healing Ministry

CHURCH HOUSE
PUBLISHING

Church House Publishing
Church House
Great Smith Street
London SW1P 3NZ

ISBN 0 7151 3837 5

Published 2000 for the House of Bishops of the General Synod of the Church of England by Church House Publishing.

Second impression 2000.

This report has only the authority of the Working Party who produced it.

Cover inset image: see acknowledgement on p. xii.
Cover design by Beatrice Brandon.
Printed by The Cromwell Press Ltd, Trowbridge, Wiltshire.

Contents

Contents

Foreword

The ministry of healing is one way in which the Church reaches out as part of its mission to the world, living out its commission from its gospel roots but in a way which is highly relevant to contemporary needs. There is a growing interest in the ministry of healing with it playing an ever-increasing – and dynamic – role in the life of many parishes.

The House of Bishops is grateful to the Bishop of Chelmsford and his Working Party for this timely report, which represents an important contribution to the Church's ministry in response to our Lord's injunction to heal the sick. I am happy to commend it for study and reflection, for action as appropriate in dioceses and parishes, and to all who are engaged in this vital part of the Church's pastoral ministry – often in partnership with others involved in healing and health care.

✠ George Cantuar

Membership of the Review Group

The Right Reverend John Perry

The Bishop of Chelmsford (Chairman)

The Right Reverend Dominic Walker OGS

The Bishop of Reading

Mrs Beatrice Brandon

General Synod member
and Researcher

The Reverend Canon John Gunstone

Former County Ecumenical Officer for
Greater Manchester and former Editor of
Healing and Wholeness

Professor Gareth Jones

Professor of Theology, Christ Church
University College, Canterbury

Dr David McDonald

Consultant Psychiatrist, Oxfordshire
Mental Health Care Trust and Home Office

Sister Hilary Markey CSMV

General Synod member,
Staff Member, Westminster Abbey

The Reverend Canon Dr Paul Nener FRCS

General Synod member,
Chairman of Liverpool Diocesan Healing
Panel
Sub-warden, Guild of St Raphael

Dr Althea Pearson

Chartered Counselling Psychologist
Psychologist in Primary Care NHS

The Reverend Michael Selman

Bishop of Exeter's Advisor on the Ministries
of Healing and Deliverance

The Reverend Canon Beaumont Stevenson

Psychotherapist, Chaplain
Oxfordshire Mental Health Care Trust
and Bishop of Oxford's Pastoral Care
Advisor

Dr Gareth Tuckwell

Director, London, Anglia and South East
England, Macmillan Cancer Relief and
former Director of Burrswood Christian
Centre for Health Care and Ministry

Assessors

The Reverend Malcolm Masterman

Hospital/Health Care Chaplaincy Training
and Development Officer

Secretary

Miss Jane Melrose

Church House, London

Mr Jonathan Neil-Smith

Secretary, The House of Bishops,
Church House, London

Preface

It would be true to say that all the members of the Review Group have welcomed the challenge that working on this report has brought. The varied expertise and experience so generously offered ensured that it was a constantly stimulating and enlightening journey together.

We also could not have done full justice to the report without the help of many outside the Group's membership. These have included the following:

> Mr Gerald Coates, the Right Reverend Graham Dow, Father David Gill, the Right Reverend George Hacker, the Reverend Paul Harris, Father Peter Hocken, the Reverend James Hollyman, the Right Reverend David Jenkins, Sister Margaret Mary SPB, the Reverend Michael Jones, the Reverend Ward Jones, Bishop Kallistos of Diokleia, Father Derek Lance, Canon Roy Lawrence, the Right Reverend Morris Maddocks, Dr Peter May, the Reverend James Needham, the Reverend Russ Parker, the Reverend Robert Payne, Canon John Peterson, Mr Edward Pinsent, the Reverend Brenda Russell, Canon Alan Wilkinson and the Reverend Valerie Woods.

In addition, we would want to express our gratitude for the time and goodwill shown by those who responded to the surveys, including the advisors from other denominations who generously shared their experience and who were eager to promote ecumenical partnership in the healing ministry. The London office of the Anglican Communion was most helpful in facilitating contact with other provinces of the Communion.

All the members of the Group contributed written material but, in particular, a special tribute is due to Mrs Beatrice Brandon and Canon John Gunstone for the immense commitment and energy that they have devoted to editing the report. Jonathan Neil-Smith and Jane Melrose from the Church House staff have also been a constant support to the Group.

No one involved in the Church's ministry of healing can fail to be confronted by the universal, inexplicable mystery of suffering. Moreover, whatever its causes, suffering is personal to us all in one form or another. As a group we often found ourselves wrestling with the questions it raises. We have responded to the need to address this issue by reflecting on the pastoral and practical responses to suffering, in collaboration with professional health care, and the opportunity for the Church to share the gracious gift of the ministry of healing.

A Time to Heal is offered as a contribution and resource to the Church's continuing ministry of healing in obedience to the commission of Jesus Christ to heal the sick. It is a gospel imperative!

✠ John Chelmsford

Chairman of the Review Group

Acknowledgements

The publisher gratefully acknowledges permission to reproduce copyright material in this publication. Every effort has been made to trace and contact copyright holders. If there are any inadvertent omissions we apologize to those concerned and will ensure that a suitable acknowledgement is made at the next reprint.

The Archbishops' Council: *Ministry to the Sick* (1983); *Lent, Holy Week, Easter* (1986); *Common Worship: Services and Prayers for the Church of England* (2000) and *Common Worship: Pastoral Services* (2000) are copyright © The Archbishops' Council and are reproduced by permission.

Cambridge University Press: Extracts from *The Book of Common Prayer*, the rights in which are vested in the Crown, are reproduced by permission of the Crown's Patentee, Cambridge University Press.

Hodder & Stoughton: Scripture quotations taken from the HOLY BIBLE, NEW INTERNATIONAL VERSION, Copyright © 1973, 1978, 1984 by International Bible Society. Used by permission of Hodder & Stoughton, a member of the Hodder Headline Group. All rights reserved. 'NIV' is a trademark of International Bible Society. UK trademark number 1448790.

The Division of Christian Education of the National Council of Churches in the USA: Scripture quotations from The New Revised Standard Version of the Bible © 1989 The Division of Christian Education of the National Council of Churches in the USA. Used by permission. All rights reserved.

Cover acknowledgement

On 23 January 1999, this image of a swirling disk of dust and gas surrounding a developing star called AB Aurigae was snapped by NASA's Hubble Space Telescope, showing unprecedented detail including clumps of dust and gas that may be the seeds of planet formation. Studying developing stars such as AB Aurigae, which is only 2 to 4 million years old and yet 2.4 times more massive than our Sun, could provide an evolutionary missing link in the planet formation process. We are grateful to NASA and Carol Grady of the National Optical Astronomy Observatories, for their help and for permission to use the image on the cover of this report and the associated handbook.

Introduction

The healing ministry is one of the greatest opportunities the Church has today for sharing the gospel. More than before in the last hundred years, many in our society realize there is a spiritual as well as a physical and a mental dimension to healthy living. 'Wholeness' is the in-word: it is what everyone longs for. The purpose of this Report is to encourage clergy and congregations in a wise and appropriate exercise of this ministry.

Three words have come to us as we have prepared this Report: **'visionary'**, **'prophetic'**, **'dynamic'**. The words came to us partly through what we have discovered in the course of our researches on what is happening in the Church and in society today, and partly through what we have learned of this ministry in the past.

We give thanks to God for those Christians in the past whose visionary, pioneering work was prophetic of what this ministry might become. And we also give thanks for the dynamic quality of their ministries – a dynamism reverberating with the authority of the kingdom of God. The Anglicans among them inherited the Church of England's traditional ministry to the sick, but as they practised it God seemed to be saying to them that there was more they could do. They obeyed him; and we are being called to that same obedience.

We are conscious that we were following in the footsteps of the earlier commission set up in 1953 by the Archbishops of Canterbury and York 'to consider the theological, medical, psychological and pastoral aspects of Divine Healing'. That commission's report was published in 1958 with the title, *The Church's Ministry of Healing.*[1] Its purpose was, said its authors, 'to guide the Church to clearer understanding of the subject; and in particular to help the clergy in the exercise of the ministry of healing and to encourage increasing understanding and cooperation between them and the medical profession' (p. 3).

In its way it is quite a historic document, for it was the first time members of the British Medical Association and of the Church of England had met officially to tackle such a subject together. Its 28 members included surgeons and matrons from London hospitals and professors from the medical departments of universities nominated by the BMA, while the Church of England was represented by five bishops, two deans, parish priests, hospital chaplains and one or two laity. The report was well received, and when it went out of print an abridged version was published in 1986 in which the editor, the Revd John Richards, commented, 'Of all the books on Christian healing being written today, none contains such concentrated wisdom as (this report)'.[2]

However, in the 40 years or so since its original publication, the healing ministry in this country has evolved considerably, particularly in the Church of England, for reasons we shall explain later. That is why a further review has been called for. But we should record that we owe much to the work done by the members of that earlier commission. They, too, glimpsed the vision of what the healing ministry might become.

The terms of reference we have been given by the House of Bishops are as follows:

> To assess the theological understanding and the state of the ministry of healing in the Church of England and to make recommendations as to its improved effectiveness, taking into account not only the activities of different groups within the Church but also of the ecumenical expression of this ministry.

Our Review Group is smaller in numbers than the earlier commission. Among us there are two bishops, several senior clergy, some with experience of working within the National Health Service, diocesan advisors on the ministries of healing and deliverance, a theologian, a consultant psychiatrist, a professional counsellor, a medical doctor specializing in hospice care, and two lay people including a religious sister. The Group first met in December 1998 and worked through until the autumn of 1999.

The different chapters were drafted by the Group working individually or in twos or threes. Whilst we worked together to develop a consensus on the content of the report and its recommendations, the expertise and experience within the group allowed us to provide an overview of the expression of this ministry from a wide range of approaches and interest within the Church and the health care professions. This variety of expression is reflected to some extent in the literary style of the individual chapters, but we would like to stress that the report has the support of every member of the Review Group. We have also shaped the report to enable its use in the medium to long term as a reference and resource book for a wide range of people, including clergy and laity within the Church of England and our ecumenical partners, health care professionals and those involved in training for ministry. Summaries are given at the start of each chapter for ease of reference. The footnotes for all the chapters may be found in the Notes section beginning on p. 388.

Today the word 'healing' is used describe all kinds of things, from acts of reconciliation and justice in nations and societies to what people hope for themselves as individuals, physically, mentally and spiritually. So there is talk of healing in race relations, in families, in institutions, among groups opposed to one another for economic, political, cultural or religious reasons, even the healing of the environment. In the ecumenical twentieth century we have also become familiar with the phrase, 'healing the wounds in the Body of Christ'.

These are themes which can be traced back to the Bible's own understanding of healing as salvation or wholeness not only for the individual but also for the nation, and indeed for the whole of God's creation. The World Council of Churches defined health in these terms in the report of its Christian Medical Commission: 'Health is a dynamic state of well-being of the individual and society, of physical, mental, spiritual, economic, political and social well-being – of being in harmony with each other, with the material environment and with God.'[3]

But what is special about Christian healing? Here we are helped by Bishop Morris Maddocks:

> Christian healing is, first and foremost, about Christ. It follows the pattern he set in his own ministry, and the commission he gave to his disciples, and the fact that it happens at all is the fruit of his work, both in the creation, and in the salvation of mankind. In both these mighty works, humankind has been created and recreated in the image of God – has been made whole. This is what distinguishes Christian healing from other types of healing. It is the whole work of Christ, in a person's body, mind and spirit, designed to bring that person to that wholeness which is God's will for us all.[4]

So far, so good. Yet this definition opens up an enormously wide field. At our first meeting, then, we decided that we were not required to discuss in great depth the social and environmental aspects of healing, nor to open up related debates on diverse and complicated ethical issues. Our terms of reference meant that we should focus on those who seek the Church's help when they are sick or distressed in body, mind or spirit, and this is what we have tried to achieve (though not ignoring these other aspects and issues when it seemed right to do so).

When we speak about the healing ministry in this report, then, we particularly refer to pastoral contacts, personal ministries or special services in which the focus is healing and wholeness through Jesus Christ. Such a ministry is the vocation of ordained clergy and suitable lay people in the Church. It is offered in prayerful settings, public services, sacramental celebrations or pastoral work. The use of prayer, sacraments, charisms and symbolic actions is thus always to be seen as part of the wider ministry of the Church; and the objective of such a ministry, offered in the name of Jesus Christ and in the power of the Holy Spirit, will usually be the wholeness of individuals, but ultimately it will be prayer for the healing and redemption of creation.

We set ourselves the goal of producing this report within twelve months so that the results of the research behind it would be as accurate and up-to-date as possible. The range of this research, as far as we are aware, is unique in this area. Nothing comparable has been done before, so it provides a benchmark against which the healing ministry can be measured in the future. The surveys and research, outlined in Appendix 6, were done on a strictly confidential basis; the replies were frank and revealed how many people within the healing ministry are concerned to see it wisely developed and more effectively resourced.

We are grateful for the time, consideration and goodwill of those who responded to the surveys. We are also grateful to those in other denominations who generously shared their information and experience and who are eager to promote ecumenical expressions of the healing ministry; what we have written about them is as up-to-date and as accurate as possible at the time of publication. However, as we collated the results of these surveys it became clear that far more could be said than what is contained in a report of this size. What we present is just a summary of the information available and the current state of the healing ministry. Several areas deserve more detailed research and review.

The surveys also showed that the healing ministry has continued to develop in the Church of England in recent years, but that there is still more to be done. Many clergy and laity need to be shown the wider implications of the healing ministry within the mission of the Church. There is need for more effective training and guidelines for good practice, with a common understanding of the theology and practical expression of this ministry. There is also need for an overall pastoring of it so that weak links are discovered, key issues raised by it addressed, and support given to clergy and laity involved in it.

Among those we contacted were the chaplains of numerous hospitals (now, we discovered, to be referred to as 'health care chaplains' in recognition of the fact that not all these priests are attached to hospital buildings). This led us to see how the Church's healing ministry is to be related to the incalculably valuable work of the National Health Service and other health and care agencies. We believe that we offer in Chapters 5 and 6 a theological as well as a practical basis for the further development of cooperation between the Church and the NHS.

That does not mean, however, that as Christians we necessarily endorse all that is done in the name of furthering health and care in these institutions. Not everything in research and practice is acceptable to the gospel of Jesus Christ. The Church sometimes has to be critical and issue warnings to conventional medicine. We have not had the time or the resources to enter into these extremely complex ethical issues (nor did our terms of reference indicate that we should), though occasionally we have had to touch on them in writing this report.

One part of our survey revealed the enormous growth in complementary medicine and alternative therapies. Although as Christians we may have serious doubts and reservations about many of these, nevertheless their popularity is something we cannot ignore. We need to learn something of what they teach and practise, partly to appreciate the reasons why people are attracted to them and partly to be able to advise those who seek our guidance about them.

Our terms of reference instructed us to take into account 'not only the activities of different groups within the Church but also of the ecumenical expression of this ministry'. This was an enlightening experience. As we listened to or read about different approaches to the healing ministry, particularly those outside our Anglican fellowship, we realized how much there is to learn from others. Our common experience of the healing ministry knows no barriers. It is significant that where some Churches Together and other ecumenical groups share in the healing ministry, they discover a new unity in the Holy Spirit.

We hope that this report will encourage all Anglicans to embrace what is sometimes called 'the full gospel' – that is, the gospel preached with the hope of healing – so that it may become central to our mission, preached and exercised in ways that are both faithful to Jesus Christ and appropriate for the culture of our time. For what our terms of reference call 'its improved effectiveness' is nothing less than this.

1

The Church's Ministry of Healing: A Century of Recovery

Throughout the twentieth century individuals and groups have been urging the Church of England to exercise a more dynamic healing ministry through sacramental and charismatic gifts. The Report of the 1958 Commission marked an important step in the Church's response to this. Since then, other factors in society's search for health, as well as developments in the Church herself, make a further report necessary. Yet in spite of these changes the heart of the healing ministry remains the same: prayer in the name of Jesus Christ.

How come you know Jesus and you no heal nobody?

The Sioux Indian Christian received no answer from his audience of American priests. We may smile tolerantly at what we regard as his simplistic reading of the biblical narratives. Yet his question leaves an uneasy feeling that we might be missing something. It cannot be easily brushed aside. Should we be doing more to fulfil Jesus Christ's commission to his disciples, 'Go preach . . . go heal'?[1]

Scholars tell us that in biblical theology there is a close connection between 'healing', 'salvation' and 'wholeness'; and in present-day English 'healing' is used to mean anything from recovering from an illness to the complex process whereby individuals, communities and societies are brought into more harmonious relationship with one another. In other words it involves a fourfold relationship: to the good earth beneath our feet (our physical environment), to other people (our living and human environment), to ourselves (a right ordering of our inner life), and to God (the source of all our being).

Pastoral theologians claim, with justification, that the Church of England is constantly engaged in this ministry through what she does in dioceses, parishes and chaplaincies as well as what is done by, and with, other Christian denominations and organizations. Furthermore, the care of the sick has always been a major pastoral concern. Visits, prayers at the bedside, intercessions in church services and practical acts of care and kindness – these have been, and still are, ways in which the Church of England ministers to the sick. But how does this relate to Jesus' ministry?

Some argue that Scripture has to be read in the light of the age and culture in which the authors lived: in those days miracles were commonly associated with stories of great leaders and therefore we must accept that the miracles of the New Testament are, if not legendary, probably based on the scrappiest of historical fact. Others claim that the healings are historically true because the New Testament era was one in which God gave the apostles a special dispensation to perform signs and wonders, powers which he withdrew once that era had passed. Many others hover between these views.

Yet even today stories persist of remarkable physical healings through the Church's ministry, especially overseas, and even after making allowance for the tendency of tales to be improved in the telling, the anecdotal evidence is impressive. When our friends tell of healings that seem worthy of the adjective 'miraculous', we find it difficult to assume they are always exaggerating.

The *vision* of a Church in which Jesus Christ is present fulfilling his preaching and healing commission 'with signs following' still comes to Christian men and women now as it has done in every age. At the beginning of the last (twentieth) century Anglican men and women were among those who were moved by that vision to exercise a *prophetic* role in reviving the ministry of healing in the Church of England. The impetus for their work was the faith that Christ's 'touch had still its ancient power'. They were instruments of the Holy Spirit in reviving a more *dynamic* ministry to the sick, but in different ways. For our purposes we will select a few of the better-known personalities, but remembering that during those years there were others like them.

The revival of the sacramental ministry

One initiative was a fresh revival of a more sacramental ministry to the sick through anointing with laying on of hands, sometimes after a private confession of sin to a priest. Among those who pioneered this revival were F. W. Puller ssje, Percy Dearmer and Charles Harris, priests of a broadly Anglo-Catholic outlook who believed that the Church of England should be encouraged to restore the Church's practices of James 5.14-16 and of the patristic centuries.

In *Anointing of the Sick in Scripture and Tradition* (1904) Puller argued for the restoration of anointing as a sacramental means by which God's healing grace is received. Dearmer supported Puller's advocacy and provided a liturgical form of a healing service with anointing in the 1907 edition of his widely read *The Parson's Handbook*. Harris, who claimed in a speech to the Convocation of Canterbury in 1931 that he had 'anointed and laid hands on thousands of people during the last twenty-five years', wrote a long essay on anointing and laying on hands in *Liturgy and Worship* (SPCK 1932), which became a standard textbook for generations of Anglican ordinands and which was reprinted several times in the middle decades of the century.[2]

The campaign by Anglo-Catholics for the right of parish priests to reserve the eucharistic bread and wine (or more often just the bread) was successful because, as a result of their teaching, increasing numbers of sick parishioners wanted to receive communion regularly at home or in hospital. The 1928 Revised Prayer Book laid down regulations for this.

The formation of organizations like the Guild of St Raphael encouraged the use of anointing the sick; the Guild published prayer manuals and teaching materials to assist parishes engaged in this ministry. Other organizations included the Guild of Health, the Divine Healing Mission and the Order of St Luke (founded in 1947 in the Episcopal Church of the USA). Such groups helped to spread the practice of using blessed oil as a sacramental sign of healing rather than as a preparation for death as it had been in the Roman Catholic Church since the early Middle Ages.[3] Nowadays anointing has become so common in the Church of England that few regard it as being distinctively Anglo-Catholic any more.

The impact of psychology

In early decades of the twentieth century the study and practice of psychology impinged on the Church's consciousness. Medical experts had been discussing for years the effect of the mind on the well-being of the physical body. The phrase 'mind over matter' was commonly used. Then Sigmund Freud's 'new psychology' came into circulation. Psychologists in general and Freud in particular were regarded with suspicion by most Anglicans; their theories seemed to rob people of a sense of sin and personal responsibility. Added to that, the popular press carried reports and advertisements about the activities of all kinds of entrepreneurs, from spiritualists to hypnotists, who advertised their claims to heal (often for a fee). Church leaders were sure that they should not be involved in practices which looked anything like that.

But the traumas suffered by men returning from the horrors of the First World War gradually caused some in the Church to recognize the need for a special ministry to those who were emotionally and mentally troubled. The Modernists were among the first to see ways of applying the lessons of the new psychology to pastoral care, and they were cautiously followed by some Anglo-Catholics. G. A. Studdert Kennedy, 'Woodbine Willie', revealed in his lectures and writings after the war that he was aware of the psychological as well as the social factors in illness.[4] G. C. Rawlinson, a curate of St Barnabas, Pimlico, for most of his ministry a noted spiritual director, assumed in his addresses that his audience would be familiar with basic psychological concepts.[5] And in his magisterial work on Christian spirituality, *The Vision of God*, the 1928 Bampton Lectures, Kenneth E. Kirk, later Bishop of Oxford, discussed the role of psychology in the confessional and in the debate about the active and contemplative Christian lifestyles.[6] But it was the Methodist Leslie Weatherhead who did most to popularize a Christian approach to psychology from the 1930s onwards. He was much sought after as a counsellor and lecturer, and his books were widely read.

Personalities

Another feature of the ministry of healing in these decades was the emergence of particular individuals who taught and practised the healing gifts of the Spirit. In the 1920s the most famous of these among Anglicans was

James Moore Hickson, who had a notable healing ministry and founded the Divine Healing Mission. He so impressed Randall Davidson that the archbishop arranged for a copy of Hickson's pamphlet, *The Healing Ministry of Christ in His Church*, to be sent to all the bishops assembled for the 1920 Lambeth Conference.[7] As a result the bishops, after noting the spread of 'Spiritualism, Christian Science and Theosophy', urged 'the recognition of the Ministry and gifts of healing in the Church, and that these should be exercised under due licence and authority'. The following year Hickson embarked on a world tour which took him to most parts of the Anglican Communion.

Dorothy Kerin, William Wood ('Brother Bill') and George Bennett were three others of a small but growing company of those who ministered to the sick through prayer, laying on hands and anointing in the period before and after the Second World War.

Dorothy Kerin (1889–1963) was amazingly healed after prayer when she was near death at the age of 22. She developed a healing ministry in and around London, then after the war she purchased Burrswood near Tunbridge Wells as a home of healing. She wrote: 'We have come to know that with God – our living God – nothing is impossible, and for those who have eyes to see and ears to hear the message is still true, "I am the Lord that healeth thee." His arm is not shortened, his power is not less than in those days two thousand years ago when he walked among us healing all who came to him.'[8] Like Harris and others, she believed that in neglecting the ministry of healing the Church had allowed spiritualists and others to steal that work from them.

William Wood, 'Brother Bill' (b. 1903), an Australian priest, came to England in 1937 'to learn more about Jesus and his healing ministry'. First as warden of the London Healing Mission and then as chaplain of the Order of St Luke, he promoted this ministry through his teaching, conferences and newsletters. Perhaps the first Anglican priest to be influenced by the charismatic renewal in this country, he combined a sacramental and a Pentecostal approach to a remarkable degree. 'Personally I can no longer minister to the sick in the name of Jesus Christ and withhold my witness to Jesus as the Lamb of God and the Baptizer in the Holy Spirit,' he said.[9]

George Bennett (1910–78) trained as a medical student. Later in life he was ordained and his healing ministry developed out of his experience as a hospital chaplain, as a canon of Coventry Cathedral, and as warden of the Divine Healing Mission. He was responsible for moving the Mission's headquarters to Crowhurst in East Sussex and he travelled extensively on healing missions until his death. He realized the evangelistic power of this ministry. Describing any priest who introduces his congregation to the practice, he said, 'His people are finding the glory of Christ through this ministry far more widely and more deeply than they could ever possibly have done when the Gospel was limited in its proclamation to speech alone.'[10]

In *Liturgy and Worship* Harris, commenting on Paul's 'gifts of healing' (1 Corinthians 12.28,30) wrote (p. 482):

> It is probable that in our age (they) are diffused somewhat widely among the devout laity. They are the endowment, either natural or acquired, of those who feel a special sympathy with the sick, and for that reason have experienced a vocation to minister to them. Devout physicians and nurses often possess such gifts to a high degree. But such lay ministrations, to prevent confusion, ought to be coordinated under proper spiritual authority. In a well-organised parish, there is no room for the eccentricities of irresponsible 'faith-healers'.

Official response

The Church of England gradually responded to these developments by providing further liturgical services for ministry to the sick. On Harris's initiative, the Convocation of Canterbury, after several years of debate (and opposition from Bishop Barnes of Birmingham, who called the proposal a 'retrograde step towards religious barbarism'), accepted a form for the *Administration of Holy Unction and the Laying On of Hands* in 1935 for 'provisional use in the Province subject to due diocesan sanction'. A similar form was accepted by the Convocation of York the following year.[11]

The Churches' Council for Health and Healing (CCHH) was founded in 1944 with William Temple's support. From his days as Bishop of Manchester Temple, who suffered from gout for most of his life, had been interested in the healing ministry. 'You cannot', he said to his diocesan conference in 1924, 'read the Gospels and cut out the ministry of healing without tearing them to ribbons . . . [Nor can you] draw a sharp line between what is physical and what is mental. The two merge into each other in most baffling ways.'[12] The purpose of the CCHH was to enable members of different denominations to bring together their experiences of the healing ministry, to reflect on those experiences theologically and to involve the medical profession in these exercises.

These, then, were the developments in the Church of England and beyond which led to the setting up of the Archbishops' Commission in 1953. Had it not been for the Second World War, and Temple's untimely death, it would probably have been set up ten or more years earlier. But when their report was published in 1958 it was widely welcomed, and within its limitations it is still today a useful pastoral guide.

The 1958 report

The Commission focused its attention on the roles of the Church and of the medical profession in healing the sick. For this reason the members emphasized both sides in the healing ministry. They refused to use the phrase 'faith healing' because they regarded it as imprecise and liable to misconceptions: faith in God is indeed necessary to salvation (which is health in the fullest sense of the word), but the phrase might lead people to assume that a cure comes through faith in a healer or faith in a particular process of recovery. 'Spiritual healing' was also ruled out for similar reasons: restoration to health is truly the work of the Holy Spirit, but in the popular mind the expression is either associated with the influence of 'spirit worlds' on invalids, or used to exclude physical healing. The Commission agreed 'divine healing' was more acceptable (it was used in their terms of reference) but they avoided it because they felt it implied there were sources of true healing which were not from God. They settled for the simple 'ministry of healing' and defined it as follows (p. 14):

> This ministry is an integral part of the Church's total work by which men and women are to become true sons and daughters of God's kingdom. In it are to be employed all the means God has put at our disposal; the administration of Word and Sacraments; the exercise of pastoral care; and the employment of all the many gifts of special kinds which God has given to individuals. Among the latter the skill and knowledge of those who have given

themselves to the discipline of medical and nursing training are by no means the least.

After defining their terms the Commission briefly discussed healing in the New Testament and the problem of evidence for healing. There is a long chapter on 'some common misconceptions', including the role of faith in healing and the notion that sickness is always caused by sin. There is sensible advice on visiting the sick and then, surprisingly in view of how uncommon they were in Anglican churches at that time, guidelines on how to organize services of prayer for healing. Dorothy Kerin, Brother Bill and Leslie Weatherhead were among those who gave evidence to the Commission so perhaps these guidelines were included as a result of their advice. A chapter on cooperation between the clergy and the medical and nursing professions followed, though only two paragraphs on cooperation with psychiatrists. Finally the Commission added appendices on services for the sick (with a liturgical text), exorcism, Christian Science and Spiritualism with the comment (p. 84):

> The Commission believes that the parish priest would be failing in his duty if he did not point out that the claim to healing power (by Christian Science practitioners or Spiritualist healers) involves beliefs which are difficult or impossible to reconcile with the gospel as received and taught in the Church of England, or indeed in the main tradition of Christianity.

The report gave some impetus to the ministry of healing. Both Houses of the Canterbury Convocation, in accepting and commending the report, requested the archbishop to refer the 1935 Canterbury service of unction to the Liturgical Commission for possible revision, and the Lambeth Conference of 1958 made suggestions about the reform of the visitation office: it should be called the 'ministry to the sick' and should include forms for the laying on of hands, anointing, Holy Communion, confession and absolution and a commendation of the dying.

Although, as we have said, this report was quite forward-looking, there have been developments in the Church and in society since 1958 which have made a further report desirable. In every generation Christians have to seek the guidance of the Holy Spirit in determining what it means for them to respond to Christ's commission to preach the gospel and heal the sick, and the 40 or so years since the publication of the previous report have seen developments which affect the way in which we minister today.

Developments since 1958

In England, as in Western society generally, there is an enormous interest in and concern with personal health. Not that previous generations were less concerned. Rather, it is that today many ordinary people are more aware of what is involved in keeping healthy, and they are also more aware of what therapies are available for different diseases. Healthy living is at the top of most people's personal agenda. The media – newspapers, magazines, TV and radio programmes – are full of information on the latest threats to the nation's health and the availability of alternative therapies. Soap operas on TV convey snippets of medical information – often misleadingly. Doctors complain that some of the patients in the surgery are liable to tell them what their problem is and suggest what their treatment should be before any examination has taken place.

The National Health Service offers a prospect of healing for many and care for all. Any political party has not only to assure the electorate that the NHS is safe in its hands – it must also explain how it will improve the Service if it wants its candidates to win parliamentary seats. Proposals for the closure of popular local hospitals are vigorously opposed and contested in court – sometimes successfully. Schemes for private medical insurance abound. Everyone assumes they have a right to a long and healthy life, and to speedy correct treatment – the issue of the *Patient's Charter* reinforcing that conviction. But some people find coming to terms with ill health and sudden disability very difficult and, if they fear they have not received appropriate treatment, a few do not hesitate to charge hospitals with negligence or ineptitude and seek compensation through the courts. The increase of this kind of litigation is indicative of the change in people's expectations about their health which has taken place in the years since the 1958 report.

Along with this interest in and concern for personal health there has arisen an astonishing array of complementary medicine and alternative therapies. Our research for this report has revealed that the market for this is huge and growing. It seems as if many are either dissatisfied with scientific medicine, or are instinctively seeking a form of healing which will meet deeper needs they hardly understand. Some of these approaches are linked with what have come to be known as New Age practices, but others take their inspiration from the treatment of illness in other cultures and the practices of earlier centuries.

A secularist might say that recent developments in the Church's ministry of healing are just another such alternative therapy in the 'get-well-quickly market'. But many in the Church recognize in the growth of complementary medicine and alternative therapies something more profound than that: among the men and women of this highly secular society there is a longing for a spiritual dimension to healing which scientific medicine cannot supply. Indeed, however we interpret the phrase 'holistic medicine', overall it is an acknowledgement that men and women are not healed by drugs and surgery alone. That is a truth which has long been recognized by most doctors – especially Christian ones – and by spiritual directors centuries before the phrase was invented.

There has been, too, an enormous growth in psychology, psychiatry and counselling. Some of this is because individuals want to understand themselves more intelligently and achieve a more balanced outlook on life. Some is the result of the stress of modern living with attendant mental as well as physical problems. Emotional dis-ease lies behind many illnesses. The breakdown of relationships in marriages, families and other human groups strains the well-being of those involved. Drug addiction and alcoholism, the abuse of the human body and mind, and the prevalence of crime, violence and racism are signs of a deep-rooted sickness in our local and national life.

All these are factors which have led the Church in recent days to seek how to minister with all that psychology can offer. The former hostility towards it has almost gone. In the 1950s and 1960s, Frank Lake and his brother were invited to run what they called 'clinical theology' courses for the clergy, often as a follow-on from post-ordination training, and this did much to dispel ignorance and reduce misunderstandings. Christopher Bryant SSJE among others helped many to see the relevance of psychology in personal prayer and spiritual direction.

During these years the Church of England along with other denominations has grasped more fully the truth that the ministry of healing is an integral part of her mission, not just one aspect of pastoral care. We have come to recognize that the healings of Jesus Christ were more than demonstrations of divine compassion: they were outward and visible signs of the coming of the kingdom he proclaimed. The members of the earlier Commission realized this (see the quotation from their report on page 18) They were reflecting the teaching of the biblical students of those days, but it has taken a generation or so for clergy and congregations to begin to act on this belief by bringing their healing ministries more to the forefront of their mission.

In the years immediately after the Second World War very few parishes organized services of prayer for healing. Those who belonged to the Guild of St Raphael met regularly for the guild office (their own special service) and ministered to individuals privately. Other groups did something similar, but acts of worship in which individuals came forward publicly for prayer with laying on of hands were considered very un-Anglican. Such practices were regarded as belonging to the Pentecostal churches.

Now a significant number of congregations regularly arrange such services. Prayer for healing is offered to individuals during or after the usual Sunday liturgy. The laying on of hands is widely used, sometimes with anointing. Counselling of various kinds is available in many parishes. The ministry of deliverance is practised in some. And, most notable of all, increasing numbers of the laity are involved – though it has to be said that, as far as we can determine, very few are properly trained or formally commissioned.

Recent years have seen the appointment of diocesan advisors and the provision of training courses for the ministry of healing and counselling in some dioceses. This is a significant development for it tries to bring this ministry into the diocesan structures instead of leaving it in the hands of enthusiasts.

A valuable contribution to the healing ministry was made by Bishop Morris Maddocks, who with his wife, Anne, founded the Acorn Christian Healing Trust and established its headquarters at Whitehall Chase in Bordon, Hampshire, as a centre for ministry and training. As advisor to the Archbishops of Canterbury and York for the ministry of healing, he has done much through his teaching and writing to encourage the Church of England to learn from what has been happening in the wider Christian community and to engage in this ministry more expectantly.

Another important factor in the past 30 or so years has been the charismatic movement, which more than anything has given an impetus to the ministry in certain parishes. The movement awoke in many an awareness that they can be equipped by God through a fresh renewal in the Holy Spirit to minister in Jesus' name. As a result of their encounter with

Pentecostal spirituality, Anglican laity as well as clergy (like charismatics in other denominations) began to pray for others with a sense of expectancy that spiritual gifts of healing will be manifested. True, there have been excesses in a few cases, but there have been many gifts and blessings as well. With this has come a greater appreciation of the Church as a fellowship in which the Spirit acts with power; the Body of Christ with an every-member-ministry.

The charismatic movement has also been largely responsible for reminding the Church that when we pray 'deliver us from evil' in the Lord's Prayer we are seeking protection from spiritual forces. This is an area where the inexperienced and insensitive can create endless trouble by failing to discern what is spiritual and what is mental at the root of an individual's distress. The Church of England has been rightly cautious in her approach to this ministry, though that caution has been interpreted by some of her members as a disinterested rejection of its validity, causing them to seek help outside her structures.

The years since the publication of the 1958 report have also witnessed a multiplication of what are usually termed 'homes of healing' in the country. Burrswood was one of the first (and still highly respected), and others have been established. They vary in character and size. Some are staffed by a resident community, others by two or three Christian leaders with a team of outside helpers. Some provide mini-breaks for short-term care; others have regular services of prayer for healing, counselling facilities and training programmes. They are almost all ecumenical in approach if not in their foundation. Since most of them are organized as privately sponsored charities, they are outside the jurisdiction of the main denominations, through some of them have chaplains licensed by the bishop. The new charity laws have given greater responsibility to the trustees of charities, and this has made it possible for the trustees of such homes of healing to oversee them more closely.

Healing also appears regularly in the programmes of such places as Lee Abbey and Scargill, and in conferences and holiday weeks such as Spring Harvest and New Wine. Those who have been helped at such events – including large numbers of Anglican clergy and laity – have returned home longing for this ministry to become a normal part of their church life.

Finally, many organizations in the UK and in different parts of the world are engaged in health and healing issues, including the World Health Organization (WHO), government bodies such as the Department of Health, and independent groups such as the National Schizophrenia Fellowship. These organizations carry out exercises and produce reports from time to time in related areas. For example, the Health Education Authority has published *Promoting Mental Health: The Role of Faith Communities – Jewish and Christian Perspectives*,[13] and the Mental Health Foundation *The Courage to Bare Our Souls*,[14] a collection of pieces written by people with mental health problems. There have also been for many years experiments to assess the effectiveness of intercessory prayer on recovery from ill health (see page 215).

However, interesting though much of this material is, any detailed study of it would take us outside the terms of reference for this report. With limited time and resources, we have chosen to concentrate on the healing ministry in the Church of England and in our ecumenical partners and the relationship of that ministry to those in professional health care. We mention this material here simply to note that research and reports like these have some relevance – if only marginal – to the way in which the Church has thought about and practised her ministry to the sick in recent years.

A work of the Holy Spirit and a ministry of prayer

These, then, are some of the reasons why a further report has been called for. Yet we must not exaggerate the differences these changes have made. The Church's ministry of healing remains a charismatic work of the Holy Spirit through sacramental and non-sacramental means. The sacramental means include baptism and the Eucharist, confession and absolution, anointing, and laying on of hands. The non-sacramental means include intercession, friendship, forgiveness, acceptance, active listening, counselling and psychiatry, nursing and medical care, and healing of emotions and memories.

But if the Church's ministry of healing includes ordinary human relationships such as friendship and listening, what is the difference between this ministry and that of secular agencies such as the National Health Service? We do not want to draw too rigid a line between them; we reject the notion of some Christians that God's healing power is located only in extraordinary 'signs and wonders'.

The difference is to be found in the expectations and faith of those involved. In secular agencies those who study and work for healing focus on creation in the belief that if the human creature is treated properly, we can in many cases alleviate and sometimes cure completely an individual's sickness. The sole objective is to enhance the quality of life of the patient as far as is possible in those circumstances. Continuing illness and then death may be regarded as a failure. 'We don't like losing a patient,' says the hospital receptionist kindly, when the family collect the belongings of a relative who has died on one of the wards.

Christians, on the other hand, minister to the sick in the expectation and faith that Jesus Christ, who came to save and to heal us, continues to do this through the Church in the power of the Holy Spirit. They recognize that much of that healing comes through medical and nursing care, even the care of those who do not acknowledge him. But they also believe that healing involves more than the alleviation of physical symptoms and the quieting of psychological problems. And continuing illness and then death, painful and tragic though these may be, can be means through which we share in the saving death and resurrection of Christ.

In other words, the difference is that the Christian ministry of healing is rooted in prayer, whereas secular healing agencies are rooted solely in human achievements. But the boundary can be blurred. Believers or unbelievers, whoever shows genuine care and compassion towards those who are sick reflects something of the love of God. And when a Christian doctor prays silently before he or she enters his surgery in the morning, or a Christian nurse intercedes quietly as he or she holds the hand of a dying patient, there is a manifestation of the Church's healing ministry.

So, then, it is Christian prayer – with all that implies in terms of relationships with God and with each other – that marks the difference. We pray with faith because we believe that God gives gifts of wholeness to body, mind and spirit. However, we also believe that what he desires most of all is our ever closer relationship with him, which may include a deeper share in the sufferings of Christ. It is worth recalling that eucharistic prayers usually end with the traditional ascription 'through Jesus Christ our Lord, by whom, and with whom, and in whom, in the unity of the Holy Spirit'. Those phrases are also fitting at the conclusion of any prayer for healing.

Prayer can only be offered because Christ first offered himself as a sacrifice for us. That is why we say *by whom*. We say *with whom* because we believe we join with Jesus in his continuous intercession for us (Romans 8.34), and *in whom* because our prayer is united with the prayers of Christ in his Body, the Church.

Although the focus of such prayer is on Jesus because it is his healing ministry which inspires and authorizes the Church's, it is prayer within the mystery of the Holy Trinity. Indeed, the revival of the healing ministry has been inspired by a prophetic and dynamic vision of the love and purposes of God the Father, Son and Holy Spirit for us. We explore this further in the next chapter.

2

Healing in the Scriptures
and Tradition

The Christian faith confesses that God was in Christ, and that this
was manifested throughout his healing ministry. We argue that
Christ's ministry was *visionary, prophetic* and *dynamic*, and that
these three qualities help us understand how and why God brings
healing to his creation. Moreover, by identifying Christ as pastor,
sacrament and charismatic, we draw attention to the belief that God's
visionary, prophetic and dynamic presence is made personal in Jesus
Christ, his Son our Lord.

Introduction

Everyone knows the harsh reality of suffering. Either personally or
through witnessing the unfortunate experiences of others, we all know
what it is to suffer. It is that part of the human condition, as philosophers
might say, which unites everyone in knowledge and understanding, sympathy and commitment. Much more than philosophical concepts, however, suffering brings us up short, thrusting us into direct and immediate
contact with the world. We cannot escape suffering, as we might try to
escape so many other things, without losing part of our humanity.

God knows that people suffer in this way. He witnesses our suffering,
calling us away from despair, towards hope. But his call is not always
heard, and people do not always escape from suffering. The history of the
world is full of people whom, it appears, God abandoned to their
spiritual deafness. We all know what it is to feel horror and outrage at
unspeakable tragedies. We all know what it is to feel anger at God's
apparent inability to prevent innocent suffering. We all know, in short,

16

what it is to call upon God's compassion, only to feel loss at the apparent silence and the void. This is part of the human condition that we all suffer and endure. And yet there is a Word spoken by God that answers this anger and frustration, though it is not always straightforward to understand Jesus Christ, his mission and his message, in this way.

One should not forget, however, that the Christian faith begins with the life of a man like us who lived in Palestine nearly two thousand years ago. Jesus of Nazareth went abroad among his fellow men and women, carrying the mission and message of God's redemption for all those who repent and believe. Over the centuries after Jesus' time, but starting with the apostles, the Church attempted to make sense of God's participation in Jesus' life. Again and again believers returned to the same point: God was in Jesus Christ. Not 'with', or 'alongside', or 'by', or 'above', but *in*: God was in Jesus Christ and therefore in all of his actions and words, his healing miracles and his parables of the kingdom.

Today, quite properly and meaningfully, the Church speaks of the doctrine of the Incarnation as God's being in Christ, and we all understand by this the mystery of faith, namely that God and humanity are one in Jesus of Nazareth. It is easy to forget, however, the drama and tragedy of Jesus' story, easy to reduce it to the kind of conceptual acrobatics that theologians love but which fail to move other Christians. When we speak of the Father and the Son, and when we speak of the Father sending the Son into the world, we must never forget that the Son was sent to be crucified, and that the cross was plunged into the very midst of the world before, victorious, the Son was raised and ascended in the power of the Holy Spirit. We must never forget this, because God's story is our story, for the same Spirit who was poured out on the first disciples at Pentecost is present with us in power today.

This emphasis on story, and thereby upon the continuity that links our time to Jesus' time two thousand years ago, brings with it another quality. In the 1958 report, *The Church's Ministry of Healing*, these words conclude the pivotal second chapter, on healing in the New Testament (p. 21):

> To the Church, then, as the Body of Christ and as the community through which the Holy Spirit works, command is given to heal the sick. Works of healing in the context of the Church's ministry throughout the ages are signs of the Kingdom of God to

17

those who have eyes to see. Each such act of healing is a direct, personal and creative act of God in fulfilment of his eternal purpose.

There are many points here that will need to be discussed in this present chapter. One of the most important, however, is the conviction that when we speak of the kingdom of God, and when we tell Jesus' story, we are not speaking of events that were completed and closed many years ago. On the contrary, *the story is not yet over.* Until the Son's return with glory and judgement, all faith, all hope, all love are provisional. We live *towards* the future, towards eternity, not backwards towards the past. And the story we confess, the story in which we participate, is one of movement, of freshness, of vigour, of health and – above all – of the Holy Spirit, for it is by the Holy Spirit that Jesus continues his saving and healing work among us, his Body, his Church.

For this reason, we have decided in this present report not to repeat the somewhat dispassionate account of Christ's ministry in the New Testament that one finds in the 1958 text. On the contrary, in concentrating upon the healing ministry of Jesus, we are trying to say something meaningful about his entire work; about God's will in becoming human, as we confess our faith in that same will. For Christ did not heal simply because it was something good and decent to do. Rather, Christ healed because healing itself was central to the proclamation of the new creation (2 Corinthians 5.17), into which we are all called as we repent and believe. This is the work of the Holy Spirit, and it is a healing work, the work of redemption.

Vision

When Jesus was baptized in the waters of the river Jordan, therefore (Mark 1.8f), and the Holy Spirit descended upon him, God inaugurated a ministry of healing that was to change the world. This baptism was an epiphany, a revelation of God's will, the seeds of a ministry and a life that were to change the world. It was a ministry that was *visionary*, because it called people towards a glimpse of the kingdom, the hope of creation renewed in perfect health and wholeness. It was a ministry that was *prophetic*, because it called people to renew their relationship with God and the world, to seek forgiveness and thereby a new beginning. And it was a ministry that was *dynamic*, because in it Jesus was proclaiming his unity with the world until the end of time. When people pray for help, for comfort, for health, they pray to God in, through and with Jesus Christ. And he is always here, responding to our deepest needs.

What, though, did people see when they saw Jesus Christ, saw him proclaim the kingdom with parables and healing? Of course, we cannot know for certain; but what we must say is that they saw a real man, for that is the Christian faith. The doctrine of the Incarnation, consequently, is central to our understanding of Jesus' healing ministry: 'The first principle, which is none the less important for being obvious, is that the human body matters'.[1] In becoming fully human, God revealed the depth of his love for the world, taking up humanity in all of its limitation in order to redeem it. Doctrinally, this event is called *kenosis*, a word that derives from St Paul's great hymn in Philippians 2. It means God emptied himself of divine power, in order to become human. And this is what Jesus is: the Son of God, healing the world, and yet one of us.

This epiphany, in which we find the seeds of Jesus' entire life and purpose, unto death and resurrection, is God's great work of compassion. That compassion is not revealed conceptually, or theoretically, but rather palpably, physically, intensely. Jesus comes into the midst of the world and heals *with his hands*. There are numerous stories to document this part of Jesus' ministry, so that we have no excuse to miss the important point: in touching people's lives with power and feeling, Jesus healed them by God's love. Whether blind or lame, leper or paralytic, Jesus embraced their physical condition totally and without limit. The healing ministry of which we speak, therefore, is not something that is 'done' to people, as if it could be transmitted by divine communication (perhaps a kind of telepathy). Rather, the healing ministry is a revelation of atonement – at-one-ment – in which Christ takes suffering into him, healing through his very being. Those who are healed are made new, because One – Christ – takes upon him their old life.

Why was such a ministry of atonement necessary? In a word, because of sin: 'He treated sickness and sin as different expressions of the one supreme evil in humanity, that evil whose overthrow was possible now that the Kingdom of God was at hand.'[2] This sin was all pervasive. It was not something that could be stepped over and ignored, as if it only affected a few people at life's margins. The suffering of those people might be the signs of the presence of evil in the world, but their misfortune could never simply be reduced to a matter of fault and punishment. On the contrary, they suffered for a far greater reason: they suffered because the world had fallen away from its true relationship with God. If we think of this situation in terms of the idea of vision, we can say that God could no longer be seen in the world. People's sight, physical and spiritual, was blighted by sin.

As well as being a ministry of inauguration, therefore, Jesus' healing ministry was also one of the restoration of vision. Jesus came into the world, and it was a place of darkness, a place of a lack of the vision of God. In this sense, Christ's ministry was one of sacramental presence: he came as that same mystery that is the light of the world, bringing illumination to the places where sin has cast its shadow for too long. Again, we do well to understand this sacramental presence not as some kind of crude 'addition' of something that was previously lacking, but rather as God's way of embracing the world. For Christ took the world up into his arms, and though those arms were to be stretched out on the cross, and though they were to lie dead in the tomb, they never let go. The health of the world depends on Christ, something the New Testament tells us again and again. This is what Matthew Arnold called 'the secret of Jesus'[3]: that our well-being lies in Jesus' hands, quite literally.

Prophecy

Of course, this was not achieved when Jesus first stepped out of the river Jordan and received the Holy Spirit, but it began at his baptism. We must remember that Jesus had to undergo many things for the sake of the world, and that his ministry was to lead first to a glorious epiphany in Galilee, but then to the apparent failure at Gethsemane and Golgotha, before the redemption of Easter and the commissioning and empowering of Pentecost. Jesus' ministry was not, therefore, a seamless robe of success, one in which people were gathered up into health and well-being without reserve and limit. Rather, as many people were called, so many did not hear, just as today many do not hear. The kingdom began with a promise, one that Christ redeems with his blood and new life. But it was also a promise that was not to be immediately fulfilled.

The gospels are particularly clear about this reality and the limits it places on our understanding of God's saving presence in Christ. The story of Jesus' baptism is one of God's approval and benediction, as revealed by the descent of the Holy Spirit and the empowerment of the ministry. It is thereby also the beginning of Jesus' struggle against evil, and therefore the beginning of his healing ministry, redeeming people from their sins. But we do not understand either that beginning or that ministry if we regard it simply as a *fait accompli,* the start of a smooth process of revelation and redemption that will ascend effortlessly to the heights of heaven with all the host intact. On the contrary, Christ came to fight for his people, for the power of evil is very strong. In this dark world, God gave the Holy Spirit to help Jesus in his ministry, and it is in the power of that Holy Spirit that Christ heals. And, in turn, Christ gave the Holy Spirit to the Church, that the fight may continue.

If we are to understand correctly the prophetic character of Jesus' healing ministry, then we must understand the bonds of continuity that relate it to what went before, and to what came after. Jesus came to restore the right relationship between God and creation, a relationship that had been lost through Adam's sin. In the time of the Incarnation, people saw Jesus' struggle against that sin, and they wept for the crucified Son as he took upon himself the sins of the world. But in that same time Christ was risen and ascended, in which events we now confess the first fruits of all salvation. That story, however, is not yet complete. The world still suffers. The Church still proclaims healing to the sick. The Holy Spirit still empowers people to embrace that proclamation. But the end has not yet been reached. We are still in the midst of the ministry.

This is a difficult thing to grasp if we regard Christ's redeeming and healing work simply as something that happened two thousand years ago in Palestine. The Church is not about what happened in the dim and distant past. The Church is about what is happening now. And what is happening now is the same as what happened in Jesus' time. By this we mean that the power that Jesus wielded for the redemption of sins and the healing of lives is the same power that the Church believes it wields today. And it has this belief because it confesses the presence of the Holy Spirit, a presence that transcends the limitations of mere time; for it is the presence of eternity. There is no way around this belief. If we confess that in Christ all things are made new, and if we believe that this reality is won through the power of the Holy Spirit, then we cannot escape the (theo)logical

21

conclusion: the healing that is now present to all time is also beyond all time. It is, in a word, eternal.

In the 1958 report this is described in the following way: 'In his doctrine the natural is not superseded by the supernatural; rather he took the natural and raised it to a new level, making it the instrument of divine grace' (p. 19). We want to sharpen this argument, reasoning that Christ's becoming human is no relative event – a raising of the stakes, as it were – but one of absolute significance. In Christ, all time bows before the revelation of eternity; all creation is judged in the sight of heaven. All suffering is healed, because all is healed. Indeed, we can make this point even clearer: all is health. This is the true meaning of new creation. But it is not a meaning that can be reduced to objective or material description. Health in this sense is the condition of the pilgrim, Church and individual together. If we speak of the supremacy of the eternal, it is not because we want to see humanity on some kind of gradual progression towards the infinite. It is, rather, because we see eternity present in the world, in the shape of one man, dead yet risen, absent yet present. We are all caught up in the middle of that dying and rising, in which sense we recognize our life as itself genuinely prophetic. For we do not acquire our full health by our own care and skills. No, we receive it solely from God as sheer gift. And yet that gift remains, in some senses, still a matter of prophecy, of hope.

These are difficult ideas, and no one argument can pin them down. Why? Because beyond the ideas there lies a new world, and that world is still breaking into our world. The new creation, into which we are baptized in Christ and the Holy Spirit, lives in the midst of the old. And in the midst of the old, there is still suffering and its *ultimate* cause, sin. We do not know why the creator allowed suffering and death to enter into his creation, but before Christ it was gradually revealed to God's people that they were still bound to him in his covenant through suffering and death and that these experiences need not separate them from him. Within the greater mystery of our redemption in and through Christ, the mystery of the suffering and death of God in Christ had its vital role in the atonement, so to be 'in Christ' is to see our human experiences of suffering and death as in some sense a sharing in that mystery, whether we do so innocently as he did or, as more often happens, as a result of our own or others' disobedience to God.

Although Christ had a miraculous healing ministry, it had its limitations. He did not cure everybody, and his miraculous powers did not save him from his own suffering and death. He was challenged in his home town to do more miracles, and the proverb that he quoted there, 'Doctor, cure yourself!' (Luke 4.23), was thrown back at him as he hung on the cross. ('He cannot save himself', Mark 15.31). So, too, as we attempt to continue in the healing ministry of Jesus in the power of the Holy Spirit, we are not able to avert suffering and death – even less so than Christ, whose obedience to the Father was perfect in a way that we, with our proneness to sin and our lack of faith, can never be. Yet, where prayer for healing is trustingly offered in the Church, glimpses of the kingdom of God are seen and experienced. Healings are given in all sorts of ways – from extraordinary cures to recoveries more rapid than expected, from prolonged sufferings gradually accepted with Christ-like patience and joy to deaths peacefully entered in the hope of God's mercy and love.

We have no complete answer to the mystery of human suffering and death (but see pages 225–7). But we have Jesus, who suffered and died like us, and who rose from death and sent his Holy Spirit to continue through us the manifestations of his kingdom where we obey him. The primary meaning of the cross is the forgiveness of sin; but ultimately linked with forgiveness is the mystery of Christ's suffering in the work of our redemption. And we want to affirm that unless the ministry of healing is exercised under the cross, it is not the healing ministry of Christ.

The mission of the Church, therefore, is nothing less than to continue Jesus' own mission, the proclamation of the kingdom, the good news that suffering may end, that health may be freely given. The hope of the world is that this truth entered it in the form of a baby, and that through this Incarnation all may be saved. But this hope is tempered by the conviction that not all know and accept Christ, and that consequently there is still need of the healing ministry, for the sake of the world.

Power

In the face of the time and distance that lie between us and Jesus, therefore, we are given a gift, and the mission of the Church is to be true to that gift by continuing Jesus' ministry in God's name. How, then, can the Church fulfil its task, and witness to Jesus' ministry? It can do this because Christ gave the Holy Spirit to be a comforter to the Church, and because at Pentecost that same comfort was poured out upon the Church, and thereby upon the world.

This is the dynamic that lies behind the Church's own mission and life, the same power that enabled Christ to perform miracles of healing in Galilee and Jerusalem. We have the wrong understanding, however, if we regard that power as some kind of force that enables the Church to do God's will, overcoming evil by dint of greater faculty or equipment. On the contrary – and as is made clear in the great farewell discourses of the Fourth Gospel – the Holy Spirit's power is that of love and comfort. It is compassion that helps the Church overcome sin. It is love that enables the Church to embrace the world in mission, just as Jesus once embraced the world in ministry. There is no hidden secret to this fact, save the one true mystery of the Incarnation itself: that God became human in order to save the world.

This reference to the Incarnation returns us to our original theme, namely that the *whole* person is healed and redeemed in Christ, not solely one part of her or him. This is very important. Jesus did not come to save simply the best bits of humanity, and from these to create a new world. On the contrary, Jesus came to redeem everyone, a mission that is yet to be completed and in which, consequently, the Church still shares. Healing, therefore, is the power of love and compassion that makes God empty himself in order to redeem humanity; healing is the gift which comes to us through his *kenosis*. And just as God becomes fully human, so God's healing grace makes people fully human. There is no one who cannot feel God's healing embrace. There is no one to whom the Holy Spirit of love and compassion is not made available. There is no one, finally, whom God has not already reached, in Jesus Christ.

We can speak of this ubiquity and presence in terms of the constancy of prayer. When people pray to Jesus for help, or when they call to God for redemption, they acknowledge their relationship with the God who is all in all. This in turn indicates that the comfort, strength and health that God gives to the world in Jesus Christ is the one universal quality upon which all people may depend. It is a power that helps people by giving them a right relationship with God. This is not a 'thing', in the sense that one person might give a present to another. On the contrary, the power of true health is nothing other than a new beginning, which in turn means a new origin. And it is a new origin that has its own beginning in a new original, the Second Adam. The Body of Christ today is mysteriously one with the incarnate body of Jesus Christ two thousand years ago. 'You are the body of Christ and individually members of it' (1 Corinthians 12.27). To be part of one is to be part of both, and thereby one with God.

It is important, then, to recognize the way in which the contemporary Church understands itself to be the Body of Christ. If we say that the new creation is a healed creation, then what we mean is that 'God's Kingdom is creation healed' (to use Hans Kung's memorable expression). And if we invoke the kingdom, then we must also invoke him who proclaimed the kingdom, namely Jesus Christ. Christ's people today, therefore, represent Christ in that they continue his work of ministry, which in large part means the ministry of healing. This will take many forms – some pastoral, some liturgical, some intellectual – but the key point is that such ministry always represents Christ. If the Church is to be vigorous, then it is because it represents Christ. If it is to heal people, it is because it represents Christ. And if it is to be holy, it is because Christ is holy. In this sense, to speak of the Church as the Body of Christ is to remember its holiest origin and memorial in the Eucharist, in which the communion of believers gathered together in Christ's Body are healed as they heal, and live as they are alive.

What we can say, therefore, is that the visionary, prophetic and dynamic qualities that we speak of with respect to the healing ministry, and which we distinguish in our confession and explanation, are in fact all one. They are all one because God in Christ is one, and because God's Holy Spirit, sent by Christ, is also one. The healing ministry, consequently, is at the same time the only true ministry, because it is the Ministry of the Word, and therefore also the right celebration of the sacraments. By this we mean that the fundamental witness of the Church is to what God has achieved in Jesus Christ, and to what God continues to achieve in Christ's Body, in the power of the Holy Spirit. And that is health, the health of new creation.

That health was to be found in the gospel that the New Testament Church lived and preached. As in the days of Christ's earthly ministry, so after Pentecost the apostles and their followers knew they had been sent out 'to proclaim the kingdom of God and to heal' (Luke 9.2). They believed they were not on their own: the Lord was working with them and would confirm their message by the signs that accompanied it (Mark 16.20). Luke recorded that, having tasted opposition for the first time, they prayed: 'Lord, grant to your servants to speak your word with all boldness, while you stretch out your hand to heal, and signs and wonders are performed through the name of your holy servant Jesus' (Acts 4.29,30). The same Holy Spirit who had been on Jesus to heal (Luke 5.17) had been bestowed on them, and in his power and in Jesus' name they healed men and women of diseases and released them from evil spirits. For Paul, the community of Christian believers constituted the Body of Christ energized through Holy Spirit-gifted services, 'spiritual gifts' or 'charisms', one of which was the gift of healing (1 Corinthians 12.4-7).

In this way, Jesus' ministry to the sick has continued down to our own day in his Church, itself a sign and instrument of the kingdom of God in the world. The parable of the good Samaritan models Christian compassion for a suffering neighbour (Luke 10.25-37). Indeed, Jesus on one occasion identified himself personally with the sick: 'I was sick and you took care of me' (Matthew 25.36). Within the ancient world, where healing practices were usually associated with magic, paganism and money-making, Christians could claim that their ministry was superior because it was the work of the one, true God through his Son, the Saviour, in the power of his loving Spirit.

In order to develop this point more fully, it will be helpful to distinguish three streams in Jesus' ministry to the sick. It is a superficial distinction, for Jesus' ministry was totally integrated with his incarnate life and his mission. But it will help us to discern how the Holy Spirit has led and continues to lead the Church in fulfilling Christ's commission to heal the sick. The three streams in the ministry reveal Christ as the good shepherd or pastor, as the sacrament, and as the charismatic. We will outline these streams to show (though only in the briefest way) how they have flowed into the Church's mission through the centuries.

Christ the pastor

In the gospels we see the love of God manifested in the pastoral concern Jesus had for those who were ill, disabled or demon-possessed. He had pity on the leper and on the two blind men (Matthew 20.34). He was angry at the callousness of the Pharisees, who were more concerned to see if he would break the Sabbath than to see the paralysed man healed (Mark 2.5). On two occasions he instructed lepers to have their cures officially certified so that they could resume normal life among their families and neighbours (Luke 5.14; 17.14).

Furthermore, Jesus' pastoral concern stretched beyond the people of the covenant to the Gentiles, foreshadowing the worldwide spread of the gospel. He healed the servant of the Roman centurion (Matthew 8.13), the daughter of the Syrophoenician woman (Mark 7.24-30), and the leper who was a Samaritan (Luke 17.11-19). No group or nation had an exclusive claim on God's healing grace.

The ministry of Christ the pastor continues in the Church in the pastoral care which her members exercised (though occasionally with grievous errors and neglects) through the centuries. It showed itself in the ordinary, practical everyday business of looking after the sick. When Alexandria was devastated by a plague in the middle of the third century, Dionysius, the bishop there, described the devotion with which the Christians tended the sick, even when some of them were infected and died, while their pagan neighbours fled.

Basil (d. 379), Bishop of Caesarea in Cappadocia and one of the leading theologians of the Church in the East, allowed his basilica to be used as a hospital during a plague and built houses around it for the aged and their attendants. His example was copied elsewhere. With the development of the religious orders, the care of the sick in the community led to the care of the sick in the neighbourhood. The names of some of the oldest hospitals in London and elsewhere reveal their origins in the infirmaries and hospices of monastic houses. Early orders of nuns were largely occupied with nursing. After the dissolution of the monasteries in the sixteenth century, the task of providing hospitals was gradually undertaken by local groups of Christians and others of goodwill as a voluntary movement that flourished in the eighteenth and nineteenth centuries.

Another aspect of the Church's pastoral care can be seen in the development of medicine. Ancient Israel had been suspicious of the medical practices of surrounding cultures because of their pagan and magical associations. King Asa was thought to have died because he consulted doctors rather than God (2 Chronicles 16.10-12). But in the intertestamental period there were signs of a growing respect for doctors among the Jews (Ecclesiasticus 38.1-4), and Jesus affirmed this by declaring himself as one who came as a physician to heal the sick (Mark 2.17). It was the beginning of a new attitude. The fact that one of the gospels and Acts were written by Paul's 'beloved physician' indicates that those who practised medicine were acceptable to the early Christian community, provided they rejected heathen methods. In the second century Cosmas and Damien were famous for their work in the city of Rome as Christian doctors. They were known as 'the moneyless ones' because they did not charge their patients a fee. (Long afterwards a hall in the Roman Forum was taken over as a church and dedicated in their honour. This church has always had a special link with the ministry of healing.)[4]

The Rule of St Benedict includes a chapter on the care of the sick. Infirmaries were to be built on the sunniest side of the cloister. Patients were to be kept warm and well fed. Herb gardens were cultivated for medicinal as well as culinary purposes. Outside the monasteries the medieval parish priest was often expected to give medical advice as well as spiritual ministrations to the sick. This role continued in the Church of England after the Reformation. George Herbert advised clergy wives to grow a herb garden and dispense prescriptions among parishioners with a prayer, and John Wesley published a book called *Primitive Physic* as a guide for his local preachers. It was only with the establishment of the Royal Colleges that the doctor became a respected figure in English society, and the advance of scientific medicine in the last two hundred years has resulted in a growing cleavage between the Church and the medical profession.

A similar story can be told of nurses. The care of the sick has always been a major responsibility for the women in a household, care which was often extended to others in need. The revival of the religious orders in the Church of England in the nineteenth century enabled unmarried women to become nurses in parishes and hostels. Florence Nightingale's name will always be associated with the emergence of nursing as a profession with nationally recognized qualifications. The strategy of Anglican missionary societies (like those of other denominations) has been based on the teamwork of priests, doctors, nurses and teachers. Over this long story we can discern the continuing work of Christ the pastor.

Christ the sacrament

The ecumenical movement has caused theologians to look beyond the former Catholic-Protestant disputes about the number and nature of the sacraments to converge in a common understanding of Jesus as the supreme sacrament. To use the words of the Prayer Book Catechism, Christ is 'the outward and visible sign' (the Word made flesh, the Incarnation) 'of an inward and spiritual grace' (the real presence of the Son of God, in the power of the Holy Spirit). In Christ the mystery of creation comes together with the mystery of salvation:

> He is the image of the invisible God, the firstborn of all creation; for in him all things in heaven and on earth were created, things visible and invisible, whether thrones or dominions or rulers or powers — all things have been created through him and for him. He himself is before all things, and in him all things hold together.
> (Colossians 1.15-17).

We read in the gospels that Jesus employed created things – water, bread, wine, olive oil, touch, the laying on of hands – in conjunction with his preaching of the gospel, and he commanded his apostles to do the same. These created things, therefore, became signs of God's grace. They were 'sacramental', as we would say today, signs which effect what they signify through the Word of God and the power of the Holy Spirit. Thus, within the faith community of the new covenant certain material objects and human gestures become 'doors to the sacred' through which the saving grace of God is offered to us. One important feature of the Incarnation is the way in which the humanity of Jesus, his physical body and everything associated with it, is central to the saving grace offered to the world, culminating in his death on the cross. He has, as Hebrews 10.19,20 states, opened a new and living way for us through his flesh (that is, the life and sacrifice of his human body). This is why the person of Christ is regarded as the sacrament *par excellence.*

Where the sick, the crippled and the demon-possessed were concerned, Jesus healed through the words he spoke, through the gestures he made, and through the things he used, giving his ministry its sacramental character. Where his speaking is concerned, we remember that in Christ the Word of God is not only a means of revelation; it is also a communication of authority. What Jesus commanded then happened:

> For as the rain and the snow come down from heaven, and do not
> return there until they have watered the earth, making it bring
> forth and sprout, giving seed to the sower and bread to the eater,
> so shall my word be that goes out from my mouth; it shall not
> return to me empty, but it shall accomplish that which I
> purpose, and succeed in the thing for which I sent it.
> (Isaiah 55.10,11)

Jesus also healed by touch. His body was an instrument of grace, particularly his hands. He reached out his hand to the sick, like the leper (Matthew 8.3; this was significant because according to the Law of Moses Christ had made himself unclean by doing this). He touched the eyes of the two blind men (Matthew 9.29). Usually the touch was accompanied by a word of command, but occasionally only the touch was mentioned, as in the healing of Peter's mother-in-law (Mark 1.31; Matthew 8.15; Luke 4.39 says he rebuked the fever). Sometimes folk were healed when they touched him, like the woman with the haemorrhage and the sick among the crowds (Mark 5.28,29; 6.56). There are a few references to the laying on of hands, suggesting a more formal gesture than a touch. Jairus asked Jesus to lay hands on his dying daughter (Mark 5.23). Jesus laid hands on the sick with various diseases and on the woman with a spirit of infirmity (Luke 4.40; 13.13).

Jesus used other signs as well. When he came to the border of the Decapolis, he spat and touched the tongue of the deaf-mute and put his fingers in the man's ears, saying, 'Ephphatha', that is, 'Be opened' (Mark 7.33,34). He spat on the eyes of the blind man at Bethsaida (Mark 8.23), and he made mud out of spittle to smear on the eyes of the man born blind (John 9.6). Twice the sick were made to do something practical: the man born blind to wash in the pool of Siloam, and the man with the withered hand to hold it out towards Jesus. There is no record that Jesus himself used oil as a sign of healing. In a sense, he *was* the oil, God's 'Anointed One'. But the twelve he sent out used oil, presumably at his suggestion (Mark 6.13). The use of oil and wine as medicaments was common at the time (e.g. the parable of the Good Samaritan), and spittle was believed to have healing properties. Christ thereby associated his healing work with the medical practice of his day.

The earliest evidence of a sacramental ministry to the sick in the early Church is found in the descriptions and texts of the liturgy. Communion of the sick is mentioned by Justin (d. 165) and that remained a regular feature throughout Christian history, either within the Eucharist itself or through receiving the sacrament at home or in hospital. *The Apostolic Tradition* of Hippolytus (c. 215), the earliest known Christian prayer book, which is believed to have originated in Rome, contains a prayer over oil for the sick which was brought to be blessed by the presiding bishop. A letter from the same period mentions a Christian who even cured a pagan with oil. In the following century prayers for the blessing of oil ask God to send 'a power of healing into this oil', that 'it put to flight every disease and every infirmity'.[5] Later prayers were along similar lines. The oil was used by lay folk for the sick at home as well as by the clergy in church services.

From about the tenth century onwards a number of factors resulted in a change in the use of anointing. One was that a series of reforms in the Western Church restricted the use of oil to the clergy. Another was that going to confession became obligatory at least once a year for all communicants. Yet another was that, in an age when life was short, healings after anointing were rare. So the anointing of the sick came to be regarded as a means of spiritual rather than physical healing which, with confession to the priest and communion, cleansed the sinner in preparation for death. A sacramental sign for healing had become a sacramental sign for dying, 'extreme unction'. The Council of Trent (1545–63) decreed that it was to be given 'especially to those who are dangerously ill that they seem to be at the point of leaving this life'. It was not until the middle of the twentieth century that Roman Catholic theologians began to recover the true nature of this sacramental sign and the Second Vatican Council ordered the rites of the sick to be revised. (This contrasted with the practice of the Eastern Orthodox Church which has always used oil in healing liturgies.)

The Anglican Reformers regarded extreme unction as unbiblical and the provision for anointing in the 1549 Prayer Book was dropped in 1552. Its use was revived, however, among some High Church Anglican groups such as the Non-Jurors and, as we have seen, at the beginning of the twentieth century Anglo-Catholics campaigned for its restoration. Since then anointing the sick has been authorized and services provided in the Church of England, as in other provinces of the Anglican Communion.

With anointing and the laying on of hands, the ministry of reconciliation (as confession in the presence of a priest is now called) and Holy

Communion are the means through which the sick may encounter Christ the sacrament and hope for his mercy and healing.

Christ the charismatic

Anglicans have always affirmed that 'we believe in the Holy Spirit, the Lord, the giver of life, who proceeds from the Father and the Son' (Nicene Creed). We celebrate the feast of Pentecost, we invoke the Holy Spirit in our prayers and hymns, and we seek guidance and equipping as individuals as well as corporately in the liturgy. But it is probably true to say that our encounter with Pentecostal as well as Orthodox spiritualities from the 1960s onwards has enabled us to understand more fully the biblical meaning of the word 'charismatic'. And it was Michael Ramsey, using the phrase 'the Charismatic Christ' in the last years of his teaching and writing career, who reminded us what we knew all along but were liable to overlook, namely that everything about Jesus, from the moment of his conception in the womb of the Virgin Mary to his ascension into heaven, was a fulfilment of prophetic proclamation: 'The spirit of the Lord God is upon me, because the Lord has anointed me' (Isaiah 61.1).

In Jesus we see the complete and perfect functioning of spiritual gifts through the obedience to God of a human life. The divided tongues of fire which, with the wind, fulfilled the divine promise that the apostles would be baptized in the Holy Spirit, also symbolized that the charisms are distributed widely among them. The Acts of the Apostles gives us a picture of various spiritual gifts guiding the spread of the gospel and manifesting the power of the kingdom (though there was an attempt to abuse a charism in the case of Simon; cf. Acts 8.18,19). Spiritual gifts operated in cases of need when an apostle discerned it was right to exercise his authority to heal in the name of Jesus Christ, often after preaching the gospel. Healings and deliverance from evil formed the majority of the 'signs and wonders' in the apostolic Church. Paul taught about the nature and purpose of the charisms in 1 Corinthians 12 – 14, stressing that they were to be exercised in love and unity for the common good, and warning about the dangers of misuse.

The charismatic ministry of healing took various forms in the Church during later centuries. Usually the gift was associated with holy persons such as the Desert Fathers. Belief in divine healing had to be set beside the other belief that suffering and death could be means of being identified with the passion of Christ, especially when faced with martyrdom (which was also a spiritual gift and from which ultimate healing was through the gate of death). The graves and memorials of the martyrs and the shrines within which their relics were venerated came to be regarded as means of healing, and so the custom of pilgrimages to holy places to seek healing grew, especially to Jerusalem from the fourth century onwards.

According to Bede two English bishops at the end of the seventh century, Cuthbert of Lindisfarne (d. 687) and John of Beverley (d. 721), were well known for their healing gifts, as was the English missionary Willibrord (d. 739). Although these and others used sacramental signs such as oil in their healing ministry, and showed a pastoral care for those who sought their ministry, they may be called charismatic because healing was experienced as a gift of the Holy Spirit through them personally.

With the decline in the sacramental ministry of healing in the West, people sought cures through charismatic persons and places associated with the saints and martyrs. Confining ourselves to England, shrines such as those of Edmund the Martyr (d. 870), Thomas Becket at Canterbury (d. 1170) and Richard of Chichester (d. 1252) all became popular centres of pilgrimage for healing (as, too, was the shrine at Walsingham). Julian of Norwich is better known for her visions and meditations on sin and suffering. But after her own remarkable healing as an anchoress she would have been approached by individuals seeking her spiritual counsel and prayers. Some historians question the reliability of the narratives of healing powers and demonic deliverances associated with these English saints. Others reply that the steady witness to such healings over the centuries cannot simply be dismissed as fiction, and that the persistence of such stories shows that the hope of receiving charismatic gifts of healing (however they were understood at the time) was still alive among the faithful.

With the destruction of many of these shrines at the Reformation, the search for gifts of healing died out until other charismatics appeared in the following centuries. We shall see elsewhere in this report how the pastoral, sacramental and charismatic streams of the healing ministry ebbed and flowed through the life of the Church of England. But our purpose in this briefest of outlines is to demonstrate how the healing ministry of Christ has continued through the centuries, especially in our own country.

Although each of those streams has at different times been neglected, misunderstood and even abused, nevertheless the Holy Spirit has recalled the Church to be faithful to the model and power of Christ's own ministry.

When the 1958 report states, therefore, that 'Whatever is to be the practice of the Church in exercising the ministry of healing it will at once be conceded that Christ's example and precept are authoritative',[6] we must concur, for in its ministry the Church believes it is continuing Christ's ministry of healing. Notions of example and precept, therefore, must be understood as real and eternal, indeed graceful associations, rather than simply being signs of something greater and unknown. The paradox of the Christian faith is that we know that which is unknown; we know the Word because of the Word. This is the miracle of the Incarnation, and Jesus' ministry of healing must be understood in the light of this miracle.

The reader will see that this theology informs everything that is written in this present report. We have revisited the main areas of the 1958 text, thinking through once again the key points that must always be contained within any Christian theology of healing. If we have developed any fresh insights, then it is in two main respects. The first is contained in this chapter, and it is the presence of the Holy Spirit in the Church which enables her to continue (although always less effectively) the ministry of the incarnate Christ, so that what we do when we pray and work for healing in his name is not rehearsing a memorial of what he achieved, but rather a taking-up of Christ's ministry. Our mission to heal is given to us by Christ, just as Christ gave us his Spirit to help us to achieve this goal. It is our holiest gift, and our most sacred responsibility, to represent Christ as the healed new creation in the midst of the suffering old creation.

At the same time, and as the reader will appreciate from the contents of this report, the situation at the turn of the millennium is somewhat different from that of the 1950s. We have tried to reflect this difference in what we have written, aware of the changed circumstances in which people now find themselves, and of their changed perceptions of such things as psychiatry and medical health in general. These reflections, however, are themselves to be understood in the light of the greater conviction, namely that new life is something that comes only from Christ.

Recommendation

We acknowledge the importance of the bishops' role as teachers and guardians of the faith. Inherent in the episcopal office is a duty and opportunity to commend the ministry of healing to the Church and to promote it within each diocese. We recommend and encourage bishops to teach the scriptural importance of this ministry and its significance in furthering the kingdom of God (see page 261).

3

The Healing Ministry
in the Church of England Today

One of the key terms of reference for this report is to assess the state of the ministry of healing in the Church of England. This chapter is a summary of the research carried out involving all diocesan bishops and their appointed advisors on the ministries of healing and deliverance, a cross-section of hospital chaplains and prison chaplains and nationally recognized training courses for ministry. We have sought to highlight the current level of awareness of this ministry, its level of support within the existing structures, the concerns and needs of those already involved, as well as the key challenges to be taken up.

The healing ministry within the parishes

Few people would argue with the view that the past 30 years have seen a significant increase in interest in the healing ministry. Although claims of various levels of increase exist, the actual increase in its practical integration into normal everyday parish life has not been accurately surveyed or quantified. People who are fully involved in this ministry tend to be more aware of areas where it is well established than those areas where it is neglected. Very few dioceses have carried out formal surveys in recent years (or at all) to evaluate the current state of the healing ministry in their parishes. One diocese which did carry out such a survey found that 'many parishes still do not place Christian healing anywhere within their structures of worship or pastoral care'.

The research for this report, carried out over nine months preceding its final draft, has included all diocesan bishops, all diocesan advisors in the ministries of healing and deliverance, a cross-section of hospital chaplains chosen by the Hospital Chaplaincies Council, a cross-section of prison chaplains and all theological colleges and courses, regional courses and Ordained Local Ministry schemes, recognized by the House of Bishops. Without a thorough and objective review of the healing ministry in every parish, carried out on a national scale by the Church of England, it is not possible to assess its precise current state at local level. But it is clear from our research carried out recently that there is still much to be done to establish this ministry as a part of normal, everyday life within every parish.

One human factor more than any other which determines whether the healing ministry has a high profile in a parish is the interest and commitment to this ministry of the parish priest. When a priest who is publicly involved in this ministry moves, he or she will take their enthusiasm with them while the priest filling the vacancy may not carry on the ministry publicly, allowing it to decline. This is one of the reasons why it is difficult to determine the state of the local healing ministry across the breadth of the Church of England. Nevertheless, while some parishes do not have a high-profile healing ministry because of the views of the priest, there are very few known cases of a parish rejecting this ministry at the request of the laity.

As we have demonstrated earlier, this ministry is part of the mission of the Church, not an optional or extraneous activity. In fact, the whole of the Church's mission could be described as healing in a very broad sense. Diocesan advisors on the healing and deliverance ministries have remarked on the difficulty of getting some clergy to take a serious and practical interest and the need for some clergy to be reminded of the call to heal the sick.

In spite of this, the Eucharist is essentially a service of healing even though many lay people do not appreciate it as such. It is helpful to highlight awareness of the aspect of healing within any service. Eucharists incorporating the laying on of hands, special services with prayers for healing and healing prayer groups are increasingly popular. Healing services in the Church of England are discussed in detail in Chapter 13. The parish priest's involvement in the healing ministry as part of pastoral care, visiting the sick at home, in hospital and hospices, and the relationships between the priest and other professions involved in health care, are also covered in later chapters.

Lay involvement in this ministry is almost always organized within the parish. Leading prayers of intercession is a way in which lay people contribute in most parishes. Prayer groups, some of which have been specifically established to pray for healing and which may be linked with one of the Guilds, are also common. Individuals who feel they have a gift in this area may be invited by the priest to take part in services, laying on hands, usually in pairs, sometimes in small groups. They have often been influenced by the charismatic movement which, as we noticed earlier (see pages 11–12), has given a considerable impetus to prayer for healing and heightened expectations that the spiritual gifts of the New Testament are still exercised in the Church today. While we acknowledge that the Holy Spirit can guide and empower individuals through such charisms for all kinds of service – sometimes in remarkable ways – yet we believe that nearly all such individuals still need training so that their ministries are exercised wisely and under proper supervision.

There are, however, limited resources available for local training of lay people to take part in the healing ministry. A few of the major charities supporting this ministry run courses at their headquarters and run day or short courses in the dioceses on request. Selection, training, involvement and oversight of lay people in this area, however, are usually at the discretion of the parish priest, who may choose (but is not obliged) to involve the diocesan advisor on the healing ministry. If there is no conspicuous healing ministry in a parish, people who feel called to serve God and the Church in this way may have little or no opportunity to become involved and in these circumstances, ordinands on Ordained Local Ministry courses training in such parishes also have little opportunity to learn about this ministry.

Lack of experience in the selection and training of people can be a serious inhibiting factor for some clergy who want to set up teams but who are untrained in this ministry themselves. Concerns about this ministry causing divisions in the congregation through differing perceptions of what it involves and offers, apprehension of apparent failure and of loss of control are also factors which can discourage clergy.

Another key factor is the churchmanship or tradition of the parish. Generally, the sacramental aspects of the healing ministry have been maintained most strongly in the Catholic parishes, so lay involvement may not be evident to the same extent as in Evangelical parishes. Catholic parishes touched by the charismatic renewal may be more enthusiastic in developing an 'every-member' ministry, even if certain aspects are reserved for the priest. Evangelical parishes are more likely to use extemporary prayer and laying on of hands, which allow for greater direct involvement of the laity.

We do not want to draw too much attention to these differences, since the diversity of practice in the Church of England gives individual members who are mobile and fit enough the opportunities to find a church community in which they feel at home and at ease. It is significant that people move around more for the healing ministry than they do for most aspects of the Church's ministry. People also travel beyond their own parish for this ministry at times, because they seek anonymity. For the barely mobile and housebound, however, there is little choice.

Some, but not all, dioceses have pastoral assistants. In this report we use this term to describe all lay persons who, after selection and training, exercise a pastoral care role in a parish under the direction of the incumbent: they do not usually have training specifically in this ministry. Because of the emphasis on the sacramental nature of much of the healing ministry, it has not been seen as a key area for pastoral assistants. There are, however, good reasons for considering how they might be used more effectively. Since much of their work involves visiting people in the parishes, pastoral assistants are well informed about and in touch with those coping with a wide range of difficulties, including ill health, bereavement and depression.

The work of pastoral assistants overlaps that of other forms of ministry, including Christian Listening, counselling and prayer groups, as well as preparation for baptism, confirmation and marriage, all of which are forms of healing. For example, baptism involves repentance, renunciation of evil and turning to Christ, which are part of the healing ministry. Since much of the pastoral assistant's work involves them with the elderly and infirm, they know the benefits of spending time, listening and sharing the burdens and needs of those they visit. When pastoral assistants visit the sick or when they are also authorized to take Holy Communion to the sick, offering to pray for healing is natural and to be encouraged.

When healing services take place, the follow-up pastoral care can be shared between priest and pastoral assistant. Pastoral assistants make up one of the few groups of laity within the Church which tend to be formally trained and licensed. Because the individual's authorization may need be renewed regularly, there are opportunities for oversight and regular review. The training and greater involvement of pastoral assistants in the healing ministry would help to ensure that it continues to be a normal part of parish life, and this ministry as it is being carried out in the parishes in which they are based could be backed up more effectively.

The healing ministry tends to have a low profile at deanery level, which may be a reflection in part, of the need for deanery synods to develop a clearer and more dynamic approach to their role in the Church of England in wider terms. A small proportion of the diocesan advisors have made great efforts to speak to all the deanery synods and chapters in their dioceses. Most of them wait until they are invited; invitations can be slow to arrive if the rural dean and lay chairman are not particularly interested in the healing ministry.

There is little evidence that rural deans and lay chairmen of deanery synods are involved or particularly interested in promoting this ministry. There is also little evidence to suggest that healing services are often organized at deanery level or that training often takes place within the deanery structure. Nevertheless, the deanery is an ideal unit on which to develop the expression of the healing ministry in rural areas or those parts of dioceses where the interest of the clergy and general availability of trained, committed laity are currently low.

The healing ministry within the dioceses

We are glad to discover that almost every bishop has some involvement in the healing ministry, particularly anointing, laying on of hands and intercessory prayer as well as taking part in the annual Chrism service during Holy Week. About half of the diocesan bishops currently chair their diocesan committees involved in or relating to this ministry, which is a clear signal of the importance they attach to its place in their dioceses. Involvement provides at least an annual opportunity to discuss health- and healing-related issues with their advisors and senior staff, as part of reviews.

Some bishops encourage and are also involved in training conferences and annual diocesan healing days and services. A few bishops are also involved with healing organizations or a particular initiative, or hold a national post related to the healing ministry. Many diocesan advisors feel that the involvement and support of their bishops is a crucial factor in promoting this ministry within their diocese. It is also important that the media see that the bishops have a keen interest in it; this helps to show society that healing is a central part of the Church's mission.

Every diocese has been encouraged to have at least one diocesan advisor for the healing ministry and for the deliverance ministry: almost every diocese has this facility, either individuals or teams, set up by and usually accountable to the diocesan bishop. These teams tend to meet regularly, usually two or three times a year, and their work is reviewed with the diocesan bishop at least annually. There is a degree of overlap in some dioceses where diocesan advisors may be members of teams for both ministries. In some dioceses, however, there is no overlap.

The post of diocesan advisor on healing is most often held in addition to a full-time post or by a retired priest. This is an indication of the current inconsistency of the allocation of resources to the healing ministry by the Church of England. Over two-thirds of diocesan advisors are carrying out their advisory role when already carrying a full workload in some other role. Lack of sufficient time to be effective as diocesan advisors is a serious concern for many of them. The disadvantage of appointing retired priests as diocesan advisors is that very few elderly priests have received any formal training in either the healing or deliverance ministries. Because of time constraints and geographical areas to be covered, many bishops have appointed more than one advisor.

Some diocesan advisors bring experience within the medical professions to their role in the diocese, while others have personal experiences on which to draw for insights into suffering. Most training received has been through the range of independent trusts, healing centres, reading, attending conferences, practical experience and being self-taught. There is no national consensus however, about the level of general awareness of healing issues such as complementary medicine and alternative therapies, what constitutes a sound understanding of good practice or what kind of broad training, including the ecumenical expression of the ministry, are needed before a diocesan advisor is appointed. For the healing ministry in the Church of England, there is no nationally recognized minimum standard of training for clergy or clear agreement about how this ministry or related guidelines for good conduct should be carried out in the parishes. Consequently, there is no consensus on what exactly, or even broadly, diocesan advisors should advise or what that advice should be, in relation to this ministry.

The work of diocesan advisors covers wide areas, though there is no clear pattern. Very few advisors work to any kind of formal job description, so there is wide variation in practice. Responsibilities and activities include

❖ assisting in setting and clarifying policies for healing;

❖ setting up and organizing diocesan committees for this ministry, and local healing groups;

❖ developing, organizing and carrying out training for clergy and laity;

❖ organizing and leading services for healing in cathedrals and parish churches, etc.;

❖ addressing chapters, deanery synods, PCCs and other groups interested in the healing ministry;

❖ liaison with hospital chaplains and to a lesser extent counsellors and prison chaplains;

❖ advising clergy and lay workers about healing issues.

The extent to which diocesan advisors are effective depends on a number of key factors. The personal interest of the bishop is a significant influence in the establishment and use of advisory groups and teams. The likelihood of a diocesan advisor being invited to a parish to talk about the healing ministry and its local development tends to depend on the interest of the parish priest. It would be helpful to have diocesan advisors on the healing ministry listed in the diocesan directories, which currently is not always the case, along with contact details for healing centres, hospices, training course coordinators, Christian counsellors, etc. This would help parish priests who are seeking assistance and advice.

Whether a diocesan advisor is effective also depends to some extent on whether he or she has been formally trained in the healing or deliverance ministry and when and where, which tends to affect his or her personal outlook and experience. Another factor is the issue of traditions and the need for diocesan advisors to be aware of their wide range and how the healing ministry is expressed within them. Diocesan advisors also need to be sensitive to the local situation and the needs of the parish they are advising, in order to help its members develop this ministry in the way which is most relevant to local circumstances.

According to the survey replies, few diocesan advisors apparently have strong or regular contacts with healing homes, hospices and local prisons in their dioceses. Contact with the National Health Service (NHS) tends to be indirect through hospital chaplains and visiting parishioners. Few diocesan advisors have formal contacts with local general medical practices. Diocesan advisors on the deliverance ministry find, however, that contacts with psychiatrists, psychologists and psychotherapists can be helpful in assessing people seeking help from this ministry. The House of Bishops' recommendations on the deliverance ministry (1975) encourage teams to be set up to include members with relevant medical expertise.

The links between the healing ministry and diocesan structures is at best weak or limited. In the case of a few dioceses, this ministry has to a small extent overlapping membership with the Boards of Mission, Ministry or Social Responsibility, or parish resource groups. Diocesan advisors have to be elected to their diocesan synods like other clergy and few diocesan advisors referred in their replies to the survey to being members of their diocesan synods, or having an active involvement in their own chapters or deanery synods. There is little evidence that advisors are elected to boards and committees in the broad structure of their dioceses, which would enable them to encourage links between the structures and the healing ministry. This situation may be a reflection on their failure to stand for election, but is more likely to be a result of already being over-stretched.

One of the factors compromising the work of diocesan advisors is the lack of adequate resources. The healing ministry is only a separate item on about half of the diocesan budgets. The most generous budget was for £2,000 p.a. in 1998 but the average is less than 10 per cent of that figure. Diocesan advisors' expenses tend to be absorbed into other budgets such the diocesan Board of Mission, or met by discretionary funds. Travel expenses are usually met, but the practical resources for organizing conferences, training and presentations tend to be provided privately, by the diocesan advisor personally or by absorbing the costs into his or her parish expenses if an understanding PCC will accept this. Alternatively, the events have to be set up to be self-funding/self-resourcing.

Such limited resources compromise and discourage initiatives to set up large events to promote this ministry. There is very little provision for study, buying books, further training which may include travelling abroad, setting up Internet web sites etc. and developing training material and courses for the parishes. Many diocesan advisors have also stressed the need for much better training for ordinands, for clergy as part of continuing ministerial education (CME), for the laity and for themselves.

Diocesan advisors need guidance and support from their bishops, advice and support from their colleagues and other diocesan advisors, and sound networks for communications. Continual, prayerful support from their friends and local communities is also needed, particularly for diocesan advisors and others involved in the deliverance ministry.

While some diocesan advisors feel that they are appreciated and that the healing ministry in their diocese is given a high profile, the majority feel that there is considerable room for improvement in the priority given to this ministry. A clear job description and recognition of their role within their diocese, based on a church-wide agreement of what these entail, would enable more people to relate to them and use their knowledge and gifts more readily. The value of working in teams and being paired with a more experienced co-worker are also noted.

Some diocesan advisors are currently working to the guidelines for good practice published by the former Churches' Council for Health and Healing (CCHH). These guidelines have not been formally adopted by the Church of England. Many advisors have commented that they would like to see the Church of England adopt and promote guidelines for good practice for the healing and deliverance ministries. The issue is a significant concern of many diocesan advisors and their bishops, since the way in which the Church ministers to people in need is one of the most important ways in which the Church spreads the message of the gospel.

Guidelines are needed to set recognizable and acceptable standards of conduct and to develop a common understanding of good practice; therefore they should be written for all people, lay and ordained, who are involved in the Church of England's healing ministry. Appendix 1 gives detailed guidance on good practice in the healing ministry, and includes the House of Bishops' draft guidelines for good practice, a list of ten high-priority guidelines. They have taken into account many of the codes of conduct and guidelines for good practice which health care professions have established and the advice of insurers and lawyers. A common understanding of what constitutes good practice would encourage everyone involved to maintain these standards. Such guidelines are also a means of encouraging and maintaining the confidence of parishioners and those ministering to them, affirming good practice where it already exists in many places.

Almost every bishop has at least one priest appointed as advisor on the deliverance ministry; approximately a third of the dioceses have a team or group to deal with cases referred to them by the bishops. These teams often include a hospital chaplain, a psychiatrist, a GP and other lay experts, to assist in diagnosis and aftercare. The membership of diocesan teams in this area is usually kept confidential but they provide a valuable, experienced resource in their dioceses. Clergy are encouraged to refer to them cases which may need the deliverance ministry; this ministry is considered in more detail in Chapter 9.

Most diocesan advisors on the deliverance ministry are aware of the House of Bishops' guidelines (1975), but there is concern that some parish priests may ignore them. There are calls to monitor more carefully the ways in which this ministry is carried out in the parishes, and to intervene in cases of bad practice or where the guidelines are being ignored.

We note that there are organizations and individuals outside the Church of England carrying out this ministry and which are not accountable to or overseen by the Church: these outside organizations and individuals are not obliged to follow the House of Bishops' guidelines. If complaints arise about such activities, the Church does not have procedures to deal with such complaints and is not responsible for them. However, the generally low public profile of the Church of England's deliverance ministry may be causing some people to seek deliverance through other organizations and individuals.

Part of the problem may stem from the tendency to keep the identity of diocesan advisors on the deliverance ministry low profile or strictly confidential. Whilst some advisors are well known as such to the clergy in their diocese, there is little evidence that advisors are being invited regularly to address chapters or synods. The result is that some clergy and most laity are poorly informed about their work and whom to contact for help. Although some individuals seeking help would be referred to the advisor through the bishop or archdeacon, the lack of readily available advice and help for clergy in some areas may be the reason why some priests 'just get on with it on their own', thereby increasing the risk of bad practice.

Concern has also been expressed by some of the clergy seeking help on the deliverance ministry that a minority of advisors are themselves insufficiently experienced and trained in this area. A few are even less than convinced of the need for this ministry at all! If a priest is appointed to advise the clergy on such sensitive issues, it is important to ensure that they are well trained, have relevant experience on which to draw, and believe this ministry is of real value for some people. Prison chaplains, for example, have commented on the need for diocesan advisors to be aware of how HM Prison Service works and the ways in which dynamics within prisons affect the ways in which the healing and deliverance ministries are carried out.

Diocesan advisors rely on a range of networks, almost all of which are independent of the formal structures of the Church of England. These include the Guild of St Raphael, the Guild of Health, the Acorn Christian Healing Trust, the Order of St Luke and the Christian Deliverance Study Group network. Whilst some are acknowledged by the Church, they are not umbrella organizations for the entire healing ministry. They represent particular groups, views, approaches or areas of activity: no single organization is representative of the entire healing ministry and fully accountable to the Church of England. This situation does not encourage coherence, the development of generally accepted good practice or the general appreciation of the wide variety of approaches, their relative strengths and weaknesses.

Most diocesan advisors have referred to the need for a national network on which they can rely, run by the Church of England through a new national advisory body which they would like to see set up at the centre of the Church's structures. They have also highlighted the need for a substructure within the Church of England of networks of diocesan advisors in every region, for organizing regional conferences, for exchanging information, for advice contacts and for mutual support on a more local and accessible level. See Appendix 2 for detailed recommendations.

The diocesan advisors are generally aware of some opportunities for ecumenical partnership at local level in the healing ministry. These opportunities tend to be 'home-grown'. Many diocesan advisors would like to see this ministry on the agenda of Churches Together in England (CTE) at local and regional levels. The advisors have some success in setting up services ecumenically but would like to see the possibility of local and regional ecumenical training schemes for this ministry explored more fully, for both clergy and laity. From time to time, diocesan advisors are invited to preach in churches of the other main denominations on the Anglican expression of the healing ministry. A similar exchange is encouraged for Anglican local churches to invite advisors from the other main denominations to preach.

There is no formal network established between the formal structures of the main denominations for diocesan advisors who have been appointed by the diocesan bishops to link with advisors on healing and deliverance in the other denominations. This is an issue which deserves serious consideration. A new ecumenical network of advisors across the main denominations would provide opportunities for sharing resources and experience, offering support and organizing joint conferences and training. It would also be helpful to those people seeking the healing and deliverance ministries who sometimes move around the denominations as well as moving around geographically to find the help they need.

Diocesan advisors have a wide range of concerns including the following:

❖ the general failure of the Church of England to respond to the gospel imperative to heal the sick and the broad consequences of this failure;

❖ the need for a sound theology of and teaching on healing and wholeness, suffering and providence;

❖ the general attitude of the Church towards those who are chronically sick or terminally ill;

❖ lack of adequate training, nationally agreed, for clergy and laity in the healing ministry;

❖ lack of resources, overwork, lack of guidance and practical and prayerful support;

❖   lack of national networks within the Church, poor or non-existent communications about the healing ministry within the Church;

❖   lack of the right kind of liturgy, specially developed for this ministry, for particular circumstances and ecumenically sensitive;

❖   divergence in practice, excesses and extremes, lack of accountability, lack of a system for dealing with bad practice and abuse, lack of guidelines for good practice to be owned and promoted by the Church of England;

❖   lack of discernment, particularly in relation to the deliverance ministry; lack of cooperation with others involved in professional health care, e.g. psychiatrists, counsellors, pastoral care workers;

❖   the challenges posed by 'New Age' approaches to healing and health.

Around half of the dioceses have produced brief diocesan guidelines on the healing ministry. Some have produced brief notes concentrating on particular aspects such as anointing and the deliverance ministry. Overall, however, there is little detailed guidance produced locally on healing and deliverance, or the ways in which these ministries relate to pastoral care.

Most dioceses have made provision for counselling facilities, which may be in the form of a diocesan advisor on counselling or team of counsellors, or through a team or network of independent counsellors. These professional counsellors often work for the diocese on a part-time or consultancy basis. Generally, these facilities are only available to the clergy and their families, although sometimes also to lay readers, pastoral assistants and diocesan staff. Diocesan counselling facilities are not usually available to the laity in the parishes. Provision of counselling in the dioceses is considered in more detail in Chapter 6.

About a third of the cathedrals have some kind of service with a particular emphasis on healing. Some of these services are annual events or held as a special celebration around St Luke's Day. Others take the form of a diocesan advisory conference with healing service, sometimes involving the bishop. A few cathedrals have regular services with prayers for healing, either monthly, bi-monthly or weekly. These services are often based around the Eucharist and the ASB Rite A has been popular. Other services are non-eucharistic and based on Evening Prayer or some specially devised liturgy. The Chrism service was rarely mentioned in the surveys as a part of the healing ministry in the dioceses.

Cathedrals have a special role to play within the healing ministry. By holding services in the mother church of each diocese, the importance of this ministry is affirmed and a good example set for parish churches to follow. The use of the nave or the high altar shows that it is regarded as a precious core part of the Church's mission. These services provide helpful models of how the healing ministry can be sensitively and effectively carried out in major centres of worship, including the attraction of people who would not otherwise attend such a service; for example casual visitors, passing tourists and foreign visitors. Healing Services in the Church of England are considered in more detail in Chapter 13.

Whilst almost every diocese has a liturgical committee, apparently only one of these has produced liturgy specifically for healing services in its diocese. For annual diocesan healing days and services, some special liturgy may be produced by the organizers, but this is not the norm. There is no evidence that diocesan liturgical committees develop liturgy for the healing ministry ecumenically.

Healing organizations, homes and hospices are scattered around the country but there are few formal links with the diocesan structures which relate to their geographic location, which means that awareness of their presence in the diocese may be limited. These resources are usually quite independent but they provide a useful service for local people, as well as those coming from outside the area. It would be helpful to have some kind of formal link between these organizations and the diocesan advisors, for referrals, advice and support.

Although some of these organizations are acknowledged by the Church of England, and some have a bishop, for example, as Patron or Visitor, we have no official or central system of review or accreditation. Consequently, it may not be practical or prudent to make official recommendations or comparisons between them. A review carried out ecumenically of the organizations seeking official recognition and approval would provide accurate information, insights into the behind-the-scenes operations and some framework on which to base recommendations to the wider Church; a kind of 'Church Standard' mark of assurance. Such a system of accreditation, however, would be time-consuming to establish and keep up-to-date and could prove contentious. Agreement would have to be reached for example, on the criteria for inclusion or exclusion.

Formal links between the dioceses in the Church of England and the NHS exist through the Bishops' Advisors on Hospital Chaplaincy although few references to these were made in the surveys. More references were made to the links through diocesan advisors and some hospital chaplains being involved in diocesan healing ministry groups or teams. According to the Hospital Chaplaincies Council (HCC), no whole or part-time appointments are made without the approval of the bishop. Most bishops however, in their replies to the survey, said they had no official links with the local health authority in their diocese. Many bishops referred to links with hospital chaplains being formed at the time of the survey.

In a few dioceses, more has been already achieved. For example, one diocesan bishop referred to his appointment of the Bishop's National Health Advisor, the Bishop's Chaplain to the Mentally Handicapped and the Diocesan Chaplain to the Deaf. A few dioceses have links with mental health organizations but little information is available on this issue. There is also a very small number of local initiatives with general practices, but apparently these are exceptional.

Hospital chaplains, their work and the role of the HCC are covered in more detail later in this chapter and in Chapter 4. An Anglican chaplain is normally a member of his or her deanery chapter and it is at these meetings that the chaplain is able to associate with other clergy to their mutual advantage. Referrals from a parish priest when a member of the congregation goes into hospital are always welcome, and if the parish priest visits the patient regularly with the sacrament it is a courtesy to inform the chaplain that this is being done.

Through the deanery and chapter networks, the chaplain may be able to recruit members for the lay visiting team in the hospital from the local congregation. The chaplain may also be a useful resource person for congregational teams of helpers who minister regularly at services of prayer for healing. Bishops and area/rural deans should do what they can to encourage chaplains and parish clergy to work together with this in view.

The healing ministry within the national structures of the Church of England

As we have said, the Church of England has no national network of healing advisors within its national institutions. Despite the fact that healing the sick is a gospel imperative along with preaching and teaching, the healing ministry does not currently fall within the formal terms of reference of any of the main boards or committees within the substructure of the Archbishops' Council, apart from the HCC in the group of boards and committees known as 'Church and World'. Within the substructure there are individuals whose work includes health, healing and related issues, including mental health and new religious movements. Given the need to reflect more fully on the integral nature of the healing ministry in the overall ministry of the Church of England, however, we ask the Archbishops' Council to consider placing it within the Ministry Division.

There is no communication network or forum established for the healing ministry within the Church of England's central structures, through which information can be communicated either to or from the dioceses and parishes. Parish-based clergy and laity involved in this ministry in the Church of England have to rely on outside organizations for information. The Central Secretariat of the Archbishops' Council has no particular brief for communication and promotion of the healing ministry. It is not an item in the national budget and there is no provision within any part of the substructure for any practical support or oversight at national level, for either healing or deliverance as they are carried out in the dioceses or parishes. We envisage that the Ministry Division could play a coordinating role, acting in particular as a central reference point for a network of diocesan advisors. The resourcing of this network could, judging by the example of similar networks (such as that for Bishops' Visitors), be relatively modest, and we hope that it might be possible to fund this element through an existing allocation through the national budget.

The only organization within the existing central structures with a clear involvement in the healing ministry within medical establishments and community care programmes is the HCC. The HCC does not cover the healing ministry as it is carried out by clergy and laity as a part of ministry and mission in the parishes. Its core work is to enable and coordinate the ministry and mission of the Church in the care of the sick and those who care for them within the very particular and complex setting of the NHS. Its functions are set out in the *Church of England Year Book*.

In 1997 the Multi-Faith Working Party was set up following the Joint National Consultation with the Secretary of State for Health, the Department of Health and the NHS Executive: its work is coordinated by the Secretary of the HCC. All organizations concerned with chaplaincy and spiritual care in the NHS are represented by spokespersons on the working party. Its primary tasks include identifying and establishing the common ground between the faith communities through chaplains and spiritual care givers working for a secular employer, the NHS, and how the spiritual care is to be achieved in a fair and orderly way. The ecumenical links between the HCC and the other main denominations are covered in more detail in Chapter 4.

Current training provided for the healing ministry

From the replies received to the survey carried out as part of the research for this report, of all theological colleges, regional courses and Ordained Local Ministry schemes recognized by the House of Bishops, it is clear that specific teaching of the healing and deliverance ministries is very limited in many cases. Interest in the healing ministry varies considerably from course to course, though most of the replies noted a significant degree of interest expressed by most ordinands. This interest was usually based on their experiences in their local church while others had no experience and wanted to know more. A few replies noted that ordinands had previously had bad experiences of this ministry.

In some colleges and on some courses, there is no specific training on the healing ministry. In others, there appears to be a recent surge of interest in developing their curriculum to include a module on the subject. During a three-year course, total time of specific teaching on this topic can be most often measured in terms of a few hours, rather than several days or weeks. In a few cases, the healing ministry is given a significantly higher profile: for example, on one course there is a module over ten weeks with a day each week devoted to a particular aspect of it, but this level of priority is unusual. Some replies referred to this ministry being implicit in their curriculum, in the form of theological training. It is not clear, however, that the need for training on how to exercise the healing ministry in practical ways in the parishes has been accepted and provided for in many cases.

The stage at which teaching of the healing ministry is given varies. For example, it may be slotted in with Pastoral Care, Liturgy and Worship, elective workshops, part of a weekend module on suffering and healing and 'sessions in the Leaver's course on the sacraments of the sick and dying'. Many colleges and courses apparently assume that the healing ministry, and particularly its practical expression, will be covered in parish placements. Few details were given, however, of the kind of teaching or practical experience in the healing ministry which ordinands gain on these placements, or how it is overseen or assessed. In some cases, this ministry is an option or elective workshop only. One reply from a course noted that 'the issue of the healing ministry has not arisen yet'.

Very few colleges and courses referred in their replies to practical teaching in the healing ministry, such as how to organize a healing service, how to establish a healing ministry team, how to train laity to be involved in this ministry or any kind of guidelines for good practice. The majority of replies did not refer to the practical training of ordinands to hear confessions, or in the laying on of hands, anointing and related prayer, and caring for the chronically sick or dying.

Few replies indicated that ordinands have compulsory visits, as part of their training, to hospitals, hospices, or prisons, to learn how the healing ministry is carried out in these environments, yet each of these areas are likely to overlap the lives of most parishioners at some stage. Such visits, where the opportunity is provided, tend to be only as an option.

In many colleges and on many courses there is no specific training on the deliverance ministry, or it is only available in elective workshops such as those on charismatic renewal. Where training is provided, it tends to be limited to as little as two hours, with a view that the ministry is covered implicitly in theological training in other areas. The stage at which training is given varies and there is little evidence that teaching of the deliverance ministry is usually directly related to the healing ministry. Only one reply acknowledged the House of Bishops' guidelines on the deliverance ministry.

Although some colleges and courses do not use outside resources and personnel in teaching the healing and deliverance ministries, others use diocesan advisors, hospital and prison chaplains, psychiatrists, psychoanalysts, professional counsellors and occasionally bishops and academics. By bringing into colleges and courses the expertise of other disciplines and wider experience of those involved in the healing ministry and health care provision in our society, ordinands may be helped to develop their general awareness of the issues involved.

In replies to the survey there were very few references to the ways in which colleges oversee ordinands' training whilst in parish placement. Given that this ministry is not regarded as part of the normal everyday life and mission of many parishes, it is unclear what ordinands are being taught. In most cases, there is little evidence that ordinands are being trained to set up local teams and oversee the healing ministry at parish level. While some would point out that the whole of the Church's mission relates to healing, others place less of an emphasis on this ministry and many newly ordained priests feel inadequately prepared for it. If priests are not trained adequately themselves, they are not able to train others. They will lack confidence and have no practical framework or guidelines for good practice to help them set up and supervise healing teams in their own parishes.

Overall, specific training in the healing and deliverance ministries has a low priority, is mainly theoretical and barely in line with its status as the gospel imperative 'Go and heal the sick' (not just a theoretical imperative but a practical one). The Church of England has no minimum standard of training or widely agreed format for preparing clergy or laity for the healing ministry in parishes. There is little evidence that the colleges and courses provide sufficient practical training or ensure that ordinands have a clear understanding of how these ministries are carried out in the parishes across the range of churchmanship. No reply referred to ordinands being made aware of the ecumenical expression of this ministry.

There has been no official link between the healing ministry and the Ministry Committees to influence selection or training of ordinands apart from the link with the HCC on issues related to hospital chaplains being involved in theological training. Apparently, however, not all colleges and courses include hospital chaplains on the teaching staff. (Training for health care chaplains is discussed in Chapter 4). Whilst the issue of training for this ministry is being considered in some depth by a few theological colleges and courses, it needs to be on the curriculum of every course as a distinct area, as a matter of urgency. By providing adequate training in this ministry the next generation of priests could be properly prepared and confident to carry it out in their parishes from the start.

There is no church-wide agreement, furthermore, on what should be taught about the healing ministry as part of continuing ministerial education (CME). Many older priests have received no formal training with a particular focus on the contemporary healing scene in our society or the healing ministry. While many dioceses have an occasional diocesan advisory conference on the healing ministry as part of CME, there is no national coordination of these courses. Very little information has been made available to indicate the breadth and depth of CME in this ministry which is currently available within the dioceses or deaneries.

Training in this ministry as part of CME tends to be optional, so those who are already interested are more likely to attend, while those who are not interested are less likely to take up the opportunities. Hence the gap is widened further between those parishes where this ministry flourishes and those where it is inconspicuous. Unless training of at least the basic practical aspects is ensured, it may be possible for a priest to avoid any training in this ministry, leading to greater risk of bad practice or of the ministry not being offered to those who need and seek it. For many years the Christian Deliverance Study Group has run annual training courses, but the take-up varies in the dioceses and has not happened in the theological colleges.

Lay involvement is nearly always left to the discretion of the parish priest. There is no nationally recognized lay training scheme. Training provided at parish level is not monitored or resourced nationally by the Church of England. Some guidelines on the criteria for selection would be helpful for those parishes trying to develop the healing ministry and encouraging lay involvement, partly to avoid the risk of any choice seeming arbitrary and partly to avoid involving people who are not suitable.

Little formal oversight takes place within the dioceses to ensure that lay people have a basic understanding of the theology and good practice which are needed to support and safeguard the healing ministry. Some helpful training material and courses have been developed by committed individuals, certain dioceses and other organizations, but currently there is no objective and independent means of gathering these options together to take an overview of which are most suitable. A soundly researched lay training course and training resources which could be used in all parishes would be a valuable asset, especially if it had the general approval of the Church of England and, in particular, the House of Bishops.

Across the dioceses, the main areas of concern include lack of accountability and oversight, lack of experience at parish level, lack of training and other resources, misunderstandings and lack of confidence, the wide diversity of practice including some excesses, and organizations outside the Church of England and the other main denominations bringing the healing and deliverance ministries into disrepute. There is no formal provision for licensing or accrediting lay people in most dioceses and no criteria or accreditation scheme nationally agreed by the Church of England. The lack of such a scheme means that if a layperson behaves in an inappropriate and unacceptable way when involved in a healing ministry team, there is no official accreditation to withdraw, to indicate that the person should no longer be involved.

Whilst this current situation does not appear to be a problem at local level for most people, the lack of a nationally recognized accreditation scheme may create difficulties for people when they move and wish to be involved in this ministry within their new parish. On the other hand, it does avoid the additional work of another layer of administration and another set of parameters to be applied. Perhaps it would be sufficient to have completion of a nationally recognized form of basic training acknowledged as a guide to suitability. For this to be fair, however, the training would have to be widely and easily available.

Training in all aspects of the ministry of healing is essential for ordinands and clergy and is also highly desirable for members of the laity who feel called by God to this ministry. Involvement in this ministry can be inspiring and uplifting, but without due preparation or training it can also be frightening, disheartening and deskilling. The theoretical and theological aspects of healing and the mystery of suffering should be covered in training, together with practical issues (for example, the importance of seeking permission before laying on of hands and using touch at other times with great sensitivity). It is essential that training provides a basic framework to be shared with others in the parishes.

Oversight of the healing ministry

Oversight of the healing ministry tends to be that of the bishop through his diocesan advisor(s) on healing and deliverance and the related diocesan teams, committees or boards where these exist. There is little evidence that archdeacons and rural deans are involved in the oversight of this ministry in their pastoral areas; it is not usually a specific part of their brief, although some archdeacons are also the Bishop's Advisor on Hospital Chaplaincy. In practice, the healing ministry at parish level is carried out with no interference from the diocese, unless there are areas for concern.

The most widely recognized guidelines for good practice, which were issued jointly by the former CCHH and the Methodist Church, are not recognized officially by the Church of England; many clergy and most laity are not aware of them. People who have used these guidelines have found them generally helpful, but many feel that they need further development and improvement, in order to be more effective. Suitable guidelines for good practice in the healing ministry need to be 'owned' by the Church of England and communicated widely if they are to be effective at parish level, as a framework within which to exercise this ministry and become a benchmark helping to make oversight more straightforward, consistent and fair.

The Church of England has no widely known procedure for dealing with cases of bad practice or abuse in the healing ministry. The complaints procedure is in itself straightforward, however, provided that it is clear against whom it is that a complaint is being made. Complaints about a layperson's conduct in the healing or deliverance ministries are not covered by Church of England legislation and only if the complaint verges on areas of criminal activity would the Church ask the police to investigate it. The issue of an effective procedure for responding to complaints about lay team members needs to be addressed. Any complaints about an ordained person are currently covered by the complaints procedure in the Ecclesiastical Jurisdiction Measure 1963.

Difficulties involved in investigating complaints include the issue of informed consent, having independent witnesses and admissible evidence, and establishing what the damage might be in tangible terms. Where guidelines for good practice are established, these may reasonably be used as a benchmark against which behaviour and related complaints could be measured. Recognition and implementation of approved guidelines would provide a framework for objective assessment of complaints and help to discourage the kind of behaviour from which they could arise. Complaints are covered in more detail in Appendix 1, on good practice in the healing ministry.

In practice, however, few complaints are brought to notice because of worries about embarrassment and not being heard sympathetically. While the healing and deliverance ministries are generally carried out with care and sensitivity in a sound way, people who feel they have been treated unfairly are unlikely to be helped by the Church, if it is not prepared to listen to their concerns and act if necessary. This issue needs to be kept in clear perspective, however, as it would be misleading and counterproductive to give the impression that bad practice is commonplace, which it is not.

Representation of the healing ministry within society

The healing ministry has tended to develop at 'grass roots' level and through the work of charities and guilds set up for its promotion and resourcing. Several private charitable bodies offer training courses and newsletters. One of these charities also coordinates an ecumenical list of healing advisors, some of whom are diocesan advisors appointed by the bishops. These private organizations do not represent the Church of England and are not formally accountable to the Church of England for their activities, unless they have a chaplain who is licensed by the local diocesan bishop or have a bishop as a patron. As there is no part of the central structures with responsibility for oversight and setting of minimum standards of good practice, it is difficult to monitor or compare these organizations constructively. To an extent, some of these organizations depend on promoting awareness of their existence for the support and increase of their funding and to fulfil their trust obligations.

In the absence of any distinct body within the Church's national organizational structure to promote the healing ministry, many of these organizations have worked hard and effectively, with great dedication, to fill the gap. They deserve recognition for their considerable contribution. However, it may be overstating their case to suggest that they are sufficient to meet the current need to promote, coordinate and oversee this ministry across the Church of England. An external, independent organization cannot be at the same time fully integrated and accountable to the central structures, carry authority on behalf of the Church and still maintain its independence. There is also the issue of whether an outside independent organization can be truly ecumenical and also claim to be truly representative of the Church of England's healing ministry.

Detailed recommendations on the integration of the healing ministry into the substructure of the Archbishops' Council are made in Appendix 2. The purpose of these recommendations is to coordinate, promote, support and resource this ministry in ways which transcend the boundaries of general approach, churchmanship, and denominations, and which are recognized, used and respected throughout the Church of England, our ecumenical partners and beyond in our society. Further recommendations are made on the kind of national networks, support and resourcing needed, according to the research done amongst diocesan bishops, their advisors, and hospital and prison chaplains. These recommendations also take into account discussions with advisors from the other main denominations, including members of ecumenical networks and joint initiatives.

The work of hospital chaplains in the healing ministry

In 1998, there were around 350 Church of England hospital chaplains working full-time within the National Health Service (NHS) in England. Their salaries are paid by the NHS and they report to the hospital management structures, but their work is supported nationally by a staff of four at the HCC based in London. In 1998 around 1,500 Anglican clergy worked approximately 4,500 sessions of part-time chaplaincy for the NHS.

In the NHS, standards have been set down and guidance issued about the employment of chaplains financed from the NHS budget. Full-time and part-time chaplains from the main denominations are employed in direct proportion to the number of patients declaring allegiance to a particular denomination. Although there have been changes in the terms and conditions of employment over the last 50 years, governments have maintained their commitment to chaplaincies, confirmed in the Patient's Charter. This charter requires NHS trusts to make provision for the spiritual needs of patients and staff.

The HCC is also involved with the recruitment, selection and training of hospital chaplains. The hospital chaplains are a strong presence in a setting which provides opportunities to minister to a very wide range of people, including members of other churches and the unchurched. They have valuable experience in the healing ministry and the spiritual care of the sick and terminally ill. The hospital chaplain's role is identified in the

Health Care Chaplaincy Standards. It includes:

❖ making provision for the spiritual needs of patients and staff, recognizing that all people have spiritual needs which are highlighted when faced with illness and suffering;

❖ providing religious ministrations distinct from more general and defuse spiritual needs;

❖ visiting patients and staff regularly, listening and caring for them;

❖ cooperating with medical, nursing and administrative staff, as part of the overall care of patients;

❖ liaising with other clergy, local churches and other faith groups;

❖ acting as a resource on spiritual and ethical issues.

A survey was carried out as part of the research for this report, which has highlighted particular concerns and challenges faced by the hospital chaplains. Our remit does not cover the detailed reporting of the results of the survey, and the HCC is aware of its results. Chapter 4 provides more information on the ecumenical nature of the Hospital Chaplaincy.

The work of prison chaplains within the healing ministry

The Prison Service Chaplaincy provides prison chaplains for all of HM Prisons in England and Wales, working within the Prison Service part of the Home Office where it provides advice to ministers and officials about policy decisions with a religious or ethical dimension. In addition, it recruits, trains, deploys and supports chaplains in their ministry to prisoners and staff.

Prison chaplains tend to regard the healing ministry as an integral part of all aspects of the work with prisoners and staff and also with people outside the system, as they address the issues which lead to people being imprisoned. For example, reconciliation is a central part of their work, through helping prisoners face up to the full implications of their offences and the related impact on the wider world, leading to repentance, forgiveness and being accepted and loved for themselves. Prison chaplains are acutely aware of the factors within our society which hurt and damage people and which need addressing as part of their healing and acceptance by the local community on their release.

Good working relationships between the prison chaplains and other staff involved in caring for prisoners, such as doctors, psychiatrists, psychologists and others with specialist expertise, are valued. The quality of these relationships is a key factor in gathering information to help with the spiritual and pastoral care of prisoners, their families and dependents. Prison chaplains are also chaplains to the prison staff, providing support and helping them cope with stress. Most prison chaplains are on the staff care teams, not however as ex officio members, but because of their ministry. A high proportion of the Prison Service's in-house counsellors are chaplains and their work includes helping people come to terms with the effects of traumatic events including riot, assault, and coping with being the first people to arrive at the scenes of suicides and murders.

During discussions with prison chaplains, the need to build better links with the hospital chaplaincies was highlighted, to help with the exchange of information, support, advice and with the care of prisoners, who often move around the prison network and are often in and out of hospital, as prisoners and as ex-prisoners. The ecumenical nature of both chaplaincies also needs to be taken into account during discussions of proposals to develop joint networks nationally and regionally.

The healing of prisoners depends to a large extent on being accepted after their release into society. Better understanding of the implications of imprisonment and the painful issues with which prisoners have to learn to deal is part of the educative process for our society and particularly the community into which they are released. The local community needs help to develop closer links with the prison chaplaincies, in order to be better prepared to accept ex-prisoners after their release. There also needs to be, however, a sensitive balance between involving the local community and protecting vulnerable people within it. The possible development of ecumenical community chaplaincies based on the Canadian model deserves serious consideration as a means of helping prisoners, ex-prisoners and their families during the sentence and afterwards, as they seek acceptance and integration: see Chapter 4 for further details on community chaplaincy.

Prison chaplains have a great wealth of experience and insights which they would like to share with the rest of the Church. Areas in which they could be more involved include training for ordination, CME, addressing chapters, synods and PCCs. It would be helpful to develop a better understanding of the work of prison chaplains throughout the Church and the ways in which the local church can help offenders.

The ecumenical nature of the Prison Chaplaincy is described in more detail in Chapter 4. Several detailed recommendations relating to the prison chaplaincies are made in Appendix 2. The ways in which the prison chaplaincies carry out the healing and deliverance ministries deserve a more detailed review.

The healing ministry and Church schools

The approach to the healing ministry in Church schools is pragmatic. Children following a religious education syllabus learn about the life and importance of Jesus and within that context learn about the healing ministry of our Lord. Prayers for healing may also be offered up in school worship, but in most schools the encouragement of awareness of this ministry depends on the individual teacher. The extent to which school-children are made aware of the healing ministry and the ways in which it is currently available is not clear.

Summary

The Church of England has no coherent approach to the healing ministry. It has no national organization or practical means of keeping abreast of the wider practice and no agreed policies to support and enable the parishes to develop the healing ministry part of everyday parish life. A major shift in the perceived importance of this ministry and its place within the Church of England's life is needed, nationally and within the dioceses and parishes.

Recommendations

We recommend that:

❖ the Archbishops' Council should be asked to address through the Ministry Division the clearly identified need for improved training for the healing ministry and the strong call for its central support and coordination (see pages 41, 47, 51, 54, 55, 59 and 62);

❖ the healing ministry should be given the weight appropriate to its importance as a gospel imperative, in the recruitment, selection and training of ordinands, in continuing ministerial education, in provision for lay training and related areas within the Church of England (see pages 38, 40, 44, 46, 47, 52, 54, 55, 56, 59 and 62);

❖ the Archbishops' Council should consider the resourcing for this ministry through an existing allocation within the national budget (see pages 43 and 47);

❖ a formal national network should be established of diocesan advisors appointed by the bishops, enabling them to be acknowledged and affirmed within the Church of England, and supported through the central structures. We envisage that the Ministry Division could play a coordinating role, acting in particular as a central reference point for a network of diocesan advisors. The resourcing of this network could, judging by the example of other such networks (such as that for Bishops' Visitors), be relatively modest (see pages 41, 43, 44, 46, 47 and 51);

❖ the Church of England should cooperate with the Churches and Provinces of the Anglican Communion in the support and encouragement of the healing ministry worldwide (see pages 84–5).

4

The Ecumenical Expression
of the Healing Ministry

In Chapter 4, we describe the ways in which the healing ministry is expressed by the other main denominations in England: the Roman Catholic Church, the Methodist Church, the United Reformed Church, the Baptist Union and the Orthodox Churches. We compare the extent and the ways in which the main denominations share and coordinate their approaches including ecumenical cooperation such as the Hospital and Prison Chaplaincies. The main concerns are considered and opportunities for further cooperation are suggested.

How do the main denominations carry out the healing ministry?

One of the key terms of reference for our Review Group has been 'to take into account the ecumenical expression of this ministry'. All the main denominations, the Church of England, the Roman Catholic Church, the Methodist Church, the United Reformed Church, the Baptist Union and the Orthodox Churches, preach the gospel of Jesus Christ, which makes clear the imperative to heal the sick. Although the denominations vary in the ways in which it is carried out, we are united in this common purpose.

All Christian churches celebrate the Eucharist, although not all of those who attend and receive Holy Communion realize that this celebration is the most common form of 'healing service' in its widest and truest sense. All the denominations similarly recognize the importance of personal and corporate prayer as part of the healing ministry. Nearly all authorized intercessions in prayer books for use at the Eucharist and at other services contain petitions for the sick. Indeed, in some places these prayers are carefully organized with up-to-date lists of names published in weekly bulletin sheets and on noticeboards.

The laying on of hands is widely used throughout the denominations, often at a Eucharist before or after the people have received Holy Communion. This is the most public and distinct form of healing ministry and it highlights the place of healing within the most important service in the parish church. Members of the Free Churches, however, tend to receive the Eucharist less frequently than members of the other main denominations. Non-eucharistic services provide an opportunity to attract a wider range of people, including those who feel disadvantaged because they are not confirmed or regular attenders at church services. These services are usually comparatively simple with prayers, hymns, readings from the Bible and a short address.

The sacrament of reconciliation or penance (which used to be known as auricular confession and absolution) is widely regarded within the Roman Catholic Church and by many people in the Church of England as a valuable preliminary step before receiving the laying on of hands and anointing. The sacrament is not so widely used, however, as it was 30 years ago. Pope Paul VI in the introduction to the revised rite of the sacrament of reconciliation refers to it as 'this sacrament of healing'.

The Methodist Church and other Free Churches recognize the importance of repentance and forgiveness in the process of healing and have developed forms of service which include these elements. This section of the service is called in the Methodist Church 'repentance and reconciliation' and in the United Reformed Church 'confession and assurance of pardon'. This penitential rite, whatever its title, is part of a normal Sunday service and an opportunity for it to be received is offered in a healing service or in ministering to the sick. Practice varies by minister; generally the Methodist Church is more formal than the United Reformed Church and the Baptist Union.

The sacrament of anointing is widely recognized although it is more commonly used by the Roman Catholic Church and the Church of England than the Free Churches. It is still generally regarded, particularly amongst the laity, as something for the seriously if not critically ill, though it has almost lost its image, acquired in recent centuries, as an immediate preparation for death. The Second Vatican Council (1962–65) restored the proper meaning of the sacrament of Anointing the Sick within the revised Rite; it is for people who are dangerously or seriously ill, and even for old people if they are in a weak condition although no dangerous illness is present. Anointing is not usually offered at the Eucharist or healing services and tends to be regarded more as a one-to-one healing ministry in private. Some concern has been expressed, however, at the increasing tendency in some parts of the Church of England to offer anointing almost as a matter of routine at regular healing services.

The Methodist Church and the United Reformed Church do not usually offer anointing as a regular part of the public expression of the healing ministry. Although its use is not very common, provision is made, however, for anointing to be done selectively and usually privately, in ways similar to the Roman Catholic Church and the Church of England. Generally, in the Free Churches, because of their very nature, decisions and patterns of ministry are determined at the local level and forms of service, for example, which are issued at national level tend to be for guidance rather than being prescriptive.

In the Roman Catholic Church, ministry to the sick has developed significantly first through the liturgical movement and later through the charismatic renewal. Through the official reception of the liturgical movement at the Second Vatican Council, the Roman Catholic Church changed the focus of the sacrament previously known as extreme unction to become known as the Anointing of the Sick, designated in the Catechism of the Catholic Church (1994) with the sacrament of reconciliation as sacraments of healing (para. 1421). The Second Vatican Council's affirmation of the corporate character of all the sacraments as celebrations of the Church (Constitution on the Liturgy, paras 26–7) has led to public liturgies of anointing for many sick people in the presence of a full congregation, often now practised for example during parish visitations by diocesan bishops.

More explicit ministries of healing in the Roman Catholic Church have been almost entirely the fruit of the charismatic renewal. Here, unlike the liturgical celebrations of anointing the sick, healing is understood as a charism (spiritual gift), given by the Lord to particular persons, and is generally exercised in a framework open to the exercise of other spiritual gifts (prophecy, words of wisdom and knowledge, discernment of spirits, speaking in tongues). It is in this context only that personal prayer ministry to the sick is practised by Roman Catholic laity, most frequently in the context of charismatic prayer groups, days of renewal, retreats and conferences. However, the imposition of hands in charismatic healing is generally not a ritual gesture.

While there are very few Roman Catholic parishes which could be described as 'charismatic parishes', there are a number that celebrate 'healing Masses' on a regular basis. These may be liturgies including the sacrament of anointing, but also including some free worship and spontaneous intercession, or they may be Eucharists allowing for charismatic-type prayer for healing after the communion. There are also some healing services during which quiet forms of prayer for the sick take place during exposition of the reserved sacrament.

The involvement of Roman Catholic laity in the healing ministry is mainly through prayer, individual and corporate. Jesus heals through the sending of the Holy Spirit, ministering to us through the Church which is all the faithful, laity and clergy. All Catholics are encouraged to pray to God to ask for healing for themselves (petition) and for others (intercession). These prayers can be offered individually in the person's private prayer. They are also encouraged to ask each other to join together and to pray for themselves and others, interceding as a group, sometimes in prayer groups, non-sacramental services and healing services and they will also, in prayer, ask saints and especially Mary to intercede for them.

There are prayers for all this at various points in the Mass; especially obvious are the Prayers of the Faithful (commonly called 'bidding prayers') which will generally include intercessions for the sick who may be named. Lay people can and should pray for or over a sick person. This can include laying on of hands, preferably by a small group of lay people, to show that it is the Church who is ministering and to avoid the danger of an individual becoming proud and treated as a 'healer'.

These forms of praying with the sick have become more common recently through Roman Catholic charismatic renewal. If a lay person in this context uses blessed oil to anoint the sick person on the forehead, it must be made clear that this is not the sacrament of Anointing the Sick. Laying on of hands and/or anointing may not be done unless the sick person asks for or agrees to it. It is also recommended that when a priest gives the sacrament of Anointing the Sick, other Roman Catholics should be present and join in the prayers (generally relatives or nursing or caring staff).

Roman Catholic priests tend to carry out the healing ministry as a normal part of parish ministry and pastoral care. There is a view that the Roman Catholic Church's approach to healing is different from that of the other churches, as it is mainly sacramental, consisting of the ministry of reconciliation, the sacrament of Anointing the Sick and Holy Communion. There tends not to be the kind of distinction made between the healing ministry and other forms of ministry which one sometimes finds in the Church of England at parish level; it seems to be naturally integrated. Furthermore, there is no separate form of code of conduct or guidelines for good practice beyond those which are an established part of each priest's ministry.

The Roman Catholic Church responded to Bishop Morris Maddocks's advice on diocesan advisors when he was the Archbishops' Advisor on the healing ministry, by agreeing that the bishops should appoint a suitable priest to the post in each diocese. The Roman Catholic diocesan advisors work in similar ways to the Church of England's diocesan healing advisors. Roman Catholic bishops also have their own advisors on the deliverance ministry. The ecumenical expression of the deliverance ministry is covered in Chapter 9.

Roman Catholic bishops have bishops' hospital chaplains' advisors. The Roman Catholic Church is a member of the Churches' Committee for Hospital Chaplaincy and sends an observer in attendance to meetings of the College of Health Care Chaplains as well as having its own organization, Roman Catholic Chaplains in Health Care.

The Roman Catholic and Anglican Churches also have a long tradition of prayer for the sick as part of the work of the religious communities. Many Roman Catholic religious orders were founded explicitly to nurse and care for the sick, which has also been an established part of the life of some Anglican religious communities.

There is a rich tradition of devotion to the saints within the Roman Catholic Church, which to a lesser extent some parts of the Church of England share but which generally is not the practice within the other denominations. The linking in intercessory prayer of a particular saint with healing of a particular ailment is not an official link; it is part of Roman Catholic folk culture that developed in the Middle Ages: this practice is far less common now. Roman Catholics tend to pray to the saints asking them to intercede in a general way; chief amongst the saints would be Mary, mother of our Lord.

Roman Catholics also sometimes ask 'prospective' saints to intercede for healing because generally a miracle in response to their intercession is needed before beatification (see Chapter 11). The devotion to saints also encourages the study of their lives, which offers in turn insights into their spirituality and suggestions for ways in which people can learn to pray and to cope with their difficulties. The saints' growth into wholeness is inseparable from their growth into holiness.

The Roman Catholic Church also has a strong tradition of shrines for devotion and intercessory prayer. Some shrines are devoted to particular saints, some of which are comparatively modern. When a pilgrimage is undertaken, the journey itself could be regarded as part of the healing process, as the pilgrim is encouraged to focus his or her attention on the illness and, through prayer, ask for help. This focus may make the person more receptive to help, although the general tendency is not to expect a cure, but to enable the acceptance of uncertainty and the mystery of healing. The most obvious example of this instance is, of course, Lourdes. Although the shrine there arose because of St Bernadette, there is more focus on Mary, whose intercession is asked for, than on Bernadette, who claimed to have had a vision of Mary there.

Of the English shrines, Walsingham is particularly associated with the healing ministry. The Shrine of Our Lady at Walsingham was founded in 1061 following a vision given to a woman of noble birth, in which she was asked to build a replica of the house in Nazareth where the Blessed Virgin Mary and St Joseph cared for Jesus in his formative years. Restored by Anglicans, it is administered by a College of Guardians and has facilities for pilgrims including sick and disabled people. In 1897, Roman Catholics began to show interest in restoring the ancient devotion and in 1934, the Slipper Chapel was restored and a statue put there; in the last 50 years, this chapel has been the centre of Roman Catholic worship. The Eastern Orthodox were also involved in the restoration of Walsingham and the former Methodist Chapel in Great Walsingham has been consecrated as a Russian Orthodox church.

Healing is a central part of the work at the shrines, where the main expression of the healing ministry is through the Sacrament of the Sick, in the laying on of hands, in anointing and in a distinctive feature of Walsingham, the sprinkling of water from an ancient well. Pilgrims who go to Walsingham receive the water in three ways. First they are given water to sip, then in the sign of the cross on their forehead and finally a little water is poured into their cupped hands. The water is a strong symbol, reminding the pilgrims of baptism and also of tears, which may be an expression of the very deepest human emotions and hidden hurts.

The shrines at Walsingham are holy ground, visited by Christians of all denominations, Roman Catholic, Anglican, Orthodox and Reformed, for whom the rite of sprinkling helps the pilgrims recognize our common allegiance to Jesus Christ in shared prayer and worship, which does not raise the issues of denominational boundaries which the Eucharist raises. Visitors to the shrines include those of other faiths, for whom water has a particular religious significance. For example, washing is part of the religious ceremonies for other faiths, and in the Islamic faith Mary has a place of significant respect. The shrines and the rite provide a holy environment for multi-faith as well as ecumenical dialogue.

Within the Church of England, there are over 40 religious communities and many more in the wider Anglican Communion. These communities range from small groups to those with more than 80 members, traditionally vowed to poverty, chastity and obedience. Their inspiration stems from the nineteenth-century Oxford Movement and more distantly from the fourth-century example of Anthony of Egypt. All centre on a life of prayer, embracing all aspects of healing. Many have ecumenical links through people formally associated with them, such as tertiaries, oblates and companions. Pilsdon and the Lee Abbey Household Communities, lay groups less formally organized and not under life vows, are also connected with the healing ministry. Similarly, the Belfast Columbanus Community of Reconciliation (a small, ecumenical, short-term residential group of laity, clergy and religious in the Roman Catholic, Lutheran and Free Churches and the Church of Ireland) forms a neutral base and house of prayer open to outsiders who may never have spoken to 'the other side'.

The Methodist Church has a formal network of advisors on the healing ministry. At the National Methodist Conference in 1993 a resolution was passed to appoint district advisors which fulfil the same role as the diocesan advisors in the Church of England. They are appointed by the district synods, however, rather than by senior churchmen or an appointments committee.

This new network was initially set up for the mailing and distribution of information and general communication. In 1999 there were 24 district advisors in 30 districts covering England and Wales. The shortfall is due to retirements and moves rather than a lack of general interest. There is little funding available and this is taken up by general administration and travelling expenses. Events and conferences are set up to be self-funding and are usually very successful. The United Reformed Church has a similar network of advisors. These are appointed by the twelve Provincial Synods. In 1995 the Methodist Church and the United Reformed Church (URC) set up a joint Health and Healing Development Group, which will be explained further in this chapter.

The link between the healing ministry and pastoral care is regarded as very important in the Methodist Church. A newly created Pastoral Care Advisory Group will work closely with the Joint Health and Healing Development Group. The aim is to enable local churches to exercise care over a wide range of needs, including those of disabled people and ministry to the bereaved. The Methodist Church has also made a feature of residential care for the elderly, with homes strategically placed around the country. Specialist care is provided for those with dementia and support given to their carers.

The Baptist Union is a union of independent churches, which have an annual Assembly. The individual churches within the Union determine for themselves the ways in which mission, ministries, etc. are carried out locally. For this reason, it is not easy to get an overview of the ways in which the healing ministry is carried out across the breadth of churches within the Union.

'Baptists for Healing' was born out of the Baptist Union Health and Healing Group. In October 1999 a team of six members met to formulate a new vision for the healing ministry within the Baptist Union. With approximately 100 members, Baptists for Healing seek to reach the local church to provide a means of teaching and support for all Baptist Communities in the denomination. The organization is resourced by members' subscription. It offers training, courses, conferences and reviews. It hopes to become involved with the Methodist/URC Joint Health and Healing Development Group.

Oversight of the healing ministry is through the Ministry Department at the Baptist Union headquarters in Oxfordshire. Ministerial training includes health and healing matters such as counselling, spirituality and worship. Additional training is provided through occasional workshops in the regions.

The Orthodox Churches, which uphold and continue the faith and practice of the Church of the first millennium, have a distinctive approach to the healing ministry, based upon the Letter of James 5.13-16. The sacrament of Anointing for Healing has a high profile in the Orthodox Churches because it is part of normal Christian life, available to everyone in an unselfconscious way. Whenever members of the congregation are sick, they are anointed. When someone is dying however, prayers would be offered rather than anointing. There is a special service for the soul about to depart from the body.

When a feast is celebrated, the congregation is anointed with the oil of the feast. Once a year, a particular service for healing is held on the Wednesday of Holy Week, when the whole congregation is invited to be anointed, to ensure that everyone has the opportunity to be anointed for healing at least once a year. This emphasizes the place of this sacrament as part of the normal life of the Orthodox Churches. The faithful may request anointing at any time for healing, or request prayers of intercession, or blessing, in the local church, before icons or at a shrine where an oil lamp constantly gives out the light of illumination and blessing.

The priest carries with him the three oils, for exorcism (baptism), for chrismation (confirmation) and for healing. The healing oil is usually a mixture of oil, prepared for the purpose, to which is added small amounts from holy relics known to exude holy oil. For example, in Kiev in 1987 at the millennium celebration of the Russian Church, several relics exuded oil (myrrh) and one of these, that of St Clement, continues to do so. Pilgrims are anointed with it at a special prayer service held daily. Certain holy relics are also reputed to bring about manifestations of healing.

The Orthodox Churches do not have formal networks of advisors, though there are many skilled in spiritual direction and counselling and some holy people have a reputation for healing powers. Whilst young men are trained for the priesthood at seminaries, older men are chosen by the bishop when a church is without a priest, according to their suitability and the support of the congregation. After tutoring by a senior priest, the man is ordained by the bishop. The understanding of the healing ministry in pastoral and sacramental training in the Orthodox Churches is guided by the detailed good practice set out in the Typika (which orders the religious practice) of the Greek Church of Constantinople. The ministry is part of normal parish life, strongly sacramental and carried out by the priest as the bishop's representative in the parish.

Lay involvement in the healing ministry within the Orthodox Churches is through public and private intercessory prayer. At services there are long prayers of intercession during which the names of those in particular need are read out. Lay people are involved in ministration to the sick through care, support and visiting but there are, however, no formal organizations such as healing ministry teams, Christian Listening or Christian counselling.

There is almost no overlap in the expression of the healing ministry between the Orthodox Churches and the other denominations. The hospital chaplaincies may, however, occasionally include Orthodox priests. Orthodox faithful in hospital are ministered to by their parish priests, members of the congregation or chaplains appointed by the diocese, who visit the person in hospital and minister to them. Generally speaking, priests in the Orthodox Churches in the United Kingdom are not involved in national church-based organizations; however, conferences on healing are arranged from time to time in other countries.

As part of the research for this report, we approached people in the New Churches to find out about their perception and expression of the healing ministry; overall the response was that forming an overview is not easy. Some New Churches seek and practise healing far more than others and that is often dependent upon the leader and the leader's experience of healing themselves.

Within the Ichthus Christian Fellowship, for example, healing is practised consistently and regularly, within the church context and with a view to the book of James; the elders of each congregation minister by coming to the people who request anointing for healing. Sometimes oil for anointing is available at the Lord's Table, giving the opportunity for people requesting healing to be anointed in the context of the community as a whole, but still the initiative is with the leaders in the actual anointing. In the context of larger meetings, laying on of hands is the method more commonly used. Healing is regarded as a regular part of ministry to people, which sometimes, but not always, links healing of the soul with healing of the body.

How is the healing ministry carried out ecumenically?

Across the Church of England, the Roman Catholic Church, the Methodist Church, the United Reformed Church, the Baptist Union and the Orthodox Churches, there is no overall coordinating body or formal linking of networks for advisors, clergy and laity involved in the healing ministry.

Churches Together in England (CTE) has a coordinating group, the Churches' Committee for Hospital Chaplaincy. The healing ministry however, is not a specific item on the agenda of CTE at national level or regional level, according to information available at the time of research for this report. In a few areas only, the healing ministry is discussed ecumenically, for example, Churches for Healing in Hampshire, but the idea of a current widespread ecumenically organized healing ministry is, sadly, a myth. Nevertheless, it is still a wonderful concept and worth pursuing from now on.

The Evangelical Alliance has an interest at a national level in healing and deliverance. The Evangelical Alliance Coalition on the Occult and New Spiritualities (EACONS) acts as a panel and sounding board on these subjects, and as a network for those working in areas of the Church's ministries which come into contact with people who have been involved in these areas, such as the deliverance ministry. Another area of interest to EACONS is the issue of complementary medicine and alternative therapies, since people within the denominations are asking for guidance on what is acceptable and what is not. The Evangelical Alliance also has a Disability Forum which falls within the remit of the Social Responsibility Department. Its main aim is to encourage effective and coordinated action by evangelical churches and agencies in this field.

The Free Churches' Council (FCC) has representation on the Health Care Chaplaincy Board, and on the Joint Methodist and United Reformed Church Health and Healing Development Group (explained in more detail later in this chapter). There is not, however, a specific Free Church network for the healing ministry.

Within the Church of England, the ecumenical dimension of the healing ministry is recognized as important, although at the time of researching for this report, the Council for Christian Unity (CCU) did not have an overview of this ministry across the denominations, partly due to the difficulty of gathering information on such a wide scale and keeping it up to date.

The healing ministry is most effective ecumenically at local level, as there are few barriers across the denominations, particularly in non-eucharistic services. These services are occasionally organized jointly as an ecumenical event. The ecumenical nature of the congregation at this type of service is a reflection of a commonly acknowledged need for healing sought at a welcoming, open and non-judgemental service. Unfortunately, at the time of writing this report there is no liturgy for ecumenical non-eucharistic healing services agreed nationally by the denominations.

In practice, people from the main denominations move around in attending non-eucharistic healing services. It is one of the few types of service where one is likely to find members of the Pentecostal Churches alongside Roman Catholics, Anglicans and members of the Free Churches – and where the differences and boundaries seem to melt away into oblivion. Perhaps the greatest opening for the healing between the churches to begin, is the healing ministry itself – but when are we going to recognize and seize this opportunity?

Some years ago, the CCHH held a multi-denominational meeting to discuss how the main denominations could work together more closely within the healing ministry. The Methodist Church and the United Reformed Church approached the issue positively, but the Church of England and the Roman Catholic Church were not so committed. Apparently one of the difficulties was finding representatives for the discussions who were in a position to commit their denominations in any serious initiative. Other attempts have been made by various bodies to set up ecumenical events, but we were told that the organizers did not consult the denominations sufficiently during the preparations to ensure their success.

The Methodist Church and the United Reformed Church pooled their resources for the healing ministry in 1995 and set up the Joint Methodist and United Reformed Church Health and Healing Development Group. This group of members, nine in 1999, plus the occasional attendance of a Baptist minister or representative from another denomination, meets twice a year to discuss a broad range of issues. These include mental health, health issues related to the Government's agenda, planning and reviewing national conferences on healing, and position papers on the denominations' approaches to healing, as well as liturgy being developed by the denominations.

This joint group also organizes a conference every two years, which is open to anyone. It usually takes the form of a three-day event with expert speakers and a wide range of topics, including seminars for the provincial and district advisors. The advisors meet separately each year and also link in with the regional day meeting organized by the Acorn Christian Healing Trust to provide an ecumenical forum.

The positions of Chairman/Convener and Secretary are rotated between the two denominations and the membership is equally balanced, a principle which is regarded as important. The joint group sends out a Health and Healing Bulletin every six months and two additional mailings each year, to keep the advisors well-informed. The bulletin is a valuable means of passing on information about forthcoming events, reviews of books and videos about the healing ministry and articles on issues such as euthanasia and the links between the healing ministry and the medical professions.

The Methodist Connexional Secretary for Health and Healing is also involved in the search for suitable people in the Methodist Church to be considered for appointment as healing advisors and to find replacements when advisors move on or retire. Healing services in the Methodist Church and the United Reformed Church are not organized or co-ordinated nationally by this joint group. Ecumenical healing ministries are local initiatives and self-starting.

Training for the healing ministry is being developed by the Methodist Church and the United Reformed Church, as part of a coordinated approach to offer suitable resources to help people engage with health and healing issues in a range of circumstances. A correspondence course open to anyone, lay or ordained, is being developed at Higher Education Level 1 through the Methodist Open Learning Centre to start in autumn 2000, with preliminary discussions taking place for further courses as Levels 2 and 3. These plans follow on from work previously completed to produce the guidelines for good practice published in cooperation with the former CCHH and the booklet *Resources for Those Involved in the*

Christian Healing Ministry. Together these provide material to help individuals and church groups who are beginning to explore this ministry or take a fresh look at what they are already doing in this area. The section on healing in the Alpha Course is used by the denominations to make lay people aware of this ministry too.

The hospital chaplaincy

Training for appointed health care chaplains is coordinated through the Training and Development Office of the Hospital Chaplaincies Council (HCC). This office is sponsored by the Church of England's Hospital Chaplaincies Council, the Roman Catholic Church, the Free Churches' Council and the College of Health Care Chaplains. NHS chaplains of all denominations with less than one year's experience in post and lay and ordained chaplain's assistants are eligible to attend. Staff on the course are members of the Church of England, the Roman Catholic Church and the Free Churches.

The HCC provides training in the healing ministry for hospital chaplains. This is coordinated through the Training and Development office, which is sponsored ecumenically. All newly appointed chaplains in acute trusts and mental health trusts are encouraged to attend an ecumenical introductory training course. The course covers areas such as the provision of the factual information required by chaplains in the performance of their work, and understanding the expectations and relationships which exist within the trust/hospital environment. The course also enables chaplains to understand and evaluate the problems and opportunities they may encounter within the trust/hospital and equips them to minister more confidently and competently. Additional courses are run on issues such as 'Chaplaincy Management and Budget Systems' and 'Spiritual Care in a Multi-Faith Society'. A Training Bulletin is published three times a year providing NHS Trusts and working chaplains with details of courses being offered.

The Churches' Committee for Hospital Chaplaincy (CCHC), which was formerly the Joint Committee for Hospital Chaplaincy, is an interdenominational consultative body and involves the Free Churches, the Roman Catholic Church and the Church of England (through the HCC), and churches from Ireland, Scotland and Wales. It has also taken in the College of Health Care Chaplains, which is not a church organization, but part of a trade union. The CCHC works co-operatively in management relationships with the Department of Health and the NHS Executive, including reaching agreement on part-time pay rates, titles and NHS grades. The Secretary of the CCHC also acts as the spokesperson and link with CTE. The roles of Chairman and Secretary are 'moved around' the participating denominations every few years. At the time of writing this report, in late 1999, there was no updated clear constitution accepted by all three of the sponsoring Churches in England. A review of all the committee structures for hospital chaplaincy may become necessary following negotiations with the NHS Executive which have been taking place during 1999 and 2000.

The College of Health Care Chaplains, founded in 1992, was the result of the merger between the Hospital Chaplains' Fellowship and the National Association of Whole-Time Hospital Chaplains. This is an interdenominational and interfaith organization based on a federation of branches formed on the boundaries of Regional Health Authorities in England. Amongst the aims of the College are the safeguarding and promotion of the work of the Church in health care establishments and issues of interest to clergy and laity working in these establishments. The College provides support in a variety of ways including an annual study course, regular journals and newsletters. The College is also an autonomous section of the Manufacturing, Science and Finance Union (MSF).

The Free Churches' Federal Council has a Health Care Chaplaincy Board, which began in 1950; it is a coordinating group of Churches Together in England (CTE), but predates CTE. This board is the official body responsible for all matters relating to Free Church Health Care Chaplaincy work. Its functions include:

❖ facilitating collaboration and cooperation between health care chaplaincy agencies;

❖ being an ecumenical point of reference for health care chaplaincy matters for the denominations and the NHS;

❖ undertaking regular joint initiatives (e.g. the annual letter to the NHS trusts on sessional payments);

❖ undertaking joint projects, such as guidance notes on ecumenical cooperation in health care chaplaincy;

❖ promoting hospital chaplaincy in ecumenical terms.

The ecumenical nature of hospital chaplaincies is promoted in various ways. For example, the members of the CCHC try to ensure that they agree general policies on chaplaincy and encourage understanding of one another's ways of regarding chaplaincy and its organization, so that the CCHC can speak for the service as a whole. Nevertheless, there are areas where the chaplains cannot be fully interchangeable on all aspects of religious provision: for example, the sacramental discipline of the Roman Catholic Church reinforced by 'One Bread, One Body'. The CCHC does not encourage rules to be broken for the sake of 'easy ecumenism'. The committee also supports the work being done to encourage and formalize the provision of spiritual and religious care for people of other faiths.

All chaplains are expected to work together as a team except for any areas in which in conscience they are unable to do so. Their work is underpinned by vision statements and working practice strategies agreed between members of the chaplaincy. The chaplains also meet together regularly to exchange information and share training and support.

Within the context of the hospital chaplaincy, the recipients' religious and spiritual needs and wishes are paramount. The tradition and wishes of the patient in relation to sacramental provision are respected and the appropriate member of the chaplaincy would normally make this provision. In order to relate to the diversity of traditions and wide expectations of the chaplaincy, a variety of traditions, skills and preferably chaplains of both genders are involved. Within this context the diversity of views is recognized sensitively and constructively.

Care is taken in relation to the activity of individuals and groups who attempt to gain access to patients in a misguided attempt to evangelize, for example, or conduct spiritual healing. Any patient has the right to receive ministry in their own tradition and can be visited by the appropriate person from their community, but no one other than the appointed chaplains has free access to other patients.

In 1997 the Multi-Faith Working Party was set up following the Joint National Consultation with the Secretary of State for Health, the Department of Health and the NHS Executive: its work is coordinated by the Secretary of the HCC. All organizations concerned with chaplaincy and spiritual care in the NHS are represented by spokespersons on the working party. Its primary tasks include identifying and establishing the common ground between the faith communities through chaplains and 'spiritual care givers' working for a secular employer, the NHS, and how the spiritual care is to be achieved in a fair and orderly way.

The prison chaplaincy

The Prison Service Chaplaincy, based in London, is interdenominational and supports the work of approximately 300 prison chaplains. Prison chaplains are involved in facilitating the observance of other faiths and every prison has an Anglican, a Roman Catholic and a Methodist chaplain. The headquarters team of the Prison Service Chaplaincy includes senior representatives of all three denominations. Outside the Prison Chaplaincy, the Anglican Bishop to Prisons, the Roman Catholic Bishop to Prisons and a Methodist Leader monitor the work of the chaplaincy and give support to Chaplaincy Headquarters. The Chaplaincy Headquarters have over recent years developed their own ecumenical covenant within the Headquarters' team. A Local Ecumenical Project (LEP) conference is usually held biannually to review the ecumenical aspects of the work.

All prison chaplaincies are now organized on an ecumenical basis with some having a formal agreement to work together in a Local Ecumenical Project, although few chaplaincy appointments are ecumenical per se. Chaplaincy duties are shared and a number of chaplaincies have explored ecumenical worship. All new chaplains coming into the Prison Service are expected to support the ecumenical ethos of the chaplaincy. Recent formal links have been developed with CTE to formalize the ecumenical aspects.

Local church communities are linked to prison establishments through LEPs. It is quite common for such local church communities to join the prison congregation on a Sunday morning. These links have proved to be invaluable in developing friendship and breaking down barriers of hostility towards men and women in prison. The diocesan ecumenical advisor may also take a new interest in prison ministry through the setting up of an LEP. Local church communities are usually impressed that the prison chaplains are able to work so closely together with them when there seems to be so much division on the outside.

A key problem is offenders leaving prison expecting the churches on the outside to reflect the ecumenical openness they have experienced in prison. Sadly, they are usually disappointed.

A key challenge falls to the denominations to look to the prison chaplaincies for a model of ecumenical working in the healing ministry that is dynamic.

Some local churches have been involved with the healing ministry in prisons. This has been done mainly on a local basis with no formal structures. According to current research, there is no known record of the healing ministry in prisons being discussed at a synod or church meeting. Prison chaplains have drawn attention to the need for simple ecumenical liturgy for use in prisons, including for healing services.

Training for the prison chaplaincy focuses on all the Christian denominations with a strong emphasis on the Anglican, Methodist and Roman Catholic groups. Chaplaincy training is managed by the Chaplaincy Training Officer based at Newbold Revel (near Rugby) and sponsored by the Chaplaincy Training Board made up of Chaplaincy Headquarters staff, Prison Service Area Managers, Prison Governors and three ecumenical chaplains working in prison establishments.

Training is divided into two parts, namely professional and spiritual. The professional training consists of an Initial Development Course, to give chaplains a basic understanding of prison ministry. Development Part 1 provides an opportunity for chaplains to discuss current issues such as drug awareness, self-harm and working with the abused. Development Part 2 is designed to give chaplains an opportunity to research and present a topic that would be of benefit to themselves and to the Prison Service Chaplaincy such as 'A Theology of Punishment', 'Ministering to Juveniles' and 'Caring for Staff'.

The Counselling Course is designed to encourage chaplains to take care of themselves before they minister to others. The World Faiths Course aims to develop a new awareness of world faith issues. Classroom-based lectures are supported by visits to various places of worship in the Coventry area. Other courses include 'Working with Sex Offenders', 'Working with Women in Custody', 'Working with the Abused' and 'Working in a Non-book Culture'. Two years ago a five-day course on the healing ministry was organized and in the past a joint training event was arranged with hospital chaplains.

Spiritual training has a strong emphasis on spiritual direction. During a twelve-month period, prison chaplains are expected to attend one training course and one retreat. The retreat may be an individually guided retreat, walking retreat, silent retreat, story-telling retreat, Celtic spirituality retreat or a charismatic retreat. Training in the healing ministry is 'in-house' and does not have any outside supervision. Prison chaplains are involved in healing through pastoral care, reconciliation programmes, formal worship, personal confession and general support.

The Prison Chaplaincy could be described as 'front-line' healing ministry. Chapel worship, groups and cell-based one-to-one conversations all provide significant time in which to minister to people in their brokenness and their lack of self-worth, responding to their need for forgiveness and the resources to change and make a new start in their lives.

Community chaplaincy (as developed in Canada)

An issue of great concern to many people in our society is what happens to people when they leave prison? A concept arousing current interest in England is ecumenical community chaplaincy, along the lines originally developed in Canada and supported by the Correctional Service of Canada (the equivalent of the Prison Service and the Probation Service in England). Community chaplains who follow the Canadian model provide a specialist resource for the wider Church for ex-prisoners and their families during the period of the sentence and afterwards, as they seek acceptance and integration. Their work includes seeking creative responses to the difficult challenges of reintegrating offenders, restoring families, healing victims and ultimately recreating community.

In consultations with the Prison Chaplaincy a request was made that local Councils of Churches or similar ecumenical groups consider sponsoring a community chaplain based on the Canadian model, to provide a focus in the community for the Churches' ministry of the affirming and challenging love of Christ to offenders, ex-offenders and their families.

Ecumenical concerns

Particular concerns shared by people, ordained and lay, across the denominations involved in the healing ministry include:

- ❖ church politics, not just between the denominations but also between different traditions, affecting initiatives to encourage the healing ministry;

- ❖ the need for an ecumenically agreed basis, to underpin existing and future initiatives and cooperation within the healing ministry;

- ❖ the lack of coordination between the denominations in different areas: for example, a lack of communication between prison chaplains and the local churches of released prisoners and the youth officers in their areas, resulting in difficulty in follow-up pastoral care for those who have received the healing ministry; lack of communication between hospital chaplains and prison chaplains at local and regional level;

- ❖ the need to develop simple forms of ecumenical liturgy for special circumstances such as worship in prisons and hospitals, where the chaplaincies are already ecumenical;

- ❖ the need for guidelines for good practice which all the main denominations would formally adopt and promote, to foster a common understanding of the healing ministry, to encourage good practice where it already exists, to inform those who wish to become more involved, to inspire confidence in those seeking healing and to discourage poor practice;

- ❖ training provision for ordained and lay people in this ministry, in particular the need to develop a wide appreciation of the varying ways in which it is carried out across the denominations and the traditions within them;

- ❖ a coherent approach to advising Christians on the issues relating to complementary medicine and alternative therapies;

- ❖ organizations which carve their own niche and earn their living through the healing ministry or associated activities, for gain rather than out of a sense of vocation, and those which are not part of the denominations, that is, not accountable for the ways in which they carry out this ministry;

❖ the need for some kind of recognized logo as a kind of Churches' guide to acceptable standards, to show where resources are approved, rather like the 'New Start' logo for the millennium material;

❖ and in particular, the need for an ecumenical organization or structure to be set up on a manageable scale to coordinate, resource, inform and promote the healing ministry across the denominations in future.

How is the healing ministry carried out in other Churches and Provinces in the Anglican Communion?

Through the London office of the Anglican Communion, a survey was carried out on the ways in which the healing ministry is carried out within the Communion. It has not been possible to draw an accurate overview of the state of this ministry worldwide because insufficient information was returned within the time allocated for this report. From the replies which have been received, however, it is apparent that this ministry has a similar state of low profile or is affected by lack of resources, in many parts of the world.

Nevertheless, in the developing countries, this ministry is regarded by many congregations as a normal and essential part of church life since although, with a few exceptions, scientific medicine is fully accepted, its costs are often beyond the resources of the poor. People come forward for prayer and laying on of hands at any service. There is the common expectation of God's intervention in curing illness. In some instances the prayer ministry may appear superficial but very significant inner, emotional healing may be experienced and a keen interest can be aroused in healing. Because occult activity is common even in sophisticated urban situations, liberation is also in some cases urgently needed.

In some parts of the Anglican Communion, the healing ministry embraces far more than the kinds of need for healing that we tend to be aware of in England. For example, in South Africa, the issues of the violence of apartheid, torture, imprisonment, abuse and exile affect people who seek help from the Church. One priest involved in this ministry lost his hands and an eye from a letter bomb sent by the apartheid police; through his recovery and witness he has established an important ministry for his country.

The theology of healing and deliverance

None of the replies provided a summary of their Province's or Church's theological approach to the healing and deliverance ministries; some replies explained that this information was not available. The need for the healing ministry to be an integral part of theological education, in order to be able to fulfil the gospel imperative, was a key concern.

Resources

In poor and developing countries the healing ministry is barely provided for by the Church in terms of practical resources. Even in comparatively wealthy countries, apart from the use of existing buildings, resources tend to be very limited. Lack of training and the necessary resources to carry this out were issues raised in many of the replies. Requests were made for help from the Church of England for training resources, such as books and videos, in some cases. No reply provided copies of guidelines 'owned' by the Church or Province, on the healing ministry. The need for guidelines is recognized widely.

Ecumenical cooperation

In some replies, there were brief references to the ecumenical expression of this ministry, but these were generally in terms of the willingness of people to mix across the denominations at healing services. There were very few indications of ecumenical cooperation at the level of organization, training, general resourcing or planned services.

Cooperation with other national organizations

There are apparently few links between the Church's healing ministry and the national organizations of the countries in which the ministry is carried out, such as health care, education and the prison service. In the poorer countries, this appears to be due to lack of infrastructure, resources, issues of autonomy and lack of good communication systems.

Recommendations

Detailed recommendations relating to the healing ministry in the Anglican Communion are set out in Appendix 2.

What can the Church of England learn from the other denominations?

None of the main denominations claims to have an ideal approach or ideal national structure for the healing ministry. The need for better organization, resourcing, promotion and oversight is widely recognized. We have much to learn from each other in order to share a common understanding of the theology and practice of this ministry, as part of its ecumenical development.

The Roman Catholic Church has a particularly sacramental approach which forms a strong basis for a priestly parish-based ministry. The Methodist and United Reformed Churches have made significant progress by forming in 1995 a joint development group for health and healing, pooling their resources and coordinating their healing ministries nationally. The Pentecostal Churches and many of the New Churches have raised awareness of the Holy Spirit working through the healing ministry. The charismatic movement has also made the link between the healing ministry and renewal and mission in the parishes.

Each of the main denominations has liturgical material worth serious consideration. If we are to work together ecumenically, we need to develop liturgy for this ministry with our ecumenical partners. In certain circumstances, such as in prisons and hospitals, the need for simple inclusive ecumenical liturgy is clearly recognized. Currently, there is no recognized forum for the main denominations to develop liturgy ecumenically for the healing ministry, which involves their representatives who are widely involved in this ministry and therefore reliably in touch with what is needed.

The Methodist Church, has developed a wide range of written resource material covering the healing ministry and its overlap with pastoral care, the NHS and social and ethical issues such as euthanasia. There is little to be gained from 'reinventing the wheel' and we need to acknowledge the contribution already made and seek to share the material already researched and proven.

It is worth noting that the main denominations have experienced similar patterns of surging interest in the healing ministry. Similar concerns are also felt, through the experiences gained, for the need for greater care and monitoring of the extremes and for the denominations to work together more closely to encourage a common understanding of good practice in this ministry.

Recommendations

We recommend that:

❖ the Church of England should work with our ecumenical partners and health care organizations to develop and establish a new ecumenical Churches' Healing Ministry Group. This group would coordinate, support and promote this ministry, at national and regional levels (see pages 49, 59, 74, 76, 81, 83 and 85);

❖ the Church of England and our ecumenical partners should develop and agree a basis for future initiatives and ecumenical cooperation within the healing ministry (see pages 74, 75, 76, 80-81, 82, 83 and 86);

❖ the Churches' Healing Ministry Group should be a springboard for interchurch initiatives and ecumenical cooperation between the Church and the health care organizations (see pages 74, 80, 81, 82, 83, 85, 87 and 151);

❖ non-eucharistic liturgy for services of prayers for healing should be developed by the Churches' Healing Ministry Group, drawing upon experience in the healing ministry as currently practised within the mainstream denominations (see pages 47, 66, 75 and 86);

❖ liturgy for special circumstances, particularly for use in prisons and hospitals, should be developed in cooperation with the hospital and prison chaplaincies, including rites for penance and reconciliation which emphasize the healing potential of the assurance of forgiveness, and for children and people with learning difficulties (see pages 81, 83, 86, 131, 254 and 255);

❖ the guidelines for good practice which are included in this report should be offered to our ecumenical partners for discussion and adaption if necessary by individual denominations, leading towards an ecumenically agreed understanding of good practice in the healing ministry (see pages 57, 83 and 87);

❖ training for the healing ministry for ordained and lay people should be developed, supported and coordinated ecumenically where appropriate (see pages 47, 54, 76, 83 and 87);

❖ the valuable work of hospital chaplains and prison chaplains in this ministry should be affirmed and a review should be considered of the relevant Church of England and ecumenical committee structures and communication networks (see pages 50, 60, 61, 77, 80, 81 and 83–4).

5

The Healing Ministry
in Professional Health Care Settings

The Church has a long tradition of working within the hospitals and other health care settings for healing in our society. This is because many of these institutions originated in the Church's care for the sick in the past. It is therefore important that cooperation between the Church and these institutions should continue to develop, especially in these days when the advantages of a multidisciplinary approach to healing is widely recognized. While the boundaries between the chaplain and other professions must be respected, nevertheless there are advantages for those within the healing ministry of the Church to be able to train alongside other professionals. Such training not only helps in their working together, but it can also lead toward a common working vocabulary. Confidentiality is a key issue in a multidisciplinary approach and this needs to be understood not only by the chaplain and his or her assistants but also by the parish clergy.

The 1958 report encouraged cooperation between doctors and clergy, and suggested that one of the ways to facilitate this was through the formation of informal clergy–doctor groups. Where such groups exist today they are likely include members of other care professions as well. But we want to discuss in greater detail the possibilities of such cooperation in the light of the developments of the last 40 years which we noted earlier. In this chapter we shall indicate opportunities for cooperation in professional health care settings (mostly hospitals) and in the next chapter opportunities in parishes. The division is a rather rough-and-ready one, for in some cases a health care chaplain is also an honorary assistant in a local church, and in other cases a vicar is a part-time chaplain in a hospital, but there are sufficient differences between institutions and parishes to make the division a realistic one.

Theological grounds for cooperation

We argued in Chapter 2 that, for the purpose of understanding the wholeness of the Church's healing ministry, it is useful to follow those theologians who distinguish three 'streams' flowing from Christ's commission: the pastoral, the sacramental and the charismatic. We traced the development of the first of these streams, the pastoral, from the apostolic Church and showed briefly how over the centuries it became a way of looking at the practical things which Christians have tried to do in looking after and attempting to heal the sick, including early forms of hospital care and medical treatment.

Until the Renaissance virtually everything done for the sick in Western Europe was provided by the Church and its members by one means or the other. But with the development of scientific medicine much of this 'pastoral' care was gradually taken out of the Church's hands. During the past two centuries the medical profession has become secularized on acquiring a special status in society with the foundation of the royal colleges and the establishment of nationally recognized qualifications. Something similar happened in nursing.

Contemporary scientific medicine, of course, has no religious allegiance. The training and recognition of medical skills is in the hands of secular bodies. Nevertheless, with most other Christians, we want to affirm that everything achieved by this profession which promotes true healing can be seen as a continuation of the ministry of Jesus Christ. The Second Person of the Trinity was active in the creation of the world, and he still sustains its life and artistic and scientific creativity. Whatever is good in the world is of God the Holy Trinity, and our hope is that the good things which emerge from medical science ultimately lead those who benefit from it to the salvation which the Father offers through Christ. In its report, *The Healing Church* (Geneva 1965), the World Council of Churches stated, 'All healing is of God, and for this very reason we accept modern medicine as a gift from God and use with the same gratitude both the spiritual and the scientific means of healing' (p. 36). The Roman Catholic *Rite of Anointing and Pastoral Care of the Sick* said the same thing: 'Every scientific effort to prolong life and every act of care for the sick, on the part of any person, may be considered a preparation for the Gospel and a sharing in Christ's healing ministry' (no. 32).[1] There is much in modern medicine for which we can thank God as potentially one current of what we define as the pastoral stream of the Church's healing ministry.

We could go further. It is traditional to identify today's doctors as being descendants of a long line of great medical persons reaching back to Hippocrates. This notable Greek is called the 'Father of Medicine', for he set a pattern for current attitudes and relationships within the medical profession which have lasted down to the present time. But Christians sometimes forget that it was Jesus who, more than any other figure in history, taught and demonstrated the essential meaning and fullness of healing. In the power of the Holy Spirit, he has brought – and can still bring – to medical methods and codes those gospel manifestations of divine love without which true healing is rarely achieved.

This understanding of the pastoral stream offers a theological undergirding for cooperation between the Church and those in the healing professions whose work can in many instances be seen to be reflections of Christ's own healing ministry. These professions include not only doctors and nurses (who figure largely in the 1958 report) but also psychologists and other paramedical therapists and social workers who provide what is known nowadays as the multidisciplinary approach to healing. And, of course, by 'Church' we do not mean only the clergy but also all of its members who belong to these professions and who assist in the medical and nursing world. The line between 'the Church' and 'the professions' is, therefore, extremely blurred; but in this discussion we shall have to limit 'the Church' to mean those who in their formal capacity teach and act on behalf of her healing ministry, and 'the professions' to mean those who because of their work teach and act within the National Health Service and other health and welfare agencies.

The Church and the National Health Service

In the middle of the nineteenth century Christians in general and the Church of England in particular were still the main agencies caring for the sick in the country through the voluntary hospital movement and other means in parishes and homes. But what they were able to do gradually became inadequate in the midst of the social changes which were taking place in the wake of the technological and commercial revolutions of that time. Many Christians of different denominations began to campaign for a more healthy environment and better care for the sick. Hospital Sundays were introduced as a means of raising finances for local institutions and of encouraging people to join the Friendly Societies as a form of mutual aid.

Some of the impetus for this came from the Christian Socialists with their strongly incarnational theology. They argued that since in Jesus Christ, God took human nature to himself, the physical, mental and environmental conditions of men, women and children were as much to do with the kingdom as people's personal, spiritual pilgrimage. John Ludlow, a friend of F. D. Maurice, horrified at the conditions of the poor in East London, called for a National Health League which would not only campaign for clean water and a healthy environment but also a doctor in every parish.[2] An Anglican clergyman, William Blackley, is regarded as the originator of the concept of 'national insurance'. He used the phrase as the title of an article in the *Nineteenth Century Review* in November 1878, though he realized that to his readers it would sound 'so extravagant, impracticable and Utopian, as to be unworthy of serious consideration'.[3]

During the First World War circumstances forced the Government to increase its control over many aspects of citizens' lives, and this continued after 1918 as the State accepted more responsibility for the health as well as for education, housing and unemployment. Slowly the concept of a welfare state emerged, promoted by the growing Labour Party. There was resistance among many Christians of different traditions to what was regarded as a takeover by the politicians of these areas.[4] But William Temple and others led the way in gradually helping the Church to accept these developments. The result was that when the Labour Government established the welfare state on the basis of the 1944 Beveridge Report and inaugurated the National Health Service four years later, many Anglicans with most other Christians came to accept it as a potentially important step towards fulfilling the Church's ministry of healing (though some bishops voted against it in the House of Lords). Under the NHS, Christian foundations were allowed to retain something of their religious character. Hospitals appointed chaplains and provided chapels. Young Christian men and women entered the medical and nursing professions with a sense of vocation. Even in the 1950s the custom of daily ward prayers was observed in many hospitals. Christian initiatives, such as the hospice movement for the terminally ill, have been assisted by state funding. It could be argued that the inspiration of the NHS – whatever its practical shortcomings – stemmed from the Christian belief that every human being, made in the image of God, has a right to be cared for and enabled to live as full a life as possible from the moment of conception in the womb to the day of his or her death.

As we have seen, it was roughly during this same period that more and more Anglicans and other Christians realized that the sacramental and the charismatic streams of the Church's traditional ministry of healing were increasingly relevant and that these two streams should be related to the pastoral one as closely as possible. So that is why cooperation between the Church and the health and welfare authorities is theologically as well as practically desirable. Such cooperation enables the Church to acknowledge God's gifts in the professions, and it helps the professions – or at least those in them who are willing to listen – to hear what the gospel has to say on the dignity, purpose and destiny of the human family whom God has created and redeemed.

Hospitals

Cooperation between the clergy and the medical profession is particularly important in hospitals and similar institutions. Both deal with different aspects of healing. It is easy to get stuck in particular specialities and forget the whole person. There have been helpful steps in the direction of coordination within the medical profession in having a 'named nurse', who is a single contact person for both the staff ministering to the patient and the patient himself or herself. If the patient needs several different specialities, the named nurse helps to coordinate their efforts and to explain to the patient what is being done and why. As patients also have a spiritual dimension, it is frequently through the named nurse that the chaplain is called because of a spiritual concern.[5]

In-service NHS training courses have begun to include courses on spirituality for medical, nursing and other professions. The courses include looking at how spiritual concerns might be presented, how the nurse or doctor might handle them and the role of and support available from the chaplaincy. People talk to medical staff as well as to chaplains about spiritual concerns, and medical staff would like to have the resources to respond to them. The courses also offer staff the opportunity to look at their own religious and spiritual beliefs and how these impinge on and support their work, especially with regard to their sense of vocation. (It may be advantageous to consider at some stage linking these courses with pre- and post-ordination training.)

With many people of other faiths working in the NHS, training given to Buddhists and Muslims about how they might be of help to Christian patients, and vice versa, might be considered as something of a high priority. There has been research on the relationship between religious belief and healing, and so it is not only in the interests of religion but also in the interests of science that steps should be taken to ensure that members of the medical profession receive at least some training in this area or have access to supervision when they need it.

Map of the relationship between professional concerns

One of the helpful maps of how different professions fit together has been provided by Viktor Frankl, a psychiatrist who was imprisoned in a concentration camp during the Second World War and who observed that those who survived best had a reason for living. They were not necessarily the ones who were most physically fit. From this he developed Logotherapy, which was a therapy designed to look at the discovery of meaning in a person's life. He talks about different dimensions of explanation for the same event. He postulates that the simplest dimension is the physical, the next highest is the psychological, and the one which is most multidimensional he calls the 'noogenic', the one where meaning is found.[6]

Taking the story of Romeo and Juliet as an example, on the physical level it can be described as a matter of hormones, on the psychological level as an example of teenage identity formation by rebelling against parents' wishes, and on the highest or noogenic level as how the tragedy of two innocent deaths reconciled two warring families. One cannot describe any of these levels as complete; Romeo and Juliet is a matter of hormones, but not just a matter of hormones. Similarly, a depression may be a manifestation of a physical illness, a psychological illness, or the result of an individual's running away from their identity or from the vocation to which God may be calling them.

Frankl suggests that the proper procedure is to start at the physical level and work upwards. The physical level is expressed in scientific language, the psychological level is expressed in psychological or humanistic language, and the noogenic level is expressed in symbols or mythical language. Specialists need to focus on their own level, but to be peripherally aware of the dynamics on the other levels. There is also a need to discuss the patient among specialists on the different levels. Frankl's thesis presents strong scientific reasons for cooperation between the Church and the medical professions.

The environment of healing

A report from the World Health Organization once said that the single most important factor for health in a hospital is the atmosphere. If this is true, then the spirit in which the medicine is practised is important. This means that many factors, such as the sense of vocation of the medical and nursing staff towards their work, the support they receive and the attitude with which they approach their work is basic. Within this situation the chaplain plays a vital role, not only in caring for the patients individually, but also in being the leaven in the medical and nursing team to ask the questions, and to identify with them what makes their work healing in its widest sense, rather than just clinical repair. This has the twofold effect of encouraging greater awareness within the general public of ways in which God works through the medical professions, health care and social services, but also in contributing to the nurturing atmosphere within the structures as part of the Christian contribution to the environment of healing.

It also means that the Church through the chaplain has the responsibility of ministering to the hospital as an institution. Sometimes the structures become less nurturing and more deprived, and this needs to be addressed. Being able to approach anyone in the system at any level who may be troubled, and therefore causing upset to those around and below them on the ward or elsewhere in the system, is important for keeping the atmosphere one in which healing can take place.

Robin Skynner talks about the dynamics of institutions as being much like those of families.[7] On a continuum they are at one end nurturing with a philosophy of plenty ('we were not expecting you, but come in and eat with us: we can add some water to the soup') and at the other end with a philosophy of deprivation ('I'm sorry, but if we do it for you, we will have to do it for everyone'). What characterizes these two extremes is that those staff on the nurturing end of the scale allow themselves to be cared for, while those on the deprivation end of the scale do not take days off, deny that they need help themselves and run up an emotional overdraft. They are then jealous of the very people they are healing and claw back what good they do with envious restrictions. Skynner's work in this area has been used in hospital settings in terms of support groups for staff or away days in which the staff receive nurture for themselves and pass on a warm philosophy of plenty to their patients. (We wonder if the Church could learn from this study for the benefit of overworked clergy!)

One issue which has to be faced within the NHS has been the challenge to the sense of vocation which hospital staff have felt when the prevailing philosophy within the health service changed from that of a public service to that of a market economy with 'users' and 'consumers'. This makes a great deal of difference to the environment which the patient senses in these establishments.

There is an immense shift from assessing the value of what was being done by many medical and nursing staff as a sense of vocation to assessing it in terms of cost-effectiveness. Chaplains (and others) have to struggle to help the staff rediscover the sense of vocation which they have to help in healing and not just to feel themselves as 'service providers'. This is an example of how the language which is being used, while valid at the physical level of bookkeeping, nevertheless leaves out the reason why people work for long hours with little pay because of their compassion for suffering people. It is essential for the Church to work with the caring professions to include the vocational within the description of the work which is being done.

The role of the chaplain in a multidisciplinary approach to healing

Some chaplains who have had the appropriate training are increasingly called upon to have a role in providing psychotherapy or counselling for those patients who have a spiritual dimension to their problems, or to help in supervision of those who are practising psychotherapy for the spiritual issues involved. Some medical people work with clergy so that an aspect of the therapy which has to do with spiritual issues can be addressed.

One such area is guilt. This comes in different forms: guilt for moral wrongdoing, neurotic guilt, existential guilt (for not being one's authentic self), and so on. Guilt also comes from distorted theological ideas. For instance, some Christian patients feel it is immoral for them to be angry, or to get any support for themselves; they regard this as a sign they are lacking faith. To be able to talk through their theological beliefs with someone who is trained in this area can be helpful. People often carpet distortions in their personality with selective quotes from the Scriptures, leaving out those which do not conform to their view. This then makes them feel guilty for going against their faith when they get better. To help a person expand their Christian perspective to a less limited one is an important ingredient in healing. Belief that someone may have committed the unforgivable sin against the Holy Spirit is another recurring theme for which the medical profession within psychiatric hospitals call in the chaplain.

There is generally good cooperation among clergy of different denominations. The chaplains work ecumenically as a rule, and either talk with patients of other traditions on the wards or will talk if they are approached by them. Sometimes the clergy will divide the wards of a large hospital so that each has its own 'chaplain'. If a chaplain of a particular denomination is wanted, they arrange this. Other chaplains prefer to visit only members of their own tradition. Chaplains on the whole do acknowledge when one of their number is trained in counselling; this is helpful when particular mental difficulties get entangled with religious beliefs. Nor is help of this kind limited to patients. Chaplains may be called in to assist the medical and nursing staff in this way. Once on a psychiatric ward the staff asked the chaplain if he could come and discuss their feelings and beliefs about death – this was so that they would be more able to provide support for a young long-term patient who was dying of a brain tumour. After a long discussion, they felt better equipped to listen to that patient as he shared with them his feelings and beliefs about dying.

Within the hospital the chapel often plays an valuable role, not only in providing a place of quiet for meditation and regular services of the laying on of hands and Holy Communion, but also – especially in psychiatric hospitals – a place where people can discover symbols which give a framework for growth. Take the case of Christian patients suffering from schizophrenia. They may be losing a coherent framework of understanding of what is happening in themselves and in the world around them. But by using events and stories from the Bible as a common language such patients may be helped to understand what is happening and to bring some order to the chaos which is being experienced.

Rediscovering the sacramental in medical and nursing care

Seeing the sacramental within the ordinary tasks of medical and nursing care is also a vital element within the work of a hospital and a general practitioner's surgery. On one occasion, after being with the chaplain as he attended a dying patient, the staff asked him for a seminar on 'how they might be able to do what the chaplain did in their work'. The result of that seminar was the idea of what might be called 'a sacramental blanket bath'. What this meant to the staff was that they would bathe a patient 'as if he or she was the most valuable person in the world' – particularly a patient who was not open to being conversed with. When the chaplain came back later, two of the staff were washing a patient with Beethoven's Pastoral Symphony playing quietly in the background. They did this, they told him, because they had observed the tender way in which he had laid hands on a patient who was dying, and invited the nurses and relatives around to do the same.

This theme was taken up in a seminar on the relationship between doctors and their patients, when there was a discussion on the symbolic nature of how prescriptions are written and handled. Some general practitioners were encouraged to perform this routine task with greater care, handing the paper over to the patient reverently with a remark such as, 'Here is some medicine I feel will help you'.

Theological students who do placements in hospitals need to be able to learn this as well. There is a lot of useful training in watching committed and caring nursing and medical staff ministering to patients. These students also need to be taught how to pray with a patient, to sit quietly holding a hand for a time when a loving presence is required, and to be able to listen for the emergence of symbols in a patient's life and handle them sensitively. This need not be only a preparation for the students' ministry after their ordination; it can also be a valid ministry by them in the hospital which receives them – a validity which is seldom fully recognized. This makes the ordinands aware of the importance of cooperation between the clergy and the health care professions through interactive sessions. Within this interactive experience the ordinand can be made aware of how what the Church has to offer – counselling, confession, anointing, spiritual direction, etc. – fits in with the total package of care in the wider aspects of healing.

Training

There is at the moment very little training going on specifically between the medical and the theological professions. There are courses on 'The Spiritual Dimension within Mental Health' which are open to different staff, but none geared towards the medical staff in particular.

One encouraging development we should mention is the opening of a special interest section in Spirituality and Psychiatry at the Royal College of Psychiatry. Approval has been given for this section; after a minimum of 120 psychiatrists have supported it, it can be made part of the formal machinery of the college. This is for those who are interested in discussing and encouraging this in the development of psychiatric training and interest among psychiatrists. A recent poll in the Southwest region indicated that 20 out of 23 specialist registrars felt psychiatric practice should routinely include consideration of spiritual concerns. Also, a recent survey by the Mental Health Foundation indicated that over 50 per cent of service users hold religious or spiritual beliefs which they see as important in helping them to cope with mental illness.

Another important element in training is the inclusion in the book *Pocket Psychiatry* by Kamaldeep Bhui, Scot Welch and Keith Lloyd of a section on 'Culture-bound Syndromes' where various psychiatric symptoms are explained by the way they are seen in their cultural contexts. There is also a section in the book on 'Possession States'.[8] They write: 'Therefore the assessment of suggestibility, ritualised and dissociative states will require consultation with those having expert knowledge about religious, cultural, spiritual and sociological aspects of possession states' (p. 189). This is a step in the right direction for the purpose of opening consultation between the psychiatrist and those whose primary interest is in the spiritual state of the patient.

Likewise there is a need for teaching not only Muslim or Buddhist doctors and nurses about ministering to Christian patients, but also the other way round. In terms of coming to an understanding of what is happening in a patient's life, all of us need to be able to put our illness into the context of our faith and culture. Since we live in a multi-faith and multicultural society, this subject should be included in medical and nursing training. These are examples of some of the ways in which clergy can relate with the medical and nursing professions so that their skills can be utilized in multidisciplinary teams.

Boundaries between the professions and the clergy

Clergy who work in the NHS are bound by the rules governing patient confidentiality. This also applies to theological students who do placements in hospitals. They are required to sign confidentiality documents. This has implications for the relationship between the clergy and the medical and nursing staff as well as between the chaplain and the clergy of the parishes where the patients live, and it is important that these should be understood by all concerned. However, it is still possible to liaise with parish priests to help the continuation of the pastoral care of parishioners who have received the healing ministry in hospital.

This places the chaplain on the same multidisciplinary team as the doctors and nurses. There is a right to be consulted. This right does not necessarily apply to the chaplain reading the case notes; however, there may be an overriding reason why the chaplain should know the background information. In fact, many chaplains prefer not to read the case notes as it allows them to be more open to hear the way the patient describes his or her illness. Nursing and medical staff are generally very willing to give background information verbally to the chaplain, and to tell them about the patient's family. Occasionally, a family gathered round a patient's bedside are at loggerheads, and they have to be put into a separate room when they come to visit. The chaplain's ministry of healing is therefore not only to the patient but to the family as well.

The relationship of the chaplain to the clergy of the patient's parish is a delicate one. The hospital chaplain cannot divulge information about a patient without his or her express permission. This includes letting clergy know someone is in hospital – unless the patient asks the chaplain to get in touch. On the other hand, chaplains like to be told by local clergy when one of their congregation is being admitted to hospital. One delicate point: it is a courtesy to inform the chaplain when a parish priest brings Holy Communion to a patient or anoints him or her. We are told that this is not done as often as it might be. It would be helpful to develop a common code of confidentiality which would be applicable to all those who minister to the patient, which would enable closer working relationships between chaplains and health care professionals, in order to maintain better comprehensive care for parishioners.

With chaplains in psychiatric hospitals the relationship between the parish clergy and the hospital must be handled sensitively when, for example, long-term patients move into group homes in the community. Ex-patients have mixed feelings about this. They may appreciate a visit from the parish priest, but equally they do not like to be marked out as different from other people. The situation can be aggravated when local residents resent ex-patients moving into their area. It is better if patients are encouraged by the hospital chaplain to make contact with the local church themselves in the first instance, as this avoids the feeling of being marked out as special. On the other hand, parishes which systematically visit all newcomers can explain to the ex-patient that he or she is just one of many who are being contacted.

It is also helpful for the hospital chaplain to form links with neighbouring parishes around his or her hospital. This enables the parish priest and chaplain (particularly in psychiatric hospitals) to talk together about patients who may be causing concern. They can also plan how particular people might be integrated into parish life. In some places the chaplains, including those of different denominations, appreciate being able to say an office together once a week in a local church.

Since much of a hospital chaplain's contribution to a multidisciplinary team can be described in the most general way as listening, it is necessary for the team to work out a common code of practice such as that found in the British Association of Counselling's *Codes of Ethics* or *The Standards of Practice in Pastoral Care* put out by the Anglican Association of Diocesan Pastoral Care Advisers.

There is also a need for the members of the other professions to know exactly what chaplains do and how they fit into the work of the entire healing team. They need to know this in terms of what they can expect from chaplains when they call upon them, and for the patients to be informed what chaplaincy is available to them while they are in hospital. There are several ways in which this can be carried out.

1. The inclusion of a session for the chaplains in the induction day for new members of staff entering the hospital service. This is an opportunity to tell them about the work of the chaplains and to distribute any literature which they might find helpful.

2. Clear guidelines in job descriptions and mission statements. This information could include things like the average time a chaplain would expect to take if called out, duty rotas, times when services are provided, further education provided by the chaplains for the medical and nursing staff on ethical and spiritual issues, availability to meet ward teams if religious issues are involved, various traditions of modesty during examination procedures of people of different faiths, varying customs and procedures surrounding someone of a particular tradition dying in hospital, how to obtain a clergy person of another tradition (or a spiritual leader of another faith) not employed by the hospital, procedures for reviewing what chaplains do, who their line managers are and how to register a complaint. The codes and guidelines for all NHS staff are stringent, but there should also be added any extra ones which might be applicable to clergy.

3. Seminars on medical ethics and healing with nursing and medical staff and chaplains (and theological students if appropriate). For example, issues around the care for family and patient when there is a question of switching life support machines off, or care of the dying patient, allow the groups to share what they know, seek out what they do not know from the others, and realize they are contributing to the healing from different perspectives.

4. A web site on the NHS computer system which tells of the work of chaplains and how to contact them, including their email addresses. NHS trusts also have web sites through which the chaplains of particular hospitals can be contacted.

Social workers and health visitors

Work with social workers and health visitors is also important. Quite a few contacts with chaplains are made through the social services when they are visiting people who have been discharged from hospital and who may have made a strong bond with a chaplain while they were in hospital. Cooperation between the chaplain, the parish priest and the social worker or health visitor can be valuable when a lonely person, newly released from hospital, feels particularly vulnerable. Care should be taken to ensure this is done with the patient's permission; confidentiality must be respected in all contacts between the chaplain and the patient's local community.

Training of priests for working with the other professions

The healing ministry is such a wide subject that training for the Church's involvement in it can vary enormously depending on the institution. It can range from how to perform an anointing to such things as an understanding of the theology of suffering and the connection between healing and personal confession of sin.

One area which ought not to be missed, however, is healing in a community. How race relations groups endeavour to heal racial tensions has obvious lessons for all. So has the work of such bodies as the Corrymeela Community and the Christian Renewal Centre at Rostrevor in Northern Ireland. Theological students and clergy also need to know about working alongside and engaging in dialogue with women and men of other professions such as medicine, nursing and social work.

Then there are practical things, appropriate ways of laying on hands, administering the sacraments in different situations, responding to requests for prayer, and so on. Most important of all, they need to know how to pray, formally and informally aloud, silently when sitting by a patient, sensitively in picking up a patient's concerns and incorporating them in the prayer.

While we do not want to suggest that prayer is a kind of psychological exercise, we think it is useful for those who minister to be sensitive to an individual's personality type and mode of functioning. For example, in the early stages of spiritual growth at least, the mainly extroverted person may find it difficult to pray alone, but a more introverted person will be drawn to a quiet time. For sensate persons the arrangement of the chapel or church will be as important as gestures such as touching, bowing and exchanging the peace. For the more intuitive introverted person, the mystery of God will be important, especially coming through the still small voice. For the predominantly thinking person an orderly pattern of devotion, perhaps with a series of Bible readings, can be helpful. For those with a strong feeling function affective prayer comes naturally. When we are engaging in healing prayer we need to understand the types of persons we are ministering to, as well as our own predominant and preferred types.

It is equally important to realize the shadow side of each personality type in what may need healing. The intuitive types tend to feel they are not understood, while the introverted thinking type may judge things in black and white. Each combination of personality type carries with it its special way of ministry, but also the possibility of the relevant difficulty. This needs to be explored in the teaching of theological students and clergy about prayer and the nature of the healing ministry.[9]

Most of us are perhaps rightly reluctant to attach ourselves too closely to one or other of the various schools of psychology which put forward different systems for analysing and categorizing personality types (we noted in Chapter 1 how suspicious of the 'new psychology' Christians were in the early decades of this century). But we would be foolish to ignore some of the basic things about our make-up which these schools can teach us. Such matters need to be explored in the teaching of theological students and clergy about prayer and the nature of the healing ministry. At least it would avoid, for example, the (by no means uncommon) blunder when an individual suffering from a clinical depression is told after vigorous prayer to believe and act as if the Lord has healed them (sometimes known as 'name-it-and-claim-it'), leaving him or her in a far worse state than before. What is probably needed in such a case is prayer which reinforces the individual's slender hope that the Lord is with them in the midst of their depression, loving them and wanting to help them out of their darkness gradually day by day.

Balance is important. Our model is the Great Commandment: 'You shall love the Lord with all your heart, with all your soul, with all your mind, and with all your strength' (Mark 12.30; Luke 10.27; Matthew 22.37 omits 'strength'). However those categories were understood by those who framed the Mosaic Law, they certainly imply that for us to respond fully to the love of God we need to be healed to the very depths of our conscious being.

Ministers need to seek from the Lord a charism of discernment necessary when responding to a request for a prayer for healing. A dialogue with the patient helps to clarify how the prayer should be offered; the brokenness and suffering from the time and perspective of where we are to God's great knowledge and will. His response passes all our understanding.

But now we are straying into aspects of the ministry of healing which are also relevant to that ministry as it is exercised in parishes and other groups of Christians, and to that we must now turn.

Recommendations

We recommend that:

❖ the relationship between the healing ministry and medicine should be encouraged on the basis of a working theology of this ministry and that a vocabulary for this ministry needs to be developed which is clearly understood and shared between clergy, laity and health care professionals (see pages 90, 91, 95, 96, 98 and 99);

❖ in order to help the medical and theological disciplines work together on healing, support should be given to making provision for medical and theological students to be trained together in pastoral aspects of collaborative health care and ethics (see pages 90, 94, 97, 99–100, 102 and 103–4);

❖ consideration should be given to mutual supervision (doctors being supervised by clergy on spiritual aspects of medical care and clergy by doctors on medical aspects of spiritual care) to work towards a holistic approach to healing (see pages 93, 94, 97, 100 and 101).

6

The Healing Ministry and Professional Care Provision in the Parishes

Cooperation between the Church and those employed in health care in the neighbourhood is best undertaken ecumenically. Pastoral care often involves some form of counselling, but the distinction between professional counselling and other kinds of pastoral listening should be understood and respected. The diocesan advisor can help in this. Codes of ethics and practice are relevant not only to formal counselling but also in different ways to pastoral care, prayer ministries, spiritual direction and the ministry of reconciliation. Ongoing training and supervision are advisable for clergy and laity alike to avoid common pitfalls in these ministries.

Opportunities for cooperation are obviously more diffuse in a parish than in a hospital. Much depends on the initiative of the parish priest, and the time and energy he or she and the congregation give to this area of pastoral care. Some clergy have taken the initiative in hosting meetings for local doctors, community and social workers, district nurses, police and councillors. Such simple acts of hospitality enable these people to consult one another on individual situations, to work together in local projects, to discuss the wider scene and so on.

Working together ecumenically has the advantage of enabling churches to undertake more ambitious projects than is usually possible for a single congregation. Churches Together and other unity groups in different places have started and staffed a variety of healing and welfare projects in cooperation with local authorities, from Relate centres to care schemes, from bereavement support to AIDS/HIV care. Or they become involved in existing projects of a similar nature set up by those authorities or by other voluntary organizations – which often saves individual congregations time and energy. Two things some churches can offer are premises and volunteers to existing and established projects. In the light of the Government's expressed desire for partnerships between the statutory and voluntary sector, together with generous financial provisions, it is possible to envisage the establishment of a variety of primary health care provisions in local church settings.

There are other ways of keeping open the lines of communication. Surgeries and health centres can be invited to have on their noticeboards a list of the names and addresses of the clergy (and leaders of other ethnic communities and faiths) who are in their neighbourhood, and members of the professions can be invited to a meeting with the local MP or other appropriate officials when matters of concern for the general health of the locality arise. Churches Together groups often play an important role in campaigns against the threat of hospital closures or in initiatives for establishing and supporting local hospices. Three hospices around Manchester – one for terminally ill children – owe their existence largely to the energies of Christian individuals and groups, assisted by others of goodwill.

Clergy also get to know members of the health care professions through their congregations. General practitioners and nurses can sometimes guess when their patients are church folk, and it is part of a psychiatrist's job to find out a client's spiritual orientation. Occasionally these professionals will turn to the clergy for information or advice. In this case, too, the courtesies and confidentialities already mentioned should be observed. A parish priest we consulted said he once had a referral from a non-Christian general practitioner, who reckoned that a patient of his did not need medication but help in dealing with guilt. Another time a Christian doctor asked the same priest to go with him to pray for and anoint a church member who had terminal cancer. We also heard of a Christian doctor who asked his parish priest if he could have a phial of oil to take with him to use when he felt it right to minister anointing with prayer to appropriate persons among his patients.

Within congregations there are members of the professions, but the basis of the relationship between the Church and the professions in this case is very different from that which we have been discussing. Doctors, nurses and others who participate in the worship and life of their church do so as Christian individuals, husbands, wives, parents, widowers, widows, and so on, seeking fellowship in their own ongoing spiritual pilgrimage. They may be glad of opportunities to discuss their work from a Christian viewpoint. Some may be willing to offer their advice to the parish's prayer ministry teams when necessary, or be members of such teams. They may ask for prayer for themselves in times of crisis or ill health. But the boundaries which they maintain between their Church life and their professional lives need to be respected. The rest of the congregation should be discouraged from using the presence of professionals in church as an opportunity for a private medical consultation. Yet doctors in a congregation may have to act professionally – as, for example, when an individual is suddenly taken ill in church, as in a supermarket or on an aircraft.

One area of healing in the parish in which many clergy and laity are now involved and which offers many opportunities for cooperation is that of counselling. The growth of the counselling profession in the years since the 1958 report has been little short of phenomenal. Large numbers of people can attest to the benefits they have derived from feeling they have been listened to; many recall the counselling sessions they have had as significant moments in their growth in personal maturity.

Sharing one another's burdens has always been an expression of pastoral care in Christian circles, and much of what we now learn through professional counselling skills was learned in the past through the experience of Christians listening to one another and through the charisms manifested by wise pastors, spiritual directors and others. But the need for this kind of pastoral care has been highlighted by the breakdown of relationships and other tensions which our present lifestyle creates, and this has led to the development of training in listening skills both inside and outside the membership of the Church. It is significant that the counselling profession's main umbrella organization, the British Association for Counselling (BAC), grew out of the pastoral involvement of some of its founder members. Not everyone who presents him- or herself as a candidate for a counselling course is particularly suitable and many such people have their applications rejected. It is prudent to note that there are also people who offer themselves for various forms of pastoral ministry, including joining a team of 'listeners' or becoming a member of a church-based 'counselling service', who are similarly unsuited to these ministries. Adequate screening procedures are necessary to protect those seeking help from possible damage caused by insensitive or even dangerous ministry by these people.

Many dioceses now have an advisor for counselling, who may be ordained or lay, full-time or part-time. Their roles vary from one diocese to another, but typically include such responsibilities as responding to enquiries from clergy and others about suitable routes of referral for parishioners and others who are experiencing psychological distress, and the management of diocesan counselling schemes for the clergy and others in need of therapeutic help. These appointments demonstrate that counselling is another of those areas of the healing ministry where local clergy and congregations often need professional assistance. While certain cases can be helped within the parish, others are more complex than a parish can handle adequately.

Part of the complexity surrounds the distinctions between, for example, ordinary pastoral care, prayer ministry, counselling and spiritual direction and the ministry of reconciliation. Another part of the complexity has to do with the psychological needs and make-up of individuals. And yet another concerns the specific ethos of the church in question and the prevailing attitude of its members towards the role of the emotions, psychological distress, psychiatric disorders, and so on. We need to look at these distinctions more carefully.

Pastoral care

Pastoral care in a parish is traditionally regarded as a primary function of the clergy, though in practice much of this is done by others. Nowadays there is an increasing awareness that such care is the duty of every Christian, though within a congregation it should ideally be exercised with the parish priest's knowledge and approval. Much of what is done in caring by clergy and others may be informed by counselling skills, yet even so formal counselling should be regarded as something distinct.

A working party of the Biennial Consultation of the Diocesan Advisors in Pastoral Care and Counselling (now formed into the Anglican Association of Advisors in Pastoral Care and Counselling) describe pastoral care as follows:

> Pastoral care is a fabric of interwoven activities and responses directed towards individuals, relationships, groups and communities, undertaken from within the overall context of the faith community. The pastoral care of others is a duty that belongs to every Christian. It is one in which we foster the well-being of all people, individually and corporately. It is not simply, or even mainly, about repairing or resolving things when they have gone wrong; it is also about sharing in community, feasting in fellowship, exchanging mutual support. It is about recognising, welcoming, affirming, encouraging and rejoicing with others and receiving this recognising, welcoming, affirming and encouragement from them . . . .
>
> The activities involved may include visiting, befriending, promoting self-help activities, giving material aid, creating opportunities for increased learning, socialisation and development and other community activities, campaigning, protesting against injustices, crisis management, conflict mediation, and so on. Formal counselling, psychotherapy and other specific disciplines are distinct and yet contained within general pastoral care activities as a whole.
>
> All the above may well use counselling skills and approaches, but they should not be confused with formal counselling as such.[1]

Counselling, on the other hand, has been described in the following terms:

> People become engaged in counselling when a person, occupying regularly or temporarily the role of counsellor offers or agrees explicitly to offer *time, attention* and *respect* to another person or persons temporarily in the role of client. The task of counselling is to give the client an opportunity to explore, discover and clarify ways of living more resourcefully and towards greater well-being.[2]

Counselling

The distinction between the informal use of counselling skills which happens (often spontaneously) in ordinary church relationships and that which takes place in the formal way just described can sometimes be a source of tension. We therefore strongly advise clergy, counsellors and others involved in this aspect of pastoral care to note the following guidelines. They also apply to similar activities in hospitals, colleges and other institutions where pastoral care is exercised.

❖ When a parishioner is receiving counselling elsewhere, it is not necessary for the clergy to know the details of what is covered in a person's therapy – even if the referral was made by the minister.

❖ It is desirable for people receiving pastoral care to have the boundaries of confidentiality made explicit. If detailed reports on their progress are to be shared between, for example, the church ministers, ordained or lay, then they need to be forewarned.

❖ If, on the other hand, their personal material will be held in complete confidence by the person to whom it is revealed, then knowing this can increase their sense of confidence and security in the process: that is, this knowledge functions as one aspect of the containment which the counsellor–client relationship provides.

A vital component of counselling is that of 'being with' a troubled person, and many people can attest to the healing power of having another human being 'come alongside' them during a distressing time. (In the book of Job we have a good example of this in that Job's friends cared enough to sit in silence with him for seven days. But afterwards they spoilt their ministry by verbally tearing the poor man to shreds.) In our churches there are many who have valued being given 'space' just to 'be' in someone else's presence, but who have then felt hurt, rejected – even abused – when that person without training has attempted to 'counsel' them. Such attempts are usually misguided in that they stem from a basic lack of knowledge and understanding of various issues which are covered in counselling training. If offering counselling, Christians should have received appropriate training, preferably to certificate or diploma level; they should also be in regular supervision and adhere to the codes of ethics and practice of a reputable counselling organization. Together these safeguards should ensure that counsellors have a working knowledge of such areas as: not counselling without permission, keeping clear boundaries around the counselling relationship; maintaining confidentiality; staying mainly in the other person's frame of reference; staying within their area of competence and knowing when to refer.

Claims that the Holy Spirit will guide those with a spiritual gift for counselling need to be tested with care. It is true that some without formal training can be wise counsellors, but this is almost always because they have had considerable experience of listening to people in the past and have learned how to follow the Holy Spirit through many encounters. Such charisms are very rarely manifested without such previous experience. Yet there is always a need to be wisely open about this. Margaret Gill expressed it this way:

> The Holy Spirit can readily work within the disciplines of listening and counselling, and frequently does. To abandon such disciplines and think that we can float free with the Spirit alone as our supervisor is not only irresponsible and arrogant, but can make his task hard if not impossible at times. God gives us guidelines, training and example to learn from, not to cast aside. However, the Holy Spirit is not bound by rules and regulations and neither, in a sense, are we. Sometimes he works outside them, against all odds, and we experience God's hand in it in a fresh and new way.[3]

Clergy and others in the churches should know that professional psychologists, counsellors and psychotherapists seek to preserve firm boundaries in their work, doing their best to ensure that the people who reveal the deepest, most intimate details of their lives to them are not then encountered in other settings. Inevitably, however, chance sightings sometimes occur such as in a supermarket or a library, but the professional therapist does not seek such meetings. Invitations from clients to social gatherings are declined, and friends are not accepted as clients.

Because formal counselling frequently involves disclosing deeply personal and sometimes shaming details of a person's life, the intensity of the relationship which results tends to evoke certain psychological processes in the client and not infrequently in the counsellor. The most notable of these are projection, transference and counter-transference.

❖ *Projection* involves perceiving in other people (or events, objects, etc.) things which exist in oneself ('You look sad today,' when it is we who are sad).

❖ *Transference* occurs when a person (in this case a client) behaves towards or perceives another person (in this case a counsellor) as if he or she is someone else, known and usually significant to the person, for example, a parent or teacher.

❖ *Counter-transference* is a similar process occurring in the other person (counsellor) towards the first person (client) and is sometimes evoked by transference. For example, a counsellor whose client behaves towards him as if he is the counsellor's son may find himself taking on a paternal role towards the client.

For this reason, it is not considered good practice for the clergy or others in positions of pastoral leadership in a local church to offer ongoing formal counselling to members of the same congregation. A preferable arrangement is for trained counsellors and psychologists in a congregation to offer a single-session contract in order to assess the situation and explore possible ways forward. Or reciprocal arrangements might be made between two or more churches so that blurred boundaries between members of the same church are avoided.

'Tea and sympathy' have an important role in church fellowships, and will continue to do so. Many churches offer pastoral care through the use of listening and counselling skills, based on some informal training in the parish or elsewhere, and again these will always be invaluable. But if formal counselling is offered, it should be carried out by people who have received recognized training, preferably of more than a minimum length, and the lines of accountability should be clear with the parish priest or the head of the counselling service or another named person exercising an oversight of the ministry. Counsellors should belong to a relevant organization which has a code of ethics and practice such as the British Association for Counselling (BAC) or the Association of Christian Counsellors and be accredited (or working towards accreditation) by such a body.

Most clergy are not trained for or engaged in formal counselling, but in their general pastoral care they often make considerable use of counselling skills. These are communication skills derived from counselling which are used in the course of a person's main profession or vocation and 'in a manner consistent with the goals and values of the established ethics of the profession of the practitioner in question'.[4] Many Christians have attended courses in active listening and 'taster' courses in counselling skills. It is important that those using these skills in churches make clear to those receiving help just what is being offered, in order to minimize confusion between these forms of ministry and formal counselling. Supportive use of counselling skills can be very nurturing and avoids the possible pitfall of an untrained 'counsellor' causing spiritual or psychological damage through the inappropriate use of such approaches and techniques, such as using confrontation or making interpretations linking experiences in infancy and childhood with present behaviour and attitudes.

BAC Guidelines for those using counselling skills in their work state:

Counselling skills are being used:

❖ when there is intentional use of specific interpersonal skills which reflect the values of counselling;

❖ and when the practitioner's primary role (e.g. nurse, tutor, line manager, social worker, personnel officer, helper) is enhanced without being changed;

❖ and when the client perceives the practitioner as acting within their primary professional or caring role which is not that of being a counsellor.[5]

This use of pastoring skills does not carry the same requirements as formal counselling. Boundaries are far less rigid. Contacts between those involved are flexible and – in psychological terms – the various roles adopted are accepted as normal. The priest and the parishioner may well meet socially, sit on committees, work on fund-raising events and minister together to someone else. There is no harm in this provided the counselling skills used in this way do not evoke the same strength of psychological reactions as formal counselling often does. Both parties can usually cope with the situation. But we believe that supervision is essential if one or the other find themselves becoming emotionally involved to a disturbing degree. It is not unknown for congregations to become divided, or even marriages broken up, through unsupervised pastoral care which has gone disastrously wrong. We say more about supervision towards the end of the chapter.

A number of catastrophic events, mainly in the 1980s, gave rise to a specialism known as 'disaster counselling'. In the early years local parish clergy and chaplains attended large-scale disasters which occurred in their neighbourhood and ministered spiritual comfort or performed the last rites as seemed appropriate. In time the role of these church representatives at such events was more clearly defined. What remains less clear, however, is the place of the healing ministry in the ongoing care of those affected by such events – names like Lockerbie, *Herald of Free Enterprise*, Hillsborough and Paddington come to mind.

Post-traumatic Stress Disorder (PTSD), first used to describe a condition affecting those psychologically affected by war, has been widened in its usage to include people suffering from the after-effects of such disasters. More recently still PTSD has been broadened to encompass the distress often experienced, for example, by those who have been sexually abused, bullied at work, involved in road accidents or the victims of violent crime.

Nightmares, flashbacks, 'survivor guilt', withdrawal from other people and anxiety can all characterize the condition, as can terrifying rages or flashes of temper. Wrongly interpreted, some of these can attract unhelpful and even harmful attempts at ministry. While we do not condone inappropriate expressions of anger, it is nevertheless the case that, for someone with PTSD, their rages can be virtually impossible to control, and may already be causing them a great deal of guilt and remorse. To be condemned as 'sinful' or treated as if demonized adds to their despair and does nothing to alter their behaviour.

Counselling is generally recognized by the other denominations as part of the broader healing ministry, although at a local level there is variation in the esteem in which counselling is held (as is the case of the Church of England). Individuals have trained as counsellors and some churches have set up counselling services or allowed their premises to be used for counselling. There is concern in these churches that counselling should be conducted according to professional standards through training, supervision and observance of boundaries between counselling and other activities such as pastoral care.

Most denominations now offer counselling support to their clergy and ministers (and quite often to their spouses and others such as adult children). The Baptist Union Ministerial Counselling Service was set up in 1992 for the Union's own ministers, and later opened up to ministers of other denominations. Renamed the Churches' Ministerial Counselling Service in 1996, it provides a confidential service on behalf of the Methodist Church and the United Reformed Church as well as the Free Churches' Council and the Salvation Army. The scheme is available to provide support to those experiencing emotional, psychological or spiritual distress caused, for example, by relationship difficulties, work problems, bereavement and other life events and adjustment difficulties. Each denomination specifies the boundaries of eligibility (ministers, spouses, etc.). It is recognized that the counsellors, who are all professionally qualified, use their skills to earn their living, so professional fees are charged. Financial contributions are invited from those individuals using the service and any shortfall is made up by the person's denomination.

The Roman Catholic Church has a specialist centre in Stroud offering psychotherapy for such problems as drug and alcohol abuse and for the perpetrators of sexual abuse. Another establishment, the Dympna Centre in Mill Hill, London, carries out psychological testing of candidates for ordination as part of the preselection process. In general the view of the Roman Catholic Church in England is that counselling is a useful form of professional therapy, not incompatible with Christian teaching. While each case would be considered on its merits, bishops may in principle refer priests to secular or other counsellors for therapeutic help, and the diocese may contribute to the fees.

Christian counselling

Christian pastoral counselling can be distinguished from other forms of counselling in at least three different ways. These are described as follows:

❖ first, that 'it belongs within the faith tradition and is specific about the values of that tradition';

❖ second, that its context is 'the whole of life, and that life as a gift of God's grace, which is not limited to this life nor confined by it'; and

❖ third, in that it is practised by *representative* people with as great a sense of the faith community of which they are a part as of their own precious 'individuality'.[6]

Many Christians say that at the time of their conversion they experience something of what Jesus meant when he said, 'I came that they may have life, and have it abundantly' (John 10.10). Some describe instant release from fears, destructive habits or harmful attitudes, others describe a process over weeks or months in which they moved more rapidly than before towards wholeness. For some it takes the form of a gradual awareness of change. Others describe a dramatic experience of struggle between good and bad, with an awe-ful sense of their greater goodness being the focus of a cosmic battle.

But for others the joy of conversion is followed by an awareness of spiritual and emotional issues which they require help in addressing. More mature believers, too, at any stage of their Christian journey can realize they have needs which can best be addressed by the ministry of others. For example, significant changes (of job, marital status, health, etc.) can trigger psychological reactions that can be helped by counselling, prayer ministry or both.

Furthermore, at some points of Christian growth people can feel themselves 'blocked' – unable to believe that God loves them, perhaps, or with a deepening awareness of the need to address an event, maybe from years previously. Listening, prayer and perhaps healing of the memories may be required to help them break through this 'block' to their wholeness. But if further ministry is required, then the individual should be encouraged to seek the help of a qualified Christian counsellor who acts under the guidance we have set out in this report.

Techniques from the secular world can be applied, such as in active listening, as can specifically Christian activities. These include the use of the imagination to enter into a passage of Scripture. The story of the prodigal can be used to take a person back to a particular event that carries traumatic memories to receive the healing Jesus brings, fulfilling his promise that whatever his followers 'loose on earth will be loosed in heaven' (Matthew 16.19). While many secular counsellors recognize the negative effects of bitterness and resentment, Christian counsellors are perhaps more aware of them, and of the frequent need for people to offer forgiveness and seek reconciliation in some relationship or other in order to be enabled to move on, both psychologically and spiritually.

For those who are in thrall to certain beliefs, practices, other people or limitations, prayer for release can be extremely beneficial. On such occasions Christians with specific charisms like 'a word of wisdom' or 'a word of knowledge' can encourage the troubled individual to permit the Holy Spirit to work in greater power (provided, of course, that like all charisms they are exercised with proper discernment).

But often there are no quick-fixes. Counselling and other means of helping people to achieve greater wholeness can be slow, difficult, painstaking work. Sadly it can be made harder when insensitive Christians express unhelpful opinions and make ill-informed judgements. Among those who were abused during childhood the belief that they were themselves at fault ('they asked for it', 'they deserved it') is often commonly and strongly held.

Such beliefs can be fuelled both by our liturgy and also by preachers who stress the status of our righteousness being 'as filthy rags' and by admonishments to instant forgiveness of those who had 'sinned against them'. A preacher's voice, raised for emphasis, can transport such people back to childhood fears, drawing them further from the loving God rather than towards him. To those who were abused by earthly fathers, eulogies about the kindness of their heavenly Father can similarly miss the mark.

Abused people's sense of not being acceptable or lovable may be reinforced when they are urged to memorize and 'claim for themselves' a verse from the Bible, or to repeat regularly a certain prayer formula. If such means do not bring about the longed-for change and the process of being restored to wholeness turns out to be more complicated, then devotional exercises can produce a huge sense of disappointment and of being beyond even God's help.

Additional pitfalls occur in those churches where charismatic forms of prayer are exercised. Patterns of ministry which smack of the conveyor belt have developed in some churches which run the risk of leading vulnerable individuals to expose their deepest needs, only to be left with just a short prayer before the person ministering moves on. 'Ministry' such as this, by people unversed in psychological processes and therefore unaware of the damage they are doing, can retraumatize those to whom

they are ministering, reinforcing terrifying early experiences of abandon-
ment and of being promised something positive but having been given
something appallingly negative instead. Professional counsellors may then
have a doubly difficult task as they attempt to 'pick up the pieces' with a
client whose early scars have been gouged deeper by their experiences in
a church.

As we shall see elsewhere in this report, the pictorial language and symbolism of the Bible, reflected in the liturgy and the ornaments of the
Church, the use of oil and the laying on of hands, and other outward and
visible signs, can aid the process of healing from spiritual and emotional
brokenness. The sense of touch is important. So tangible objects such as
stones can be used to represent burdens during a prayer and then laid at
the foot of a cross.

For many people a sense of closure is very important. Having disclosed
certain things in a counselling setting, it may be appropriate for them to
write what they have said and then burn the paper. This can help to sym-
bolize that they are finally closing that particular chapter in their life.
Others have been aided by writing a letter to the one who has hurt them,
then sealing the letter with wax as a way of reminding themselves that
they have now put the past behind them.

Prayer ministry

We need also to distinguish what we understand by the terms 'prayer ministry' and 'prayer counselling'. In prayer ministry the situation is presented to God in words spoken aloud or silently with little or no comment.
A typical situation for this would be during a service of prayer for healing when those ministering may ask the individual who has come forward
no more than, say, their name and what it is they wish to be prayed for.
In prayer counselling a time of intercession to God follows counselling,
during which some of the facts and feelings revealed in the session are
drawn into the prayer with a view to seeking the Lord's healing and guidance.

Prayer ministry tends to invite fewer problems than prayer counselling
because, as we have just said, the situation is more or less presented to
God with little comment from the person ministering. On the other hand,

prayer counselling, with both its emphasis on the human relationship and its focus on God, may sometimes evoke even stronger psychological reactions than does counselling; and in this case the guidelines we have described must be carefully observed.

Some churches which have developed a healing ministry use members of the congregation who are psychologists or trained counsellors in the team of people who minister healing during or after services. While this is no doubt very helpful in certain cases, caution should be exercised so as to maintain appropriate boundaries between the relatively short periods of prayer ministry and episodes – potentially far longer – of counselling. The same kind of boundaries also need to be kept when members of the medical professions are involved in prayer ministry.

Spiritual direction

Spiritual direction is only part of the healing ministry of the Church in the widest sense since it is a continuous ministry to the healthy as well as the sick. It may be described as the exercise of a spiritual gift of discernment which enables a Christian to help others to grow in their faith in Jesus Christ through prayer, worship and a disciplined life.

In the Catholic tradition since the Reformation it has often been combined with the hearing of confessions and the giving of spiritual counsel. In the Orthodox tradition spiritual help was sought through the advice of those who were regarded as living close to God, especially the members of religious communities. But in practice spiritual direction has been sought and given in all kinds of informal situations. What distinguishes it from, say, confidential chats among friends (which can, of course, be very helpful) is that it usually involves making personal appointments with known spiritual guides in retreat houses and elsewhere.

Superficially, there may seem to be a close connection between spiritual direction and counselling. The director, like the counsellor, knows he or she can only be him- or herself by depending on God's forgiveness, love and acceptance of his or her current state of being, and so the director is released to be an instrument of God's forgiveness, love and acceptance of the directee. And the director, also like the counsellor, has to resist the temptation to dominate or dictate to the directee in order to become more open to the Holy Spirit.

Moreover, certain skills of counselling can offer important lessons for the spiritual director and the directee. For example, direction like counselling can involve the disclosure of very personal details, and the director and the directee should be aware that the same psychological reactions can take place between them as in a counselling session. Tendencies towards projection, transference and counter-transference are just as likely to be present and need to be watched.

But there the similarity ends, for spiritual direction has a different purpose from that of counselling. The spiritual director is not a therapist, and the therapist is not a spiritual director. Counselling aims to help clients to understand themselves and to be healed to be more fully human. Spiritual direction aims to help directees grow in their relationship with God through prayer and discipleship. There is a time for counselling and a time for spiritual direction, and the boundary needs to be understood and observed. 'Spiritual direction is therefore a means to an end. The end is God, whose service is perfect freedom.'[7]

The ministry of reconciliation

The ministry of reconciliation, whether or not it is associated with spiritual direction, is in itself an aspect of the healing ministry. Going to confession is nearly always a liberating experience when done faithfully, and for many with troubled consciences it is sufficient in itself. But, again, it needs to be distinguished from counselling. This confusion may arise more because these days the hearing of confessions tends to be more informal, with the confessor (the priest hearing the confession) and the penitent sitting at chairs and only using a kneeling desk for the liturgical prayers of confession and absolution. It is necessary to remember that at the heart of this ministry are the confession of sin made by the penitent to God in the presence of his people (represented by the priest) and the prayer of absolution, pronounced by the priest with the authority of the Church, through which the penitent is reconciled to God and to his people.

Where a difficult case arises, when the confessor thinks that the penitent would benefit from a session with a trained counsellor, the confessor can suggest this, or seek the penitent's permission to discuss the matter further outside the confessional. If, however, the penitent rejects the suggestion, the seal of the confessional obliges the director not to pursue it any further.

We believe that in their training courses ordinands, clergy and laity who are preparing for pastoral responsibilities should be made aware of the distinctions in counselling, spiritual direction, ministry of reconciliation and prayer ministries. We are concerned that from time to time we meet lay people who have had unhappy experiences of counselling by those who have lacked the necessary instruction, sensitivity and supervision, and priests who complain that they were 'never taught to hear confessions'. We hope it is possible for such training to be given both before and after ordination or, in the case of the laity, before and after commissioning or permission to minister.

Supervision

The various codes of ethics which apply to counsellors and psychologists, such as those laid down by the British Association for Counselling, the Association of Christian Counsellors and the British Psychological Society, all require that those covered by the codes have regular supervision for as long as they are in practice. As a minimum, these therapists must have one and a half hours of individual supervision per month (or the equivalent, if receiving group supervision). For trainees and novice practitioners, supervision may consist largely of exploring different therapeutic methods; troubleshooting; professional 'housekeeping' and case management; constructive feedback; the establishment of their own clinical 'style' and the monitoring of boundaries.

As they progress, and supervisees become more able to reflect on process rather than content, more time is likely to be spent considering themes which recur, relating theory to content across a variety of contexts, exploring the dynamics operating in the counselling room and perhaps exploring the relationship between themselves and the supervisor.

Good supervision is a collaborative relationship in which empathy, respect and unconditional positive regard provide a safe environment in which the therapeutic work can be discussed openly and honestly, and in which supervisees can reveal their feelings about the demanding, frustrating but also extremely rewarding work they do.

Where churches offer formal counselling, supervision such as this should be an essential part of the package. However, we also strongly recommend that both clergy and laity in churches offering pastoral care, which includes listening, prayer ministry, spiritual direction and the ministry of reconciliation, and those who are members of healing ministry teams, should consider carefully the advantages which that supervision affords and explore appropriate ways of introducing it into their own situation.

We have alluded elsewhere in this report to some of the pitfalls which can occur in the healing ministry and pastoral care, many of which can be avoided if supervision is offered, received and well used. Those ministering healing may be overwhelmed by their own feelings about the situations they encounter, and these feelings may affect the quality of the ministry they can offer; there may be issues of sexual attraction or overdependence. Carrying such burdens alone is exhausting and isolating – and unnecessary if supervision is provided.

The future

We introduced the previous chapter by suggesting that the theological undergirding for the Church's cooperation with the professions is to be found in the stream of pastoral care for the sick over the centuries, which is a continuation of the ministry of Christ the pastor. Of course, the pastoral stream cannot be separated from the sacramental and the charismatic streams in this ministry for Christ as pastor, sacrament and charismatic is one and, indeed, we have noticed the sacramental and charismatic streams appearing in our discussion of cooperation both in institutions and in parishes.

But as we look to the future of the cooperation, especially amidst all the advances in scientific medicine and modern therapy, the role of the Church in the ministry of healing as visionary, prophetic and dynamic becomes even more relevant in working alongside the professions. She could be visionary because she will still be called by God to declare the good news of the divine purpose for which individuals and humanity have been created, and of the salvation which Jesus Christ has brought them. She could be prophetic in seeking and proclaiming God's Word in the midst of all the advances and changes, whether of encouragement for what is good or of warning for what is evil. And she could be dynamic because it is the Holy Spirit who energizes her in this ministry, sometimes taking initiatives in demonstrating more Christ-like ways of caring for the sick and dying, ways which are eventually recognized and accepted by the professions.

For her to fulfil these roles in the midst of cooperation with the professions, the Church must continue to be a Church at prayer – not just the Church as she relates officially to the institutions and the parishes, but the whole community of the faithful, those in the health and welfare structures as well as all others among her membership. They should be helped and encouraged to pray for guidance, discernment and boldness for what is done for the sick and the dying in this nation, asking that all involved will be filled with the Spirit of Christ. In this task she will be aided by the various Christian organizations among the medical and nursing professions who have had much experience in helping their members to see their work as a Christian vocation rather than just an employment. In this way cooperation between the Church and the professions can become a John the Baptist mission, making straight the way for the coming of Christ the healer.

Recommendations

We recommend that:

❖ clergy and other church representatives should be encouraged to initiate and maintain links between themselves and others working in the community, such as doctors, police and the social and voluntary services; for example, through occasional lunches or seminars. In the light of the Government's expressed desire for partnerships between the statutory and the voluntary sectors, this recommendation may suggest creative use of church premises (with appropriate funding) in wider health care provision for the community (see pages 107–8);

❖ all those using counselling skills in pastoral care should receive adequate training and supervision (see pages 110, 112, 113, 114, 115 and 122–3);

❖ those offering formal counselling should receive adequate training and supervision, work with a recognized code of ethics and practice and be accredited by or working towards accreditation by a reputable body (see pages 110, 114, 117 and 122–3);

❖ boundaries between counselling and other forms of pastoral care and between people in dual and multiple roles (that is simultaneously in more than one relationship with one another) should be monitored and regularly reviewed (see pages 109, 110–11, 112, 113, 114, 118 and 121–2);

❖ given the wide variety between dioceses in counselling services provided for clergy, their spouses and dependent children, standards should be established which ensure that at least basic provision is available in every diocese (see pages 110 and 118–19);

❖ courses of training for lay and ordained ministries should include an introduction to the ministry of spiritual direction, and individuals who develop a special gift for this ministry should be encouraged and helped in further studies and practice (see pages 110, 113, 119, 121 and 123–4);

❖ courses of training for lay and ordained ministry should include an introduction to the ministry of reconciliation (hearing confessions), and priests should be helped to develop this ministry through appropriate supervision and guidance in their continuing ministerial education (see page 121).

7

The Impact of Limitation and Illness

The impact of limitation and illness on the Church's healing ministry is such that Christ's presence and purpose have to be sought within each situation. Christian healing relates not solely or necessarily to the restoration of function but also to the restoration of the possibility of fulfilling the purpose for which we were created. Those with persisting disability and illness may need protection from inappropriate evangelism. Carers have to learn to leave the burdens of the day at the foot of the cross, and understand that caring is a vital expression of the Church's ministry of healing. It is in caring for one another that a healing community is born.

The reality of unremitting limitation and illness

Be merciful to me, O Lord, for I am in distress, my eyes grow weak with sorrow, my soul and my body with grief. My life is consumed by anguish and my years by groaning; my strength fails because of my affliction, and my bones grow weak . . . I am a dread to my friends – those who see me on the street flee from me. I am forgotten by them as though I were dead; I have become like broken pottery.'

(Psalm 31.9-12, NIV)

If the Church's healing ministry is to have relevance in the world of the twenty-first century, a world that demands instant cures and lasting pleasures, then it has to bring meaning and hope rather than a sense of guilt and failure to people with unremitting limitation and illness.

Christian faith is not problem-solving but mystery-encountering, so that any particular sickness is part of a much wider and deeper picture. A common mistake is to suppose that the Christian approach to healing is problem-solving – the illness or disability being the problem. This puts something called Christian healing in the marketplace along with all the other competing therapies which seem largely unaware of, or intolerant of, one another's claims.[1]

It is important to beware of any picture of healing as merely the restoration of function. A focus on function places value on performance and ability rather than on the individual. Dysfunction and disability then leave the person concerned feeling discarded.

Any particular illness or limitation acquires a distorted significance when it is made the centre of the picture. A problem-centred approach assumes there is a solution, but Christian faith invites us further and further into the mystery. The fact that someone for whose cure we pray is not cured makes us look to the sovereignty of God in every particular of human life, and calls forth a deeper trust, often dearly bought, that the gift is in the ordeal. Our identity is being forged in the crucible of whatever sufferings turn out to be inextricable from the particular journey of each person, and of us together, into the fullness of life.[2]

In responding to Psalm 31 and the writer's faith in the almighty God as protector, many will cry that God does not defend his people from worldly evil, and indeed he seems powerless or unwilling to protect them. Reflecting on this and the reality of persisting illness, Margaret Spufford writes: 'The trust one has to develop in God lies far deeper, in the knowledge that he will be present in the deepest waters, and in the most acute pain, and in some apprehension of his will to transform these things. No cheap belief in him as "insurance" will serve'.[3]

People suffering from illnesses and disorders which show little prospect of abating, either with treatment from health care professionals, or as a result of Christian ministry, often feel marginalized and come to wonder whether the care of the Church (or the National Health Service) really extends to them. Churches all too quickly erect barriers against people with disability rather than enabling and empowering them. Congregations fail to see that such people have as much to offer as anyone else. Disabled people tend to be objects of ministry, rather than providers of it. People with difficulties of an intellectual, emotional or psychiatric nature often feel unseen and unheard in the churches.

Both a return to health and unrelenting sickness or limitation are realities of life. In this paradox, the mind of Christ has to be sought, knowing that within the purposes of God, who one day will make all things new, is a beautiful harmony between the power of prayer and the God-given offering of medical understanding that opens the way to wholeness.[4] That wholeness may have to be experienced within the reality of sickness of some kind. People do not have to get up out of their wheelchairs to show the healing power and presence of God at work in their lives.[5]

Ministry to people whose illness or disability seemingly has no horizon places the highest demands, not only on the caring capacity of the Church, but also on the teaching ministry within local congregations in the areas of healing and suffering.

Christian healing in these situations is helpfully seen as 'the restoration of the possibility of fulfilling the purpose for which we were created'.[6] It has been said that 'wholeness is a perfection of relationships such that to be me I have to be me in such a way that I help you to be the you are meant to be'.[7] The challenge is in allowing God to make each other whole – disabled or 'differently-abled' people and those who are able, people who have unremitting illness and those who enjoy a freedom from ill health; they all have the potential to make each other whole. It is not all one-way.[8] In a congregation that understands this there is a mutuality in giving and receiving and the love of God abounds. This love is a call to action and that action will speak of relationship. Perhaps valued relationships matter more than results – there is no place for 'doing good' but always a place for 'sharing with' on the journey into wholeness.

In a personal letter, Anne with multiple sclerosis wrote: 'When things are unbearable, to know people care and share your pain is like the knot at the end of the rope – you can literally hold on! When there is no answer and things are desperate, it is knowing that I do not have to travel alone that is life giving.'

The challenge in pastoral care here is to identify with suffering people and to offer companionship on their journey, being expectant of receiving from them for they have a gift to be shared. The challenge for people with persisting limitation is to 'live' their grief and loss rather than just to 'feel' it. Merely to feel their grief could bring someone to the brink of destruction. To live their grief could become an act of human dignity.

It has been said that 'until we get a sense of proportion about miracles and disability – until we get miracle and disability into the right perspective of salvation – the greatest handicap for disabled people will continue to be other people'.[9] Each church needs to bring an understanding of health in the context of salvation, so that it is better equipped to show those very people its loving, accepting, all-inclusive face and grow in the depth of its ministry.

Moltmann suggested, 'Experiences of powerlessness are now the order of the day'.[10] If this is so, maybe we need to turn to those who have a deep experience of powerlessness to find out how to live. People who are dependent in one way or another and those who are marginalized by a society which sets the norms are also a powerful people. Power in such people has a positive and a negative aspect, like all power. With negative power, the fruits are negative; power to instil fear, anxiety, stress, distress, to project helplessness onto so-called normal people, so that they feel helpless before those who distress them. Their positive power lies in the challenge they provide but also in the comfort they can bring: 'Look, you can be human, even if your body, your mind, your emotions do not work well!' That is so often the fear in 'normal' people: 'Can I still be human, be loved, be myself if I recognize and allow others to recognize all the weakness, all the disability that is within me?' If the negative power of people with disability is to give place to the positive, then all have to change.[11] Moltmann again:

> If they want to be truly human, people who are not themselves handicapped must be liberated from the illusion that they are healthy and they must at the same time be freed from their fear of people who are handicapped. . . . Handicapped people help us to achieve true humanity for they compel us to stop basing our self-confidence on health and capability and to seek it through trust in God.[12]

Challenge in disability

Learning disabilities

Most church services are inevitably heavily weighted towards those in the population who are literate, can comprehend symbolic language and who have a sufficiently long attention span (not to mention grasp of standards of conventional behaviour) to be able to sit, stand, recite and be silent as required for over an hour. For many people in our society, these things are not possible. Clearly toddlers and young children may lack sufficient cognitive and social skills to follow a church service with all its nuances. Some people have learning or socialization disabilities which prevent them from following the service. Spontaneous utterances, interruptions and other disinhibited behaviour may cause embarrassment. Parents and other family members can feel that the child or person concerned is unwelcome within the congregation.

Such a situation brings challenge and opportunity for a church. If responded to with compassion, understanding and sensitivity, even a small response can prove to be a focus for healing. Parents and carers can be reconciled with the rest of the congregation and the self-esteem of the person with disability can be increased.

Example: Where some adults with learning disability, living in sheltered accommodation, are going to begin attending a local church, some of the carers could be invited to 'pave the way' by introducing themselves and the work of their charity at a church service. Church members could be invited to a coffee morning to meet the residents. Bridges of understanding and the beginnings of relationship can dispel incipient fears.

Perhaps the churches which most closely resemble the level of fellowship of the early Church are those which regard the children in the congregation as the joint responsibility of those present – not just that of the parents. Extended to embrace children and adults with learning disabilities or with other special needs, this challenges churches to provide suitable help during services (perhaps a designated helper in the crèche, Sunday school or a 'quiet' area) so parents can attend services rather than staying at home because they 'can't take Stephen'.

Practical help of this kind (and, for example, offers to babysit or to be a Link family providing respite) can make a huge difference to families struggling with the demands of a member with particular long-term needs. Coupled with prayer, both for the family as they seek to juggle the various calls on their time, and for the person with disability, such measures as these form part of the Church's ministry of healing.

The Lord's healing power can, of course, reach to any situation, but it is preferable to show his love and compassion in practical ways, rather than to wait expectantly for cure, a move which puts its own additional pressures on the family. Enfolding the family in prayer, with particular focus on disruptive and exhausting behaviour patterns, should be but part of the response of the caring congregation. Communities and congregations have much to receive from these people that will help them to a deeper understanding of wholeness and relationship.

> The most significant values in the Christian tradition are summed up in St Paul's list of the fruit of the Spirit: love, joy, peace, patience, kindness, generosity, faithfulness, gentleness and self-control. These values can only flourish in community. Furthermore, they imply a healing from self-interest and self-pity, a reorientation from the self-concern that comes from guilt, a turning that opens up to receiving grace and acceptance from others. Experience is that those who are 'different', those whose lives are simpler and in some ways more basically human, are precisely those who can generate the relationships in which the truth emerges and those values are realised.[13]

The possibility of these people being specifically used in the ministry of the Church must be borne in mind and the appropriateness of this assessed in each individual situation. They have gifts to be recognized and emotions to be shared within their congregations and communities.

Psychiatric illness

People who suffer from disorders of thoughts and emotions, perception and judgement, range widely from those who have mild depression and abnormal grief patterns to those with major psychoses or dementias. Most commonly, many people within a congregation will experience degrees of ill-effects of neuroses at one time or another. They will be greatly helped by active listening, prayer and pastoral concern. During times of anxiety and depression, these people may be particularly enabled and supported by the availability of healing services or regular opportunities for specific prayer.

During such illnesses, some people become disinclined to attend their own congregations. They may lack motivation to get there or feel they may be judged by others in the church. The latter feeds their sense of guilt and failure, often leading them to seek help from church services where they feel anonymous – at a Christian healing centre, for example. A triumphalist approach with a prescriptive dose of 'Jesus is here for you – there is no need to worry' or 'there must be unconfessed sin in your life' can tip an already self-denigrating person into more serious illness, accompanied by an abyss of despair.

It is in the areas of severe enduring mental illness and some personality disorders that the greatest challenge comes, both for those who are afflicted and those who attempt to offer help. Church members may feel distanced from people with such conditions; unable to identify with their problems, responses, attitudes or behaviour and fearful of aggravating the situation, they react by marginalizing them.

One or two well-meaning people in a congregation can easily become overburdened in trying to help a person suffering with a psychiatric condition. Local churches or Churches Together could establish a network of people who are trained in offering support. With informed support, prayer, companionship and even round-the-clock care during crises, trust is established and the frequency of hospital admissions will diminish. Professional teams, in primary and specialist services, can welcome this involvement in community care.

The Greek lexicon suggests three meanings for the root word 'psyche': breath, especially the sign of life; life, spirit, the soul of a person, as opposed to the body; the soul, mind, reasoning, understanding. Hence there is a sense of appropriateness for priest and psychiatrist to work together, sharing in understanding and ministry where this is practicable[14] (see Chapter 9 regarding the deliverance ministry). Reluctance to do this may come from a mistrust of the other's expertise or from difficulties in the area of confidentiality.

Disorders of adult personality and behaviour

Much that is written about pastoral care of people with illness applies to ministering Christ's love and healing to those who have personality disorders. There need to be safeguards and supervision, and close professional liaison, as the impact on other individuals and groups may be considerable. These conditions comprise deeply ingrained and enduring attitudes and behaviour patterns, as inflexible responses to the broad range of personal and social situations. They represent extreme or significant deviations in how individuals think, feel, and particularly relate to others. Such people commonly find it difficult to be accepted in social groups within the community but, ideally, find welcome and acceptance within their churches. Their problems may be internalized in excessive self-regulation or avoidance, and not impact on others significantly (e.g. obsessional and schizoid personalities) or may be characterized by histrionic or overdependent behaviour, or aggression, with demands and challenges.

In particular, people with 'borderline' or antisocial personality disorders, and addictive or impulsive traits, may make the strongest impact on those with whom they relate. This is one context in which church members do well to heed Jesus' words about being 'wise as serpents and innocent as doves' (Matthew 10.16) if they are to avoid being manipulated or exploited. People with these conditions have the greatest level of disturbance in personal boundaries, often with a fragmented sense of self and lack of empathy with others, and an egocentric need to gratify their desires or to discharge inner tension and hostility. Safety is paramount. Pastoral supporters need to know when and how to hand over to responsible professionals for statutory interventions, under mental health or child protection regulations, when these individuals threaten or actually harm others.

Yet, at the same time, these are the very people for whom Jesus had the greatest compassion – the poor in spirit, outcasts, even perhaps the 'oppressed' and 'prisoners' that Jesus refers to as he proclaims his ministry (Luke 4.18-19, NIV). People with crippling low self-esteem, with no value or regard for themselves nor, therefore, for others; deprived, disadvantaged and damaged in their own development, maybe as much victims themselves as they are perpetrators of an offence against others; prisoners within their own minds, and sometimes within co-dependent relationships, locked into self-defeating patterns. Only perfect love can cast out fear, and begin the building of trust. There will usually be relapses and disappointment, testings, interpersonal 'woundings' and grievances, and much conflict on the painful road to recovery. This can all be a source of creative tension for church members commanded to show love, grace and acceptance to people whom they do not understand, or sometimes fear. Pastoral failure through overreaction and an attempt at vigorous deliverance ministry will be harmful. A prayerful community will provide strength and containment through firm loving boundaries and support for professional workers.

Physical limitation and progressive physical illness

Perhaps the greatest impact on thinking relating to the healing ministry has been made by those who have had the courage to share their experiences of living with and alongside human disability. In many congregations the Bible is read as declaring that God's will is for our wholeness and perfection, with an emphasis on sufficient faith resulting in healing. Salvation belongs to the here and now. Liberation theology preaches the possibility of change. But where does that leave people whose circumstances are unchangeable, whose conditions remain uncured, whose disabilities constitute the reality of their existence?[15]

One who lives with profound physical impairments writes:

> The resurrected Jesus Christ, in presenting impaired hands and feet and side to be touched by frightened friends, alters the taboo of physical avoidance of disability. Jesus Christ, the disabled God, is not a romanticised notion of 'over-comer' God. Instead, here is God as 'survivor' . . . a simple unself-pitying, honest body, for whom the limits of power are palpable but not tragic.[16]

Continuing disability is a reality of life for many. Those ministering to people who specifically seek Christ's ministry of healing see many who return again and again for prayer and the laying on of hands. These people may carry the marks of outward disability or the inner burden of destructive emotions. Some receive only the strength and desire to keep going, while others appear to move on and grow into new areas of fruitfulness, despite their disability.

Example: 'George' comes for the laying on of hands every week, transferring from his car to his wheelchair and then being pushed into church to receive ministry. He has been doing this for 14 years and has missed few services. He lives with depression, his own physical disability and his wife's obsessional neurosis. How should one pray for him? What is the expectation? When should a longing for physical and emotional healing lead those who pray to hold George and his needs before God and 'making no special requests – neither asking nor beseeching but lifting him to God . . . desiring nothing but that our Lord may be glorified in all'?[17] Perhaps the breakthrough comes when George in his wheelchair becomes, for those ministering, the Christ figure in their midst. From there the notion of community becomes of paramount importance for understanding the idea of God's image. If Christ is in God's image and Christ's body on earth is the Church, a corporate body in which the least regarded members are as important as the best to the functioning of the whole, then it is as community, each individual embodying some different aspect, that we constitute God's image. And the 'Georges' of this world are essential, for they represent the crucified body, which is essential to the whole Christ.[18]

To be alongside those with persisting illness and limitation, to see Christ crucified in them and to free them from inappropriate burdens that some interpretations of the healing ministry can impose on them, it is vital that congregations and communities have a good understanding of the usual responses to loss. A better understanding of loss and its effect on the individual will build bridges between prayer and ministry teams and the one requesting help from the Church.

Responses to loss often follow a recognizable pattern, beginning with shock and progressing erratically through denial, questioning, anger, guilt, grief and anxiety to a state of acceptance or resignation. A similar pattern is seen in grief and people facing death.[19] Movement tends not to be linear; people move backwards as well as forwards in the process of adjustment, particularly in illnesses like multiple sclerosis, where symptoms come and go. Because emotions are ever-present, the process of adjustment goes on at varying levels 24 hours a day. At times this will be exhausting. It is a process which has to be 'gone through' rather than 'got over'.[20] Losses to be coped with often include:

- ❖ normal family life
- ❖ independence
- ❖ career and status
- ❖ mobility and use of the senses

❖ continence
❖ sexual expression
❖ motivation
❖ employment.

Understanding of the responses to loss can enable a shared journey and open the door to healing. Hence they deserve individual attention. *Shock* causes emotional numbness, and is particularly marked when the consequences and implications of a diagnosis are imparted without warning. The 'anaesthetizing' of the mind allows the person to assimilate bad news gradually. The challenge here is to provide a dependable, accepting and enabling environment that allows truth to be faced without inappropriate dependency.

Denial allows what cannot be endured to be ignored. Life is lived as if in a dream because reality is hell, and the face smiles as if to prove that nothing is wrong. Denial is a necessary defence or coping mechanism which we all use, albeit in different ways. The challenge is to open up new opportunities for purposeful and creative living that remove the need for denial. Denial is usually eroded in time by the inescapable consequences of disability. One teenager with sickle-cell anaemia wrote: 'I remember when I used to think that this was just a passing phase I was going through and that things could only get better. How wrong I was.'[21]

Questioning begins the search for meaning and purpose despite disability. In his frustrations, Job cried out to God:

Why was I not stillborn,

why did I not perish when I came from the womb?

Why is life given to those who find it so bitter?

(Job 3.11,20, REB)

A diving accident which left Joni Eareckson paralysed from the neck down when aged 17 caused desolation, depression and a wish to die. Out of her physical immobility and mental confusion she repeatedly cried out, 'Why did you let this happen, God?' It was years later before she was able to let go of the questioning, but eventually she wrote, 'Only God knows why I was paralysed . . . but now I am really happy. It was only when I stopped asking "Why?" that I began to move on.'[22] The challenge in care is to avoid offering superficial answers or untruths that only feed the unanswerable 'Why me?' 'There's no point in trying to understand; it's all a mystery. You just have to live the mystery.'[23]

Anger is a powerful response in loss and consequent vulnerability – a plea for restoration of that which is lost. Even 'nice' people reveal anger towards a nasty world. Once the response of denial is past, anger finds a target. The young man with sickle-cell anaemia wrote:

> During a painful episode when I am bedridden and can't move a muscle, my alter ego seems to appear. I find myself incredibly angry and almost vengeful. I despise my friends because they have never had to go through half of this and never will. Their lives seem so free of problems and yet I hear them talk about the pressures of school.[24]

As anger seeks a target, little is right – the food, the nurse, the doctor, the friends who visit for too long, God – all are in the line of fire. More positively, anger may be a cry for clear communication and a true meeting together in loving understanding:

❖ anger directly expressed is a mode of taking the other seriously;

❖ anger is at its greatest when it is a cry for love; the person who suffers silently, stoically, has usually settled for hopelessness.

The challenge is to enable the sufferer to pinpoint his anger and to identify what is needed from the 'community of carers' – anger expressed may then be a gateway to hope. Those offering pastoral care have to avoid defending God on every side, lest they reveal their own doubts and uncertainties. They have to beware seeing the 'good patient' (or parishioner) as the one full of smiles and thanks and the 'bad patient' as the one who is angry and demanding.

Guilt is often an expression of inverted anger, targeted at oneself in the form of self-blame. Appropriate ('true') feelings of guilt may grow from the realization that one's chosen behaviour or activity caused the illness. On the other hand, much guilt is inappropriate ('false') and relates to feelings or concern that:

❖ faith is not standing the test of endurance;

❖ there is anger with God;

❖ thoughts are sometimes of suicide;

❖ there is a sense of letting others down (not helped by trivial asides from those whose own inability to accept the situation are transferred to the one who is sick);

❖ 'If only I had more . . . it would not have happened';

❖ the lack of physical healing is a judgement from God.

The challenge is to discern appropriate guilt and to facilitate repentance and forgiveness, as well as to bring love and understanding, which impart the 'courage to accept oneself as accepted in spite of feeling unacceptable'.[25]

Grief brings a time of loneliness, depression and withdrawal, which is dominated by a feeling of being unloved and unlovable. The latter is accentuated if the ability to achieve is lost. A feeling of being abandoned may be reality as friends shy away from a prolonged grief reaction. Resentment of dependence on others may prolong grief, and increasing dependence may precipitate further grief, often coupled with the desire that the end will soon come.[26]

> 'Want to play hangman?' asks my son, and I ache to tell him that I have enough on my plate playing quadriplegic. But my communication system disqualifies repartee: I guess a letter, then another, then stumble on the third. My heart is not in the game. Grief surges over me. His face not two feet from mine, my son sits patiently waiting – and I, his father, have lost the simple right to ruffle his bristly hair, clasp his downy neck, hug his small, lithe, warm body tight against me. There are no words to express it . . . suddenly I can take no more. Tears well . . . [27]

Tears may act as a catalyst on the journey to acceptance and should not be discouraged. Crying, as an expression of physical, psychological or spiritual pain, is a natural, God-given function, which often brings a sense of relief and relaxation. Tears are beyond words and yet may also help in finding words. The ability to cry, however, is affected by physical state, social environment and the expectations of others. Some people who have had a stroke have little control over their emotions and cry when one would expect them to laugh, or vice versa. With such people communication may be difficult. Visitors may attempt to comfort them superficially, instead of allowing an opportunity to give vent to these uncontrolled emotions. Contrastingly, Christians who naively believe that Christianity should be lived only with a smile will need permission to mourn and cry. The challenge in pastoral care is to acknowledge the appropriateness of grief and to 'weep with those who weep' without attempting answers. It is costly to enter into solidarity with the person who is grieving their loss of health and the challenge is to stay and not to walk away.[28]

Anxiety may accompany any of the above responses to loss. It is often coupled with anger and fear. Anxiety, whether admitted or displayed, may be in response to:

❖ separation from an 'attachment figure';

❖ difficulty in adjustment to a changed environment;

❖ seeming loss of control, of either self or circumstances;

❖ poor communication;

❖ unresolved past experiences;

❖ unmanageable pain;

❖ a loss of privacy.

Anxiety is hard to help until it is acknowledged and identified. The Christian may feel that to show anxiety is a denial of faith, and help needs to be given to show that anxiety is in fact a God-given, sometimes life-saving, response to stress. However, if inappropriate, it may undermine reality. The challenge is to provide stability, reassurance and understanding which bring a sense of control and rebuild self-esteem in the sick person.

Acceptance or resignation eventually comes. Some seem to become stuck in their grieving and enter a sullen resignation that longs for death. This is more likely in the face of uncontrolled physical pain. Pastoral care here can be draining but the challenge is in believing that no one is entirely helpless and that everybody reacts to love and care, demonstrating that their lives are of inestimable value to God. Viktor Frankl concluded that 'mankind has one thing that cannot be taken away – the ability to choose one's attitude in any set of circumstances – to choose one's own way'.[29] Love and care enable many to choose a place of positive acceptance, enabling their loss and limitation to become as a gift, used in a tangible way to ease the suffering and loneliness of others. Some enter into a belief that their suffering is used intangibly, enabling them 'to cooperate in the transformation of human suffering'. Professionals and family also have to hold the balance of hope and realism and know and accept when limits have been reached.[30]

For many, with time and appropriate support, a realization comes that despite permanent loss of health, life can still be lived – 'that letting go is not at all the same as giving up and that going with the situation is not to be confused with giving in to it'.[31] Helen Keller in her deafness and blindness was able to say, 'I thank God for my handicaps, for through them I have found myself, my work and my God'.[32] Frances Makower, who was afflicted for more than 20 years with a progressively disabling disease of the spine, wrote:

> While on the more superficial level I fight both pain and dependence, deep down I find myself grateful for my situation which draws me ever deeper to the pierced heart of Christ, to whom I am consecrated and who continues to be reflected in the lives of the powerless, the suffering and the outcast.[33]

Margaret Spufford wrote:

> The acceptance of limitation seems to me one of the most important, and also one of the most dangerous, of disciplines. If you live in a prison cell, it is foolish to spend energy beating yourself into a pulp against the walls; but before accepting those walls, you have to make sure they are there, and you have to make every effort to escape from them. Only the inescapable should be accepted. Everything that can be amended, transformed, healed or ameliorated has to be done first.

Later she reflected that:

> We have to allow ourselves to be open to pain. Yet all the while we must resist any temptation to assent to it being other than evil. If we are able to do this, to act, as it were, as blotting-paper for pain, without handing it on in the form of bitterness or resentment or of hurt to others – then somehow in some incomprehensible miracle of grace, some at least of the darkness may be turned to light.[34]

Acceptance of incurability can:

* ❖ open up new possibilities through new discoveries about oneself;
* ❖ lead to a sense of liberation, despite the limitations;
* ❖ restore a sense of control;
* ❖ transform the individual's sense of purpose;
* ❖ restore self-esteem;
* ❖ reduce feelings of isolation;
* ❖ restore relationships;
* ❖ ease physical pain;
* ❖ impart to those who care the courage to go on;
* ❖ enable one to participate in the reconciling work of Christ.[35]

The challenge in ministry

The challenge in ministry and care is to meet people where they are and not to force them into an outward show of acceptance to ease the distress of those around them. There is a need for the walls of fear which separate them from those offering help in any form to be broken down, so that there is a true meeting on the ground of our common humanity.

There are key points for ministry and care teams:

* ❖ Touch restores love, security and a sense of being valued. It communicates where words fail to, but 'all who tend the sick will bear in mind the maxim: To touch is not a technique; not touching is a technique'.[36] Touch may be healing or wounding; it is vital to be sensitive and prudent about what is appropriate in each situation.

* ❖ Humour, used sensitively, allows a sense of the ridiculous to lighten the load. Laughter can make the unbearable seem bearable. Both are used of God to bring healing.

* ❖ Do not encourage people with disability to live in a dream because reality is hell. It is preferable to attempt to transform reality or give support to face the hell.

❖ Avoid being condescending:

> Do not be surprised at rejection by broken people . . . They have suffered much from broken promises, from people wanting to learn from experiments or to write a thesis and then . . . going away and never coming back. Rejected people are sick and tired of 'good' and 'generous' people, of people who claim to be Christians, of people who come to them on their pedestals of pride and power to do them good.[37]

> 'Hell is other people visiting,' said a lady in a Cheshire Home. 'I am patted on the back and told, "There, there, you'll be all right." I just want to hide when the do-gooders come round.'[38]

❖ Do not collude with relatives whose own needs may bring pressure with comments such as, 'It's time you got over the shock of your illness now.' On the other hand, relatives may need help not to dilute the prognosis unrealistically for their own comfort.

❖ Do not encourage living in the past. Emphasis on the joy of past events and achievements may promote feelings of guilt and serve to deny the reality of the present experience. To encourage the belief that 'I am who I am' equates identity with past productivity and success. This opens the door to bitterness.

❖ Avoid offering 'good advice' because this may create a barrier rather than facilitating involvement. People up against it need to find their own answers. Paul Tournier commented:

> Advice may put people back together again, but it cannot change them. Advice touches the surface of personality, not the centre. To give advice is to place oneself above one's follower, thereby obstructing the spiritual fellowship in which he can be helped.[39]

❖ 'Chronic niceness' in priest, doctor or carer will tend to elicit comparable niceness in the disabled person, with the result that negative feelings are not readily shared and resentments accumulate.

❖ Beware of limiting expectation to the medical prognosis, and of focusing solely on physical well-being. On the other hand it is important to avoid making exaggerated claims of physical healing (in the context of cure) where there is no evidence to support this.

❖ It is easy to react to doubts expressed by overstressing the truths of the Christian gospel. Fanaticism is born out of doubt. Doubt allows for personal spiritual growth and has to be lived with as a travelling companion.[40]

Breakthrough

Breakthrough in the ministry of healing within the Church comes as it is realized that people with persisting illness and disability may need protection from insensitive evangelism and ministry. Robert Foxcroft wrote: 'Prayer is asking God for the power to do his will; magic is asking him to do your will.'[41] In seeking God's will, maybe the priest and carers have to spread out their sense of helplessness before God, with the knowledge of the enabling prayer support of the wider Church. It is the power and presence of Jesus that transforms lives. This transformation may be manifested physically, emotionally, spiritually or in relationships. Those who receive will recognize God's power at work. They will experience the care of a loving Father and be healed in ways that they did not expect.

They will soar on wings like eagles; they will run and not grow weary, they will walk and not be faint.

(Isaiah 40.31, NIV)

The climax, the goal, is not soaring, it is not running, it is walking. For each person, it is carrying on faithfully, no matter what. Occasionally something happens to make the spirit soar like an eagle; now and then someone will get up and run; more often we will see people becoming whole, able to carry on more fully in their everyday lives. In reality, lives are not lived on signs and wonders, nor on a race track with runners, following a God found only in the supernatural, but in the day-to-day responsibilities and practicalities of living – in the ordinariness of life – and that is surely where everyone, with or without physical limitation, needs him most.[42]

At the end of the day, no human mind can encompass God. Spirituality is in principle a never-ending journey in which new heights and depths are always still to be discovered. Human perfection lies in limitation. Wholeness involves the acceptance of limits, for we are all limited in one way or another. The gospel is not a magic wand that guarantees miracles and removes every disability. Rather it is the story of how our limitations can be transformed, how our struggles can paradoxically become the very places where we discover the deepest truths and values of the Christian gospel.[43]

The cost of caring and the need for healing

'. . . where's your boat?'

'I ought to say' said Pooh . . . 'that it isn't just an ordinary sort of boat. Sometimes it's a Boat and sometimes it's more of an Accident. It all depends.'

'Depends on what?'

'On whether I'm on the top of it or underneath it'.[44]

For the Church's ministry of healing to be more than prayerful, sacramental and prescriptive, there has to be an awareness of the demands placed on individuals, particularly when they are involved in ministry to people with continuing illness and those facing death. The 'needy sick' pull at our heartstrings but the toll on the 'gracious carers' may go unnoticed.

There are particular areas of stress that are likely to arise in this kind of caring:

❖ difficulty in accepting that some things cannot be controlled;

❖ frustration when one is not heard or free to do what seems best;

❖ disappointment when one feels let down or rejected;

❖ anger at the unreasonable expectations of others or when faced with the death of the one being cared for;

❖ indecision when faced with drawing limits around one's involvement with another.

Rest, relaxation and self-discipline are important. Engines are fuelled in stillness and not on the run! Jean Vanier warns that:

We can become like rolling locomotives, fuelled by anguish, and perhaps by the fear of stopping. And when we do stop, it is just to sleep more or to potter around, not knowing what to do . . .

Each one of us must find our own secret rhythm of how to rest, relax and find re-creation, for we are all different. We need personal space and time and that is why God gave the Sabbath as a day of rest. We have all to discover our own Sabbath, our real nourishment. This is all the more important as we are called to live with the tension and carry the stress of being with wounded people.[45]

C. S. Lewis wrote:

To love at all is to be vulnerable. Love anything and your heart will certainly be wrung and possibly be broken. If you want to make sure of keeping it intact, you must give your heart to no one. Wrap it carefully round with hobbies and little luxuries. Avoid all entanglement; lock it safe in the casket or coffin of your selfishness. But in that casket, safe, dark, motionless, airless, it will change. It will not be broken – it will become unbreakable, impenetrable, irredeemable. The only place outside Heaven where you can be perfectly safe from all the dangers and perturbations of love is Hell.[46]

Burn-out in carers

This is a syndrome of physical, spiritual and emotional exhaustion that is particularly likely where there is an experience of discrepancy between expectation and reality.[47]

Three stages of burn-out have been described:

❖ In the first stage there is an imbalance between the demands of work and personal resources, which results in hurried meals, longer working hours, spending little time with the family, frequent lingering colds and sleep problems. This is the time to take stock, seek God and the advice of those around us. *Ordering your Private World* by Gordon MacDonald is helpful, but there is probably no time to read it![48]

❖ The second stage involves a short-term response to stress with angry outbursts, irritability, feeling tired all the time and anxiety about physical health. This stage highlights a real need to get away from it all.

❖ 'Terminal' burn-out, stage three, creeps up insidiously. The carer cannot re-establish the balance between demands and personal resources. He or she goes into overdrive, works mechanically, by the book, lacking the fresh inspiration of the Holy Spirit. They tend to be late for appointments and to refer to those they are caring for in a derogatory manner, using superficial, stereotyped, authoritarian methods of communication.

On an emotional level, the carer becomes exhausted, incapable of empathy and overwhelmed by everyday problems. Emotional detachment becomes a form of rejection, which can develop into irritability and even aggression towards those nearby. Persons in this situation put themselves down, feel discouraged and wonder how they ever achieved in the past. Problems pile up and paralyse the mind. Disorganization results in more precious energy being expended to make up for lost efficiency. Fatigue deepens and thought processes slow. Physically, an inner tension, an aching across the chest, weakness, headaches, indigestion and a lack of sleep are often experienced.

Prevention is better than cure! Supervision should be the norm for all involved in pastoral work and spiritual direction should also be encouraged. These are the kind of questions which can be asked:

❖ Has caring/pastoring become your identity?

❖ Do you so need to be needed that you make yourself indispensable to others?

❖ Are you caring for others as a way of vicariously caring for yourself?

❖ Are you striving to heal the world because your own needs remain unhealed?

❖ What do you need to care for yourself? What drains one person energizes another. Can you delegate? Who is out there especially for you?

Objectivity is provided by relationships outside normal situations. Not only the carer's own internal world but the world of their immediate communities has its own self-deluding madness; objective dialogue is vital.[49]

Pastoral carers need to register what is happening for them when they go to someone in need of care – only by being aware of themselves can they be available to others. If they easily 'fuse' with others, this can be used by

God to help them but pastoral carers need to recognize their need to detach and separate out – boundaries help.[50]

'Pastoral lust' is a danger. With inappropriate giving to others, those who really need attention are deprived – spouse, parents, siblings, children ... this kind of giving can easily be disguised as a virtue and the carer can be deluded into believing that too. The carer has to prevent his or her own needs from determining his or her actions and to hesitate from acting without knowing his or her deepest feelings and wants. Carers need to meet their own legitimate needs, watching the fine line between dedication and overdedication. Although most people are intuitively aware that there is such a line, they may need help to set finite boundaries to their involvement.

For those who are in burn-out, help can provide a way through that is life-changing for the better. But rather than get there unnecessarily, it is important to see that support structures are in place both for the priest and the carers, so they should:

❖ have a local support group;

❖ have 'support people' in related professions (or mentors);

❖ communicate and seek prayer support within the Church;

❖ ensure carers are in touch with each other;

❖ besides praying for sick people, what about a group specifically to pray for those who are on the sharp end of care?

We need to be aware of the consequences of burn-out. It:

❖ consumes the carer's illusions and false expectations (God alone is their hope and expectation, their vision and joy);

❖ is a refining fire that can detach the sufferer from an excessive identity with the results of his caring and the impact that is made in the world;

❖ can teach a deeper trust in God by forcing the person concerned to withdraw all hope, ideals, vision and expectation from every other object, situation, thing or person – except God;

❖   becomes not just stages of disillusionment but rather a maturing process of faith;

❖   disestablishes illusions and establishes true faith.

Burn-out holds the potential for making the carer either cynic or saint. In the midst of burn-out he or she has a choice, either to swing from the heights of current expectations to the detached withdrawal of no expectations at all, or to learn to grow in faith and transfer misplaced expectations to his or her proper focus on God alone.

The healing God wants to bring

Jean Vanier wrote:

> We must learn, as the mother must learn in front of the never-ending needs of her children, how to respect our energy and relax in all the moments of our day, filled as they may be with arduous work and often tiresome meetings and crises of all sorts, and the hundred and one things that have to be done. To do this, we must discover how to harmonise the active and the passive in us. If we are just doers, feeling terribly responsible and serious, we will crack up one day. We must look to the corporate rhythm within our communities. We must nourish the passive part of us, our hearts made for a personal love, learning to marvel at nature, to rest a moment in the presence of Jesus, to receive the love of those around us and be nourished by their trust, enjoying the little things of each day, not taking ourselves too seriously, accepting to become like little children.
>
> Once we know that we are poor, the Kingdom of Heaven is ours. So when our lot is cast with somebody who is finding his Cross, his desert, his poverty overwhelming, we are on holy ground.[51]

Despite having structures in place to care for themselves, in offering God's love to sick people, carers may feel emotionally and spiritually drained, as well as open and vulnerable. They are faced with personal limitations and a sense of inadequacy in trying to discern the activity of God in the crushing defeats of everyday life. There are, however, occasions of immense joy. Not every experience is Gethsemane, although carers often find themselves in a place of pain, wounded by the paradoxes and conflicts of life. Carers need to learn to leave the burdens of the day at the foot of the cross, and to hold up the situation to God in prayer. Carers are among the pain-bearers of today's society.[52] They have to bear the cost of caring if they are also to bear its fruit. Christians caring in this way are a vital expression of the Church's ministry of healing and should look to be part of a local congregation.

The conflicts of life have to be recognized as part of the Easter mystery, in that there is a necessity for death before resurrection. This is true for all. Only by the experience of repeated small deaths in their own lives can carers know the meaning of resurrection. If the caring community is to be a sign of the kingdom of God, it must reveal a new kind of humanity. It is not just a collection of people, perhaps with a personal faith, who have been called to be alongside sick and wounded people. Rather, it is the relatedness of these individuals that is at the heart of caring and is the key to living the gospel. In caring and self-care, healing and a new self-understanding will be received. Thus, it is in caring for one another and ourselves, in working out the Church's ministry of healing in practical ways, that a healing community is born.

Future opportunities

Priests in the Church of England are reluctant to seek help for their own emotional and spiritual needs, yet their high profile in the local community, accompanied by unrealistic expectations placed upon them, can leave them stressfully isolated and exposed. The network of psychiatrists offering expertise through their association with St Luke's Hospital for the Clergy provides an invaluable resource. Yet help at this level is often inappropriate and requires referral from a general practitioner. The GP is often a personal friend but not a confidant of the priest in need. Clergy need ready access to skilled Christian support that is affordable, confidential and assures anonymity.

Christian centres offering this kind of resource, whether it be of a psychotherapeutic or a sacramental nature, should be able to approach the relevant diocesan bishop on occasions, for a discretionary financial contribution towards the cost of services provided, whilst retaining the anonymity of their client. Should any centres be particularly well equipped to provide this form of counsel and ministry, they could be formally authorized to offer support to incumbents in this way. A way forward that would increase the counselling support available across the dioceses would be for the Church of England to apply to join the Churches' Ministerial Counselling Service.

Many excellent overtly Christian organizations are involved in offering social support and health care of one form or another. With an ageing population and overstretched resources in social services and primary care, such organizations may have an increasing opportunity to step in where the Government of the day sees it unnecessary to respond. They can offer, for example:

❖ rehabilitation of people suffering from psychiatric illness;

❖ treatment for people with addiction and eating disorders;

❖ respite, physical rehabilitation and terminal care.

The Church of England, along with other denominations, should actively encourage partnerships between the statutory and voluntary sectors where the result would bring new opportunities for Christians to live out the gospel in practical and caring ways. This outworking of the Church's healing ministry at the point of practical need could bring the love of God and the compassion of Christ to those people whose lives are challenged by limitations, progressive illness and terminal disease.

Recommendations

We recommend that:

❖ churches should remove barriers to people with disability, when appropriate, enabling and empowering them for ministry (see pages 128, 131 and 255);

❖ local churches or Churches Together could helpfully offer a network of people who are trained in offering pastoral support to those who are mentally unwell (see pages 133 and 134);

❖ people with persisting illness and disability need protection from insensitive ministry; hence the importance of training in this area for ordinands and of including it in continuing ministerial education (see page 144);

❖ the Church of England should continue to support specialist ministries to those with disabilities (chaplaincy to the deaf) and encourage initiatives to study the relationship between physical and mental disabilities and Christian faith (see page 142).

8

Healing for Those Who
Are Dying or Bereaved

The importance of addressing our own mortality is emphasized so
that carers are wholly available to those who are dying. The prominence of the hospice movement has drawn attention to the inevitability of death and the ingredients required for dying with dignity.
The grief journey needs to be understood in order to offer meaningful pastoral help to the bereaved.

Healing in our dying

The death of Jesus on Good Friday is an event in history that lies beyond
mere words. Treachery, denial and flight revealed to the disciples the truth
about themselves and their relationship to Jesus. The death he achieved
left them shocked, abandoned and hopeless. They felt let down. But the
death of Jesus is the key to life. The whole meaning of life is decisively
reinterpreted by the death of Jesus. His death brings healing, forgiveness
and the possibility of a living relationship with him. Jesus puts into
reverse today's Western, secular culture's flight from death. He lived with
an unrepressed awareness of death, and always for him incarnation has
appeared as a limitation beyond which his powers would be released for
the whole world. So he was able to set his face to go to Jerusalem and on
to Calvary.[1]

In one sense we are all dying. Most people have probably seen death all
too close and many have to come to terms with the fact that they have a

progressive and possibly fatal disease. The anticipation of death can be a positive experience in the light of Christian belief, especially if one realizes that the time to look at the reality of our own mortality is now. If people fail to look at the fears surrounding their own death, they will only share their anxieties and vulnerability, leaving those they love to die alone, even when they remain at their side.[2] The challenge for the Church in the twenty-first century is to encourage those in training for ministry to explore along this path, so that the teaching on death, resurrection and eternal life has more impact. Provision should be made for ordinands to be exposed to the needs of dying people and their families in palliative care. There, they could be involved in experiential and interactive sessions as a powerful tool for learning.[3] Across the denominations, the Church needs to address the deep change of values involved in preparation for church membership. An intellectual approach alone is not enough. Christian conversion is akin to a Calvary experience as old perceptions die and transformation of the person takes place. Reaching a point of acceptance of death as desirable, even if dreaded, frees the individual from slavery to fear.

The human response to loss of many kinds is like dying to the old life and rising to the new. Life's great negative experiences may prove to be enhancements. In these events the fingerprints of a dying/rising God at work may be recognized. Those who share in the life-through-death changes of growth in daily life may also see in the face of their biological death a familiar pattern. These people will already have learned to endure, to face the unknown with courage, and joyfully to anticipate through death a gift of new life, a communion with God, whose nature cannot be foreseen.[4]

Today people fill their lives with preoccupations in order not to face death. If they become free to look at the eventuality of their own death in the midst of life now, then the energies caught up in maintaining a denial of reality can be released for trusting, hoping and loving within their Church, their family and their encounters in life. Hospices of high reputation serve many communities across the country and bring not only a visual reminder of our mortality but also an easing of fears that surround the moment of death.

The hospice movement

The hospice movement has developed rapidly over the last three decades, lifting the taboo of death and offering expert care that is individual to the patient, detailed, sensitive and time-consuming. The modern hospice is historically rooted in Christian belief, although in practice most are broadly theistic.[5]

Hospice care offers an interdisciplinary approach focused on the needs of the dying patient and their family rather than the active treatment of the disease process.

St Joseph's Hospice in London was founded by Mary Aikenhead in 1905. Dame Cicely Saunders founded St Christopher's Hospice, London in 1967 and this became the first teaching and training centre for hospice care. She chose the word hospice, 'a resting place for travellers', to imply the bringing together of skills demanded by hospital care and the compassion, companionship and hospitality found in the intimacy of home and family. There are now 230 hospices in the United Kingdom, mainly charitable organizations, partly reliant on independent funding.

Whilst a hospice does not need to be a religious organization, when looking for a sense of purpose and hope in the midst of suffering and death, it is hard to avoid addressing the spiritual dimension of life in the search for meaning.

Hospices are generally available to people suffering from cancer and sometimes to people with AIDS and motor neurone disease. It is likely that the application of hospice care will eventually be opened up to a much broader group of people, particularly those people whose progressive illness has a predictable path.

The prominence of the hospice movement in medical care has drawn attention to the inevitability of death and the ingredients required for dying with dignity. Hospice care has opened the door to the humanization of medicine in the face of ever-increasing technological advance. This in turn introduces possibilities for healing even as death draws closer. It forces Christian ministry away from an emphasis on cure, to looking at the needs of the individual in terms of their body, mind, spirit, emotions and relationships.

The following letter highlights the unique impact of the hospice experience on the Church's healing ministry:

> As a full time hospital chaplain . . . I am becoming increasingly concerned about some of the teaching regarding the Christian healing ministry, which I frequently find is being presented, especially to some of the terminally ill patients with whom I come into contact. In fact it seems to me there is an almost fanatical emphasis on physical healing, and that no matter how serious the condition of the patient, faith in God is all that is necessary for that person to be restored to radiant health. Now, I am not denying that faith is important, although I know of some cases where remarkable healing has taken place when there has been little or no faith; neither am I saying that miraculous healings do not take place, I know they do. I am saying, however, that healing is not as simple as some people make it out to be, and that God heals in different ways; and the way is his choice, not ours.[6]

Hospice care is not limited by the 'tyranny of cure'. Hospice both affirms life and recognizes dying as a normal process. It seeks neither to hasten nor to postpone death. The care of the dying and the ministry of healing are but different aspects of one ministry. Both centre on bringing the love of God to where it is needed for each and every person.

The movement has developed a model of teamwork that may be a prophetic statement for the modelling of health care, and care of the dying in particular, in the wider community. The needs of the sick person are best met when the different professionals involved seek permission from the individual concerned to share together, whilst respecting their individual professional codes of confidentiality. Priest, doctor, nurse, social worker, health visitor and other carers need to be able to harness their knowledge and skills for the good of the one who is sick and their family.

Once the medical team has relieved the physical pain, then the pain that has social, spiritual or emotional roots may surface, making it vital for good communication across the disciplines of care. Effective ministry, as with good medicine, demands the care of the whole person – body, mind, spirit, emotions and relationships; a whole person cannot be broken into parts.

The community of carers

Healing occurs in an environment that allows growth towards wholeness. Thus attending to the many dimensions of pain brings opportunity for skilled church members to be involved in creating space for that person's growth, even as death approaches. The 'community of carers', with the one who is sick, has to work to hold space within which the Holy Spirit is free to work.[7]

At Burrswood, Christian Centre for Health Care and Ministry, it is observed that dying people need the community, its skills, fellowship, care and love. Yet the community needs those who are dying, to keep its eyes on eternal issues, so as not to be focused on the minutiae which seem critical to everyday living. This eternal perspective can bring healing and a purposeful focus in congregations that are wrestling with the dying of one in their midst.

Sheila Cassidy writes:

> The world is not divided into 'needy sick' and 'gracious carers'; we must all take our turns in playing these roles. Once we have grasped this truth, we are much freer because we are able not only to accept one another but also to value our own vulnerable humanity.[8]

Those offering pastoral care have to realize that for the family, coping with terminal illness is more than a challenge; it is all-consuming and entangles every corner of life. There are so many people to talk to, so many questions to ask, so many tasks to do. The hopes of different treatments can quickly change into fears and failures. There is an exhausting emotional rollercoaster. It is like having an unwanted and uninvited stranger in their home who seems to take up every moment of the day.[9] An unscheduled visit from the vicar or their team may be anything but healing! Pastoral care and ministry in this situation have to be well tuned to the needs of the family concerned. For example, a telephone call asking if and when it is all right to visit leaves the household with a greater sense of control at a time when life often feels out of control.

Carers need prayer, ministry and understanding just as much as the sick person. They need to be helped to let others share the burdens and responsibilities as well as the joy and sadness. They need help to maintain their rhythm of life with rest, food and exercise and to feel free to spend time in prayer and in doing what they enjoy. They need someone alongside who will actively listen to them so that they can help identify the source of their anger and their fear (see Chapter 7).

Having been heard, carers are set free to listen; to listen with ears, hearts and open minds. Trained listeners from the Church who are accepted within the 'community of carers' can be alongside the dying person, if appropriate, listening for issues that need resolution, issues that need healing and reconciliation – with people, with God, with themselves. They will hear of the pain of parting, of dependence, of practical concern for the family, of hearing God and wondering how to respond. All this needs expression with the confidence that the depth of the agony will be heard and understood. The Christian Listeners' training, available through the Acorn Christian Healing Trust, is an invaluable resource to church congregations, enabling healing in many different situations. 'The fact is,' wrote Michel Quoist, 'none of us can reveal ourselves to ourselves, unless we first reveal ourselves to another, who listens to us with love.'[10]

There may be no space for spiritual growth until the whirling of the mind is stilled and the fears that encircle and torment are shared and their reality examined. There may be the fear of something unbearable, of deep sleep being mistaken for death, of failing to get help in a hurry, of being a burden, of being rejected in ugliness, of dying alone, of having no say in treatment decisions, of loss of control, of being misunderstood: all these fears can overwhelm and disable the rational mind.[11]

Listening is a key ministry at this time. It reveals unfinished business, incomplete reconciliation, a lack of assurance that the family is ready to cope; hearing and ministering into these problems brings release. 'Healing the dying' is about enabling the sick person to be released from all the issues that hold him/her in this life so that a peaceful journeying on into death is achieved. Listening allows the mind space to untangle thoughts, concerns and relationships. It gives value to the one who feels of no value: it allows an entering into the other's pain. Dying people are not so much dying as people, men and women, living whatever time is left to them with a sense of urgency.[12] They have messages for those they love but sometimes need to share these with their priest, or someone outside the family, as these things are perhaps too hard to communicate face to face.

Stages of loss

Church members involved in the care of the dying must be well versed in the different stages of loss previously outlined, so that denial is respected, anger is not taken personally, depression is not glossed over with 'but you've had a good life', and acceptance is not mistaken for an opiate-induced euphoria. In-service training for clergy would help to develop an understanding of the grief journey.

As death approaches there are key points to be borne in mind:

❖ Even when, to the professional eye, life is near to its close, a frustrating conspiracy may arise in which everyone pretends that the sick person will recover. It takes tremendous energy to sustain this fiction and inevitably it increases a sense of isolation. Should the opportunity arise, priest and doctor together are uniquely placed to break this conspiracy, bringing a combination of medical knowledge and pastoral skill to bear.

❖ The dying person often becomes detached and contentedly draws away from those they love. This can be painful and feel like rejection, but it is very normal.

❖ Permission to die, granted by the closest member of the family, often eases agitation. People not unusually know when they are about to die.

❖ Not infrequently, the sick person may share, 'There are others in the room.' They may sense the presence or companionship of family members who have already died or speak of angels, the presence of light or of love beyond description. Although this may stretch understanding, respect for what is shared helps and enables a participating in their joy: death often follows swiftly.

❖ The times when priest or carer are lost for an answer may be the very moments when true companionship is shown, with the sick person perceiving those in the caring role to be as vulnerable and naked as they are.

❖ Those who are prepared to receive will find so much being offered: a sense of being valued, a realization of which things in life are really important, the infectious sense of peace, being included in the 'family', inspiration to continue through difficult situations of life. Also reassurance that what might seem chaotic is still all right; all that imparts courage and provides encouragement to keep going.

It has been said:

> At death's door only one person can go through at a time, but it makes a great difference to know that on this side of the door there is a loving presence to accompany you and to prepare you for the presence that welcomes you on the other side. That seems to me to be the real mission of the new caregivers in this field – to be that loving presence as fully and humanly as possible.[13]

As the family are left deserted on the touchline, they need help to see that gradually healing comes as they release the person who has died into Jesus' loving arms, and then love Jesus and those left behind with that same love that otherwise could be stifled in loneliness. They need help to ensure that the questions that cannot be answered are not a barrier to acknowledging the joyous certainties of the gospel. God's purposes for each person are not measured by the length of their life. The best is yet to be: there is nothing more glorious than to be with Christ. Nonetheless, it is not sufficient just to say, 'That person is now with Jesus' because something is broken in the one who is grieving. Jean Vanier reminds us that when we love, that person has in some way filled us, led us, healed us and then there is the wrenching and pulling apart. So death is painful and we must never spiritualize death too quickly. Somewhere in that pain is what we have to discover: the tiny seeds of resurrection, the tiny seeds of peace.[14]

The grief journey[15]

> The trouble is my friends at church think I should be over it by now.
>
> I feel I should be able to cope.
>
> If only my faith were stronger I wouldn't still be like this.

It is heartfelt comments like the above that suggest that Christians, as well as others, need educating about a natural and God-given process called grief. A survey of clergy revealed an appalling ignorance of the bereavement process. What is needed, therefore, is a more informed awareness and a greater acceptance of the grief journey. If it is natural and God-given then Christians cannot expect to be exempt from it. It is a factor in many situations of loss or pain, as well as in the death of a loved one. In the New Testament grief is a real and expressed emotion (e.g. Luke 19.41; John 11.35; Mark 14.34; Acts 20.37,38; Romans 8.26; Hebrews 5.7). Indeed tears can be a form of praying.

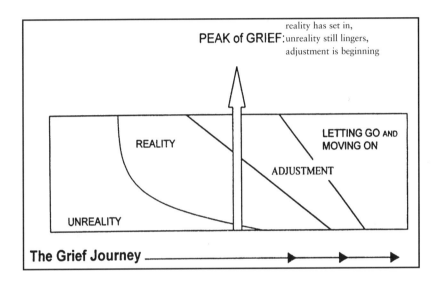

The bereavement process

The experience of loss is different for everyone, but it has certain common factors, and indeed seems to follow a similar pattern. So the 'stages' of grief have often been identified and labelled in different ways. For simplicity the process can be seen as a fourfold one. It is worth noting that people do not move from one stage to another at clearly defined points. As the illustration above indicates, the stages give way to each other more subtly, and at times the force of a stage that appeared to be over returns with unexpected poignancy. It is also true that the journey of grief may begin *before* a loved one dies, if, for example, it is known that he or she has a terminal illness. On the other hand sudden or accidental death will prolong the early stages of grief and those alongside may find themselves saying things like, 'I don't think it has really hit him yet.' The diagram suggests that there is a 'peak' of grief, which seems to be when everything is going on at once. No one stage is completely resolved and there may be a sense of confusion, stress and tension. It is always guesswork to put this in terms of the passage of time, but usually grief 'peaks' about six months to a year after it first begins. The whole process of the diagram may take one to two years, or considerably longer in the case of losing marriage partners, parents or children. Years later the pain of a sorrow may suddenly feel as real as yesterday.

Stage 1 – unreality: 'I don't believe it'

When painful truth dawns no one can absorb it in one go. So the early stage of grief is one of numbness, not unlike suffering from shock. People have described it as feeling 'like cotton wool' and to some extent it is a kind of natural anaesthetic which wears off slowly as the individual begins to be able to absorb the pain. There may be a sense that the dead person has 'just gone on a long journey' from which he or she will soon return. There may also be a kind of euphoria which carries people through this stage and which causes others to say, 'They are coping absolutely wonderfully.' When this is linked with a strong Christian faith it can be regarded by onlookers as a sign that the person has overcome their grief by means of their faith.

It is important for helpers to realize that the stage of apparent well-being will not last. What may last for quite a long time is the feeling deep within that 'somehow I still can't believe it'. This unreality theme will continue to recur at some level and at different moments through the whole grief process. A good example is the desire to share something significant with a loved one. 'When I get home,' people say to themselves, 'I will tell him about this . . .' and then suddenly they realize there is no one to tell. This kind of experience can catch people unawares months after bereavement begins.

Stage 2 – reality: 'I can't bear it'

Gradually the pain of loss and the reality of the loved one's absence become more and more acute. This is the stage when the grief will express itself and weeping from deep inside may feel endless. Many cry and cry but do not exhaust the grief. Rather it exhausts them, and all kinds of physical, mental and spiritual symptoms can occur. Tiredness, dizziness, sleeplessness and a kind of 'cloak' of despair may overwhelm. Depression at this stage may be viewed as a protective cloak, which people need in order to let them get on with grieving.

It is not unusual to be unable to cope with the smallest of everyday demands. Some may feel they are going out of their minds. The mind is likely to feel sluggish and confused. Many forget things or forget the word they wanted to use. It is important to be reassured that this is all perfectly normal. This is the stage of processing memories, sometimes playing them over and over again, and often saying 'if only this' or 'what if that?' Feelings of insecurity creep in, expecting others around us to be ill or die, because the secure foundations of the individual's world have been shaken.

This acute stage of grief is when the support of friends who will simply listen, listen without comment or criticism, is vital. People need to talk about their loved one and express strong feelings of sorrow, guilt, anger or fear. Often anger will be directed at others, for example, doctors, vicars, God himself. Expect those grieving to be on a short fuse with little time for the needs of others. Carers need to realize that if those they are alongside are self-absorbed, they need to be self-absorbed at this stage of the process.

Stage 3 – adjustment: 'What can I do to handle it?'

Slowly there is a move towards the possibility of adjusting to loss. The depth of pain has been reached and there is some energy for working at how to move forward. Still there will be times when people seem to take one step forward and ten back. Often others will notice that those grieving are 'coming through' the worst before they do. The process of adjustment may well include tying up unfinished business. Regrets, hurts, things said or not said – somehow these need to be resolved. Skilled counselling may be helpful in this phase. Prayer and ministry can move people on as the Lord heals some of the loose ends and hurt places. The gradual task of letting go begins. There is a time to let go of a loved one and to commit him or her wholeheartedly to God. All along the grief journey there are symbolic moments which may help and bring meaning.

The funeral service is a letting go and a commendation of the departed, at a point in the journey when probably people are unable to enter into that process. But if they have participated in the funeral it remains there in the memory as a powerful symbol to draw upon. And there come moments when it is right to 'let the coffin go' as they may have seen it go at the service. Tasks like clearing out a bedroom or the wardrobe also help the moving on. Literally moving house can be the occasion when people turn a corner on the journey. Or they may go away, perhaps to a quiet place of retreat, where God can minister, and bring resolution to some of the inner conflicts.

Anniversaries and special days like birthdays and Christmas are turning points. Every time another one goes past people find themselves (painfully) letting go a little more. The celebration of a Eucharist may be of great help, especially if those grieving were not able to be at the funeral, and especially too where traumatic death has occurred (accident, suicide, termination of pregnancy, miscarriage, etc.).[16]

At the Eucharist we are intensely aware, in more than one way, of the presence of Christ, and the reality of his sacrifice which brings victory over death. We are able to offer him the deepest cares and concerns of our hearts, and to express the love we have for those who have died. In that moment, knowing his closeness to us, we can be assured of his closeness to those he holds safe in his heavenly presence. This helps us to be at peace about them, and we can take further steps in the process of letting them go.[17]

Stage 4 – moving on: 'I feel better but I'll never be the same again'

The length of time which it takes to come through the grief journey varies from situation to situation. Individuals are never the same again. It is not simply a question of getting back to normal. Something within them has died relating to the loved one and something also comes back to new life as they chart a new course without them. Certain pockets of grief are likely to remain so that experiences of rejection or loss can awaken the pain. It remains a vulnerable area. Insight is still needed into the ways aspects of grief are unresolved. Many need skilled help even years after a bereavement.

Help on the journey

What help do we need to offer? People need:

❖ the permission to grieve;

❖ the awareness that grieving is natural and that Christians are not exempt from it;

❖ a gentleness on themselves and a gentleness from others;

❖ others to understand that time often stands still for them – the painful loss is as real as if it were yesterday, especially when they are at the peak of their grief;

❖ others to listen without overreacting;

❖ to be able to repeat themselves until they have got the acuteness of the pain out of their system;

❖ people who understand and accept that living with a bereaved person is hard work.

The ultimate help is in God himself. But the pain of the whole process may include the sense of his absence. Prayer may be dry or difficult. Many do not necessarily experience the uplifting that some people know through the prayers of others. It may be a long time before light and love and faith blossom again.

> God's capacity for restoring life is beyond our understanding. Forests burn down and are able to grow back. Broken bones heal. Even grief is not a permanent condition. Our tears can be seeds that will grow into a harvest of joy because God is able to bring good out of tragedy. When burdened by sorrow, know that your times of grief will end and that you will again find joy. We must be patient and wait. God's great harvest of joy is coming! (Psalm 126.5,6, *Amplified version*)

165

Recommendations

We recommend that:

❖ theological colleges, courses and schemes should make provision for ordinands to be exposed to the needs of dying people and their families. Ordinands could helpfully be involved in experiential and interactive sessions in palliative care as a powerful tool for learning (see pages 153–4);

❖ the needs of the sick person are best met when the different professions involved seek permission from the individual concerned to share together, whilst respecting their individual professional codes of confidentiality (see page 156);

❖ in-service training for clergy should help to develop an understanding of the 'grief journey' (see page 159).

9

Deliverance from Evil

One aspect of healing is deliverance from evil. Evil is manifested in society in such things as racism, violence, poverty and in various forms of discrimination. It is also experienced by individuals who feel personally afflicted by evil and who turn to the Church for ministry. The New Testament describes Jesus' own battle with evil, a battle which is linked with healing the sick and establishing the kingdom of God. Whilst the reality of evil is not to be doubted, there are different aetiologies and models used by Christians in trying to understand it; therefore in trying to combat it, there is a variety of approaches to this ministry. How are such terms as 'demons' and 'possession' to be understood in the third millennium? Are these appropriate terms for describing social and personal evil? The ministry of deliverance is helped by a multidisciplinary approach in which pastoral and sacramental care and the insights of theology, psychology and psychiatry lead to holistic and good practice.

A report like this would be incomplete without addressing the issue of the ministry of deliverance. This ministry certainly has its place in the modern Church, but we must be careful neither to underestimate the power of spiritual evil nor to overemphasize its importance. We want to stress that it is a ministry which requires both a multidisciplinary approach and charisms of discernment. It also requires caution and expertise, for sadly it is open to abuse and it can attract a great deal of unhelpful and speculative publicity. Nevertheless, the need to renounce and combat evil continues to be one of the foremost tasks of the Church, whether the evil is in the make-up of individuals, organizations and society in general, or whether it is of spiritual origin.

In 1965 Dr Robert Mortimer, Bishop of Exeter, appointed a commission to examine the ministry of exorcism. It comprised theologians and psychiatrists, and it was ecumenical in its membership. Its report, *Exorcism* (SPCK) published in 1972, recommended that diocesan bishops should appoint a suitable person to undertake this ministry in each diocese. This recommendation was accepted, and today every diocese has an appointee and often a team of advisors including psychologists and psychiatrists to deal with such cases.

The possible dangers associated with deliverance ministry attracted widespread media attention when in 1974 an exorcism was linked with a tragic death. The following year Dr Donald Coggan, the Archbishop of Canterbury, issued guidelines for good practice on behalf of the House of Bishops. These were that this ministry should be done (a) in collaboration with the resources of medicine, (b) in the context of prayer and sacrament, (c) with the minimum of publicity, and (d) by experienced persons authorized by the diocesan bishop, and then (e) followed up by continuing pastoral care.[1]

Developments since 1972

Since the Bishop of Exeter's commission there have been a number of developments which have brought attention and new insights to this ministry. First, there is the charismatic renewal. This movement, emphasizing the promise of the Holy Spirit, has caused many to take more seriously the reality of evil. It is not uncommon for Christians who are trying to be more open to the Spirit to experience spiritual oppression in a new way; they say that as they become more aware of the reality of the Holy Spirit they also seem to become more aware of the evil forces in opposition to God. Charismatics and others see the need to counter this by addressing issues of social justice as well as discerning evil in society and in people's personal lives. Parishes do this through intercession, social action and protest, and also by including the prayers for deliverance within their overall healing ministry.

Second, there is the growing public interest in the occult and the paranormal which tends to sensationalize the subject. The re-release of the film *The Exorcist* and similar productions is symptomatic of this. Occult shop sales and magazines, video and Internet material are now widely available, and they can be damaging to the vulnerable. The result of this is a growing demand for the churches' spiritual help in this area from those who have been seriously disturbed or hurt.

Third, there are now in this country ethnic groups from countries among whom the power of spiritual evil is regarded as a hazard of everyday life and prayers for deliverance are an accepted feature of their pastoral practice. These groups have caused some Anglicans to review a little more sympathetically the views and activities of a small minority in the Church of England clergy who exercised a deliverance ministry when they believed it was appropriate to do so.

Thus the deliverance ministry has spread in the Church of England. It must be emphasized that this often takes place within an accepting and caring environment and in a non-sensational way. A number of dioceses have helpful guidelines regarding the deliverance ministry. These guidelines usually recommend professional counselling, prayer and absolution, anointing, the laying on of hands and Holy Communion. Elsewhere, however, there have been allegations of inappropriate ministry and spiritual, physical and sexual abuse. Whilst such allegations are thankfully very rare, they do indicate the need for accountability and good practice based on sound theological and pastoral principles.

The place of Satan

In former times people believed in a world of serpents and dragons, good and evil spirits, and angels and demons. This is reflected in some of the earlier parts of the Old Testament where it gradually developed into the people of Israel's conviction of the uniqueness of Yahweh and his victory and control over evil. In the later books Satan (meaning 'adversary') is viewed as an angelic being. The book of Job portrays him as a fairly neutral character, acting as the prosecution counsel in Yahweh's court where he puts Job to the test, but in Zechariah 3.2 he is no longer neutral and is fiercely rebuked by God. By the intertestamental period (paralleled in neighbouring religions) Satan had come to be viewed as in direct opposition to God. It was in this period the tradition arose that Satan had been ejected from heaven for pride and rebellion, and had come down to continue his rebellion on earth. So in the New Testament Satan is portrayed as the spiritual opponent of God.

The Synoptic Gospels and the Acts of the Apostles show Satan tempting Jesus in the wilderness (Matthew 4.1; Mark 1.13; Luke 4.2) and biding his time (Luke 4.13) until he enters Judas to betray him (Luke 22.3; John 13.27). Satan has a band of angels (Matthew 25.41), and sometimes illnesses, diseases and natural disasters are attributed to him (Mark 9.17; Luke 8.29; Luke 13.16). The Synoptic Gospels portray Jesus healing many people and also casting out demons or unclean spirits on numerous occasions. In contrast John's Gospel contains no exorcism accounts: there is just one reference to Satan (John 13.27), one reference to the devil (John 8.44), two to 'the prince of this world' and three to people having a demon (John 7.20; 8.48-52; 10.20,21). In one place Jesus describes Judas as being a devil (John 6.70). The writer of the fourth Gospel depicts the spiritual battle between good and evil as between light and darkness (John 3.19; 12.35,46), life and death (John 3.36; 10.28) and truth and falsehood (John 1.17; 8.32; 18.37).

In the Church today, some understand the concept of evil in terms of light and darkness. Others believe in Satan as a personal devil and, although accepting Christ's victory on the cross, think that Satan has not yet been finally banished and that the Church therefore has a duty to confront his activity. And others, while rejecting premundane accounts of fallen angels as too mythological, and viewing Satan as a personification of evil, nevertheless accept that there is a place for deliverance ministry as identifying and naming the evil and mentally exorcising it from the human mind.

In the New Testament Jesus comes to establish the kingdom of God. He does this by healing diseases, casting out evil spirits, by giving sight to the blind, curing the lame, cleansing lepers, opening the ears of the deaf, forgiving sins, raising the dead and preaching good news to the poor (Luke 7.21-23). His coming initiated a battle between the two kingdoms. 'The Son of God was revealed for this purpose, to destroy the works of the devil' (1 John 3.8). In the Synoptic Gospels, his mission is opposed by the forces of Satan and in the fourth Gospel by the spirit of darkness, untruth and unbelief. Whilst Paul no doubt shared the world-view of the evangelists, he does not record any exorcism accounts. In his letter to the Romans it is human sin rather than Satan that is in opposition to God, although that is not to say that he did not see demonic influences behind human disobedience. For Paul, cosmic and demonic powers were dealt with decisively at the cross (Colossians 2.14), although he recognized their continuing presence and influence even on Christ's followers (Ephesians 6.10f; 2 Corinthians 2.11; 1 Corinthians 10.20f).

Exorcism in the early Church

In Matthew 10.1 the divine commission given to the apostles is to proclaim the good news of the kingdom and have authority over unclean spirits, to cast them out and to cure every disease and every sickness. Exorcism and healing are linked. It is however, not altogether clear as to how widely the ministry of exorcism was carried out in the early Church. Harnack wrote:

> The Christians made their appearance throughout the whole world as exorcists of demons, and exorcism was a very powerful missionary and propagandist weapon. They were concerned not merely with exorcizing the demons which inhabit man, but also with purging them from the atmosphere and the whole of public life. For the century (the second) was under the dominion of the spirit of darkness and his legions . . . The whole world and the atmosphere surrounding it was peopled with devils; all the formalities of life – not only the worship of idols – were governed by them. They sat upon thrones and surrounded the infant's cradle. The earth, God's creation though it is now and forever, became in very truth a hell.[2]

In contrast, some of the early Fathers like Irenaeus believed in the goodness and blessedness of God's creation and some scholars, whilst accepting that exorcism was performed by the early Church, conclude that first-century congregations would have varied in the emphasis that they gave to this ministry so that, for example, the Johannine churches would have had less to do with exorcism than the Lucan churches.[3]

Early liturgical texts indicate that catechumens were exorcised as part of their preparation for baptism, since it was assumed pagans needed to be set free from the control of the demons they had previously worshipped. Later liturgical rites included prebaptismal prayers for protection and defence from evil, but it did not necessarily imply that candidates were considered possessed or following baptism were about to be invaded by demons.[4] In today's *Common Worship Initiation Services* candidates for baptism are required to reject the devil and all rebellion against God and they are commissioned to persevere in resisting evil. The Lord's Prayer itself contains words of exorcism, 'but deliver us from evil'. The office of exorcist was the second of the minor orders leading to the priesthood.

Theological opinions

There is a wide range of theological opinion about the value of the deliverance ministry. The Church has always been challenged with the task of interpreting the gospel as it has come down to us in the Scriptures in the light of contemporary culture, and many argue we can no longer think and speak in terms of evil spirits, Satan or even spiritual evil. Others, while acknowledging that some demythologizing of the scriptural texts may be necessary, reply that the primitive symbolism points to spiritual evil as a reality which we cannot ignore, because even today such an evil can so dominate the lives of certain people that they need the Church's authority and power in Christ to liberate them.

One side is put by Dr Michael Wilson:

> I feel under no pressure to believe in possession by evil spirits just because Jesus believed in them. I feel under no obligation to exorcise anyone simply because Jesus and his contemporaries did so . . .. A great deal of disturbed behaviour was then perceived as if caused by possession. It was the usual way to perceive it in those days, in that culture. This raises for the pastor the important question as to how he or she uses the Bible. How far are Jesus' attitudes to things like illness, evil spirits, race and marriage, a sociologically determined part of his Jewish culture? How far are his teachings divine insights? How do we discover truth in the culturally created language in which truth must be expressed?[5]

At the same time it should be noted that Jesus was able to take a radically different position from his culture, for example, in his attitudes to women and on matters of ritual purity. In raising the issue of belief and culture we do not wish to imply that modern opinion is right and the biblical view is wrong; rather, that we are as culturally conditioned as the New Testament writers and that we need to acknowledge our own presuppositions. Particular sensitivity and respect should therefore be shown in ministry towards members of minority ethnic groups with their different cultural backgrounds.

Modern medical and psychiatric insights have led to suggestions that the biblical exorcisms point towards various forms of psychiatric ill health such as dissociative hysteria, catatonic hysteria or to epilepsy. Perhaps the man with the evil spirit in Acts 19.16 was suffering from schizophrenia. Whilst such diagnoses cannot be conclusive, the place, methodology and limitations of medical science must be recognized. Equally it is important to recognize the spiritual and psychophysical components in illness and the complexity of human nature. There may sometimes be two equally valid ways of describing the same phenomenon, the medical and the spiritual.

But, as we have said, other Christians take a different view. One of these is Dr Harvey Cox, the American theologian whose book *The Secular City* outlined a theology for what he called 'the post-religious age' and was a best-seller in the 1960s. A few years ago Cox spent a sabbatical among the Pentecostal and Black churches in four different continents and wrote about his experiences in *Fire from Heaven*. He was deeply impressed by what he observed of their teachings and practices of the deliverance ministry, and he introduced his book with the well-known dictum of C. S. Lewis:

> There are two equal and opposite errors into which our race can fall about devils. One is to disbelieve in their existence. The other is to believe and to feel an excessive and unhealthy interest in them. They themselves are equally pleased by both errors, and hail a materialist and a magician with the same delight.

Then he continued:

> I am convinced that modern liberal theologians have too easily discarded the idea of trans-personal forces of evil. Instead of trying to fathom what references to evil spirits in the Bible point us to in our own age – which I believe is something quite real – they have dismissed the whole notion of the demonic as implausible. But in my opinion a century that has witnessed Auschwitz and Hiroshima and the Gulag is in no position to laugh off the ugly reality of diabolical forces that seem capable of sweeping people

up in their energies. I also believe, however, that we must ponder these destructive currents that surge through our psyches without pretending we know much about them and, most of all, without locating them in people we oppose. . . . What annoys me about the experts who catalogue and chart different devils today, and who are sure the demons are at work in their opponent, is that they are making a very serious religious question seem trivial and ridiculous.[6]

The question of whether evil influences come from outside ourselves and even from outside the society in which we live remains an important theological issue. If we believe that all evil is subjective and can be explained as being brought about by behaviour on the part of an individual or by society, or that evil is the result of behaviour resulting from psychiatric illness or disorders of the personality, then exorcism will appear to be inappropriate. The appropriate way of ministering to an individual will be through pastoral counselling, the sacraments and medication, or by tackling the evils in society that lead to disorders and injustices.

But if we believe that spiritual influences are at work for evil as well as good, then some form of deliverance ministry may be appropriate. We should acknowledge, however, that within the Church there is a wide range of opinion of how this is understood and addressed. Some will be able to accept and work with the biblical model, language and imagery. Others will prefer to demythologize some of the biblical language but nevertheless accept the underlying belief that there can be objective evil forces at work in people and in society, and that with the right professional safeguards the Church has a unique contribution to offer. Nevertheless, both groups minister in the belief that the gospel witnesses to the incarnate Christ who, through the victory of the cross and resurrection, triumphed over evil to empower the Church to bring the fruits of that victory to others. This it does in a variety of ways through its pastoral, preaching and sacramental ministry, ministering to those afflicted by evil and leading them into the peace of God.

We recognize that there is a real danger of seeing evil only in personal terms and of ignoring evil oppression brought about by social structures and injustice. The Church has a prophetic role in unmasking demonic forces when exercised by governments, multinational corporations, advertisers or even religions as well as individuals whose behaviour or abuse of power leads to such evils as poverty, cruelty, racism and discrimination. A person may be oppressed because, for example, he or she is a victim of racism and the Church would be failing in its prophetic task if it only ministered to the victim and did not unmask the victimizer. It is possible to be so preoccupied with demon possession as to miss the real spiritual battles that matter and the real conflicts between the kingdom of God and the kingdom of darkness.

Christians also accept that we live within an imperfect world, a world of suffering, and whilst we believe in the victory Christ has won for us through the cross, we await the fullness of that victory. In the meantime we are co-workers with Christ, fixing our eyes on him and his cross. There is a danger that exorcism can become a form of Christian magic and a means of denying evil rather than encountering it and doing something practical about it. In our understanding of the deliverance ministry we must keep a healthy balance, recognizing the power of evil as well as the lordship of Christ and his victory over demonic forces.

Deliverance and psychiatry

Some theological writers have used the word 'demonic' to describe powers or influences which are not evil in themselves, but which, when diverted from their proper ends, become destructive of human life and its possibilities. Thus structures and powers in society may be seen to be capable of being either good or evil. Using the word 'demonic' loosely about general wrongdoing, however, could obscure the reality of spiritual evil. Following this, we must look more closely at possible misinterpretations of the 'demonic' in troubled persons.

The Greek word often translated as 'possessed' is more accurately translated as 'demonized'. Today, the words 'oppressed' and 'possessed' are used to describe the degree of spiritual distress encountered. *Possession* normally means that a person will appear to be no longer in control of his or her own will, whilst *oppression* indicates a degree of self-control. The terms *trance disorder* and *possession disorder* or *possession syndrome* are used in psychiatric diagnosis in which there is a temporary loss both of the sense of personal identity and of full awareness of surroundings. In these cases an individual may act as if taken over by another personality, spirit, deity or 'force', but these are experienced as involuntary and unwanted and outside accepted religious or cultural contexts. The medical classification is used strictly when these states are not self-induced or feigned but are truly involuntary. They are dissociative states but not a form of delirium. These diagnoses are not appropriate for such phenomena arising during other illness, intoxication or in personality disorders. *Possession states* which are not medical or psychiatric have been recognized in diverse situations ranging from mystical practice to teenage pop idol fans. There are various suggested explanations for the phenomenon of possession.

It is possible for a person to feel possessed as a result of receiving the projections of another person or a group of people so that the individual becomes a 'scapegoat' and believes him- or herself to be evil. Such a state can be brought about by long periods of psychological and sometimes physical or sexual abuse so that a person's self-esteem and confidence is eroded. Exorcism is inappropriate in such cases; indeed, it may be even be harmful by enforcing the delusion that the person is evil rather than the object of the evil projections of others. Nevertheless, through appropriate ministry a person can be delivered from the projections and released from the projected evil.

Someone may appear possessed or to be suffering from a trance disorder as a result of mental illness such as schizophrenia or depression, temporal lobe epilepsy, psychoactive substance abuse, organic or borderline psychosis or personality disorder. The term 'hysterical' has varied connotations and is generally avoided now in psychiatry, with a preference for *dissociative disorder* where intolerable stress of insoluble problems has been converted into symptoms. Bizarre or symbolic acting-out can readily lend itself to supernatural interpretation. Many sufferers complain of being tormented by voices or images of demons or of feelings of guilt or punishment by God. Such perceptions are brought about by altered mental states and in most cases can be successfully treated with the use of prescribed medication and psychiatric care. Counselling and psychotherapy may bring an underlying problem to awareness and so to a solution or better control.

A particularly difficult problem is the appearance of possession when part of an individual's personality has been repressed as denied or disowned, and this takes on a life of its own or dominates the person and his or her relationships. This may range from destructive character traits or addictive behaviours, sometimes colloquially known as 'inner demons', through to the rare 'multiple personality'. The apparent possession is due to fragmentation of self, usually as a result of organic traumatic events but subsequently exacerbated by stress or even in therapy, relaxation or hypnosis sessions. Integration through pastoral care is needed, not exorcism, which would only serve to collude with the deceptive explanation the person has sought or which others may believe.

It is vital for people to face responsibility for their own selves and parts of their personalities, as far as possible within the limitations of treatment. Responsibility may have to be shared but that is still within the wholeness which God wills for us. A claim of 'possession' may be used to evade personal responsibility by blaming the behaviour on some external source rather than facing the need for repentance, confession and reparation.

The use of hallucinogenic substances, brainwashing, hypnotic suggestion or some mystical or occult practices may lead to mind-altered states and an appearance or feeling of being possessed. More likely, the complaint will be of being influenced or controlled by evil forces or spirits, and psychological reaction has to be distinguished from a true spiritual problem. Spiritual oppression may genuinely be experienced as a result of such things as a personal trauma, painful memories, bereavement and loss, occult involvement, family influences, abuse or sinful practices. Careful discernment is needed to address the root problem. In many places the Church has recognized the need for specialist pastoral care and counselling in, for example, bereavement, healing of memories and post-trauma care. In situations of spiritual oppression, when paranormal activity such as apparitions is said to be experienced, it is important to consult the appropriate diocesan advisor. Many phenomena, such as poltergeist activity or apparitions, may have psychological causes.

Places

In many cases, requests for deliverance ministry are made by those experiencing unusual phenomena in their homes or other places. They may describe what they perceive to be unexplained noises, poltergeist activity, strange happenings or apparitions. These experiences, which can sound bizarre when described, may nevertheless instil fear and alarm and need to be handled with sympathy and respect. Such symptoms are frequently linked with personal or family anxieties or trauma requiring a holistic approach.

What is described as disturbances to places may have a psychological causation with people projecting images or energies onto a place. More rarely, it may be a paranormal phenomenon where the causation is unknown or has no scientific explanation. Such cases should be referred to the diocesan advisor who may suggest prayers for the people and a blessing of the place, and in some cases the celebration of the Eucharist.

Exorcism and deliverance

However, we do not wish to reduce or explain away evil oppression or possession simply in medical or psychological terms. We recognize that there are evil forces at work which cannot be psychologically integrated and where the resources of medicine and psychology are only partial solutions. Prayers of deliverance or exorcism, with all the necessary safeguards, may in some cases be appropriate and beneficial.

The term 'ministry of deliverance' is preferred today as being more accurate than 'exorcism'. Indeed, the word 'exorcist' is only used in the New Testament (Acts 19.13) to refer to charlatans: it was not a term applied to Jesus or the apostles whose ministry of casting out was part of a wider ministry. Sometimes people describe feelings of oppression by an evil force resulting in guilt, victimization, oppression, anger, alienation, paranormal or psychic phenomena, profane thoughts and a rejection of God, his representatives and religious objects. Such people may be spiritually afflicted by evil although emotive terms like possession and exorcism are not helpful. The Church can offer deliverance ministry to them through prayer, sacraments, counselling and practical help and support. Modern health care will often seek to identify a person's health needs, including a spiritual assessment, in order to establish a care plan. It is also becoming more common for health care staff to be taught how to recognize spiritual distress in patients, as we noticed in Chapter 5.

The early Church saw the need to identify spiritual evil and to cast it out in the name of Jesus Christ. But they also recognized that the struggle with spiritual evil continues throughout the life of every Christian.

According to the Prayer Book catechism the devil as well as the world and the flesh are the source of personal temptations and sins. So the Christian confronts them with self-examination, repentance and confession as well as reflection on the Scriptures, prayer, fasting and the use of the sacraments. This process does not involve exorcism of evil but resistance to it, as in the case of Jesus in the wilderness (Luke 4.13).

Manipulation and abuse

In the ministry of deliverance there is the danger of manipulation and spiritual, psychological and physical abuse. A number of people have turned to mainstream churches for help because they have received inappropriate ministry elsewhere. Some groups have developed complex demonologies – like those criticized by Harvey Cox. Some view demons as having physical as well as spiritual properties which enable them to enter a person through bodily orifices and they are then expelled physically. Others have been told (often quite inaccurately) that their troubles were due to the influence of witchcraft in previous generations. Such beliefs and unorthodox teachings contain the possibility of inappropriate and even abusive ministry, particularly if informed consent is not, or cannot be, given.

In the course of the Church's ministry, most clergy and authorized lay people will encounter individuals or situations where evil is at work or where people are oppressed by evil. Many will express the need to be heard and to be treated with seriousness. The Church has much to offer such people by way of pastoral care and counselling, but such ministry should be firmly rooted within the wider ministry of healing and its disciplines. Prayer addressed to God for protection and deliverance from evil may be appropriate, but pastors should be careful to observe professional boundaries and to seek help and advice when needed. Pastors (authorized priests and laypersons) should avoid colluding with urgent and sometimes dramatic requests for the deliverance ministry, so as to be able to make a considered judgement of the situation. Nevertheless, it important to provide those in need with assurance and a commitment to help.

Over the centuries the Church has traditionally distinguished between a greater and a lesser exorcism. In a greater exorcism the demonic is itself addressed in the name of Christ; in a lesser exorcism prayer is addressed to God to banish or protect someone from evil. Whilst it is true that the New Testament does not appear to make such distinctions (even the distinction between exorcism and healing is not always clear, e.g. Luke 4.39 and 13.16), it has proved very useful in setting boundaries in pastoral practice.[7]

The service

People receiving the deliverance ministry need to be prepared to examine their own lives and recognize any need to change their relationships, lifestyle or direction. Only then can they take responsibility and be willing and freely consent to take part in this ministry. Pastors also need to listen sympathetically to those who, rightly or wrongly, feel themselves to be afflicted by evil forces, and not to allow caution to be misinterpreted as rejection.

The decision to perform a service of exorcism should only be taken after other avenues have been explored and the risks assessed. An exorcism should only be carried out by a priest or other minister who has the authority of the bishop to do so.[8] Counselling should form an important part of the process, and pastors should ensure that they are supervised and that they work closely with medical and other professionals. Where a person is already receiving other professional care, it is desirable to work collaboratively in a multidisciplinary approach, respecting one another's professional boundaries. There should be provision for pastoral care and counselling following the service. In each diocese people should be carefully chosen and authorized for this ministry and we recommend that they have access to consult and work with other clergy and medical colleagues.

Finally, the service itself should be simple and may include the ministry of absolution, Holy Communion, anointing and the laying on of hands. The welfare of the subject is paramount and as far as possible the service should not be emotionally charged. The service is one of authority and love, not magic or manipulation. It sets people free from fear and false belief and brings them to truth and freedom.[9]

Diocesan guidelines for ministerial practice should be followed and we endorse the guidelines issued by the House of Bishops in 1975 (paragraph 3). We also commend the importance of keeping careful and confidential records.

The issues surrounding the deliverance ministry are complex. They raise questions about epistemology, theodicy, cosmology, Christology, anthropology and sociology. It is an area in which there has been a great deal of study in recent years and it is likely to be an area which will continue to attract academic and critical attention. Whilst such studies are welcomed and we trust will lead to a better ministry, we also recognize the present need to minister to people who are or feel themselves to be afflicted by evil so that they may be set free. The Church must proclaim the sovereignty of God and Christ's victory over demonic powers and avoid too narrow a view of evil, which can blind us to other evils in the world.

Recommendations

We offer the following recommendations:

❖ we endorse the normal practice of suitable people having episcopal authorization for deliverance ministry and the widespread appointment of diocesan teams (see page 168);

❖ we endorse the guidelines issued by the House of Bishops in 1975 (see pages 168 and 180–81);

❖ we commend the practice of keeping careful and confidential records, within the constraints of the Data Protection Act (see pages 180–81);

❖ clergy and lay people involved in this ministry should have appropriate training and supervision (see page 180);

❖ a multidisciplinary approach is to be desired and we recommend that those authorized for this ministry should have access to consult and work with other clergy and with doctors, psychologists and psychiatrists (see pages 168 and 180);

❖ services involving deliverance ministry should be simple and use appropriate pastoral and sacramental ministry whilst always ensuring that the welfare of the person being ministered to is of paramount concern (see page 180).

10

Complementary Medicine and Alternative Approaches to Healing and Good Health

This chapter looks at alternative approaches to healing and good health, in particular complementary medicine and alternative therapies, what they offer, how they are widely regarded and the reasons why people are attracted to these approaches. It is estimated that four to five million people a year in the United Kingdom go to complementary practitioners. Because of this we felt that we ought to devote a chapter to them as one of the significant features in our society within which the Church exercises the healing ministry. The issues surrounding the extent to which they are compatible with Christian teaching are explored and questions suggested which may be asked of practitioners, to guide people in their choices. The chapter compares and contrasts these approaches with the healing ministry and acknowledges the opportunities through this ministry for the Church of England to respond to people's needs in their search for healing and wholeness.

As we have stated several times in this report, our understanding of the healing ministry begins with Jesus' own ministry, which is in turn established in Jesus' proclamation of the kingdom of God. To repent and believe in the gospel of the kingdom is to repent and believe in Christ. And to repent and believe in Christ, in the words of St Paul, means being a 'new creation in Christ' (2 Corinthians 5.17). Everything we have to say about a Christian understanding of good health must be understood in terms of this new creation.

We have also repeatedly acknowledged, however, that this new creation is encountered in the midst of the old, that is, in the world. Today, and specifically with respect to the healing ministry, this means that the Christian understanding of good health must be seen in relation to other, worldly therapies. There are different aspects to such a discussion, and some of them have been considered in previous chapters. It would be remiss of us, however, if we did not consider the relationship between the Christian healing ministry and what have come to be known as complementary medicine and alternative approaches to healing and good health.

It is important to be clear about the way in which we approach this subject. At first sight, the Christian healing ministry is about the revelation of God's will in Jesus, and any healing ministry that does not also confess Christ crucified and risen is not Christian. There are many such difficulties with various forms of complementary medicine and alternative therapies, some of which are obvious, some of which only arise as one encounters them. At the same time, however, the overwhelming evidence that we have received from ordinary Christians is that they have questions about complementary medicine and alternative therapies, and conflicting beliefs and thoughts about their efficacy. There is, in short, a substantial range of difficulties surrounding this relationship that preoccupy many Christians, which is why they are considered in this chapter.

That said, and with the proviso that the reader will identify a variety of judgements in what follows, what we have tried to do is consider the issues as openly as possible. If we have always considered them from a Christian perspective, that is because we are Christians! But at the same time we recognize that this entire area is in a state of flux for the Church at large, and that consequently the most valuable task we can undertake is the clarification of the issues and questions involved. In so doing, we believe we are being consistent not only with the Church's present circumstances, but also the intentions of the 1958 report which we have been charged to review.

The 1958 report included an appendix on Christian Science and Spiritualism because 'among the many modern religious and quasi-religious movements these are the most influential of those whose exponents make claims about the healing of disease'.[1] After giving an outline of the teachings and practices of these two movements, it advised every parish priest to become familiar with them so that they could then help members in their congregations who were thinking of going to them for help.

> The Commission believes that the parish priest would fail in his duty if he did not point out that the claim to healing power in these cases involved beliefs which are difficult or impossible to reconcile with the gospel as received and taught in the Church of England, or indeed in the main tradition of Christianity.[2]

Forty years on, the scene has become much larger and more complex. Information about complementary medicine and alternative therapies, including commercially motivated promotional material, is widely available. This is a popular area of interest in the media and an area of considerable commercial growth over the last 20 years. It is estimated that four to five million people a year in the United Kingdom go to complementary practitioners.[3] Because of this we felt that we ought to devote a chapter to them as one of the significant features in our society within which the Church exercises the healing ministry, and then suggest ways in which we decide which can and which cannot be reconciled to the gospel.

Despite the widely varying world-views and different religions on which many of these approaches to healing are based, there has not been much interest in the underlying trend of the introduction into everyday life of multi-faith concepts related to health care, through this process. Comparatively little has apparently been done to assess objectively the spiritual implications of such widespread interest and acceptance by our society. Discussion within and between the denominations has tended to be on the relationship between the Church and non-Christian religions in multi-faith dialogues.

In general, complementary medicine and alternative therapies are regarded as closer to the issues of health care than spiritual care. To develop a sound appreciation of complementary medicine and alternative therapies is a challenging task, particularly for non-practitioners, because of the wide range of information available. This is confusing to some extent because there is no clear glossary which is accepted by all involved. Furthermore, the spirituality affecting a particular approach may be unclear. The Church needs an ecumenically agreed basis on which to develop a sound and constructive approach to the provision of guidance in this area, which is also sensitive to interfaith dialogues. Christians need guidance from the Church on the kind of questions that could be asked about these approaches to healing, health and wholeness.

Some forms of complementary medicine and some alternative therapies are not particularly concerned with spirituality. It is, however, implicit and in some cases explicit that many of these therapies are non-Christian in origin. Many types of therapy seek to encourage clients to reconsider their lifestyle, fundamental orientation towards themselves, general values and world-view, so far as these affect their health and well-being, as part of a broader or holistic approach to health and wholeness. A review of one's lifestyle and values is very difficult to carry out in a way that is completely divorced from any spiritual belief. Some therapies go further and encourage people to reconsider their belief in the supernatural. It must be noted that the Church does all of these things too, as part of the healing ministry.

These are not new issues; they have been around for millennia. For example, Jesus was born into a multi-faith society which employed oils and ointments using ingredients such as frankincense and myrrh which are now used in aromatherapy. Frankincense and myrrh were considered amongst the most highly prized substances of the ancient world and were used for a range of purposes. The Egyptians used frankincense as incense to fumigate sick people and drive out the evil spirits that were thought to cause the illness; the Romans and the Egyptians also used it in beauty products. Myrrh was used by the ancient Egyptians at noon every day when it was burnt as part of the sun-worshipping ritual. It was also used for embalming, cosmetics and perfumery and was valued for its antiseptic and anti-inflammatory qualities.

Comparatively recently, since the 1960s, there has been a general trend in conventional medical thinking towards acknowledging the need to link the body to mind and to spirit, to develop a holistic approach which treats the client or patient as a person with many dimensions to his or her life. This restoration of the relationship between health care and the spiritual or mystical has provided opportunities for a wide range of complementary medicine and alternative therapies, including the introduction of paranormal and New Age approaches and new therapies resulting from experimentation and innovation. While spiritual awareness is apparently on the increase, there is little evidence, however, of a commensurate increase in spiritual discernment.

In the climate before the 1960s, however, the healing ministry had a low profile in most parishes, which has allowed many people's awareness of the spiritual dimension of healing to be influenced by other approaches, including those which are incompatible with the Christian faith. Because their needs in relation to healing and wholeness have not been met by the Church in clearly recognizable and readily available ways, some people have searched for healing, health and wholeness elsewhere. Nevertheless, they often come to the Christian healing ministry after trying other approaches, and even when they have come for the wrong reasons they have found the right answers.

From the viewpoint of many people outside the Church, it is one of many organizations offering healing and a model for a healthy lifestyle. To those who are not already committed to the Christian faith and the Church, it has to compete with other approaches, to convince them that it offers something unique, something far beyond holistic health in the worldly sense. Within the Church we do not encourage comparisons between the Christian healing ministry and complementary medicine and alternative therapies, but there are lessons to be learnt by considering why many people are attracted to them, and why some of them are apparently successful in meeting people's needs. A sound understanding of these approaches and their underlying spirituality and world-view is also necessary to help to discern which ones are not incompatible with Christian teaching, which ones may be more likely to distract from or undermine a person's faith in Christ and which approaches are clearly incompatible.

The Bible and its religious teaching and philosophy, for all its wisdom, is not a technical, medical or scientific textbook. It does not contain, for example, all the necessary factual information to ensure or restore perfect health in a yet imperfect world. Furthermore, there is the danger of identifying the Church with only one culture. Over the last 2000 years, our scientific and technical knowledge has increased dramatically. Many people recognize God working through research and development in a vast range of areas, not just those related to medicine and health care, to enable our better understanding and appreciation of his creation.

It is possible, that as God has revealed through cultures other than our own aspects of how creation works, non-Christian cultures have developed approaches to physical and mental health and healing which will, in time, be proven by scientific means to be soundly based and effective, when measured according to agreed scientific criteria. The Church has always been aware that God can reveal aspects of how creation works through peoples of other languages and cultures and this is particularly so in the realm of medical treatment.

The challenge for Christians is to discern whether a particular approach to healing, health and wholeness can be made compatible with our biblical and theological understanding of what God wills for us at the present time. We need to test everything, hold on to the good and avoid every kind of evil (1 Thessalonians 5.21,22). It is appropriate that scientists and the medical profession assess the physical and mental benefits and risks associated with complementary medicine and alternative therapies, but the effects on the spirituality, faith and world-view of Christians are the key issues which the Church needs to consider seriously.

Why do people seek alternatives to conventional medicine?

People seek attention to their overall needs, including those which are not always clearly expressed; mental, emotional, spiritual needs and dis-ease, with themselves as well as others. Many doctors and nurses are unable to spend as much time listening and expressing personal interest as they and their patients would like. Many people are disenchanted and uncomfortable with conventional medical approaches which can tend, despite good intentions in many cases, to treat the patient more like a biochemical mechanism which can malfunction, rather than a whole person: body, mind and spirit. Physical illness and disease are still frequently seen, including by those coping with suffering, in terms of biophysical defects, even though many health care professionals are supportive of the holistic approach to health. Sometimes the links with other areas of ill health, 'dis-ease' and distress are overlooked or paid insufficient attention, because of pressures on resources, particularly time.

By paying for therapies and health care, people tend to believe they can expect more personal attention, expertise and time during which their particular needs are considered paramount. For many people, having the opportunity to try to relax and have someone listening while they talk through their concerns is as important as improvement in their physical health. Assumptions may sometimes be made by clients, however, about the fine details of the codes of conduct, for example, to which the practitioner may be professionally bound.

Because of the highly technical nature of much modern health care, people sometimes feel confused, suspicious and vulnerable. Being seriously ill, for example, can be a frightening and bewildering experience, for which most people are unprepared. The alternatives of 'natural' therapies and related products, 'ancient wisdom' and treatments which involve spiritual energy and mystical imagery can sometimes seem less intimidating, less invasive, safer or more 'wholesome'. The value of caring human touch in an appropriate professional setting can also be much appreciated by lonely people. These approaches to healing and health may seem more pleasurable, particularly for those who have had long-term, unsatisfactory or depressing experiences of conventional health care.

Many people worry about taking prescribed medication because of concerns about side-effects and seek some relief or cure through non-drug-related means. A healing approach which does not involve surgery or 'chemicals' may be regarded as comparatively safe although this assumption may not be supported by widely accepted, independently and professionally researched evidence. Even if an approach uses 'natural' substances, that does not mean that it is always safe. Caution is needed, for example, in using herbal preparations, since they may contain naturally occurring toxic components. If a health problem can be improved by non-surgical physical treatment or a change of attitude, it may seem an attractive option, even if the treatment depends upon unqualified energy sources or leads the client towards adopting (with a few carefully considered questions or answers) the values or spirituality of a different religion or world-view.

The need to find a sense of purpose and self-worth can prompt an interest in approaches to health and healing which emphasize self-satisfaction and comforts. The body also tends to be regarded as a sensual medium for pleasurable activities and experiences. An aromatherapy treatment, relaxing massage or reflexology treatment is often appreciated as an enjoyable treat, reward or consolation which the individual can give to him- or herself or to someone else. There is a sense of being 'kind to oneself', being relaxed, revitalized and restored to 'normal', whatever that might be.

As a society we are continually presented with images of beautiful and healthy bodies to which we are encouraged to aspire and to which many of us appear to fail to match up. This can lead people to feel dissatisfied and ill at ease with their bodies. Many people also regard their bodies as a means of working; if a body does not 'work' properly the person feels 'let down' by it. Since our society places such a high priority on efficiency and productivity, there is an unfortunate tendency to regard those who are ill or disabled as of less value and a drain rather than as 'net contributors'. People who suffer from chronic ill health and/or cope with disabilities often feel uncomfortably aware of, and are made more vulnerable, by the impatience or lack of understanding of others.

Pressure can be put upon people to find a manageable level of good health sometimes at almost any price; to get a 'quick-fix' so than the normal business of living and working can be resumed. In the search for healing, people are often inundated with well-meant but poorly informed advice from friends and family and are pressurized in various ways to try almost anything: otherwise it may be suspected or even suggested that they do not really want to get well. Pressure from within is another factor, when trying to cope with the limitations of illness and the effects of suffering; if someone is really desperate he or she may be willing to try almost anything for relief.

What are complementary medicine and alternative therapies and what do they offer?

Most, but not all, health care provided nationally is based on conventional Western medicine. Conventional medicine can be described as the wide range of diagnostic and therapeutic concepts and their practical applications which are founded upon and employ modern scientific knowledge and techniques. There has been some absorption of other approaches since the beginning of this century. This gradual trend reflects our multicultural society, the recognition by many people of the limitations of traditional Western medical approaches, and the desire to bring relief and comfort, if not always cure, to individuals suffering from ill health and disease.

There is no widely accepted or clear dividing line between conventional and non-conventional approaches to healing. Currently, the range of healing and health care approaches beyond the conventional could be classed as:

❖ **complementary** – 'in support of conventional medicine'; some forms of complementary medicine are increasingly regarded as conventional; the term embraces a wide diversity of therapies and diagnostic methods;

❖ **alternative** – 'instead of conventional medicine'; many people, however, use alternative therapies in addition to conventional medicine.

Holistic medicine or therapeutic approaches to healing are those which aim to treat the whole person: body, mind and spirit. Disease is thought to be the result of imbalance or disturbance at a combination of levels; physical, psychological, spiritual and social/environmental. The purpose of holistic medicine includes the restoration of balance and helping the body to heal itself. Holistic approaches to health and healing are not restricted to complementary medicine and alternative therapies; good conventional medicine follows similar practices.

The most widely practised forms of complementary and alternative medicine therapies in the United Kingdom are:

❖ acupuncture
❖ Alexander technique
❖ aromatherapy
❖ chiropractic
❖ healing
❖ herbal medicine
❖ homeopathy
❖ hypnotherapy
❖ massage and bodywork therapies
❖ naturopathy and nutrition
❖ osteopathy
❖ reflexology
❖ shiatsu
❖ yoga.[4]

The particular approach of each of these forms to healing and health varies in emphasis and directness in relation to body/mind/spirit and the extent to which they are holistic. Some forms of complementary medicine and alternative therapies concentrate mainly on the physical state of the client. They include forms of physical manipulation and realignment, such as postural and movement therapies of Alexander technique and Feldenkrais method, chiropractic, osteopathy and other bodywork or massage approaches. Others involve treating clients with products which are digested or absorbed through the skin such as herbal medicine, phytotherapy, organic and mineral remedies. Clinical ecology, for example, treats ill health through detecting and eliminating irritant and allergenic foods from the person's diet, while macrobiotics is based on diets according to the principles established in Zen monasteries. Homeopathy treats the symptoms of the person in need of healing with minute doses of remedies which would create similar symptoms in someone who is healthy.

The mind–body link is the primary concern of therapies such as hypnotherapy, and autogenic training and therapy. Autogenic training and therapy, for example, is a mind–body technique for physical and psychological healing and rebalancing, is holistic in approach, links with homeopathy, psychotherapy and counselling and functions as an alternative or a complementary therapy. It is taught to clients, who are then self-directed; once learnt it is a lifetime skill and the client is not dependent on the therapist. Anthroposophical medicine, pioneered by Rudolf Steiner, believes that diseases are caused by astral and ego forces that impair natural healing. It uses eurythmy (sound and movement harmony), art and music therapies, as well as herbal and homeopathic remedies.

Bioenergetics uses the concept of body–mind energy, as is common to many alternative therapies. These aim to release tensions and psychological blocks, through relaxation, breathing and posture. Biofeedback trains one's reading of bodily signals to consciously control the automatic nervous system. In primal therapy (sometimes called rebirthing or primal integration therapy) a person relives some of his or her earliest memories, then integrates them into the present. Primal therapy is sometimes used by Christian therapists, mindful of the truth that God is sovereign of the past as well as of the present. Meditation, visualization and yoga exercises are used to maintain a calm centre, positive self-image and lifestyle. They are sometimes combined with Bach flower remedies, and aromatherapy which involves massage, inhalation and occasionally digestion of essential oils which have beneficial effects on body and mind.

Some forms of complementary medicine and alternative therapies are analytical or diagnostic methods and may lead to the recommendation of a range of other methods and remedies of herbal, homeopathic, mineral and vitamin composition. For example, the Radionics Association in its publication *Radionic Journal* (Winter 1998) describes radionics as

> a method of healing at a distance through the medium of an instrument using the ESP faculty. In this way, a trained and competent practitioner can discover the cause of disease within any living system, be it human, an animal, a plant or the soil itself.

Iridology is another diagnostic method, which involves carefully studying the client's eyes for signs of disease and changes in the body, where energy and circulation are impaired. Acupuncture and acupressure (shiatsu) and reflexology use energy points in meridians of the body, or soles and palms, for diagnosis and treatment of organ disease. Kinesiology uses a system based on testing at certain points of the body's muscular strength and balance to determine where weaknesses exist in the body.

Some approaches to healing draw on a variety of healing systems. Polarity therapy, for example, is described as a 'complementary therapy' and a 'preventative health care system'. It is a health care system founded by Dr Randolf Stone, who trained in chiropractic, naturopathy and osteopathy, and studied Ayurvedic medicine and yoga. His polarity therapy is based on the Indian (compared with yin–yang) balance of 'life energy' where ether, air, fire, water and earth correlate with parts or organs of the body. Treatment, using therapeutic bodywork, awareness skills, diet and nutrition and stretching exercises, claims to provide a basis for rebalancing and unblocking the restrictions to the body's vital energy, thereby restoring good health.

Complementary medicine and alternative therapies also include forms which are primarily concerned with the spiritual dimension. They are usually based on the transmission or rebalancing of some form of energy for therapeutic purposes. These are the approaches to healing which the Church needs to consider carefully in order to provide advice to Church members. Some people assume that the energy source is from God as understood by Christians, but that is not necessarily the understanding of the practitioners. The energy is often referred to as 'life force' or 'vital energy'. For example, therapies which refer to 'Chi' energy are rooted in the ancient Chinese religion of Taoism; shiatsu is based on Shintoism, which refers to the energy as 'Ki'; yoga, which is based on Hinduism, calls the energy 'prana'. In some approaches, however, the energy source is less clearly defined.

How are these approaches organized and regulated?

The European Commission and the World Health Organization take an interest in the regulation of the marketing of alternative and complementary medicine and related products. For example, at the time of the preparation of this report, guidelines are expected in the near future on the definition of a medicinal herbal product. There is also the All-Party Parliamentary Group for Alternative and Complementary Medicine which includes Members of Parliament and peers. There is, however, still little statutory regulation specifically for complementary medicine and alternative therapies. For example, osteopaths and chiropractors are state registered and regulated, following the acts of Parliament to establish the General Osteopathic Council and General Chiropractic Council, but apparently there is no statutory obligation on practitioners of other approaches to join an official register before setting up their practice. Some disciplines recognize the disadvantages of having several or many registering organizations and are working towards having a single main regulatory organization and towards statutory self-regulation. Nevertheless, statutory regulation involves bureaucratic procedures and parliamentary legislation, which can be time-consuming and expensive.

Many practitioners of complementary medicine and alternative therapies are members of one or several of the accrediting or regulatory bodies which have been established. These bodies vary in size and have different criteria and standards. Some therapies are overseen by governing bodies for the profession and its suppliers, such as the Aromatherapy Organizations Council. These governing bodies offer members the status of belonging to a professional organization/register and they often facilitate arrangements for professional indemnity insurance. They also arrange meetings for members with lectures and workshops, and the agenda may include business issues affecting the profession and related policies. Furthermore, newsletters, journals and bulletins are often produced to provide information on changes in the related fields and the activities of the governing body.

Many of the regulatory and governing bodies have codes of conduct and procedures for dealing with complaints which affect their members. It is widely recognized that such steps are necessary to build up and retain the confidence of the public and the authorities. Whilst the terms vary, there is clearly a desire to be seen to be setting acceptable standards and providing a framework for good practice for practitioners. But like the Church, these bodies cannot enforce disciplinary measures against independent organizations and individuals who are not members.

How does the mainstream medical profession regard these alternative approaches?

Complementary medicine is now an established part of health care nationally. It is increasingly provided within the NHS; for example, it is estimated that nearly 40 per cent of GP partnerships provide access to complementary medicine and alternative therapies for their NHS patients.[5] Around 75 per cent of the public support NHS access to complementary medicine.[6] Furthermore, there is strongly expressed interest among some practitioners of complementary medicine and alternative therapies in developing their work within the NHS. Nevertheless, doctors and patients trying to find the most suitable health care can face a confusing range of information from a wide range of sources, on issues such as what the particular approach offers and how, training and regulation of practitioners, whether the therapy is proven effective, how and by whom, and in what circumstances the therapy is inappropriate.

Several universities and colleges run courses in complementary medicine ranging from diploma to Ph.D. level. It is important that such courses are properly accredited to the relevant professional body. In time, it is hoped that this development will lead to a more integrated system of health care provision and a sounder academic foundation for these approaches. Some medical schools already include some content on complementary medicine as part of their curriculum.

At present, however, there are concerns including:

❖ the increasing number of organizations and professional bodies representing and regulating the very wide range of complementary medicine and alternative therapies;

❖ the need for further research carried out to widely acceptable and sufficiently high standards on the safety, efficacy and effectiveness of these approaches to healing and health;

❖ a lack of training in complementary medicine and alternative therapies as part of training in many medical and nursing schools; on the other hand, concerns that some courses for complementary medicine and alternative therapies do not include enough training on the principles and practice of conventional medicine;

❖ a common lack of effective integration of complementary medicine and alternative therapies with conventional medical practice in primary and secondary health care;

❖ fears that people may rely on alternative therapies and only seek conventional health care as their condition worsens, by which time treatment may be made more difficult or the delay lead to unnecessary suffering.

The Foundation for Integrated Medicine on behalf of the Steering Committee for the Prince of Wales's Initiative on Integrated Medicine published a discussion document in 1997, setting out objectively the current situation in terms of research and development, education and training, regulation and delivery mechanisms. The document sets out a summary of carefully considered and constructive practical proposals in relation to these areas to improve on the current situation.[7]

A key factor affecting the recognition by the medical profession of complementary medicine and alternative therapies is the need for more rigorous research. New conventional types of medicine have to undergo very thorough test procedures to establish their efficacy, side-effects and interaction with other drugs for example. Medicines which pass the tests then need to be approved by the licensing authority to ensure the safety of patients. Questions are being asked about what the priorities for research should be, what might be the most appropriate methods and how this research should be carried out and supported. Following on from this issue is the question of how the information should be gathered, studied, organized and disseminated.

Some forms of complementary medicine are now largely accepted by the medical profession on the basis of existing information. More research information is available than is widely supposed but it is limited by a range of factors, for example, lack of funding, lack of relevant research skills and academic infrastructure, the difficulties of recruiting patients from private practices and issues surrounding methodology. It is possible in certain circumstances to study and evaluate the effects of spirituality on physical healing and health. The medical profession is not, however, able to assess the spiritual effects or benefits, tensions, challenges and even possible spiritual dangers of complementary medicine and alternative therapies, only the ways in which these are reflected in someone's physical or mental state of health. The Church has an important and urgent role to play in clarifying the spiritual dimension of such approaches to healing, health and wholeness.

Practical health care is often seen by Christians as an area where physical and mental well-being are the overriding aims. Doctors do not always explain all the options, but neither do the clergy always explain the wide expression of the healing ministry. Perhaps this highlights the need for the Church to work to ensure that its members are better informed about conventional and complementary medicine and alternative therapies and that we are all encouraged to be seriously holistic in our own approach to health. The healing ministry is both complementary to conventional medicine and holistic. In response to research carried out for this report, however, it was noted that some doctors are more suspicious of the Church's healing ministry than they are of complementary medicine and alternative therapies, particularly if they have encountered patients who have suffered from inappropriate ministry.

To what extent are other approaches to healing compatible with Christian teaching?

It is difficult to assess and present in a report of this length a wide overview of the range of complementary and alternative approaches to healing and health. The issue is further complicated by the fact that new therapies are continually being introduced and established and some of them are a combination of existing therapies, since innovation and inspiration are encouraged. Crucially from the point of view of researching for and writing this chapter, at present there are no criteria agreed by the Church of England or ecumenically with the other main denominations for assessing the approaches of these alternatives. In order to consider these approaches, the main denominations need to agree on appropriate terms of reference and the criteria which are relevant.

For example, is the approach compatible with, ambivalent towards or incompatible with Christian teaching? Should the framework for criteria be theological, medical, social/pastoral? Should the criteria be, as many Christians believe, that for a form or approach to healing to be acceptable it must be in the name of Jesus? How would the criteria eventually chosen compare with those against which conventional medicine is evaluated? If, for example, scientific proof of effectiveness is insisted upon, would we accept such criteria for the assessment of the Church's healing ministry?

At the beginning of this report and in Chapter 2, the healing ministry of Jesus is described as **'visionary, prophetic and dynamic'**. These distinctive characteristics of his ministry are a valuable and relevant way of reflecting on the nature of alternative approaches to healing, health care and wholeness. For example, is the form of complementary medicine or alternative therapy 'X' visionary, prophetic and dynamic in the same terms or not? Does it give a glimpse of the kingdom and call us to reflect on our relationships with others and with God; does it answer our deepest needs? Or is its approach more limited or more diffuse? Some approaches, for example, may be falsely prophetic, through obscuring the real vision, causing people to look elsewhere from God for another source of healing, thereby being dynamic in a harmful way.

It is not always clear, however, what the complementary or alternative therapy is based upon, what principles and spiritual values underpin it or if there is a wider agenda and what it may be. People considering a particular therapy need to make detailed enquiries about its principles, sources of healing and spiritual values. The International Self-Realization Healing Association (ISRHA), for example, states in its 'Code of Conduct for Healers' that the 'ISRHA embraces all expressions of spirituality, encouraging individual members in a personal understanding and connection with the source of life. Healers should at all times respect the spiritual, religious, political and social views of any individual irrespective of race, colour, creed or sex, remembering that within we are all souls of the same light.'[8]

Rather than making sweeping generalizations about alternative therapies and complementary medicine, such as 'Eastern', 'superstition', 'New Age' or 'incompatible', each approach needs to be thoroughly reviewed by the Church, according to the approach's principles, claims for efficacy, underlying spirituality and world-view, and in particular, its claims for spiritual benefits and improvements to recipients. For example, explanations of how complementary medicine and alternative therapies work may be incompatible with Christian teaching but some or all of the techniques and materials used may not be incompatible.

Not all approaches to healing and health have a spiritual dimension; some attempt to address physical or mental/emotional conditions by physical means. Some approaches appear to fit this class but nevertheless are based on older approaches which have a spiritual dimension. A therapy may claim its healing power is from God, but the Christian client needs to know what is the understanding of God in that case. For example, 'Integrated Chronotherapy is the result of a symbiosis of oriental traditional wisdom-knowledge of bio-energy, the western scientific knowledge of phyto-medicine with the ancient knowledge of astronomical movements and exact universal timing.'[9]

Other forms of therapy and medicine are more clearly underpinned by particular spiritual beliefs and may be based on other world-views or faiths which are distinctly non-Christian. This raises challenging questions about whether Christians are compromised by taking advantage of these approaches. For example, Reiki is an energy healing system apparently of Tibetan Buddhist origin rediscovered in the late nineteenth century. The source of the energy which is channelled through the practitioner's hands is not clearly defined, but the system is claimed to be holistic, leading to progress in one's spiritual life. Training of practitioners takes place over several stages, at financial cost, and involves a 'sacred ceremony' in which the recipient's aura is accessed and implanted with Reiki symbols which open up and clear the healing channel; it is not clear how this works and the training has (apparently) always been an oral tradition.

'New Age' is a blanket term used to refer to a movement which seeks self-improvement and personal wholeness through a variety of means including non-conventional and alternative health care, therapies including the use of crystals, astrology, techniques to heighten awareness and spiritual teachings from a variety of faith traditions. At its most benign, it refers to a desire to achieve an integrity of body, mind and spirit in health and healing, and to promote a balanced way of life, to redress materialism by pursuing altruistic and 'green' policies. But it may be interwoven with the tares of occultism and opposition both to worship of God and to co-operation with God's ministers and healers. New Age approaches tend to move away from the belief of God the creator and healer, towards the belief that healing comes from within one's own body, from 'spiritual energy'. These approaches are considered by some Christians to be fundamentally hostile to biblical Christianity. It is important in the ministry of Christ to discern what is sound and in support of God's holy purposes.

Certain alternative therapies offer healing through various energy sources, or 'life forces'. These energy sources are ambiguous; there may even be different views on the source of the energy amongst the practitioners of the therapy. The underlying principle is that the healing source is available for channelling through some people for the benefit of others. The psychic dimension, however, is not fully understood. It could be described as morally ambiguous or ambivalent; it is not entirely bad or entirely good. It does not carry a 'British Standard' assurance of safety. Those practitioners of alternative therapies who are dependent on energy from vague sources may take risks in ways which few people are able to discern reliably. The links between the use of psychic techniques, energy sources and the occult can be strong, but not necessarily made obvious to clients. Therapies related in any way to occult practices are incompatible with the Christian faith. Christians are warned in the Bible to avoid mediums and spiritualists and any connection with the occult. The word 'occult' means 'hidden' and its practitioners believe that there are within ourselves and our world hidden powers and forces which can be harnessed and be used for good or evil. Occultism is sometimes criticized as being an attempt at spiritual manipulation and oppression in contrast to the Christian view that spiritual gifts are given by God in response to the relationship he has with us.

At this stage, with no agreed approach to complementary medicine and alternative therapies by the main denominations or the Church of England in particular, some guidance for Christians might be found through asking questions of practitioners such as:

❖ How would you reassure a Christian client that the complementary medicine or alternative therapy is compatible with Christian teaching and practice?

❖ Is the approach holistic and, if so, how does it heal body, mind and spirit?

❖ Is there a rational scientific basis for the approach and, if so, what is it? How does it relate to the practitioners' claims?

❖ How is its effectiveness measured? Is there scientific proof and who did the tests? How will the practitioner measure the effect on the client?

❖ Is the approach based on or influenced by a spirituality other than Christianity and, if so, what is it?

❖ To whom or what is the appeal for healing being made? If the healing power behind the approach is not God's, where is it coming from?

❖ Does the approach involve the occult in any way?

❖ If the healing power is based on visualization techniques, how do these relate to Christian symbols and the name of Jesus Christ?

❖ In what ways might the approach challenge my values, world-view or self-perception and encourage me to change?

Two pertinent points worth consideration at this stage are:

❖ The personal spirituality and world-view of the practitioner may be different from that underpinning the therapy he or she is offering.

❖ Most people do not deeply question medical or health care professionals involved in conventional medicine about their personal spirituality, and their professional expertise is not usually assessed according to this issue; few Christians would refuse conventional medical treatment from a non-Christian doctor or nurse, for example, simply because he or she had a different faith. The lack of a shared world-view or faith does not rule out cooperation, trust and mutual respect.

Questions which the Church needs to address include:

❖ Should a Christian refuse complementary medicine or alternative therapy treatments based on beliefs which are not compatible with Christian teaching? Or should they go ahead, aware of possible pressures, to take the practical benefits, if they need them?

❖ If Christians receives treatment based on a spirituality other than Christianity, is his or her faith or spiritual growth undermined, and if so, how?

❖ How would the Church of England regard the integration into the National Health Service of therapies which are not compatible with Christian teaching? How would these be reconciled with the teaching of the Christian faith by the established Church? What implications does this issue have for the national Church and the NHS? How does this issue affect hospital chaplains and prison chaplains?

What are the limitations of alternative approaches to healing?

While some forms of complementary medicine and alternative therapies are supported by scientific evidence of how they work and the extent to which they are successful, others rely more heavily on the claims of the individual practitioners, who may have a commercial interest in attracting clients. It should be acknowledged that most practitioners have a strong and genuine desire to help their clients and bring about a measure of healing in them. Nevertheless, the issue of whether or not a particular client benefits in any tangible way and the extent of success may be a matter of subjective reaction rather than scientific proof.

Although increasing amounts of formal research on complementary medicine and alternative therapies are being conducted, the limited evidence available is not widely accepted within the medical profession. There are, for example, apparently almost no reports of direct adverse effects from naturopathy or homeopathy. On the other hand, many people would like to see more independent and professional scientific research done on the safety and effectiveness of individual forms of complementary medicine and alternative therapies.

Most practitioners of complementary medicine and alternative therapies make financial charges which can be substantial, and sometimes recommend regular and/or follow-up sessions or additional types of therapy for successful treatment of an ailment. The costs of some treatments, which could be compared with private medicine, may be more than some people can reasonably afford and so they may need to make choices about how they spend their money, perhaps affecting their well-being in other ways: for example, 'Should I pay for a course of "X" or save up for a holiday when I can rest?'

Many alternative approaches to healing are not concerned primarily with spiritual health. They attempt and sometimes succeed in helping to relieve symptoms, bringing about physical healing and making life appear more pleasant. Some approaches concentrate on changing the state of the client's mental health and others address the broader issues of lifestyle and environment. Spiritual health is sometimes one of a wide range of factors taken into account by people who are not usually primarily spiritual directors. A person's spirituality tends to be regarded as a source of potential physical or mental ill health, but not usually as the key potential source of good health overall.

What can the Church learn from complementary medicine and alternative therapies?

The considerable interest nationally in complementary medicine and alternative therapies shows the extent to which people are seeking a personal approach to healing and good health. People want to be in control of their lives and well-being. This leaves little room for coping with chronic problems which may be interpreted as a loss of control or lack of effort on the part of the individual. Many people regard complementary medicine and alternative therapies as activities in which they can consent and participate in an informed way, where they matter as people and where their needs can be met. They often see themselves in a partnership with the therapist rather than as a biophysical object to be treated or restored to good working order.

People need time and attention and deserve to be properly valued for themselves, rather than, for example, primarily in terms of what they can contribute to others, to organizations or to our society. Within the

Church of England we face the challenge to make more time for people, to give them more personal attention – to find out more about what concerns them, their problems and their burdens. Many people involved in the research for this report linked spiritual direction with the healing ministry as a means of encouraging spiritual good health and a closer relationship with God. The Church of England needs to consider the link between spiritual direction and holistic approaches to healing and good health in more detail and how spiritual direction may be made more widely and easily available for those who seek it.

People feel valued when someone is willing to give their time and full attention to listen to them. The healing ministry is not an impersonal ministry, to be done hurriedly and as a matter of routine: sufficient time should be available for those carrying out Jesus' ministry and those who are receiving it. Christian Listeners, Christian counsellors and pastoral assistants have an important role within the healing ministry working as part of local collaborative ministry. This has implications for the role of diocesan advisors too, as many of the advisors are struggling to find time for the healing ministry on top of other responsibilities, including full-time posts in their parishes.

The success of complementary medicine and alternative therapies reflects the speed and efficiency with which the various organizations have marketed their approaches. National organizations overseeing many of these approaches and most individual practitioners are professional in the ways in which they make people aware of what they have to offer. The media are aware of this national interest in healing and health and it is frequently featured in magazines, newspapers, television and radio. Practitioners are usually active in promoting their approach locally too.

We need to recognize that these approaches tend to be in competition for people's attention and commitment. Currently the Church's healing ministry is rarely covered by the media unless it is as part of a critical review. The healing ministry needs to be promoted effectively in order to attract the attention of these groups of people in our society. If we do not promote it actively and effectively, it will be overshadowed in the media by those approaches to healing and wholeness which are fashionable or which are high profile through professional marketing, celebrity supporters, media interest or novelty, for example.

The Church of England needs to consider how this ministry is most effectively communicated, particularly to non-church-attenders, including those of other faiths. Preaching about it occasionally from the pulpit is not enough. We do not specifically recommend that the healing ministry is promoted in the same ways as complementary medicine and alternative therapies, but we do emphasize that lack of awareness of this ministry among the public is a serious issue. Carefully considered ways of communicating about this ministry, which distinguish it from medical and alternative therapeutic approaches, are needed for the range of groups within society, taking into consideration issues including their current needs, interests and perception of the Church and its mission.

Effective communication about the healing ministry is also an effective way of spreading the gospel. In fact, it can be one of the ways in which the Church of England can break through many people's disinterest in the Church and its message. Great sensitivity is needed, however, to avoid putting people under pressure when they are ill and at their most vulnerable. Part of this task involves finding ways of encouraging accurate reporting and ensuring that those working within the Church of England's communication networks, nationally and in the dioceses, are well informed and enthusiastic about the healing ministry.

We also need to acknowledge that many alternative approaches to healing and health care are sensuous and pleasurable in their own right; the use of touch, scent, music, natural products and personal attention encourages people to use them. Many people think that if something feels good, it must be good for them, and to some extent this is often true. If a treatment helps someone relax, relieves pain and helps them to be more hopeful and optimistic about their life, they do tend to feel better, at least for a while.

The Church of England needs to consider how the healing ministry can be carried out in ways which will attract people. In order to ensure that the experience of a service with prayers for healing is a pleasant one, the issues of physical comfort and uplifting surroundings which appeal to the senses should be addressed. It needs to be an experience which people remember as helpful, pleasant and spiritually uplifting. The healing ministry is not just for the elderly and seriously ill either; it is for everyone, including children, young people and people who do not normally attend church services. If a healing service is not a pleasant experience, people are unlikely to return.

Suitable seating and its sensitive arrangement, adequate heating and fresh air, suitable lighting and a peaceful atmosphere are basic requirements, not luxurious options. Easy access and appropriate facilities for disabled people should be incorporated into every church building. People with hearing and/or sight difficulties need to be treated with consideration and provided for adequately. The use of appropriate scents and gentle music can help to create an atmosphere of serenity and sanctity. Those people carrying out the healing ministry need to be aware and sensitive to the ways in which their appearance and behaviour can inspire confidence and set people at ease or, on the other hand, put people off.

Another feature of some forms of complementary medicine and alternative therapies is the privacy in which people can relax and be vulnerable. Not everyone wants to display their vulnerability publicly and many people feel more able to seek help on a confidential basis. Public healing services, particularly in the local church, will not offer this privacy to those who need a more discreet environment: opportunities to receive the healing ministry in private, following the guidelines for good practice, should be made known generally, not just for the housebound and in-patients.

The Church does not 'charge' for the healing ministry so it may be difficult for someone who is not a member of the Church to appreciate its true worth and the wider vision of the message it proclaims. By setting the healing ministry in clear partnership with preaching and teaching in the parishes, the message of the awesome price which Jesus paid for our healing can be put across clearly. For this reason, collections or encouragement for donations at healing services may give the impression that the Church does make a charge or expect financial payment; it may be preferable to avoid taking collections during healing services.

The healing ministry is the ministry of Jesus Christ, who has already paid the highest price for our healing, in every sense. He continues to heal through the power of the Holy Spirit. The integrity of this power is clearly defined in Christian teaching and is not in any way ambivalent, but an expression of God's love for us. This ministry enables the individual seeking healing to become more aware of the divine and leads to a closer relationship with God. It is outward-looking and leads through spiritual growth as well as healing towards wholeness and eternal good health. In our research, we were frequently reminded of the link between spiritual direction and the deeper understanding of suffering. People coping with disease ask 'Why me?', 'Why now?', as they try to make sense of their situation, cope and learn from it. The Church can provide invaluable help through spiritual direction, as well as the healing ministry, to people seeking healing or graceful acceptance of their situation.

One of the features of several forms of complementary medicine and alternative therapy is the encouragement to reassess the client's lifestyle. They may encourage the adoption of lifestyles and values based on other world-views or faiths rather than on Christianity. Yet the Christian faith offers far more than physical healing as its end and cannot be bettered as a model for lifelong living. In this sense the Christian healing ministry could not be more holistic. Furthermore, it is incomparable with complementary and alternative approaches to healing, because the healing ministry is unique in its offer of healing for the Christian soul in the context of eternity.

While the Church of England has much to learn from the rapid growth in success, in recent years, of alternative approaches to health, it would be a mistake to respond by developing approaches to the Church's healing ministry which may give the impression that it is in any way commercial, or in competition with the alternatives in a secular way. In the ways in which it is visionary, prophetic and dynamic, the healing ministry is unique and priceless. We must ensure that the message is conveyed in total clarity, that healing the sick is a most precious expression of Jesus' ministry and it is an key activity within the mission of the Church in this world. The healing ministry is one way in which the Holy Spirit drives the shafts of light from Jesus' love into the darkest depths of our lives and reveals the true nature of our personal relationship with God.

Recommendations

We recommend that:

❖ the Church of England, working ecumenically with our ecumenical partners, should establish a Review Group, with agreed terms of reference and criteria, to assess in the longer term the compatibility with Christian teaching of widely used forms of complementary medicine and alternative therapies, taking into account interfaith issues (see pages 47–8, 83–4, 183, 184, 192, 196 and 198);

❖ the Church of England should provide ecumenically agreed guidance for Christians who are considering or using these approaches, including the kind of questions that might be asked about these approaches to healing, health and wholeness (see pages 74, 183, 192–3, 196 and 199–200);

❖ the relationship between the healing ministry and those forms of complementary and alternative approaches to healing which are becoming integrated with conventional health care should be reviewed, in cooperation with the HCC and health care professionals within the NHS (see pages 60, 190, 194 and 201);

❖ training for ministry, particularly for hospital and prison chaplains, should include an appreciation of the range of complementary and alternative approaches to healing and the issues which surround them (see pages 41–2, 55, 184, 192–3, 201, 203 and 204–5);

❖ the relationship between spiritual guidance/direction and health care provision should be reviewed and recommendations made for the increased availability of spiritual direction as part of total health care (see pages 85, 192, 203 and 205);

❖ local churches should be encouraged to communicate effectively information about the healing ministry to raise awareness particularly amongst non-church attenders; for example, putting notices in surgeries and providing leaflets (see pages 186, 196, 203, 204 and 206).

11

Evidence for Healing

The healing ministry of the Church is constantly questioned by those who demand medical evidence that a miraculous cure has been experienced in answer to prayer. According to their understanding of how the Bible is to be interpreted today, Christians often give widely different answers. Yet such evidence is almost impossible to obtain. There is a mystery in the way God deals with us which cannot be expounded through scientific testing. And in any case, the real evidence of a healing is a change in the individual as a result of knowing the risen Christ's saving and healing grace within themselves. For them, that can be a miracle indeed.

We have already said in this report that the Christian understanding of healing is far broader than a miraculous physical cure in the commonly accepted sense of that phrase. We want to encourage a proper appreciation and practice of this ministry, not one aimed at producing more miracles and then using the evidence to prove the authenticity of the gospel.

Nevertheless, the question of evidence has to be faced. If we teach that the Church is continuing the healing ministry of Jesus Christ in the power of the Holy Spirit, then it is not unreasonable to be asked, 'Are you expecting the same sort of cures as sick people did in Jesus' day, and can such cures be shown to be miraculous after being subject to medical criteria?' We live in an age that expects scientific evidence for what is claimed.

New Testament miracles

Approaching this question we need to remember that in the New Testament Jesus' healings are inextricably linked with his preaching of the gospel of the kingdom of God. The good news is the promise of wholeness for humanity, through the great saving acts of God celebrated in the Church's calendar from Advent to Pentecost. That wholeness is demonstrated in the different layers behind the New Testament stories of the healings.

At one layer they testified to God's love for suffering humanity (Mark 1.41; 8.2). At another layer they fulfilled the Old Testament promises of the coming time of salvation when God would heal people's bodies as well as their souls (Luke 7.22; Isaiah 29.18,19; 35.5,6; 61.1). And at yet another layer they demonstrated that the kingdom of God which Jesus announced was coming into the world to conquer evil and to bring the forgiveness of sin (e.g. Mark 1.23-26; 2.1-12). Relief of suffering, the promise of healing, the forgiveness of sins and the conquest of evil – these layers added together make up much of what we mean by 'wholeness' today.

But it was only those who accepted Jesus as the Christ who recognized the healings as signs of the kingdom. To those who might be described as 'outside the community of faith,' he was not the Messiah but a stumbling block, and his healings were only 'wonders' which aroused astonishment and admiration – and antagonism among his opponents. The difference faith in Christ makes to our approach to the miraculous is extremely important, as we shall see presently.

The overriding impression given us by the New Testament is that the healing miracles were not *compelling* signs of God's power. Jesus rejected the temptation to work miracles to dazzle people or seduce them into believing in him (Matthew 4.5-7; Luke 4.9-12). Not everyone recognized them as signs of the kingdom. The Pharisees attributed Christ's healings to the power of Satan (Mark 3.22). Jesus challenged the official at Capernaum about wanting to see signs and wonders (John 4.48), and told the Pharisees and scribes, 'An evil and adulterous generation asks for a sign' (Matthew 12.39). Furthermore, Jesus himself asked many of those who were healed not to publicize what had happened: 'Go on your way rejoicing, give thanks to God, tell nobody, make the customary offerings and sin no more' paraphrases his follow-up instructions to them.

But it is important to note that rebukes against seeking signs are always directed against hostile unbelievers, those who were looking for a miracle only as an opportunity to criticize Jesus. Never does Jesus rebuke anyone who comes in faith or in need, seeking healing or deliverance or any other kind of miracle for him- or herself, or for others.

We must also note that in their New Testament context the miraculous healings were not isolated from the wider healing of relationships with God and with others. So, for example, the paralysed man's sins were forgiven (Mark 2.1-12 and parallels). The story of Zacchaeus must be set alongside those of physical healing and deliverance from evil spirits because the result of this little man's encounter with Jesus was that he became a changed man, a 'healed' person. The townspeople recognized that although he had not been made any taller physically, he had become bigger in every other way (Luke 19.2-8). Similarly with the story of the woman with the issue of blood. She was cured but she was also a transformed person, able to be united with family, society and God in a new way (Mark 5.25-34; Luke 8. 43-48). The forgiven, changed person – and the effect that change makes on others – is at the heart of these healing stories. And the ultimate response which authenticates the miracle is to give glory to God (Luke 7.16). In Irenaeus' dictum, 'The glory of God is manfully alive. And man fully alive is the glory of God' – that is to say, a human being developing into the wholeness for which he or she was created and redeemed, and which is the heart of the healing ministry.

So although we need to heed warnings about seeking evidence for the authenticity of the miraculous, yet it is true that, for those with eyes to see and ears to hear, the healings constituted signs that the risen Christ was working in fulfilment of his promises. And, as signs, they awakened and confirmed faith in him. The same applies to the miracles in the apostolic Church. The Book of Acts reveals how through the Holy Spirit Jesus was working with his disciples, confirming their message of salvation with signs following. After the healing of the crippled man at the gate of the temple and Peter's witness before the Sanhedrin, we are told that the apostolic community prayed and 'the place in which they were gathered together was shaken; and they were all filled with the Holy Spirit and spoke the word of God with boldness' (Acts 4.31). Other healing miracles, such as those in Acts 9.17 (Paul's sight), Acts 9.33,34 (Aeneas), and so on, were powerful signs of encouragement to the Church.

Views on the miraculous

In the wake of the Enlightenment and the post-Enlightenment rationalist debate, the Church came under pressure not only to defend the possibility of the miraculous but also to prove with scientific evidence that miraculous signs are, and always have been, a part of God's dealing with humankind. From the latter years of the nineteenth century and throughout the twentieth a spectrum of responses has been made by Anglicans and other Christians to this pressure. Without giving labels these different responses can be roughly categorized as follows.

Response (a) The New Testament healing narratives are historically accurate and similar miracles would happen today if the Church still had faith that Christ would work through her members in answer to prayer. Such miracles do happen even if it is difficult to prove them medically.

Response (b) The New Testament healing narratives are generally accurate but healings no longer happen in the same dramatic way because at the end of the apostolic age God ceased to work miracles. The reasons for this are varied: some argue that once the gospel was established it suited God's purposes to withdraw miraculous interventions (this view was known as 'dispensational' but nowadays is more often called 'cessational'); others that God's grace is now manifested in other ways through the Christian community.

Response (c) There is a hard core of historical fact behind the New Testament healing narratives but we cannot be sure that the details, passed down by oral tradition before being written by the authors, are accurate in every case. Besides, we now recognize that many of the symptoms attributed to demonic activity in the first century are now in the twenty-first century seen as having physical or psychological causes. However, God who raised Jesus from the dead must surely have worked wonders through his earthly ministry, and we can still hope that he may do so now through the Body of Christ.

Response (d) In the intellectual climate within which we live today, we have to accept that the New Testament healing narratives are an integral part of the Christian faith as it has been handed down to us but, while they are immensely valuable as such, we should not expect to find much historical fact behind them. As an outstandingly charismatic personality, Jesus no doubt exercised an enormous influence over those who came to him, and one of the effects of that encounter may well have been remarkable 'healings' such as are sometimes experienced today, especially among those in societies which have had little contact with modern medicine. But we cannot call such 'healings' miraculous for, if all the facts were known to us, we would probably be able to attribute them to medical, psychological or communal causes. The notion that God intervenes directly in the world is incompatible with what is known scientifically about the universe, even if some things have to be attributed to chance. If the word 'miracle' is to be used at all today in connection with healing, it is more fittingly employed to describe such things as marvellous advances in medical science which bring cures hitherto thought impossible.

Although it is difficult and perhaps misleading to attempt to categorize the views of Anglicans today on these matters, it is perhaps generally true to say that some would want to say that *(a)* is substantially true but with qualifications, many would agree with *(b)* or *(c)*, and others hold that *(d)* is nearer the truth for contemporary men and women. Such expectations – or lack of them – will obviously influence the ways in which they minister to the sick.

It is among the *(c)* category that anecdotal claims of miraculous healings continue to circulate. Hardly a lecture is given on the healing ministry without at least one such story being narrated. They make best-selling paperbacks. The media occasionally invade this area with investigative equipment and emerge with 'evidence' that is not usually satisfactory.

However, we need to be discerning about these. What is miraculous to one culture or generation may not be so extraordinary to another. For example, one of our members who has worked overseas described how simple therapies can be regarded as amazing events by the local people because they had never experienced or understood anything like them before. Seriously disabling conditions, including long-term blindness and speech impediment, were healed by ordinary medical common sense, but to the persons involved and to their families and friends they were miraculous.

But not all such healings can be explained in that way. Among the peoples of the developing world there is often a communal awareness of the spiritual dimension of life which is notably higher than it is in modern Britain. People expect God to answer prayers, and quite inexplicable healing signs are experienced among Christians and also sometimes among those of other faiths or none. Among our members are those who have both seen in others and known personally rapid healings after prayer, though it has never been possible to prove that such healings were *solely* the result of the Church's ministry. Today many Christians have discovered the wonder and mystery of God's relationship with his people through intercession for their sick friends. As Morris Maddocks wrote, 'Possibly the greatest contribution the healing ministry is making to the life of all the churches in our time is this recalling of Christians to deep prayer'.[1]

Other denominations

Faced with this problem we made enquiries to learn how Christians of other denominations dealt with the matter of evidence for miraculous healings.

The Free Churches

Our informant in the Methodist Church told us that it has no formal procedure for assessing claims of miracles. We learned this is also the case in the United Reformed Church and the Baptist Union. Generally speaking, they are as cautious as Anglicans in accepting unreservedly such claims. A Baptist suggested the following dialogue:

> 'Can God heal?'– 'Yes.' 'Does God heal?' – 'Yes.' 'Do we always see it?'– 'No.' 'Is it common?' – 'It depends on what kind of healing you are looking for.'

The New Churches

The New Churches (formerly known as House Churches), like the Pentecostal and Black churches, have a far higher expectancy of physical healing as a result of prayer than many in other denominations, but their stories of miraculous cures are largely anecdotal. However, their more experienced leaders are well aware of the dangers of unsubstantiated claims and advise those who make them to seek verification from their doctors. Wayne Gruden, an American theologian much respected in these circles, warns:

> Christians should be very cautious and take extreme care in their reporting of miracles if they do occur. Much harm can be done to the gospel if Christians exaggerate or distort, even in small ways, the facts of a situation where a miracle has occurred. The power of the Holy Spirit is great enough to work however he wills, and we should never embellish the actual facts of the situation simply to make it sound even more exciting than it actually was. God does exactly what he is pleased to do in each situation.[2]

The Orthodox Churches

The Orthodox Churches do not have any formal and official procedure for substantiating claims for miraculous healing. Centres of pilgrimage such as Tinos, where miraculous healings are often reported, keep records of such events, usually collating evidence from the person involved and from other eye witnesses as soon as possible after the event occurs. How far such accounts are supported by reports from qualified medical experts depends on the initiative of the religious institution concerned. For a canonization process in the Church of Greece, it is the responsibility in the first instance of the local diocesan bishop to collect evidence of the person's life, together with accounts of any supposed miraculous healings, during his or her life or afterwards. How detailed such reports are depends on the judgement of the bishop in question and his advisors. If the bishop thinks there is a case for canonization, the dossier is then referred to the Holy Synod of the Church of Greece, which examines it in detail. In general, however, the Orthodox Churches do not require evidence of miraculous healings as a necessary condition for the proclamation of a saint, although it is normal for such evidence to be included in any request for canonization.

The Roman Catholic Church

The Roman Catholic Church has the most sophisticated process of all the denominations. Evidence for miraculous healing is one of the conditions required for the process of canonization, and as early as the first half of the eighteenth century, a gifted theologian and lawyer named Prospero Lambertini, who became Pope Benedict XIV (1740–58) and whom Eamon Duffy described as 'a supreme papal exponent of common sense realism'[3], wrote what remains the standard textbook on canonization. He demanded, among other things, that when claims were made about healings as a result of the intercessions of a candidate for canonization, there must not be found in the cure any valid explanation, medical, scientific, natural and usual.

The system of verification at Lourdes is probably the most refined. Qualified doctors are involved in the Lourdes Medical Bureau and the criteria used in both the diagnostic and the 'evidence' part of an investigation are as for any that would be required in a scientific analysis of miracles. For the medical study to be able to find in favour of a cure to be 'certain, definitive and medically inexplicable' it must be established that the fact and the diagnosis of the illness are correct and that:

> the prognosis must be permanent or terminal in the short term, the cure is immediate, without convalescence, complete and lasting, and the prescribed treatment could not be attributed to the cause of this cure or be an aid to it.

There is also a further level of verification through a large International Medical Committee, and no decision can be made for years. In the end it is the person's bishop who makes the final decision as to whether or not the cure is to be announced publicly. Between 1947 and 1998 some 19 cases were judged to be miraculous. Of these only three have been so declared at Lourdes, and the most impressive of these has raised controversies about the original diagnosis. And as medicine has advanced, the criteria evolved at Lourdes have correspondingly produced a degree of doubt among doctors.[4]

Tests

It is very difficult to use medical techniques, such as controlled trials, double-blind studies and the administration of placebos under scientific conditions, when studying the effect of Christian prayer and sacramental and charismatic administrations. Whilst writing this report we have heard claims that in double-blind conditions the well-being of those who are prayed for is enhanced, when contrasted with those who are not the subject of such intercession. We have also heard of attempts to assess the effects of praying for one group of patients and ignoring another group. Research of this kind raises questions, such as how do those conducting the research 'screen out' the prayers of other people, locally, at a distance, and around the whole world, in general intercessions for the sick in the Church. Such projects also seem to reject the apostle's injunction, 'Rejoice always, pray without ceasing, give thanks in all circumstances; for this is the will of God in Christ Jesus for you' (1 Thessalonians 5.16-18).

Nevertheless, this area of research is of increasing interest to the medical profession, as well as to those who are seeking to prove the value of healing prayer. The media occasionally reports on research into the health of Christians compared with that of their neighbours. For example, an article with the headline 'Church-goers blessed with long life' appeared in the *Daily Telegraph* on 12 February 1996 (This topic has since appeared elsewhere in the media.) Recent research does indicate that prayer for healing is effective, but this is something that those involved in the Church and her healing ministry have always recognised, and for which believers do not require scientific proof. Carefully conducted research can be helpful, however, in establishing for those who do doubt the value of prayer, that it is worthwhile and that prayers for others, particularly those which do not 'tell God what to do', but are open to his will, are heard. Such research may also affirm the value and expression of unselfish compassion and love, in the care for those needing healing.

From time to time evangelistic rallies are organized by Christian groups with publicity about 'healing miracles'. Some Christian doctors have interviewed those who were told when they attended such rallies they had been healed and failed to discover medical evidence for it. From this, and from other evidence we have seen, we seem to be moving towards the view that, whatever happened in the past, today God does not normally work through that which can be defined as miraculous.

And yet, despite the elusiveness of such evidence, Lourdes[5], Walsingham and other places continue to draw people unfailingly in the search for healing. Homes of healing, services of prayer for healing, healing campaigns and missions attract ordinary Christians and others, and the anecdotes of remarkable healing experiences abound. Few Christians would eschew medical help in their diseases and disorders, and yet more and more seek the ministry of the Church in specific ways. And they seem well able to draw clear conclusions about the part played in their personal healings through the Church's ministry of prayer, sacrament and spiritual gifts.

The 1958 report included a chapter on 'Evidence and Healing'. In it the Commission discussed in detail categories of evidence and accompanying investigations and concluded that, because miraculous healings were of a different order from cures effected by medicine, and because the causes and effects of healings after prayer are far too complex to be attributed solely to that ministry, evidence for such healings is of an entirely different order from medical evidence. 'Scientific testing can be a valuable corrective of rash claims that healing, ordinary or extraordinary, has occurred,' the Commission said, 'and it may bring to light natural healing virtues in religious rites; but it is idle for the Church, or anyone else, to appeal to science to prove the reality of supernatural power or the truth of a theology or metaphysic.'[6] They added, however, that 'there are valid reasons for believing in a different order (of healings)' – in other words, they did not dismiss completely the possibility that God might act directly to heal in response to prayer. 'The main strength of the testimony of God's healing action through his Church lies not in the occasional marvel but in the numerous cases where, though nothing medically surprising is noted, faith sees God acting through the ministry of grace as well as through medical means.'[7] In short, their answer is equivocal.

Searching the mystery

Hopes for and stories of healings remind us that in this ministry, as in other ministries, we are encountering the mystery of God's grace which is far beyond our understanding. We can only rejoice that through this ministry hearts and lives are changed and bodies and minds made whole. If people ask for evidence, then all we can do is point to the ongoing life and worship of the Church in the midst of creation and her witness to the risen Christ in this sinful and suffering world. The chief miracle remains the fully converted person filled with the shalom which is God's gift. What is clear, and even more difficult to verify, is that lives are so transformed that as a result of this ministry many are able to respond obediently to God whatever comes their way, including the facing of death itself.

So what are we to make of the anecdotal evidence? Let us return to the mystery of God's grace and reflect a little further. In Chapter 2 we said that Christ's healings must be seen within the context of his whole redeeming ministry, offered in obedience to the Father and in the power of the Holy Spirit. The healing ministry of Christ is a mystery within the greater mystery of that redeeming work.

The Incarnation shows that God respects the integrity of his creation. According to the well-known saying of Thomas Aquinas, his grace perfects nature and completes it. So it is erroneous to make a sharp distinction between the natural and the supernatural. If we do, we imply a dangerous division between what medical science achieves and what prayer for healing achieves. The Incarnation also shows that God works for total healing. When God became man in Jesus Christ, he took the whole of our humanity – body, mind and spirit – to himself, and his saving grace reaches everything about us, including our emotional responses to the care of others and our reaction to the environment as we experience it.[8]

Christ's sacrifice on the cross and the triumph of his resurrection extends far beyond the mediation of forgiveness of sin. He has taken sickness and sinful humanity through suffering and death and raised it up again into newness and wholeness of life. The cross shows that the only power Jesus works is that of self-giving love, and a Church in which healing can happen will be open to receive and to communicate that love.

And then it remains a hard fact that all our healings, however remarkable, are still only temporary. In our theology of the Church's healing ministry, therefore, we have to make a place for illnesses which are not healed and those which are terminal (see Chapter 8). So it is that a healing ministry which does not have the cross at its centre cannot be the ministry of Christ. Just as the Father took the prayer of the obedient Son in the garden of Gethsemane and used it in the mystery of our salvation, so God's purpose is not always achieved by taking us out of what threatens or hurts us, but sometimes by taking us through it. At the edge of this mystery we are halted, puzzled and maybe doubtful, but the Lord's words to Paul encourage us: 'My grace is sufficient for you, for my power is made perfect in weakness' (2 Corinthians 12.9).

Signs for the faithful

So we return to the biblical picture of Jesus' miracles being recognized for what they were by the community of faith, 'signs' of the kingdom. The same is true today. A miracle can only be seen with the eye of faith, just as the redeeming work of God in Jesus can only be accepted in faith. So it is possible for the believer to experience or witness an unexpected or rapid cure and assume that, if it had happened under clinical conditions, it would have been possible to explain it medically (or at least to explain it medically when science has advanced further).

But then our medical friends remind us that from time to time there are astonishing occurrences, remissions of tumours, sudden recovery of paralyses, cures of various physical disorders. When these are reported, it is commonplace for the medical attendants to express surprise and even wonder, but at the same time they are usually able to comment, quite truthfully, that such can be the way of this or that disorder.

Also in the world of scientific evidence, there is little doubt about the positive value of the placebo effect during double-blind trials, nor about the healing power of tender loving care (TLC). While it would be untrue to the New Testament simply to reduce the healing ministry to a placebo or an extension of TLC, we cannot just ignore their role in our spiritual ministrations. They are, after all, an integral part of the humanity which God has created, and who are we to deny that they have a role in the Lord's answer to our prayers? It should therefore come as no surprise that there are overlaps between the healing ministry and such empirical observations.

But to those who have prayed in faith for a cure and who experience it in ways that cause them to regard it as an answer to prayer, it will seem like a marvellous intervention by God. If it strengthens their faith and they want to call it a miracle, they have every right to do so.

So a healing miracle might be defined as an inexplicable cure which, seen with the eye of faith, itself builds up faith: *inexplicable* because at that time and in those circumstances it is beyond scientific explanation; *seen with the eye of faith* because without faith it can be explained away; *builds up faith* because it should result in giving glory to God (the effect of New Testament miracles).

219

Towards an answer

Theologians and others when discussing 'evidence' for healing have to be careful not to do what some investigators do: that is, extract the subject under investigation (the disease) from its milieu (the person) and, having investigated it rigorously, place it back in its position with either a positive or a negative result. The true scientist always conceptualizes the object of study. The human person likewise is too complex to be studied in parts. When dealing with the human being, created in the image of God, we are not dealing with any merely mysterious phenomenon, but rather with the divine mystery itself. Such phenomena are not readily amenable to objective, scientific study.

Christians assert that all human persons are in need of wholeness in Christ. This is not a 'scientific' statement but a theological one. The good news is that such wholeness is the free gift of God in Jesus Christ. This is the work of healing; it operates at all levels of the person, and much is too deep to plummet by logical criteria or statistical parameters. God heals, and he heals at all levels of our being. There are many who will testify to that fact. God heals through ordinary means assisted by the medical, nursing and other caring professions. We believe this to be undeniable. The empirical and scientific evidence for medical advance is always before us. Reports in medical journals about successful drugs or beneficial operations are all evidence about the working of God in his creation. Such advance in medical science, where it has treated humanity in accordance with God's purposes, in the last few decades has been in itself miraculous.

At the same time we wish to affirm that in whatever condition people find themselves, there is need for attention to their spiritual lives for the fullness of health. This is the experience of all those involved in the Church's ministry of healing, and it is also the experience of medical attendants who are willing to look beyond pathology to a more holistic view of their charges (as we have seen in Chapter 5).

We conclude, therefore, that it is practically impossible to provide scientific evidence to prove without question the effectiveness of the Church's healing ministry. As we have said, a Christian may claim to have experienced a miracle, and if the experience strengthened their faith, that claim should be treated with respect. But other Christians would be wise when they repeat the story to say something like, 'So-and-so *believed* it was a miracle.' And if the claimant declares that they are going to throw away their medicine as a result of their experience, they should be warned to consult their doctor first.

Yet even if God will not allow his works to be the subject of human investigation beyond what he wills to reveal, he continues to surprise us when we turn to him in faith. So although we answer the question posed at the beginning of this chapter negatively, yet we agree with an unnamed Christian surgeon who, when asked the same question, replied, 'I have learned that when the Spirit of God touches and penetrates the human spirit, there is no limit to the responses the body can make.'[9]

12

Questions People Ask about the Healing Ministry

Many people would like to know more about this ministry, and some have been misinformed. This chapter has been included to help clarify the answers to frequently asked questions and to provide reassurance and guidance based on the wider content of the report.

How much faith should I have to be healed?

The idea that healing is just a matter of faith is very misleading. It leads to cruel advice such as, 'You'll be healed if you have faith' (implying that if you're not healed it's your fault!). This is completely contrary to the teaching of the New Testament. The use of the term 'faith healing' is also misleading. That is why we don't use it in this report, preferring the phrase 'healing ministry'.

Certainly faith is important. But we must ask, faith in whom, or in what? It cannot be just faith in those who minister. Nor can it be faith in my conviction that 'I will be healed' (for that implies faith in one's own thoughts and feelings). The only faith needed is faith in the saving, healing grace which God revealed in Jesus Christ and which the Church is commissioned to proclaim and demonstrate in the power of the Holy Spirit.

But such faith need not necessarily be the patient's. It is true that in the gospels and Acts there are some instances of healing in response to the sick person's faith in Jesus' ability to heal; but there are other occasions when only the faith of the relatives or the friends is mentioned, and still others where no faith seems to be shown either by the one healed or by anyone else except Jesus. The one constant factor in the healing narratives is Jesus' complete trust in his heavenly Father. And similarly in Acts: the apostles' ministry of healing is dependent only on their trust in the risen Lord.

So if we don't feel we have much faith ourselves, that should not prevent us seeking prayer for healing. Certainly we need to trust that the Holy Spirit will work through those who minister to us conscientiously (as indeed we trust our doctor for his medical skills, which are also God-given). Beyond that we simply put ourselves into the hands of God with as much or as little faith as we have at that moment. He has revealed his love and his purposes for us in Jesus Christ, and his love and purposes remain whether we are healed as we hoped to be or not. And that is true, also, of those who minister to the sick. They may not feel they have much faith as they pray and perhaps lay on hands – but all that is required of them is that they prepare themselves for this ministry and trust God in what they are doing.

If God loves me, why does he allow me to suffer?

Christian thinkers have long pondered this question (see page 225f.), but in the end we have to admit that there is no answer to the mystery. Suffering is universal; this is the way the world is. We know that God does not deliberately inflict suffering on us like some vengeful deity. Nor does he stand aside from it. The Scriptures reveal that in his love for us he sent his Son to share our human life, and as man Jesus did not escape the experience of suffering and dying in agony on the cross. But Christ's resurrection meant his suffering had not been in vain. It had become the means through which he won salvation for us, so that faith in his cross – in all that he suffered – has become a central article in the Christian creed ('He suffered under Pontius Pilate, was crucified, died, and was buried. He descended to the dead. On the third day he rose again'). The New Testament teaches that our suffering, whatever form it takes, can be a means through which we are united with Christ in his redemptive work through the Holy Spirit and begin to taste his victory ourselves (Colossians 1.24; Philippians 3.10, etc.).

We certainly do not want to treat insensitively the effects of a prolonged and painful illness. However much faith and courage patients have, there are times when illnesses of this kind can drag them to the depths of despair. But we do want to affirm that many Christians have been able to look back on their suffering as a time when they were drawn close to the cross, and when they experienced God's blessing for themselves and for others in a new way. It is as if they have had a foretaste of what Paul meant in Romans 8.18: 'I consider that the sufferings of this present time are not worth comparing with the glory about to be revealed to us.'

I've been told that I'm suffering because I've sinned. Is that true?

Being unforgiven and/or unforgiving is always an unhealthy condition to be in. So when we are sick we should especially seek God's forgiveness and, if necessary, the forgiveness of others as well, besides being willing to forgive those who have wronged us. And we should also remember that a sense of guilt can be debilitating in all sorts of ways. Sometimes we need to forgive ourselves as well! But it is unkind even to hint to an individual that his or her particular sickness is the result of his or her personal sin. We are all subject to various ills and accidents which cannot reasonably be regarded as the results of, or as punishment for, our wrongdoing. Jesus had to refute his disciples' belief that the man was born blind because of his sin or his parents' (John 9.1-3).

Nevertheless, sinful attitudes and actions can contribute towards or cause much sickness and suffering, selfishness, abuse, carelessness or neglect on the part of the community, or of individuals. It is not difficult to add to the list of sins and see the consequences both to the sinner and to the one sinned against. In this sense, then, we can say there is often a general connection between suffering and sin. And we have to admit there may be occasions when some personal sin causes our sickness and blocks our healing.

Jesus pronounced the forgiveness of sin to the paralysed man before telling him to take up his bed and walk (Mark 2.1-12). If we persist in sins such as continuing in patterns of behaviour and self-neglect which we know undermine our health and happiness and that of others, excessive consumption, unforgiving attitudes, uncontrolled emotions and so on, without seeking God's grace to forgive us and to change us, we should not be surprised if these have physical, emotional and spiritual ill-effects on our lives. We note that in James 5.15,16 prayer for healing and the forgiveness of sins are closely linked, and that formal confession of sins to a priest can often lead to different kinds of healings.

Why do people suffer anyway?

Two early Fathers are the source of two traditions about this: Irenaeus (c.130–c.200) and Augustine (354–430). Here are brief and oversimplified outlines of them.

In the centuries when the story of creation in Genesis was regarded as historically true, the Augustinian tradition saw suffering as a direct consequence of human sin. God created a good and perfect world, and its present imperfections – including suffering – are the consequence of Adam's sin. In the last two centuries, however, as scientific evidence showed that suffering was experienced long before the appearance of the first human beings on this planet, some teachers have developed this tradition further by arguing that before the fall of humanity there was a cosmic rupture caused by the rebellion of Lucifer and his followers against the creator, and that this affected creation from its beginning. As a consequence the world became a place of pain and suffering, and this was the kind of world in which humanity evolved. Having the freedom to choose between good and evil, men and women tended to choose evil and in so doing increased the degree of suffering experienced in this life.

The strength of this tradition is that it reflects the biblical story of evil being present in creation from the beginning (e.g. the serpent was already in Paradise to tempt Eve) and that it preserves the truth that men and women have free will. Its weakness is that it relies on highly mytholo- gical images and language which many today find difficult to accept.

The Irenaean tradition sees the origin of evil in what might be called more evolutionary terms. According to this view, we are not to think of a primeval human fall from perfection. Rather, we are to understand that in God's purposes creation, with humanity at its centre, is moving towards fulfilment and perfection without having yet attained it. Adam and Eve are not completed creatures who fall away from perfection, but pilgrims created to move towards completion. Since they fall short of their goal, creation itself, being intimately bound up with them, must fall short of its goal, too.

Christ was sent to trace all the stages of Adam's experience and all the process of Adam's transgression, at each stage and in each act obeying where Adam had disobeyed. In Irenaeus' famous phrase, 'Christ became what we are that he might make us what he is'. It is therefore with, through and by Christ that the world is being drawn towards its consummation so that all things (in another Irenaean phrase taken from Ephesians 1.10) are 'recapitulated in him'.

The strength of this tradition is that it allows us to think of the world as being in the process of development and it fits in with God's mandate that human beings should multiply and subdue the earth. Creation was declared to be 'very good' (Genesis 1.31) because it suited God's purposes, not because it was perfect. It provides a suitable environment within which human beings could grow to realize their freedom – supremely the freedom to choose to respond to God's word and to cooperate with him in his purposes. But it also allows room for the theory that creation, not yet perfected, is a place of suffering, and that pain and suffering will remain the experience of humanity and the other living creatures until the world reaches the end for which God has destined it.

Although the Irenaean tradition certainly does not take us far into the mystery of suffering, it offers a sort of mythological backdrop to our geophysical and biological knowledge, which tells us that in the world there is a balance between the destructive and the creative. The sun that burns and destroys also gives life and promotes growth. The seasons that delight and feed us can also affect climatic conditions dangerously. Bacteria are a necessity for healthy life, but they can overpower and kill us. Certain forms of suffering can also act as a necessary warning to us so that we avoid greater pain. Creating, living, suffering and dying are woven together in the universe, and as creatures we are inescapably part of it.

The photograph on the cover of this report shows a young star, and superimposed on it is a dark cross. That was no trick photography; it was what the camera saw. Maybe it was just an optical illusion, but it is an amazing pictorial parable. Its message: even as new-born worlds rise, there is a cross at the centre of creation, the cross of Christ. And that cross is also at the centre of the mystery of suffering – vindicated in Christ's new resurrection life by the power of his Holy Spirit. The reason for a healing ministry at the heart of the gospel is the faith that, in spite of suffering, Christ's resurrection life can touch us now, often in unexpected ways. The great paradox is that so often human suffering brings out all that is good in people, and that if it were absent we might find ourselves in a world without selfless love, a place with an empty cross without resurrection.

Do I need to seek prayer for healing if I am being well cared for medically?

It used to be assumed – and perhaps still is in some quarters – that modern medicine is the fulfilment of the New Testament promises about healing, and that the healing work of the early Church was just a temporary dispensation before the arrival of scientific medicine and skilful nursing. We do not believe this assumption is justified. It ignores the fact that to be truly healed people need to know that God loves them and forgives them, and this profound spiritual need cannot be supplied by medicine. Counselling can, of course, go some way to help troubled people to find inner peace, but we can only hope for wholeness in the truest sense of that word through the grace of God's Holy Spirit. Besides, as we have seen in our discussion of the biblical meaning of salvation (see Chapter 2), there is no distinction in the New Testament between the healing of body, mind and spirit.

However, we should not forget that there has always been a close partnership between the Church and medicine and that, while the Church from time to time questions or opposes certain medical experiments and therapies (e.g. cloning, euthanasia), nevertheless the partnership has been a very fruitful one. Christian teaching on the goodness of God as creator, on the potential for healing within his creation and on the dignity and worth of each individual has encouraged many initiatives in the care and treatment of the sick. At the same time care and treatment using the latest scientific resources have led the Church's mission in many lands. Neither should we forget that Christian doctors and nurses are often involved in the Church's healing ministry today as members of prayer groups and informal advisors for them.

My mother says she's too old to receive a ministry for healing. What should I tell her?

Try to find out what is the real reason for her attitude. Some people don't believe in God and don't want to be prayed with; that attitude should be respected and the care offered them should be strictly practical. But is that your mother's reason? Is she is hesitant to ask others to do something for her because she feels she is giving them extra tasks? Has she inherited from the past the mistaken idea that this ministry is only for those who are dying? Does she believe this ministry depends on the amount of faith she has – and she doesn't think she has much? Some of the other answers in this chapter may help in discussing these things with her.

Then, more positively, you can remind her that the ministry of healing is essentially a ministry of prayer and that there's never a time in our lives when we don't need that! Tell her that those who act as ministers in praying with people – not only the clergy – regard it as a special privilege to be able to do this, and they would not have offered themselves for it if they had not had a strong sense that God was calling them. And, if she has never witnessed a service of prayer for healing, or seen anyone being prayed with, describe what happens and then leave her to think about it further. Perhaps you can give her a leaflet about the healing ministry.

Do you have to be ordained or have a special gift to practise the Church's ministry of healing?

Some would argue that since in James 5.14-16 it is the elders of the Church who were summoned to anoint the sick and pray for them, only those who are ordained should exercise this ministry. And indeed in the past it has usually been the clergy who have prayed formally with the sick, anointed them and laid hands on them. But since the ministry to the sick is essentially a ministry of prayer, there is nothing to prevent any Christian praying for a sick person on an appropriate occasion. In many homes a parent prays for a sick child or relative, and friends pray for one another.

When the ministry to the sick takes place publicly, as in a church service, however, it is necessary to have safeguards against misunderstandings and abuse (as with any ministry). That is why the ministry of healing should be exercised under the supervision of the pastoral leadership of the congregation (which is how we apply the practice in James 5.14-16 today). And it is also desirable that those who pray with others should have been trained to do this.

Over a period of time it may become clear that certain individuals are particularly gifted in praying for people and counselling them, and it may be right for such individuals to have further training for the benefit of the congregation's ministry. We understand this to be an example of a special 'gift of healing' which Paul includes in his list of charismata in 1 Corinthians 12.8-10. A few of them may be led by God into a wider, personal ministry. If they are, they should exercise it with the clergy or some other Christian group, who can assist them in discerning that their programme is a 'manifestation of the Spirit for the common good' (1 Corinthians 12.7).

In the discipline of the Church of England the anointing of the sick is normally administered by the clergy. In some dioceses pure olive oil is blessed by the bishop in Holy Week for use on such occasions. The regulations about this can be found in Canon B 37 in diocesan regulations.

Should we expect a miraculous healing when we receive ministry for an illness?

The word 'miracle' has been used so injudiciously in recent years that we advise it be avoided in reference to any healing except when such a manifestation can be justified scientifically. A sudden and unexpected healing may seem miraculous in the experience of the one who receives it (and therefore they may understandably refer to it as 'a miracle'), but it is extremely difficult to prove medically that sudden and unexpected cures do not have some natural explanation at present unknown to science. We have to be open to the possibility that the reason for such a healing may one day be discovered. We also need to remember that some patients enjoy remissions from serious diseases, and that the use of a placebo in therapy shows that other patients are inexplicably healed without drugs.

Nevertheless, we believe that those who act as ministers in praying for healing and those who receive their ministry should be open to the possibility of God's gracious surprises. For in the ministry of healing we invite

God to enter into a new and dynamic relationship with his creation in which he respects it, claims it and restores it, making it whole. We believe that the Incarnation reveals that God works in and through our humanity, neither exclusively 'naturally' nor exclusively 'supernaturally', but by enabling things to happen which extend and enhance but do not contradict the healing processes which he has built into it from the beginning. Furthermore, this prayer is offered 'in the name of Jesus Christ' with the total healing of the cross, resurrection, ascension, Pentecost and the coming of the kingdom in view, and there is no limit to what God might do through the power of the Holy Spirit in response.

So although none of the doctors among us could recall any healing in response to prayer which matched the spontaneous miracles of the New Testament, this does not mean we do not believe the Lord could still so act in this way if he wished. We have heard stories of such healings from friends who have ministered in Africa, South America and the Asian subcontinent as well as in the West; and even allowing for the human tendency to embroider tales in the telling, we still believe remarkable healings are experienced when Christians pray.

My friend thinks he is demonically oppressed, but his vicar tells him that's impossible. What should I advise him to do?

Evil spirits figure prominently in the healing narratives of the New Testament (e.g. Mark 1.21-28, 32-34; 3.10-12), but today many Christians would argue that symptoms which were then attributed to evil spirits would now be treated as having a psychological cause and dealt with by drugs, psychiatry, counselling, etc.

Some of them would go further and claim that the biblical references to the devil and his minions can be dismissed as examples of how a primitive society tried to explain the problem of evil by ascribing it to malevolent spiritual forces outside human control. Consequently the gospels, written in the first century AD, speak of Jesus Christ's authority over these spiritual forces. This was the religious and cultural milieu into which Jesus was born and which he accepted as a human being of that era. People sharing this point of view regard the concept of a spiritual warfare, so deeply embedded in Christian teaching, as a hangover from this, enshrined in the Bible. They urge us to abandon such outdated concepts and recognize that, if we knew all the evidence, everything that is evil can be traced ultimately to natural causes. For them, therefore, there is no such thing as being 'demonically oppressed'.

This view is not accepted by other Christians. Even those who do not accept the New Testament understanding of healings as just outlined still believe that Jesus' teaching on evil and his personal spiritual battle against Satan cannot be explained away just to satisfy the assumptions of a science-dominated world-view. Jesus included in the Lord's Prayer the words, 'Deliver us from evil', and in the experience of millions of his followers over the centuries the spiritual battle is very real indeed. Not all evil can be attributed to personal upbringing, psychological make-up, genetic programming, social pressures or other natural causes. For these Christians the words 'Satan', 'the devil' and 'demons' may have a primitive mythological flavour about them. However, they represent the reality of evil influences which affect the lives of people to varying degrees – influences which often seem so mysteriously aimed at particular individuals, families, groups and nations that the adjective 'personal' is appropriate in describing them (e.g. in the phrase 'a personal devil'). The appropriate ministry for people troubled by such evil influences is prayer for deliverance or formal exorcism in acute cases. We have discussed these ministries in Chapter 9.

Your friend should be advised that it is extremely unusual for anyone to recognize demonic oppression in themselves and that he should first seek the advice of his medical practitioner, who may suggest counselling or perhaps psychiatric treatment. However, if he follows the doctor's advice for a while and is still troubled, he should seek spiritual help. Then, if the vicar (for whatever reason) is unable or unwilling to minister to him, he should ask the vicar if he can make an appointment to see the bishop's advisor for the healing ministry (or write to the bishop himself).

Is it realistic to expect God to give us perfect health in this world?

Perfect health is as unlikely as perfect living, but that doesn't mean we should not expect God to give us his healing grace when it is his will to do so. The word 'health' was once used generally to denote the normal working of the body as a living, physical organism with respiratory, motor, digestive and other functions. A 'health check' is usually limited in that way. But the word is etymologically connected with the word 'whole', and this is included in a cluster of Old Testament and New Testament words which bring together a number of concepts showing that health is God's will for his people and his creation. Such health is his gift. It is about being a whole person in every way, it is about right relationships between oneself, God, other people and the environment, and it is measured by the standard of Jesus Christ.[1] If you are familiar with the 1662 *Book of Common Prayer* you will know that in the general confession at Morning and Evening Prayer we acknowledge our sinfulness by saying 'there is no health in us'.

Is there such a thing as faith healing?

We would advise against using that term; it is liable to give rise to dangerous misconceptions. Many who use this phrase mean that healing is achieved either through belief in the healer's personal powers, in some healing power within, in healing by ambiguous energy source, or simply that the sufferer is going to be healed because of something heard or read. A more subtle error is believing that God has already determined that recovery from a particular disease will happen – that is, when such a belief depends solely on human instincts and not on any authentic word from the Lord. Faith in God is what is traditionally known as a theological virtue necessary to salvation (which is health in the fullest sense of the word), but we cannot dogmatize about the casual connection between personal faith and recovery from particular bodily ailments.

Well, then, what about the phrase 'spiritual healing'?

When carefully used within the Christian community this phrase is intended to emphasize the belief that restoration to health is the work of the Holy Spirit, but the phrase is too imprecise to be used today for the Church's ministry. The words 'spirit' and 'spiritual' are used in all kinds of contexts, often far removed from what is understood when Christians use them ('spirit world', 'spirit zone', etc.). It is commonly used to denote spiritualist healing.

Can anyone go to a healing service?

Yes, of course, but they ought to be warned that although the phrase 'healing service' is often used in conversation and notices, it can be very misleading. For one thing, it might suggest to them that attendance at such a service might earn them a healing for being there! For another, every act of worship ought to be a 'healing service' for those who participate in it, even if it is only that they leave the church 'feeling better for having been'. Where the Word of God is proclaimed and a congregation responds in confession, intercession, praise and sacrament, there is an encounter with the healing Christ. That is why we prefer the more accurate if slightly more long-winded title of 'a service with prayer for healing'. It would indicate that what we are about is seeking God's mercy and grace for healing – and being willing to accept in faith whatever answer we receive as a result of that prayer.

Isn't the healing ministry just a placebo?

A placebo is a very useful device for testing the effectiveness of new drugs (or, in certain extreme cases, for satisfying a patient who demands an unnecessary drug from the doctor). It is possible that some regard the healing ministry a similar kind of device. But behind the question is a bigger one, namely, does God answer prayer? If we have no faith that he does, then we are treating this ministry the same as a harmless pill. And, like a placebo, it might help some to feel better and so, at this level, assist in their healing.

Yet such an attitude is ultimately dishonouring to God. The healing ministry, as we have said often in this report, is fundamentally a ministry of prayer, and there is much in the Scriptures and in the experience of Christians over the centuries to encourage us to pray in Jesus' name for our needs and for the needs of others, and then to trust that God will answer our prayer in his time and in his way.

Do I have to be seriously ill before I ask for the healing ministry?

This idea seems to have stemmed from the former practice of the Roman Catholic Church, when confession, anointing and Holy Communion were given to persons who were dangerously ill and thought to be dying – hence its title, the 'last rites'. What had originated in the early Church as a ministry of healing changed over the centuries to become a ministry to the dying, because many had little hope of healing in ages when life expectancy was short and mortality rates were high, especially among children. In this century, however, more enlightened Roman Catholic theologians and priests have struggled to recover the proper use of this ministry, and the Second Vatican Council (1962–5) affirmed their efforts by saying it 'is not a sacrament for those only who are at the point of death' (Constitution on the Church, c. 73). The negative expression of this statement reflects the extreme caution with which the Council inaugurated change, and Roman Catholic priests and others have seized the opportunity to offer this ministry to those who are just ill and feel in need of prayer for support and healing.

This is the Anglican understanding of the ministry of healing. At what stage in an illness or a period of mental and emotional trouble we should seek that ministry depends a good deal on what we feel the Lord is leading us to do and how far that is confirmed by our parish priest and/or by those with pastoral responsibilities in the parish. In very general terms, for a minor ailment or trouble the prayer of a couple of friends may be sufficient. If it is something which persists and affects the way we live and pray, then it may be appropriate either to go to a service of prayer for healing or to seek prayer (perhaps with the laying on of hands) from the parish priest or others. Many priests follow the traditional custom of reserving an anointing for time of crisis, such as the diagnosis of a life-threatening disease or admission to hospital for an operation.

Can anointing be administered often?

The Church of England gives no official guidance on this matter, leaving it to the discretion of the clergy. We advise that it is appropriate on the kind of critical occasions such as those just mentioned. Since anointing by the elders is linked with a confession of sins in James 5, anointing is normally preceded by an act of penitence in which the person examines their conscience and makes an act of confession. This can be done by using a form of the general confession, but if there are things on their conscience they may be helped greatly by making their confession to a priest. They are then anointed using an authorized liturgy and, if they can, receive Communion afterwards. If the critical condition persists, it may be appropriate for them to be anointed regularly at appropriate intervals.

13

Healing Services
in the Church of England

Since the 1958 report was published there has been progress in that
more parishes now integrate the healing ministry into their regular
programme. Practices vary, some churches holding separate 'healing
services' whilst others incorporate opportunities for ministry in their
regular services. This chapter looks at some of the forms and varieties
of ministry in use and considers the wider liturgical context, together
with some practical issues arising from the exercise of ministry and
prayer for healing in public worship. Finally, it notes the new services
for the ministry of healing in the Church of England.

The 1958 report declared that, as a result of the replies it had to its
questionnaire from about 100 priests in 21 dioceses, 'the considerable
development in the Church's ministry of healing in recent years has given
rise to a variety of practices. In the absence of clear guidance from the
Church the clergy have had to work as they thought best in this sphere.'
The Commission recognized that this was understandable given the fact
that different situations required different pastoral methods. But then it
added a note of caution: 'Clearly, however, certain more recent developments pose a number of urgent and important questions both to the
Church and to the medical profession, and this is specially true of the
practice of conducting healing services and demonstrations.'[1]

It noted that the healing ministry had spread in three ways:

❖ *Intercessory groups* – a group of instructed persons who met regularly in a parish, hospital or religious house to pray for the sick. The Commission said that some of the priests who had answered the questionnaire had stressed the importance of such groups, and strongly commended them.

❖ *Private healing services* took place in a home or a hospital. The distinctive features about these were that they were not advertised, that the sick could be prepared for the service beforehand, and that those who attended would be known personally to the priest.

❖ *Public healing services,* on the other hand, were open to all and ministry was offered to any who attended, usually without any private preparation, and who may or may not be known to the priest personally. The Commission thought such public healing services were very few and far between, and they saw dangers in them. They had listened to claims that such services demonstrated the Lord's love for suffering people and had an evangelistic value, but they felt the disadvantages far outweighed these. Lack of preparation, misunderstandings, unjustified claims, and emotionalism leading to subsequent disappointment caused the Commission to advise parish priests to treat these services with caution. 'Mass demonstrations as some healers organise have no equivalent in Church of England practice.'

However, the Commission was not entirely negative. It recommended that the Church's healing ministry should be closely related to the parish's normal worship and pastoral work and that the priest should always conduct services himself. Where possible the celebration of Holy Communion with the laying on of hands and anointing should take place in the church building: 'The objectivity of the Church's worship in Holy Communion is . . . a salutary corrective to the subjective and emotional tone which can easily become dominant in healing services.'[2] Individuals who received ministry should be prepared beforehand, doctors should be informed, especially where an illness involved emotional and psychological problems, adverts in the secular press were undesirable, and healing services should not be arranged without the bishop's permission.

As we have shown in the third chapter of this report, the three categories identified by the report still exist in parishes today, but with greater numerical variation. Intercessory groups – prayer groups as we now call them – are much more common, though healing may be only part of their agenda. Private healing services of the type the Commission described are less common, unless we include those organized in conferences and homes of healing. But the Commission's caution about public healing services no longer prevails in many parishes. Public services of prayer for healing are much more numerous than they were 40 years ago, though their availability across the country is patchy. In urban and suburban deaneries there are often two or three parishes which organize them regularly, but that is not so in all deaneries in predominantly rural areas.

One of the main reasons for this increase is the influence of the charismatic renewal. Nowadays more lay persons as well as clergy are familiar with and seek to exercise the gifts of the Holy Spirit, and trained 'ministry teams' of lay persons who have a special concern for the sick are common in some churches where regular healing services are held. Indeed, such teams are an essential in such services, not only for sharing with the clergy in prayer but also in the pastoral follow-up. Furthermore, prayer for healing is offered at meetings and conferences almost as a matter of course. The popular Alpha and Emmaus courses include sessions on healing, bringing to many the awareness that God still heals today. All this has created a climate in the Church where there is a higher profile and acceptance of the ministry of healing.

This ministry now encompasses a wider range of possibilities on offer than was the case in 1958. In this chapter we shall consider that ministry in relation to the overall worship of the parish church. Appendix 1 on good practice in the healing ministry applies in the examples we list below, so we will not repeat the advice and the cautions we have given there.

Ministry outside public worship

Small prayer groups, mentioned and commended in the 1958 report, are more common nowadays in parishes of all traditions. Numbers in them vary from two or three to nine or ten. At their meetings members usually pray for one another informally, though this can occasionally lead to more formal ministry and some use of counselling skills. It takes place mostly outside of the liturgical context, in home and hospital visiting, or perhaps by appointment in church rooms or at the parsonage.

This small group ministry offers many opportunities for trained lay persons or formally appointed pastoral assistants to use their gifts. There are also opportunities for more extended prayer ministry to individuals. These range from sessions for the 'healing of memories' and prayer counselling to formal counselling with qualified persons. Although this kind of ministry usually relies on spontaneous prayer, we commend the texts provided in the liturgical rites as outlines or templates for it. There is much to be said for ending a time of spontaneous prayer with an appropriate collect and the Lord's Prayer.

The suspicion of spontaneous prayer, which was a characteristic of many Anglicans at one time, has practically disappeared. The liturgical revisions of recent decades have made provision for creative forms of prayer within public worship, especially during the intercessions. While this flexibility and freedom is necessary in small group ministries, nevertheless formal liturgical prayers provide valuable models for those who pray spontaneously. Their Trinitarian structure and their biblical foundations and imagery offer lessons for all kinds of spontaneous prayers of intercession, penitence, thanksgiving and praise. The Holy Spirit is not bound by such forms, of course, but often we can be more discerning of him if we take note of how he has inspired those whose prayers have helped previous generations.

Larger informal prayer groups consisting of, say, ten or more can often be helped by the use of more formal prayers. The bigger the group, the more difficult it is for everyone present to pray spontaneously. A more corporate participation is achieved through the shorter forms of the daily office, such as in *Celebrating Common Prayer*. The shorter versions of Morning and Evening Prayer introduced Anglicans in the experimental years of the *Alternative Services* to the value of psalm, a canticle, a Scripture reading and one or two formal prayers as a fitting framework for a period of intercession leading to ministry to individuals.

In some parishes prayer meetings such as these are supplemented by the provision of prayer chains in which intercessors are mobilized by phone calls and emails. 'Requests for prayer' boards are now found in churches and cathedrals. But an individual's confidentiality and privacy have to be respected. There are occasions when it is better to pray for certain persons without mentioning their name or the nature of their illness.

Like the 1958 report, we strongly commend groups of this kind both for the individuals who are blessed by them and also for the prayer support they give to public forms of the healing ministry. Such groups incidentally provide valuable experience for those who are being trained to take part in this ministry; in them they can learn from their mistakes in ministering to one another without causing much anxiety! Through these larger prayer groups the injunction of James 5.13-16 is now probably closer to the experience of many Anglicans than it has ever been before, and they are often proactive in prayer for and with individuals.

After-service ministry

An increasing number of churches make arrangements for individuals to be prayed with after a service, in a side chapel or other less public part of the church. In most cases this is staffed by a trained team, two or more members of which will be on duty week by week, their names joining those of the sidesmen and the servers on the rota. Quite often the priest will be otherwise occupied at this time, though he or she can be called in if necessary.

This after-service ministry is not usually suitable for serious counselling. Rather, it provides an opportunity for the 'Christian Listening' promoted by bodies such as the Acorn Christian Healing Trust. It involves a friendly ear and sensitive prayer which affirms the person and helps them to clarify what they need and to gain a perception of how they might deal with it. The session is not usually very long. When it seems advisable, the recipient might be encouraged to arrange for a longer period of ministry, or to consider referral to an accredited counsellor.

In some parishes the after-service session will be based on a prayer ministry of the kind we have described on p. 241. It is similar to the listening ministry but more time is spent on praying about what has been said and invoking the guidance and healing of the Holy Spirit into the life of the recipient and their situation. In most cases those who minister will ask if they can lay hands on the person while they pray, and this is usually acceptable, though occasionally someone will say they prefer not to be touched.

Ministry within regular worship

A variant on the above is the provision at some point in the service of an opportunity to receive prayer ministry with the laying on of hands (and in some churches, anointing). In most cases this will involve lay people as well as the clergy, but this will be affected by the nature of the service, the timing of ministry and the geography of the church. So in a small congregation at, say, a weekday celebration of the Eucharist, the priest might be the only suitable minister. He or she would lay hands on any who wished to receive this before the service, after communion, or at the end of the service.

With a larger congregation, a more appropriate pattern is for the ministry to be administered by members of a ministry team at the communion rails following the intercessions, or in a side chapel during the continuing administration of Holy Communion. The frequency of such ministry varies according to the needs and expectations of the parish. In a few churches, it is offered at every act of worship; in some, it is offered weekly, at the Sunday service or a midweek service; in others it is available once a month at a particular service, on Sunday or a weekday. Within a Eucharist, the ministry is usually organized after the Communion. Liturgically it is perhaps more fitting before the Communion (like the ministry to individuals in a baptism, confirmation and marriage within the Eucharist), but it is usually more convenient after the recipients have received the sacrament.

A further variant comprises those parishes where there is a service in which healing ministry is very much the main focus, probably once a month (either on a Sunday evening, or during the week). These are the circumstances for which the liturgies authorized by the Church of England are provided.

Although the 1958 report was cautious about such services, many Anglicans have now had enough experience of them to avoid many of the dangers and mistakes associated with the larger rallies. The benefit of them is threefold:

❖   there can be some specific teaching on Christian healing;

❖   more adequate preparation is possible;

❖   pastoral follow-up can also be more easily dealt with.

In the first chapter we mentioned the services passed by the Convocations of Canterbury and York in the 1930s for use in the parishes. The 1958 report printed a form of service for use in the sick room which followed the pattern just outlined. It included prayers for the laying on of hands and anointing taken from the 1549 *Prayer Book of Edward VI*. It also expressed the hope that the service would be a useful resource if and when the Liturgical Commission revised the Church's services. The 1958 Lambeth Conference recommended that the Provinces of the Anglican Communion should revise their prayer books so that a service of 'ministry to the sick' be included together with forms for the laying on of hands, anointing, confession and absolution, and a commendation of the dying.[3]

In spite of these hopes and recommendations, it was many years before the Church of England got round to the task. The period of liturgical experimentation before the authorization of *The Alternative Service Book 1980* was lengthy, and it was not until 1983 that the ASB *Ministry to the Sick* was published. It followed the recommendations of the 1958 Lambeth Conference in providing forms for home Communion, and a commendation at the time of death, together with prayers and readings. It also gave forms for the laying on of hands and anointing. The publication of *Patterns for Worship* in 1995 provided another service for healing, and this has been issued in leaflet form.

Further expressions of pastoral need led to the commendation by the House of Bishops of forms of service and prayers in *Ministry at the Time of Death* in 1991. This provision makes a clear distinction between the normal expectation of prayer for healing as resulting in some blessing of body, mind and spirit, and the particular type of ministry that is appropriate in preparing someone for a 'good death'.

It is difficult to assess how far the ASB *Ministry to the Sick* has been used. Those who have been used to devising their own services probably ignore it, while those who are trying to introduce a healing service in their parish do not always realize that it can be used flexibly like other Alternative Services.

Liturgical structure

It might be worthwhile pausing here and examining the traditional structure of these and other liturgical rites. This structure goes through a series of movements (to borrow an analogy from the world of music) between two major themes – the proclamation of the word of God and the response by the congregation in faith to that word. This structure is used in any liturgy involving a sacramental act – baptism, confirmation, marriage, ministry to the sick – with or without Holy Communion – as well as the Eucharist itself. The movements are as follows.

The Preparation or Gathering: the congregation assemble with prayers and songs which express their joy at being together and their faith that God is present with them.

The Reception of the Word: the Bible reading(s) leading into a sermon and other contributions such as an interview or personal testimony. This movement is to encourage the congregation and those who are to receive ministry to listen to God and to prepare themselves to submit to God's purposes for them. The readings need not always be selected from one of the healing stories; equally suitable are passages revealing God's love for and care of his people.

The Act of Penitence: confession of sin and the assurance of God's forgiveness are a vital part of the healing ministry. This takes place before the word or immediately before the ministry.

The Intercessions: these can start for those who suffer in the world and the nation and then turn to those who are sick in the parish, especially members of the congregation and their relatives. Sometimes the congregation is invited to call out names.

The Healing Ministry: organized so that individuals are prayed over with the laying on of hands and perhaps anointing in the most convenient way, while the rest of the congregation continue in prayer for them.

The Dismissal: a prayer of thanksgiving, an act of praise and the final blessing and dismissal. This helps both the congregation and those who have received ministry to depart in a spirit of faith and hope in God.

Not everyone seeking prayer for healing wants to do it publicly. For them there should be opportunities for private ministry. But for many, public healing services help to demonstrate that this ministry is a central and normal part of the Church's life, and it is also recognized to have an evangelistic impact, as some of those who gave evidence for the 1958 report indicated. 'Healing and Mission' is a phrase much heard these days (though the majority of Anglicans want to avoid the kind of hype that accompanies certain much-publicized rallies).

Ministry in other contexts

A number of cathedrals now hold healing services on a quarterly or annual basis, sometimes with seminars earlier in the day. Frequently a distinguished preacher is invited. Ministry is made available to all who present themselves. These services are a valuable affirmation from the heart of a diocese of the acceptability of healing ministry, and bring it to the attention of people on the fringes of the Church, who might be more challenged or helped by what is seen to be 'safe and respectable'. Some welcome the relative anonymity of such an event. If the bishop can take part, this is helpful and meets the recommendation of the 1988 Lambeth Conference.

On the other hand, there is the danger that since the people attending may be known to nobody present, their needs cannot be dealt with in the context of normal pastoral care. This can be a problem, particularly if emotional wounds are stirred and left unresolved, or if there is confusion about what can be expected. People with psychological problems like depression may be discouraged if 'nothing happens' after their receiving ministry. Similarly large charismatic renewal events at which ministry is available call for careful management so that the more vulnerable participants are not left unsupported after being prayed with.

We note that Spring Harvest, New Wine and similar meetings make the healing ministry available to a growing number of people, especially young people, who do not otherwise frequent such services.

While we agree with the 1958 report that 'healing rally' events are not an integral part of the Anglican scene, we should note that they are, however, attended by many Anglicans who may need to be warned that, while beneficial to some, these rallies can also be manipulative and unhealthily emotional.

A very different context for ministry is the healing retreat available in some centres, conferences and retreat houses. If led by experienced Christians, they can be very helpful, especially to those who come from parishes where the healing ministry is not established. Pilgrimage centres like Walsingham also offer healing services.

Visitation of the sick

The 1958 report contained a whole section on this subject, much of which is still valuable, including its assertion that the priest ministers with confidence in the name of Christ, as a representative of the Church, and 'ordained of God for this very thing'. This is a reminder that strictly speaking no parish is ever without a healing ministry, for in one way or another, the sick are visited at home or in hospital, prayed for and offered the sacraments. This is a corrective for the impression that is sometimes given that the ministry is absent if a church does not have public services for healing.

The Book of Common Prayer (BCP) 'Order for the Visitation of the Sick' regards sickness as 'the chastisement of the Lord' and 'our heavenly Father's correction'. The primary purpose of the service is that the sick person be moved to repentance and to greater trust in God's mercy. These are not unworthy objectives, but the service is virtually obsolete. The 1928 Prayer Book provided a wider selection of prayers for the sick and, as we have already noted, various other services have appeared since. There are also many private collections of prayers. Some of these are used in sick visiting, but usually it is informal; if any liturgy is involved it is most likely to be a home Communion.

However, these older rites remind us that there is a proper place for repentance in healing services: guilt and resentment can affect our emotional and physical health. Care should be taken, of course, not to give the impression that ill health is caused by personal sin, still less that it is a divine punishment. Rather, the rites should affirm the truth that God's forgiveness is an essential element in his healing grace, and that we all need 'healing' from sin whether we are ill or not. That is why the rites for the ministry of reconciliation are in the true sense always 'healing services'.

The ministry of reconciliation

One of the most significant ways in which we can talk of the presence of healing ministry in every church is through the availability of the assurance of forgiveness. The BCP's 'comfortable words' implanted in the consciousness of generations of Anglicans the good news that 'if any man sin, we have an advocate with the Father, Jesus Christ the righteous, and he is the propitiation for our sins' (1 John 2.1).

The BCP 'Visitation of the Sick' provides for confession of sins to the priest, who is to absolve the penitent with the words:

> Our Lord Jesus Christ, who hath left power to his Church to absolve all sinners who truly repent and believe in him, of his great mercy forgive thee thine offences: And by his authority committed to me, I absolve thee from all thy sins, In the Name of the Father, and of the Son, and of the Holy Ghost. Amen.

These words are often used in those churches where confessions are heard, together with one or two other prayers and a dismissal such as: 'Go in peace and sin no more; the Lord has put away your sins. And pray for me, a sinner too.'

A more updated form is provided in *Lent, Holy Week and Easter* (1984):

> God, the Father of all mercies,
> through his Son Jesus Christ
> forgives all who truly repent and believe in him:
> by the ministry of reconciliation
> which Christ has committed to his Church,
> and in the power of the Spirit,
> I declare that you are absolved from your sins,
> in the name of the Father, and of the Son, and of the Holy Spirit.

As that formula indicates, sacramental confession is more usually (and more accurately) called 'the ministry of reconciliation' these days. Although practised quietly and informally in some places in the past, teaching about it influenced by the Oxford Movement aroused great controversies, especially the wording of the absolution formula. However, since the Second World War it has come to be recognized as being of great value in appropriate cases. In churches where it is practised, the set-up nowadays is usually more informal; the priest hearing the confession sometimes concludes the little rite by laying hands on the penitent's head and praying for a fresh infilling of the Holy Spirit.

The healing value of the assurance of forgiveness, which is at the heart of the gospel, should not be underestimated. Our culture does not take sin seriously. But separation from God is a 'sickness unto death'. To be released from the power of sin is healing. Jesus emphasized his right to offer forgiveness, and expected his disciples to forgive others – both in the sense of proclaiming forgiveness, but also in the more difficult area of personally seeking reconciliation. Yet balance is essential. For while we need to proclaim the need for forgiveness, people must not feel 'rubbished'. A healing church affirms people's essential value, for they are made in the image of God, and they are those for whom Christ suffered and died. Nevertheless, it is hoped that future liturgical developments in the area of reconciliation will recognize and emphasize the healing potential of ministering Christ's forgiveness.

The penitential sections in church services emphasise the corporate need for forgiveness and reconciliation, and the simple gesture of sharing the peace underscores it (particularly when an individual wonders why he or she tries to avoid giving it to a certain person in the congregation!).

Services of reconciliation proposed in schemes of reunion convey the same message: 'healing the wounds in the Body of Christ'.

Laying on of hands

The laying on of hands is a sign of the Church's solidarity with a person in praying for the healing power of Christ. But for those unfamiliar with it some explanation is helpful. The practice has biblical roots, though its function there is mostly the 'ordination' of a successor or the consecration of an animal for sacrifice. It functions as a form of blessing, and this can be appropriate in understanding a prayer for healing. But it needs to be clearly distinguished from so-called 'therapeutic touch' as exercised in some forms of complementary medicine and alternative therapies. It is an expression of God's abundant love and desire to bless.

The normal form is for one of those ministering to lay hands on the head or shoulder of the recipient. In practice it is best to place the hands on either side of the head: one over the forehead and the other at the back. This is more comfortable and reassuring for the recipient than pressure from the top by more than one. Others who are ministering can touch the shoulders. Care needs to be exercised; people do not want to be over-whelmed by insensitive enthusiasts! Inappropriate physical contacts must be strictly avoided.

In a healing service the recipient may want to mention what the problem is, and this can be incorporated into a spontaneous prayer, but care should be taken not to allow the moment to develop into a mini-listening session. Otherwise it may be better to use formal words such as those in the 1983 service (*Ministry to the Sick*):

> In the name of our Lord Jesus Christ,
>
> who laid hands on the sick that they might be healed,
>
> I lay my hands upon you, N.
>
> May almighty God, Father, Son and Holy Spirit,
>
> make you whole in body, mind and spirit,
>
> give you light and peace and keep you in life eternal. Amen.

The new healing service (*Common Worship*) uses these words:

> In the name of God and trusting in his might alone,
>
> receive Christ's healing touch to make you whole.
>
> May Christ bring you wholeness of body, mind and spirit,
>
> deliver you from every evil,
>
> and give you his peace. Amen.

In small group situations spontaneous prayer is nearly always used. But not all such prayer needs be vocal; laying on hands for a few moments with inner attention to God can be very appropriate.

The phenomenon known as 'resting' (or, less felicitously, 'being slain') 'in the Spirit' is encountered in some meetings, when a recipient slips to the ground during the laying on of hands, and remains there for a while.

Some may weep, or burst out laughing or react in other unexpected ways. Although in recent years these phenomena have been associated with the so-called 'Toronto Blessing', they have in fact been a feature of religious revivals in different centuries, as well as in the early days of the charismatic renewal. It is difficult to determine the reasons – or, more likely, different reasons – for them. But they need not cause undue concern, provided neither the recipient or others are hurt or alarmed. For many the experience has been an occasion of deep refreshing, with a new sense of love; and a few claim they were healed as a result.

Anointing

This, too, is an ancient and biblically attested practice of blessing and empowerment. The kings of Israel were anointed and so the act became a sign of an outpouring of divine blessing and the Spirit of the Lord. Jesus in the sermon at Nazareth took the text of Isaiah 61.1,2, speaking of the year of the Lord's favour, to introduce himself as the Lord's Messiah, the anointed Servant (Luke 4.18f). The disciples sent out by Jesus used oil (Mark 6.13) and the epistle of James mentions the use of oil in prayer for healing, perhaps reflecting the medical practice described in the parable of the Good Samaritan.

The early Church used oil in a number of ceremonies including the rites of Christian initiation as well as in healing and exorcism. In time in the Western Church the sacrament of unction came to be largely associated with preparation for death, until a renaissance of its role in healing in the earlier part of this century and in subsequent liturgical reform. The post-Second Vatican Council Roman Catholic Ritual places it firmly back in its place as a sacrament of wholeness. This is also apparent in the order in the ASB *Ministry to the Sick*.

The episcopal blessing of oil for the anointing of the sick is frequently observed in Holy Week. As there is still no official rite for this in the Church of England, many Anglican bishops use the Roman Catholic order, with its impressive prayer over this particular oil:

> Send the power of your Holy Spirit, the Consoler, into this precious oil,
> this soothing ointment, this rich gift, this fruit of the earth.

Bless this oil and sanctify it for our use.

Make this oil a remedy for all who are anointed with it;

heal them in body, in soul and in spirit

and deliver them from every affliction.

The new Church of England services for healing and wholeness include this prayer for the president when oil is to be used:

By the power of your Spirit may your blessing rest

on those who are anointed with this oil in your Name;

may they be made whole in body and spirit.

Traditionally, oil is sacramental and reserved to priests. This is the position implied in Canon B 37 'Of the Ministry to the Sick'. The Roman Ritual takes the same stance, but allows oil to be blessed by a priest for his own use: 'Lord, bless this oil and bless our sick brother (sister) whom we will anoint with it.'

There are a variety of forms of words that can be used at the imposition of oil, among them those of the 1983 service:

N, I anoint you with oil

in the name of our Lord Jesus Christ.

May our heavenly Father make you whole in body and mind,

and grant you the inward anointing of his Holy Spirit,

the Spirit of strength and joy and peace. Amen.

The revised service provides these words:

N, I anoint you in the name of God who gives you life.

Receive Christ's forgiveness, his healing and his love.

May the Father of our Lord Jesus Christ

grant you the riches of his grace,

his wholeness and his peace. Amen.

The Roman Catholic rite for the anointing of the sick allows for the anointing to be administered firstly to the forehead, and then to the palms of the hands.

Other traditions

Many other denominations hold services of prayer for healing. The Church of Scotland, the Baptist Union, the United Reformed Church and the Methodist Church have all in recent years provided services with ministry through the laying on of hands (and in the case of the Methodist Church anointing with oil). Such services in the Roman Catholic Church usually take the form of special Masses with ministry given privately. It is valuable for us to listen to and learn from the liturgies for healing services developed by other Anglican Provinces and from other denominations.

Of special interest are the customs of the Orthodox churches, which are faithful to their patristic foundations in the provision of healing services. Typically these contain anointing, surrounded by prayer and readings from Scripture. Customs vary between patriarchies, but in the Romanian Church, for example, regular healing services are very common in parishes and cathedrals. People are anointed at the end of the celebration of the Divine Liturgy every Sunday. A feature of the Romanian practice is the custom of placing those most in need of healing closer to the priest for the laying on of hands. This is mediated through the imposition of the gospel book and the priest's stole. The laity also take part in the laying on of hands. The healing ministry is widely interpreted as being for the healing, not only of the body, but also of the mind and the spirit.

The ecumenical dimension of the ministry of healing can be an impetus to greater cooperation with other denominations as well as a means of mutual learning. We encourage more Churches Together groups to explore ways of celebrating the healing ministry together, not only for the benefit of individual members but also as a witness to the desire to heal the divisions in the Church.

Pitfalls and dangers

Many of these are dealt with elsewhere in this report where good practice is also considered, but so far as healing services are concerned some of the main issues are these.

1. Public services can raise unrealistic expectation, if they are attended by people with little church background who have not received any

teaching or preparation. This is not to endorse scepticism, but harm has been caused by people who have assumed that ministry would bring a particular form of cure and have felt cheated and abandoned by God when what they desired has not been experienced. This is exacerbated when the service itself contains any attempt to stir up emotions. To meet this danger public ministry should be offered as far as possible with due preparation and teaching, and in particular with conscientious follow-up and pastoral care. Not everyone grasps the truth that prayer is answered in different ways and times, or that God's healing work is deeper than the curing of symptoms, desirable though that might be.

2. Those involved in ministry need to be acceptable to the Church as a whole and under a clear authority. So the selection and training of ministry teams is important. Few dioceses have any formal require-ments for membership of these teams, leaving it to individual par-ishes and clergy. Some guidelines for accreditation would be welcomed. At the very least those in the teams should receive teach-ing on the theological aspects of healing ministry, even though the main requirement is the spirituality and personality of the potential ministers. Not everyone who offers is necessarily acceptable. To be involved in the healing ministry calls for maturity in faith, commit-ment to prayer and a readiness to receive ministry and continuing oversight. Training can take place working and praying with more experienced Christians. We refer to the additional safeguards in the section on good practice in Appendix 1 and also to the section in Chapter 7 on ministering to those who suffer from long illnesses.

The wider context

The healing service and other ministries find their true place within the wider context of the Church's worship. Christ is the only 'healer' and God's grace cannot be limited to our categories. All acts of worship and sacramental administration have a healing potential. The daily office puts us in touch with the living Word, the source of all healing and wholeness. Christian initiation (baptism, confirmation and first Communion) declares a healed relationship with God in Jesus Christ through the for-giveness of sins, the renunciation of evil and the gift of the Holy Spirit.

Holy matrimony contains great possibilities of healing through growth in maturity and grace to give and receive human love through all the joys and pains of family life. Funeral rites give opportunities for affirming faith in the risen Lord and for expressing grief within a loving fellowship. And there are other ways in which there can be healing through the services around the time of death.

Prayers of commendation for the dying can help them to lose fear and let go in peace, finding a deeper healing which comes through union with Christ. There is also scope in the funeral service or in the later memorial service to enable those grieving to acknowledge unfinished business: for example, areas where forgiveness is called for. Many from all traditions appreciate a celebration of a Eucharist of the resurrection specifically to commend the departed to God's mercy.

When God's people meet for the breaking of bread the gospel is proclaimed, sins are forgiven and each person is affirmed as one for whom Christ died. Everyone is invited to take and eat in remembrance of what the Lord has done. The acclamation, 'Christ has died! Christ is risen! Christ will come again!' reminds us of Christ's victory, setting us free from the fear of death and its power. In some churches the invitation to Holy Communion is given in these words:

President: Jesus is the Lamb of God who takes away the sins of the world.

Congregation: Lord, I am not worthy to receive you, but only say the word and I shall be healed.

So it is that the Eucharist is, among other things, in the memorable patristic phrase the 'medicine of immortality'.

All Christian worship can bring healing through which we meet the living Christ and touch the hem of his garment. But healing services can help us to see the possibility of seeking God's grace for our illnesses and troubles in every act of worship. In fact, some churches which have organized regular healing services over a period of years find that they are led to reduce the number because the members of the congregation are discovering this wider context. The after-service ministry continues, but individuals begin to ask for prayer from each other spontaneously before, during or after an act of worship, so that the ministry becomes as 'natural' as singing a hymn or going to the communion rail. Healing services, though fewer, remain in the Church's calendar as a reminder of this aspect of worship and for those who are not used to the informal and spontaneous ministry.

Practical considerations

We have already discussed the importance of the setting of healing services (and, indeed, of all acts of worship). Some other practical matters are worth noting. Besides obvious things like publicity ('in house' or wider?), stewarding, service sheets, suitable music and hymns, and so on, the preparation of those taking part is important. In the introduction to one of the new services the Liturgical Commission suggests that 'Before the service it is normally appropriate for [those ministering] to pray together for grace and discernment.'

Equally important is the preparation of the congregation, either printed or announced beforehand, telling them of the purpose and nature of the service and explaining their part in it. Experience shows that when significant numbers of the congregation as well as the ministry team have been carefully instructed and learned how to pray expectantly, their corporate presence and faith does much to inspire the worship of the healing service and open people's hearts to God's word and grace. Healing services often attract people unversed in traditional forms of worship. There may be things which need explanation and should not be taken for granted. What is needed on these occasions is simplicity, brevity and a sense of the accessibility of God's healing love. Worship material is needed for use in a variety of contexts, including hospitals and prisons.

The Church of England Liturgical Commission has produced new services for healing and wholeness, including services for healing, for use at diocesan and parish level. Other Anglican Provinces have produced a variety of services, which may be studied with advantage, as may the publications of other denominations, already mentioned. Parishes should seek to provide 'user-friendly' services and service sheets, adapting the liturgical material to their own setting.

Our culture is increasingly less book-orientated and, to be accessible, liturgy has to use more than words to communicate. Healing concerns more than the mind, so the use of symbolic acts like the laying on of hands and the use of oil, and creativeness in music, song and visual arts can be inherently therapeutic. Penitence and the healing of the past can be focused in different ways: stones representing wounds brought to the cross, negative experiences written down on paper to be torn up or burnt, washing of hands, lighted candle as a sign of persistent prayer – a variety of source books are now available to suggest the kind of symbolism which might be appropriate in different settings.

Children should not be excluded from healing services, but there are concerns about their comprehension of what is involved, and what response is expected. They are a joy to pray with and for, provided it is done with sensitivity; but difficulties arise in the case of chronic or terminal illnesses, where their expectations may be unrealistic. (This is a possibility for anyone, of course, but may be more acute when children are involved.) Yet many who have experience of working with children can attest to the depth and reality of their faith, which can often challenge adults. If we are to take children's membership of the Church seriously, we need to explore their role in exercising ministry and being part of prayer groups.

People with disabilities should also be regarded first as members of the Body of Christ and helped to find their appropriate role in the ministry. There can be an assumption that they need to be 'healed', so giving the impression of marginalizing them and not accepting them as they are. To think of them as 'differently abled' rather than 'disabled' is a good step towards changing attitudes to them. Indeed, it may result in a certain healing of relationships in those who are 'abled'.

We note, in the new forms of services for wholeness and healing, some interesting features:

❖ The overall title sets this ministry within the context of the emotional, spiritual and social restoration of the person as well as the physical, as encouraged in this report.

❖ The ministry of healing is seen in relation to baptism. The sacrament of Christian initiation is an individual's first 'service of healing' since it 'points the way in which God in Jesus Christ is overthrowing an order of life corrupted by sin and death and bringing to birth a renewed creation, a creation alive with the healing presence of God's Holy Spirit' (Introduction). We understand that Rites for

Reconciliation – another obvious aspect of healing – will be submitted for authorization later.

❖ A variety of forms of service are provided: for diocesan or deanery occasions; for the laying on of hands with prayer and anointing at a Eucharist; and for ministering to those who are sick at home. There is also a choice of many Scripture readings and prayers to enable flexibility in planning and presiding at services.

❖ A section on 'Prayers for Protection and Peace' includes one or two traditional texts which can be used for those who believe they are troubled by an evil spirit. A note at the beginning of that section says, 'On occasions when exorcism and deliverance is administered, it is for the bishop to determine the nature of the rite and what forms of words should be used.'

❖ Naturally, liturgical texts do not provide detailed instructions on pastoral matters for clergy and laity who engage in this ministry, but what is in these texts fits in well with the guidelines for good practice in Appendix 1 and other safeguards we have set out in this report.

❖ These services could be a valuable aid for those who are being trained to exercise a ministry of healing. Much can be learned through studying the Scripture passages and the texts of the prayers, as well as the introduction and notes that accompany them.

To summarize, we welcome these services as yet another sign, with this report, that the Church of England is encouraging its members to see the healing ministry as central and normal in the life of every parish church. Resources for help are available in the diocese and in other recognized organizations. Our vision is that every church can become a 'centre for Christian wholeness and healing' in the neighbourhood.

Recommendations

We recommend that:

❖ a wider range of worship resources for services of prayer for healing, appropriate for use in parishes, hospitals and prisons, should be developed; flexibility, for use in different contexts, is essential and ecumenical cooperation desirable (see pages 243 and 254–5);

❖ better communications should be established with other Anglican Provinces and other denominations to facilitate awareness of different material available in the ministry of healing (see page 251);

❖ services of penance/reconciliation which acknowledge the healing potential of forgiveness should be promoted (see pages 246–7).

14

Developing the Healing Ministry in the Parish

The preceding chapters set out the current state of the healing ministry in the Church of England and give an overview of its range of expression within the wider context of our society. This chapter takes the theological strands within this ministry and its description as 'visionary, prophetic and dynamic', which are set out in Chapter 2, and relates them to the practical, prayerful development of the healing ministry in the parish. We draw attention to the wider issues which affect people's healing and health, including their relationships with themselves, their families and the community and environment in which they live. We also offer suggestions to help the broad development of this ministry, including working collaboratively with hospital and prison chaplaincies, people involved in professional and voluntary health care and the other main denominations in the local community.

Where the healing ministry is already familiar to the congregation, it needs support and encouragement. Whilst, however, it is already clearly established in some parishes, it is not a part of normal everyday life in others, as we have explained in Chapter 3. Although this ministry is integrated in many aspects of the Church's activities, it needs to be clearly identified at local level. There are also considerable variations in the ways in which this ministry is exercised in the parishes. Across the Church of England, we need to develop a common understanding of good practice, with effective guidance and well-informed oversight. We also need to encourage wider awareness of the many ways in which this ministry is expressed, by the various traditions and denominations, by the chaplaincies and those involved in professional health care and by ordinary people in everyday situations.

Overall, it is crucial to develop a common understanding of the healing ministry as part of the Church's mission. This ministry is not an isolated activity at parish level: it is part of the wider mission to bring healing to the Church as the Body of Christ and to our society. Ultimately we are being led towards the healing of God's creation and the coming of the kingdom. This ministry is not simply about sacraments and services – it is a way of life and our expression of the gospel in everyday settings which involves all Christians. The local church needs to become 'a healing church' but it can only be effective as such inasmuch as it is 'a church being healed', – that is, a community which is open to God's healing in all its fullness and not just somewhere where a healing service is held on the third Wednesday in the month for a handful of people. To take a simple illustration; a congregation which is known to be quarrelsome and divided is hardly likely to be seen as a community which can help towards the healing of relationships. People in the parish might well say to such a congregation 'Physician, heal thyself'!

Before attempting to develop this ministry in a parish, questions need to be asked about why it has not been part of normal parish life so far, since the answers may give insights into the issues which need attention early on. Are there inhibiting factors such as disinterest and disbelief, misconceptions, misunderstandings, bad experiences and lack of confidence? These factors can be overcome: none are insurmountable, but they are important and need to be addressed.

We recommend that clergy and laity interested in developing the ministry of healing review how it is currently expressed in their parish. Some of the questions which could provide a practical framework for the review are:

❖ How effective is the expression of the theology of this ministry through preaching, teaching, pastoral care and personal example in the parish?

❖ In what forms is the healing ministry available in the parish and to what extent are the congregation and parishioners aware of this ministry?

259

❖ To what extent is the expression of this ministry ecumenical and what is known of the healing ministry of the other denominations in the local community?

❖ To what extent does this ministry address the issues which affect people in the local community and environment?

❖ What training has been undertaken by those involved and what is provided currently?

❖ What guidelines, advice and referral networks and oversight are in place?

❖ What kinds of healing and supportive prayer networks exist locally?

❖ What links exist between those involved in the healing ministry in the parish and those involved in professional and voluntary health care, hospital chaplaincies and prison chaplaincies?

❖ What kinds of resources are available for promoting wider awareness of this ministry?

The healing ministry in the parish is visionary . . . because it beckons us towards the future and a glimpse of the kingdom, the hope of creation renewed in perfect health and wholeness

The healing ministry within the parish must be founded on the theology of healing and needs to be expressed through preaching, teaching, personal and corporate example. The vocabulary we use in explaining this ministry is crucial to the task of informing people about it; however our common vocabulary in relation to this ministry needs clarification. Words such as 'spiritual' and 'spiritualist', 'incarnation' and 'reincarnation' are sometimes used carelessly in everyday conversation and on occasions they are swapped about, leading to confusion and misinformation. The tendency for people to be more aware of language associated with complementary medicine and alternative therapies means that many people, including regular church attenders, are confused about the meaning of key phrases and words. The vision needs to be clearly described.

The ministry of healing gives us a glimpse of the kingdom – hope for the future – creation renewed and in perfect health. What does this mean for the local church? It means a shift of focus. We are being offered – in this world – healing for our souls for all eternity. 'We know that the whole creation has been groaning in labour pains until now; and not only the creation, but we ourselves, who have the first fruits of the Spirit, groan inwardly while we wait for adoption, the redemption of our bodies (Romans 8.22,23). This ministry encourages each person in the parish to consider carefully and then look beyond their own circumstances and needs, to put their problems, challenges, weakness and suffering in perspective, and to seek healing and closer relationships through and with God, for themselves and for other people.

Sharing the vision with the congregation is an essential part of the preparations to establish and develop the healing ministry. How its members respond to those seeking healing and wholeness, comfort and support is part of the way in which the good news of God's love is spread. Every member of the congregation has a role in this ministry. By understanding its purpose and expression through prayer, each person can be helped to discern how they and their particular gifts from God may be most effectively involved and used. Individuals with time to spare can, for example, visit people suffering with illnesses which keep them housebound, providing friendship and a practical link with the local congregation. Those who are housebound through illness or other circumstances may be able to set up and maintain healing prayer networks, by phone or email. A group may form to offer support for carers, respite from the day-to-day pressures of caring for others. Pastoral care is not just an activity for the clergy; it is a fundamental expression of Christian fellowship.

Sharing the vision with the parochial church council (PCC) is another important preliminary stage. The support of the PCC for this ministry will affect, for example, the type of liturgy used, the style of service, the membership of the healing team and the support and interest within the congregation for this ministry. Nevertheless, care should be taken to ensure that setting up services for healing does not cut off this ministry from the overall message of the gospel, or allow it to deteriorate into a comfort zone for a minority interest group.

The issue to be addressed from that point is 'What needs to be done to establish and develop the healing ministry as part of normal parish life in *this* parish?' The local vision of this ministry should not be blinkered; it is necessary to see the needs of individuals within the wider expression of healing in society and reflect the prophetic dimension. The bishop can help establish and develop this ministry and encourage confidence by his involvement in services with prayers for healing in the parish church: a visible sign that the leadership of the Church regards the ministry of healing as part of normal parish life.

The ecumenical vision of the healing ministry shared between the denominations, nurtured by God's grace, is both prophetic and dynamic. It draws attention to the differences and the similarities of the ways in which this ministry is carried out. We need to be aware of our weaknesses, failures and need for healing in order to build wider and stronger ecumenical partnerships. A shared perception of its expression amongst our ecumenical partners shows how much we have in common and how our differences generally pale into insignificance compared to the opportunities to work together in this ministry. The Holy Spirit is calling us towards a unity which is visibly expressed through words and action.

The glimpse of the kingdom revealed through this ministry gives us a vision of creation renewed. The parish church, its congregation and the local community need to be aware of the healing needed within the whole of creation, particularly the local environment, how it suffers and how this affects the people living within it. Misuse of God-given resources affects us all, not just in the present but in the future too. If we close our eyes to these issues now, the vision could become a nightmare. Recognition of where and how these issues arise locally is the first step towards the healing of the local environment.

The healing ministry in the parish is prophetic . . . because it calls us to reconsider our relationships with God, each other and the world, and to seek forgiveness and a new start in our lives

Preaching the prophetic message of reconciliation and its theological foundation sets the healing ministry in the right context. So much unhappiness and ill health is connected to the state of our relationships with each other, our environment, ourselves and with God. To avoid this ministry being seen only in terms of the individual and his or her apparent well-being, it needs to be set in the prophetic context, through preaching and teaching and effective communication within the local community.

What are the local issues? What kinds of reconciliation are needed? For example, the issues of greatest or most widespread concern may be broken relationships and families, unemployment, crime, social decay and vandalism, poverty, self-neglect, racism, the effects of imprisonment on families and ex-offenders. On the other hand, the key issues may be more covert, such as substance abuse, child abuse, domestic violence, AIDS, homophobia, infidelity, incest or occult involvement. The reasons for individuals seeking healing are very diverse and sometimes not conspicuous; for example, bereavement, loss through separation and divorce (which affects children and grandparents as well as the wider family), mental illness, physical illness, coming to terms with chronic or terminal disease, rejection because of sexual orientation, loneliness, anger and unresolved guilt. Disease may also be caused by social mismanagement, over-indulgence, oppression, fear and stress.

Such a wide range of concerns deserves more than one approach to healing. Jesus set us an example by using different approaches for different people, sometimes in public and sometimes after taking the person aside. Sometimes they came to him for help and sometimes he went to them. The parish needs to consider the key local problems and how the Church can bring healing through ministry, pastoral care, mission and engaging with the local challenges in prayerful and practical ways.

The preparations for the third Christian millennium have been shaped around the concept of new starts. The prophetic dimension of the healing ministry calls us to new starts in our relationships with God, each other and the world and to seek forgiveness and a new start in our lives.

Baptism and confirmation create a new start by incorporating an individual into the Body of Christ. Confession and absolution create a new start by restoring relationships within that Body (which is why this discipline is more appropriately called 'the ministry of reconciliation'). Each of these gifts from God through which the Church formally enables people to make a new start with God are expressions of healing of the relationship between the individual and God. Unfortunately many people, including those who attend church services, fail to fully appreciate these opportunities: they need encouragement and inspiring teaching in order to do so.

A new start with family and friends can be through the sacrament of marriage, when two people are joined together for life in a new relationship with God. The 'Service of Prayer and Dedication after Civil Marriage' also helps to bring healing and a closer relationship with God, through the recognition of public vows and commitment to each other, including 'in sickness and in health'. Services for the renewal of vows and thanksgivings for marriages at times of anniversaries are also opportunities for reconciliation and healing. 'For the Christian couple, their "yes" in marriage becomes a "yes" to God, to each other, to their children and the community and finally to the Earth.'[1]

Many marriages sadly end in separation and divorce. The damage to those involved, the pain and repercussions, may affect them for the rest of their lives. Whilst the Church of England tries to reach agreement on the issue of remarriage, the question of how to bring about healing to those who have been affected by divorce ought to be addressed urgently. The local church is not just for those who are happily single, married or widowed: it is in the parish for everyone. How the church relates to divorcees will affect many people in the local community, including children of broken families and grandparents. Each congregation needs to consider how to bring reconciliation and healing to broken families through the healing ministry, pastoral care, counselling, support groups, mission and fellowship.

Healing may be brought to individuals and families through what is sometimes called a 'Healing the Family Tree'. Psychologists and therapists have used a person's family tree (genogram) as an aid to exploring family background and history and enabling people who feel alienated to have a sense of belonging. Some clergy have also found the study of a family tree to be a useful means of discovering broken relationships, traumatic events and family traits as well as disowned, lost, forgotten or unmourned relatives. Pastoral counselling centred around a family tree may later be focused in a service of Holy Communion in the parish church, where members of an earthly family are remembered and brought into the healing love which is found in the Holy Trinity. Many have found that such prayer for the healing of the past and for the peace of departed forebears can bring a sense of release from oppressive influences.

People may also be helped by the 'healing of memories'. This is a term in common currency to describe a situation in which an individual is unhappily influenced by things which – though not necessarily consciously remembered – continue to affect their attitudes and behaviour. The

Church, through its ministry, can help individuals to be freed from their effects. Diplomatic and counselling skills are helpful in enabling the local community, and families and individuals within it, to identify, recall and articulate memories from the past and to move forward to discover ways of forgiveness, confession, reconciliation and healing. However, specialist professional skill is usually necessary for survivors of personal abuse and trauma.

A new start for the local community may be found through addressing the key issues affecting local people. Racism and other forms of prejudice for example, can be immensely painful and damaging. Memories may be very long and old resentments can burn away unresolved until a concerted effort is made by the local community to address the issues and seek reconciliation. The parish church has a role to play in bringing about the healing of deeply held memories which divide communities: the congregation at the heart of the community is called to bring people together and enable this to happen – 'Blessed are the peacemakers'!

As part of this dimension of healing within the community, the issue of how to welcome and re-integrate ex-prisoners and offenders is important. We have a duty to welcome people into our congregation and especially offenders, though this should be part of a carefully thought-out policy. For example:

> The three theological questions which any congregation will have to face are first, whether they believe personal change is possible for this person given the power of past habits; secondly the place of anger and how this can be worked with; and thirdly the nature of the call of God, as seen in Jesus, to a new life empowered by the forgiveness of God.[2]

Restorative justice is the name given to the process of bringing the perpetrators and victims of crime together to try to find healing for both. Often the victim's suffering is made worse by feeling powerless in not being involved in the criminal justice process and those who carry out acts of violence or burglary fail to realize the extent of the emotional and psychological damage they have done. Restorative justice schemes aim to bring the criminal and the victims face to face and to meet one another as fellow human beings rather than remaining the impersonal victim or 'demonized' criminal.

The advice of the prison chaplain should be sought to see if it is appropriate to consider inviting a particular prisoner or ex-prisoner to such a meeting. This kind of meeting brings about an encounter where listening, forgiveness, contrition, reconciliation and healing can be achieved, and hopefully lead to a situation where the victim is less traumatized and the criminal is less likely to reoffend. This form of healing needs to be carried out with great care and expert help, in order to protect those who are vulnerable.

Can the healing ministry bring about a new start for the parish church? The Church is to be a sign and instrument of God's will, a divine reality, but because it is still imperfect, it is called to repentance, reform and renewal as part of its own healing. Realizing the visionary, prophetic and dynamic nature of the healing ministry provides a wonderful opportunity for the parish to review its priorities and mission.

A number of questions arise. How do the congregation, the PCC and the clergy relate to the key issues in the local community where healing is needed? How does this affect the services and liturgy used? What are the implications for reordering of the church building and providing facilities for disabled people? How does the healing ministry relate to existing ministry groups, lay training provision, parish mission statements, financial budgeting, outreach, family care, pastoral care, lay visiting teams for the local hospital, links with local prisons, support for health-related mission overseas, care for the chronically ill and terminally ill in the community and their carers? Through the ministry of healing in the parish, Jesus meets people at their point of need: not necessarily where the Church would like people to be, but where we truly are, in our brokenness and vulnerability. The healing ministry and its links with pastoral care within the parish need to be considered, in the light of local needs and resources. Few parishes can do everything they would like to do or need to do. With prayerful reflection and practical appraisal, however, the local priorities can be agreed.

The ecumenical expression of this ministry can be a new start for reconciliation between the denominations at local level. They are being called toward unity as part of the healing of the Church. The local congregation is a 'being healed community', that is, a community that shows the way forward towards healing by submitting to the healing grace of God in all his merciful ways. As a congregation which is seeking healing and manifesting signs of being healed by God, the local church can then in Jesus' name and in the power of the Spirit beckon to other people and communities and invite them to follow.

How we express this ministry ecumenically is part of this healing: the parish church can be a catalyst in this process, by finding prayerful, practical and visible ways of sharing this ministry. Clergy, ministers and laity within the denominations need to meet locally to discuss and plan the most appropriate ecumenical approaches. Issues to be considered in relation to joint healing services include the sharing of training, resources, information and support networks and conferences, ecumenical hospital lay visiting teams. Wherever appropriate, opportunities to work ecumenically should be created and taken up, particularly in relation to healing, health care and related areas of pastoral care.

God's plan involves healing creation through Christ, the reconciler of all things: he is Lord and Servant who lives for the sake of the whole of creation. Issues such as animal welfare, minimizing pollution and protecting wildlife, for example, are part of our being reconciled to the rest of creation. The parish is the local environment and the parish church has a role in encouraging awareness of environmental issues and good use of resources. Furthermore, caring for and healing the local environment as part of God's creation is a task for the parish which often attracts the keen interest of young people.

Within the wider context the healing ministry is also expressed through the support of overseas mission and charitable projects, including the financial backing which these require, particularly that related to health care provision, evangelism and education, through projects such as Mercy Ships, which is a charity which uses medically equipped ships to take medical care and evangelism to countries around the world.

The healing ministry in the parish is dynamic . . . because Jesus is with us to the end of time: when we pray for his help, he comforts, strengthens and heals us, responding to our deepest needs

This ministry is an integral part of our relationships and fellowship within the Christian community and beyond. Jesus meets us at our point of need through each other.

Christ has no body now but yours, no hands but yours, no feet but yours. Yours are the eyes through which Christ's compassion must look out on this world. Yours are the feet with which He is to go about doing good. Yours are the hands with which He is to bless us now.[3]

Many of the gifts within the parish church are given by God to build up this ministry of healing within the Church and to share in its wide range of expression. The diocesan advisor on this ministry is a valuable resource for the parish, including through presentations to the congregation, preaching, providing training and helping to set up local healing teams. He or she can also advise on the various ways in which this ministry is carried out and its wider implications, and help individuals within the parish to discern their vocation within it. Diocesan advisors also have useful contacts for information, resources, referrals, specialist advice and ecumenical contacts.

Healing services, already described in Chapters 3 and 12 and earlier in this chapter, are a particular public expression of this ministry, usually within the parish church. Many helpful books and other resources are available to provide inspiration and basic information on the necessary preparation and form of these services, so they are not covered in detail in this chapter. It is important that these services are not allowed to become the only expression of this ministry in the parish, also that they are carefully established to meet the local needs and reviewed from time to time.

The laity should be involved in this ministry if it is to be truly collaborative. Lay people may be interested in forming a healing team for services: care should be taken, however, to ensure that only suitable people are involved. Whilst the positive qualities which are needed, such as compassion, reliability, discretion, and a regular worship pattern, may be obvious, factors which indicate unsuitability such as a record of child abuse, emotional difficulties, substance abuse and conflicts of interest tend to be less apparent. Within the congregation there may already be people with relevant training and professional expertise, such as professional counsellors, psychiatrists, psychotherapists, whose gifts may be used through this ministry. Licensed lay workers such as pastoral assistants and youth officers may also be interested in involvement with this ministry. The section on good practice in Appendix 1, the detailed recommendations in Appendix 2 and the guidelines for recruiting healing team members in Appendix 3 provide further information to help clergy and PCCs select, train and support the most appropriate people for the team.

Once people are chosen to be part of the healing team, they need proper training which should be ongoing and kept up to date. If clergy are not confident or prepared to train people for healing teams, or are untrained themselves, they should seek the help of the diocesan advisor, and consider inviting him or her to come to the parish to help to provide training to an acceptable standard. Everyone involved in healing services should also be aware of and support the guidelines for good practice in the appendices of this report. Those who are actively involved need the prayerful and practical support of the congregation, PCC and clergy. If, however, someone behaves in an unacceptable way, they should be withdrawn. Bad practice left unchecked brings the healing ministry and the local church into disrepute and can lead to serious consequences for all concerned. Teamwork, clear and shared understanding of areas of responsibility and accountability are important and depend on good communication with all those involved.

One effect of the liturgical revision in recent years has been to reveal more clearly the Eucharist as the healing service *par excellence*. There the word of God is read and expounded; sins are confessed and forgiven; intercessions are made for the needs of the Church and the world, including the sick; the mighty acts of God in Christ are recalled and we partake of the sacrament of Christ's body and blood. The Peace exchanged during the Eucharist is a sign which, perhaps more than anything else in this revision, has impressively reminded us that what we are engaged in is a service for the healing of relationships through the grace of God.

The ministry of healing can be incorporated into the main Sunday service, offered through the laying on of hands either before or after receiving Holy Communion. Anointing is not usually regarded as a sacrament to be offered routinely as part of a Sunday service: it is sometimes offered after the service for those who need or request it. Whenever the laying on of hands or anointing are part of the service, the congregation need to be properly instructed about what those who are ministered to should do and how those not directly involved should support the ministry with prayer. An explanation is necessary because there may be newcomers to the service who know nothing or very little about this ministry.

Non-eucharistic services are ideal opportunities to involve members of the other denominations and the parish is encouraged to co-operate ecumenically in the planning and sharing of these services. At the time of the writing of this report, the tendency has been for services of this kind to 'just happen'. But this ministry is too important to be arranged without preparation beforehand and review afterwards. Types of liturgies need to be studied, the theme of the sermon discussed, and the follow-up planned. A service of healing can be authentically Anglican without being exclusively Anglican; some tangible expressions of ecumenical sensitivity can make a big difference, showing a real willingness to work together.

Some people prefer to maintain a degree of anonymity; their attitude should be respected, even though it makes effective pastoral care more difficult or not possible. On the other hand, others may feel unable, too shy or afraid of showing their emotions, to receive this ministry in a public setting. As well as offering this ministry as part of services, there should be opportunities to receive it afterwards or in private, according to good practice set out in this report. These provisions need to be made known to the congregation, so that no one is left feeling that there is no sensitive setting in which they can be ministered to. Care needs to be taken, however, when prayers for proxy healing are requested. Although sometimes people wish to receive the laying on of hands for others, opinions differ as to the appropriateness and use of this practice. This issue should be discussed with the PCC and healing team members, to form a locally acceptable view and to ensure that the privacy and dignity of those being prayed for is protected. There is a risk of confidentiality being breached if information about others is passed on in this context, particularly in a public service.

Overall, however, the healing ministry needs to be seen to be part of normal parish life and not something hidden away or strictly private. The ministry to the sick, for example, can involve if appropriate the friends and family of the person who is sick, in home communion and prayers for healing. Common sense is important; if someone, for example, seeks this ministry repeatedly in private with one person, it may be that there are other issues which ought to be addressed and the safety and good reputation of those involved should be considered. For this and other reasons, it is recommended that, whenever and wherever appropriate, the healing ministry is carried out by trained teams or people working together in pairs, preferably male and female, rather than two of the same gender.

Because people seek healing for a wide range of ailments and suffering, clergy and laity may find themselves praying for people with such problems as serious psychiatric illnesses, personality disorders, chemical and other dependencies, and learning disabilities. In these circumstances, it is important to pray for discernment as to how to pray, since although the symptoms may be lessened and the stresses relieved, it is unlikely that the condition itself will disappear. Care needs to be taken that those suffering from serious psychiatric illnesses, for example, do not suffer through attempts to bring about healing which have been undertaken unwisely.

In situations involving people with personality disorders, the issues of safeguards and supervision need to be addressed, and close professional liaison is encouraged because of the impact on other individuals and groups, which may be considerable. Pastoral supporters of individuals with personality disorders need guidance on when and how to hand them over to responsible professionals for statutory interventions, under mental health or child protection regulations, when these individuals threaten or actually harm others.

The deliverance ministry should not be exercised publicly; it is dangerous and pastorally insensitive to minister to anyone in this way, without careful and prayerful consideration and discernment. This would be contrary to the House of Bishops' guidelines (1975) and the House of Bishops' draft guidelines for good gractice in the healing ministry, in Appendix 1.

Christian Listening is a form of pastoral care related to the healing ministry, based on the ability developed through training to listen to others, to God, to the world and to ourselves. It is a skill which many people can use to help others, within the Church and the local community, as a form of ministry, which could be defined as 'gift, hospitality and healing'. In Chapter 10 we considered the attraction of alternative therapies for many people and their need for time, someone to listen and to put them 'first'. The parish can meet this need by encouraging, recruiting and training suitable people for this ministry.

Christian Listening provides the opportunity for someone to be listened to and heard: it can be appreciated as a precious gift, a sign that they matter, not just to the listener but also to God. It is an expression of hospitality, through making oneself available for someone else, based on a sincere welcome, a sense of space and trust. This ministry of listening helps to bring about healing because it offers compassion and discernment, an opportunity for those who hurt to open up and tell their story of suffering to someone in a safe environment. This ministry is also, in a sense, the ears of the Body of Christ and can help in a broad way to inform the parish church of the needs of the local community (whilst ensuring that confidentiality is not breached).

Chapter 8 has already covered, in detail, the healing ministry and professional care provision in the parishes, including Christian pastoral counselling, prayer ministries and prayer counselling. It should be borne in mind, however, that while all clergy are pastors, not all pastors are counsellors. These are valuable ministries which should be carried out by people who are properly trained and under supervision. Counselling and related areas are referred to in 'Good Practice in the Healing Ministry' and the 'House of Bishops' draft guidelines for good practice in the healing ministry' in Appendix 1.

Pastoral care, which has great value and is one of the ways in which we carry out the mission of the Church, should not be confused with the work of professional counsellors and psychotherapists, who will have their own guidelines and indemnities. Clergy and laity who are trained in counselling should make clear to parishioners what they consider appropriate and whether they are offering pastoral care or professional counselling. People who work in professional health care and related areas and who live in the parish can be valuable members of the healing ministry within the local church. Nevertheless, they deserve to be treated with care and consideration since their work may make heavy demands on them and they should not be overburdened.

In pastoral situations and healing services, individuals may indicate the need for or be invited to receive 'healing of memories' or prefer to recall them in silence before God. Prayer, the laying on of hands, anointing, confession and Holy Communion are among the appropriate means of bringing about the healing of memories. Specialist professional skills such as counselling or primal therapy are frequently required, however, when memories are of sexual, physical and emotional abuse.

We have shown elsewhere in this report that God works through people beyond the Church, through professional health care and social services. The healing ministry should be carried out in a collaborative and co-operative manner, with health care professions and others involved in providing care whose particular contributions to the care of parishioners deserves to be recognized and respected.

Since this ministry is both complementary and holistic, wherever possible, links with the local health care and medical centres and surgeries should be encouraged. As complementary medicine and alternative therapies increasingly become available through local health care provision, the healing ministry needs to be seen to be available and attractive too. It is helpful to arrange from time to time local meetings of clergy and laity involved in professional health care in the local community, perhaps with a guest speaker, to encourage cross-disciplinary communication on health, healing and reconciliation issues.

Complementary medicine and alternative therapies are used by many people, as we have already described in Chapter 10. In order to be objective about these approaches to health, it is important to be accurately informed about them. Whilst the Church needs to address the issue of advice on these matters, questions have been suggested which parishioners may ask of practitioners. Those involved in the healing ministry in the parish and in areas related to this ministry, particularly healing teams, pastoral care, counselling and listening, visiting and support networks should be aware of the range of alternative approaches and particularly those which are linked with or involve the occult and other factors which are incompatible with Christian teaching.

The parish may contain a hospital or hospice, in which case the hospital chaplain should be encouraged to be a member of the parish church and he or she will be a member of the local chapter. As already mentioned in Chapters 3, 4, 7 and 8, these local links can be valuable to both the parish healing team and to the chaplain. Through local networks, for example, hospital visiting teams may be formed. When parishioners are admitted to hospital it is courteous to inform the chaplain; this also helps to ensure that the spiritual needs of the parishioner are cared for properly while he or she is an in-patient. Links between the chaplains and the parish clergy also help to ensure the continuation of the healing ministry and pastoral care when parishioners are able to return home.

Prison chaplains have highlighted the benefits of links between local prisons and the parishes, as set out in Chapter 3. Healing in the lives of prisoners depends to a large extent on being accepted after their release into society. The parish can help by developing closer links with local prison chaplaincies, which are ecumenical, in order to be better prepared to accept ex-prisoners. There needs to be, however, a careful balance between involving the parish and protecting vulnerable people within it. A better appreciation of the work of prison chaplains and how the parish can help them and the prisoners, their families and ex-offenders after release can be enabled by discussion between the parish church and the local prison chaplain, since the restrictions and opportunities for support and action will vary from prison to prison.

Whilst we are used to interceding for people who are sick, dying or in some other specially needy situation, there is a wider responsibility and serious need for prayers for those involved in healing, within the Church and our society. Prayer support within the parish for everyone involved in the healing and deliverance ministries, the hospital, hospice and prison chaplaincies, in health care provision and pastoral care is essential. Every person in the congregation is part of this prayer ministry, through private and corporate intercession, in personal prayer, prayer groups and in services. This is a valuable way of reassuring people who do not feel that they have 'special gifts' that they are a precious and valuable part of Jesus Christ's healing ministry.

It is helpful to have wide awareness of the prayer ministry in each parish, so that when people are sick, those who love them and are concerned know whom to contact and can keep those praying up to date about their condition, within the boundaries of confidentiality. Some parishes for example, have a phone network through which news of patients can be spread for prayers. At the same time, many people are concerned about confidentiality and care needs to be taken to ensure that details are not made public or shared without the person's consent. Information which relates to people's suffering should be treated with great sensitivity.

The healing ministry depends to some extent on the formation and use of networks, for effective exchange of information, sharing of resources, fellowship and support, and developing a common understanding. It is helpful to have for use in the parish a readily available list of contacts, including professional health care experts, psychiatrists and psychotherapists, diocesan advisors, charitable organizations specializing in this ministry, details of the Guilds and of diocesan staff, including senior clergy for advice on pastoral issues, legal advisors, communication and youth officers. The details of relevant contacts in the other denominations present in the local area are also useful.

As part of this report, we have responded to many people who have requested guidelines for good practice to be formally 'owned' and promoted by the Church of England for the healing ministry. These guidelines are widely drawn but are particularly appropriate for use in the parishes by all clergy and laity involved in this ministry and related areas. Every parish is encouraged to adopt the guidelines because we need to develop a common understanding of what is good practice and to uphold it where it already exists.

Training, already mentioned in several places in this report, is a key concern in relation to this ministry. At the time this report was being researched, there was clearly inadequate provision made by the Church of England at national, and at diocesan level in many areas, for training in the practical expression of this ministry in the parishes, its wider implications and its ecumenical opportunities. Parish-based clergy should take up opportunities for training which are available through CME, training programmes for clergy and laity by diocesan advisors and the recognized charitable trusts, as long as they are in line with the guidelines for good practice. Clergy are also to be encouraged to attend conferences and meetings with others involved in this ministry in order to keep up to date and aware of its wider expression. In this way the parish priest keeps an open mind and not a narrow view of the ministry in his or her parish, and of the ways in which it can be expressed more effectively and ecumenically.

When lay training programmes are being developed in the parishes, it is helpful to invite the diocesan advisors and also to include people from the other main denominations in the planning of programmes and modules and related teaching and to provide opportunities for learning from each other. Training should also include a wider appreciation of this ministry as it is carried out by the other denominations and by the different traditions which span them. In this way, the local expression of the healing ministry can be ecumenical and attractive to the widest range of people possible.

Ordinands, particularly those on Ordained Local Ministry (OLM) training schemes, currently depend heavily on their parish placements to gain practical experience of this ministry. Such parishes should do all they can to ensure that ordinands are involved in it and provide them with opportunities to learn and appreciate its diversity of expression, according to different circumstances.

The right environment is important for the healing ministry. The introduction of the Disability Discrimination Act 1995 has already established that disabled people should have access to all buildings, including churches and church halls. The ways in which many of our churches and buildings have been designed over the centuries have made it difficult for these people to be part of the congregation. Aspects of the design of the building which need reviewing include the approach and car park, ramps and steps, entrances and reception areas, movement and level changes, doors, lavatories, fixtures and fittings and means of escape. Apart from legal obligations, the parish church and its site needs to be audited and reviewed in the light of the recent legislation and the guidelines produced by Church House Publishing for the Council for the Care of Churches. A church that makes serious practical efforts to welcome disabled people gives them a sense of being wanted.

Effective communication is also important. Hearing loops, for example, are not a luxury but a basic need for those who have hearing or learning difficulties and need to be used properly with an adequate sound system. Service sheets in large print are helpful to those who are partially sighted. The congregation, particularly those who are newcomers, need to have some idea of how they will be ministered to, in order to trust and to feel at ease. Information should be in a readily accessible form which people, including the unchurched, can understand; for example, pew leaflets written with clarity and without jargon can be very helpful. People involved in this ministry should also be prepared to provide information for those with learning disabilities, language problems, older people and those with mental health problems. The language used must be inclusive and sensitive to the situation.

In Chapter 10 we considered the reasons why people are attracted to alternative therapies and what the Church can learn from this. When the reordering of churches is being considered, the issues raised by the healing ministry need to be taken into account. Thought should be given to the environment in order to make healing services and other expressions of this ministry a safe and pleasant experience. A clean, well-lit, suitably heated and ventilated location, with comfortable seating, and easy access and facilities for disabled people and children, are basic requirements, as is a welcoming, peaceful and reverent atmosphere.

Pastoral care for those who receive the healing and deliverance ministries is particularly important. Although some people seek anonymity, many find that they benefit from receiving the healing ministry over a period of time, as healing is brought about at different levels and previously unacknowledged needs for healing may emerge. People's privacy and dignity should be respected and care must be taken over confidentiality, the safe keeping of records, the issues of consent, and general safety, for those ministering and those receiving, whether in the church or elsewhere.

When setting up healing teams and introducing this ministry into services, provision should be made for the pastoral care needs which will follow. It is helpful to have vergers and sidespersons, for example, who are sympathetic to this ministry and who have been trained or briefed to deal with enquiries and requests for help in this area. To have someone on hand who has professional medical training is also an asset, though not always possible.

The care of people who are housebound is often left to members of the immediate family, creating a situation where someone may be forced to give up his or her job or career and lose friends and hobbies, working for long hours without relief or respite. Caring for the carers is part of pastoral care; often they feel guilty about their situation and the resentment which can sometimes arise. Caring for someone who is frail, senile, seriously mentally ill, physically or mentally handicapped, for example, is a demanding task which some people have little choice but to accept.

The ministry of healing can help carers within the parish to find a sense of peace and spiritual support which is much needed to cope with the day-to-day demands on their time, energy and emotions and the strains which have been placed on their lives. It can help to heal, for example, the pain of lost opportunities and the fear of being 'left out'. These areas of caring for the carers and 'burn-out' are covered in more detail in Chapter 7.

It is clear from the range of people who attend healing services that they attract people of all ages and social backgrounds, economic groups, races and spiritual traditions. We need to acknowledge, however, that we live in an ageing population; issues related to ageing will become higher in priority and increasingly reflect people's concerns. Part of the challenge facing this ministry is how to help people in the parish come to terms with the different stages in their lives and the ways in which their need for healing may change. As people get older, they have to come to terms eventually with their own mortality. Few people in our society are really ready to face death without fear and even fewer regard death as the ultimate healing opportunity. Within the parish, the implications for the local community and the impact of our ageing society should be discussed in relation to this ministry.

The healing ministry is also for young people and children, and there are particular issues which relate to their needs for healing. The pressures of examination times, trying to cope with the breakdown of family life (due to divorce or a member of the family having a custodial sentence), bullying, sexual abuse and peer pressure, for example, are areas where young people may seek help through the Church. Unfortunately, this ministry is not often explained to them and they may be quite unaware of it. The ways in which it is communicated and explained will affect the perception of those who are on the receiving end; the method of communication needs to match the recipients. Almost every parish includes young people and children; this ministry needs to be expressed in ways which they can appreciate.

Many young people are involved with drugs and other forms of substance abuse, which in turn affect their families, friends, studies and working lives, physical and mental health, spirituality and world-view. The local church can help them through this ministry, prayer, related forms of pastoral care and loving compassion to overcome addiction and substance abuse. A former drug addict has testified:

> What eventually made me give up drugs then? Two things helped me: prayer and love, two things which each and every one of us in this room can do. Most people within the Church rejected me – they just couldn't be bothered – except for one person. This person looked past the drug habit, looked past the sin in my life and saw me as Jesus saw me. This person loved me with the love of Christ.[4]

Young people come into contact with the occult, through friends, the media's interest in this area, youth culture including computer games and heavy metal music. Some may only dabble on the fringe, but others go on to become more involved and in increasing danger. The local church is one of the few organizations which can help those affected, through the healing ministry and in some cases, the deliverance ministry, to renounce their involvement and lose the influence of the occult. We strongly advise however, that the deliverance ministry only be carried out in accordance with the House of Bishops' guidelines (1975) as set out in Chapter 9, and that this is not an area of ministry for the untrained and unauthorized to 'have a go'.

Occasionally those involved in the healing ministry may become aware of claims or proven cases of abuse. They are recommended to follow the guidance for dealing with complaints set out in Appendix 1. It is also important that clergy and laity involved in this ministry are aware of current laws and Church guidelines relating to the protection of children, and adults with learning disabilities, and the issue of confidentiality, for example.

Clergy and laity alike need to be alert to particular spiritual dangers. They include:

❖ concentration on self – wanting to be a 'healer' rather than a channel for healing;

❖ residual doubt about the authority of God;

❖ uncritical use of the gift of discernment and lack of discernment concerning those who claim they have this gift;

❖ enthroning, through overemphasis, the powers of evil rather than Christ;

❖ personality cults; it is advisable to work in pairs and/or teams and change partners when appropriate;

❖ power and control seeking.

Religious addiction and spiritual abuse, for example, can lead to people becoming fettered in their attitudes and increasingly judgemental – 'spiritual bullies'. When people use Christianity to reinforce the shame and spiritual abuse of others in order to escape their own inner reality, shame and pain, they are behaving in ways contrary to the healing ministry, which is non-judgemental, non-exploitive and non-discriminatory.

The healing ministry is an expression of God's healing love, and how it is carried out in the parish is part of the message of the gospel.

Regular reviews of the way in which this ministry is exercised within the parish, including all those involved, are a valuable way of highlighting the issues to be addressed before they become a problem. For example, without a review, support for a particular type of service may wane while the need for a different approach may be ignored. The parish church needs to learn from experience in this ministry as with everything else it does. Being a pilgrim church involved in a dynamic ministry means being prepared to adapt and move on, not staying in the same place and being left behind.

One challenge sometimes overlooked by clergy and laity is the willingness to be healed themselves when necessary. We may be much encouraged ourselves when we are channels or instruments of others' healing; our loving empathy with others and our desire to help them through Jesus is a blessing to us. Nevertheless, it is important that we do not become so concerned about the healing and health of others that we neglect our own health and needs for healing. All of us need the healing ministry for one reason or another.

Recommendations

We recommend that:

❖ the healing ministry should be clearly defined as part of the Church's mission and ministry, effectively led, overseen, resourced and supported through diocesan structures (see pages 258–9, 261–2, 268, 269 and 274–5);

❖ the Church of England should adopt and promote nationally and within parishes the guidelines for good practice in the healing ministry as incorporated in this report (see pages 268, 269, 271, 272, 275 and 279);

❖ bishops should review the work of diocesan advisors on the healing ministry and, noting the additional workload involved in carrying out the recommendations in this report, consider the future needs within dioceses and the required number and quality of advisors (see pages 264–5, 268, 269, 272, 273, 274 and 275);

❖ each diocese should conduct a survey, in cooperation with the Ministry Division and central support of the healing ministry, to evaluate the current state of this ministry in parishes (see pages 259–60, 266 and 276);

❖ deanery synods and chapters should be encouraged to review the current state of the healing ministry in their area, develop and support proposals for increased effectiveness, including ecumenical cooperation (see pages 262, 266–7, 270 and 274–5);

❖ each parish should evaluate ways in which the healing ministry is being carried out as part of mission, and make proposals for improved effectiveness, noting local needs and challenges and expressions of this ministry in ecumenical partnerships (see pages 259–60, 262–3, 264, 265, 266–7, 270, 271, 273–4, 275–9 and 280).

15

Summary and
Main Recommendations

In this final chapter, we have gathered together the main recommendations from each chapter with their page references. The aim of the following proposals is to move from the current situation where the healing ministry is not coordinated, overseen, supported or promoted nationally within the Church of England, to a situation where it is an effective and integrated part of normal daily parish life in every parish, supported and coordinated at diocesan and national levels. The recommendations support the ecumenical expression of this ministry and the need for more cooperation. We also take into consideration the need for improved training for ministry and for lay people and the importance of adopting throughout the Church of England the guidelines for good practice in the healing ministry. Recommendations also support the relationship between this ministry and the caring professions, in institutions and in the parishes.

This report is the first of its kind, an overview of the healing ministry, its expression within the Church of England and the other main denominations in England, its place within our society, the other forms of health care and healing which are available, and the wider view across the Anglican Communion. It is based on extensive research involving bishops, clergy and laity who are actively involved in this ministry. The information was gathered between the autumn of 1998 and the summer of 1999 and reviewed and incorporated into this report by the autumn of 1999, to ensure that as far as possible the overview which it provides is up to date, balanced and accurate.

The recommendations at the end of each chapter relate to the points made in the text of this report. Because of the extensive research carried out and the surveys conducted on a confidential basis, Appendix 2 sets out in more detail the recommendations and how they cross-relate between the groups and organizations involved in this ministry. We envisage that it would take several years to develop and establish the sub-recommendations, depending on resourcing available and on the speed with which the main recommendations are implemented. Nevertheless, this overview provides a unique opportunity to affirm, enable and develop the healing ministry throughout the Church of England and in closer ecumenical cooperation with the other main denominations. We expect that the House of Bishops may wish to set up a small Steering Group to oversee the implementation of the recommendations, it having a strictly limited life until such time as other bodies (as appropriate) are identified to take the recommendations forward.

The improved effectiveness of the healing ministry needs to be addressed simultaneously at each level within the Church of England and also ecumenically. The necessary changes in approach cannot be achieved simply by a hierarchical drive down or out from the central structures, a grassroots-led revival or an individual diocesan scheme. Furthermore, to develop this ministry within the Church of England isolated from the ways in which it is carried out ecumenically would be to waste precious opportunities and would be a failure to respond to the call to unity. The success of the recommendations depends on a coordinated approach for momentum, clear communication and cooperation. Sections in Appendix 2 are relevant to particular groups within this ministry and may be used to facilitate discussion. They are intended to help shape the development and resourcing of this ministry centrally and within the diocesan structures.

We strongly recommend, however, that the draft guidelines for good practice in the healing ministry should be approved by the House of Bishops and that they should be actively promoted and implemented within the dioceses and parishes. For this reason, we have recommended that they should be published separately and made available, attractively priced, in order to encourage parishes, organizations and individuals involved in this ministry to buy copies for general use and in order to promote a common understanding of good practice. We also recommend that these guidelines should be introduced into training for ministry, and for lay people in the healing ministry and related areas. The guidance in Appendix 1 has been developed to 'stand' in its own right and the text includes some information which has already been provided earlier in this report.

The new Services for Healing and Wholeness were given final approval by the General Synod in February 2000 and we look forward to their publication within a few months of the launch of this report. We recommend that consideration is given to linking the discussion of the services with this report, since the publications are mutually supportive.

The main recommendations from the relevant chapters are listed with page references.

Chapter 2:   Healing in the Scriptures and Tradition

We acknowledge the importance of the bishops' role as teachers and guardians of the faith. Inherent in the episcopal office is a duty and opportunity to commend the ministry of healing to the Church and to promote it within each diocese. We recommend and encourage bishops to teach the scriptural importance of this ministry and its significance in furthering the kingdom of God (see page 261).

Chapter 3:   The Healing Ministry in the Church of England Today

We recommend that:

❖   the Archbishops' Council should be asked to address through the Ministry Division the clearly identified need for improved training for the healing ministry and the strong call for its central support and coordination (see pages 41, 47, 51, 54, 55, 56, 59 and 62);

❖   the healing ministry should be given the weight appropriate to its importance as a gospel imperative, in the recruitment, selection and training of ordinands, in continuing ministerial education, in provision for lay training and related areas within the Church of England (see pages 38, 40, 44, 46, 47, 52, 54, 55, 56, 59 and 62);

❖ the Archbishops' Council should consider the resourcing for this ministry through an existing allocation within the national budget (see pages 43 and 47);

❖ a formal national network should be established of diocesan advisors appointed by the bishops, enabling them to be acknowledged and affirmed within the Church of England, and supported through the central structures. We envisage that the Ministry Division could play a coordinating role, acting in particular as a central reference point for a network of diocesan advisors. The resourcing of this network could, judging by the example of other such networks (such as that for Bishops' Visitors), be relatively modest (see pages 41, 43, 44, 46, 47 and 51);

❖ the Church of England should cooperate with the Churches and Provinces of the Anglican Communion in the support and encouragement of the healing ministry worldwide (see pages 84–5).

Chapter 4: The Ecumenical Expression of the Healing Ministry

We recommend that:

❖ the Church of England should work with our ecumenical partners and health care organizations to develop and establish a new ecumenical Churches' Healing Ministry Group. This group would coordinate, support and promote this ministry, at national and regional levels (see pages 47–8, 59, 74, 76, 81, 83–4 and 85);

❖ the Church of England and our ecumenical partners should develop and agree a basis for future initiatives and ecumenical cooperation within the healing ministry (see pages 74, 75, 76–7, 80–81, 82–3 and 86);

❖ the Churches' Healing Ministry Group should be a springboard for interchurch initiatives and ecumenical cooperation between the Church and the health care organizations (see pages 74, 80, 81, 82–4, 85–6, 87 and 151);

❖ non-eucharistic liturgy for services of prayers for healing should be developed by the Churches' Healing Ministry Group, drawing upon experience in the healing ministry as currently practised within the main denominations (see pages 47–8, 66, 75 and 86);

❖ liturgy for special circumstances, particularly for use in prisons and hospitals, should be developed in cooperation with the hospital and prison chaplaincies, including rites for penance and reconciliation which emphasize the healing potential of the assurance of forgiveness, and for children and people with learning difficulties (see pages 84, 85-6, 89, 135, 259 and 260);

❖ the guidelines for good practice which are included in this report are offered to our ecumenical partners for discussion and adaption if necessary by individual denominations, leading towards an ecumenically agreed understanding of good practice in the healing ministry (see pages 59, 85-6 and 89);

❖ training for the healing ministry for ordained and lay people should be developed, supported and coordinated ecumenically where appropriate (see pages 48, 55, 79-80, 85-6 and 89);

❖ the valuable work of hospital chaplains and prison chaplains in this ministry should be affirmed and a review considered of the relevant Church of England and ecumenical committee structures and communication networks (see pages 51, 62, 63, 80, 82, 83 and 85-6).

Chapter 5: The Healing Ministry in Professional Health Care Settings

We recommend that:

❖ the relationship between the healing ministry and medicine should be encouraged on the basis of a working theology of this ministry and that a vocabulary for this ministry needs to be developed which is clearly understood and shared between clergy, laity and health care professionals (see pages 90, 91, 95, 96, 98 and 99);

❖ in order to facilitate the medical and theological disciplines in working together on healing, support should be given to making provision for medical and theological students to be trained together in pastoral aspects of collaborative health care and ethics (see pages 90, 94, 97, 99–100, 102 and103–4);

❖ the consideration should be given to mutual supervision (doctors being supervised by clergy on spiritual aspects of medical care and clergy by doctors on medical aspects of spiritual care) to work towards a holistic approach to healing (see pages 93, 94, 97, 100 and 101).

Chapter 6: The Healing Ministry and Professional Care Provision in the Parishes

We recommend that:

❖ clergy and other church representatives should be encouraged to initiate and maintain links between themselves and others working in the community, such as doctors, police and the social and voluntary services; for example, through occasional lunches or seminars. In the light of the Government's expressed desire for partnerships between the statutory and the voluntary sectors, this recommendation may suggest creative use of church premises (with appropriate funding) in wider health care provision for the community (see pages 107–8);

❖ all those using counselling skills in pastoral care should receive adequate training and supervision (see pages 110, 112, 113, 114, 115 and 122–3);

❖ those offering formal counselling should receive adequate training and supervision, work with a recognized code of ethics and practice and accredited by or working towards accreditation by a reputable body (see pages 110, 114, 117 and 122–3);

❖ boundaries between counselling and other forms of pastoral care and between people in dual and multiple roles (that is, simultaneously in more than one relationship with one another) should be monitored and regularly reviewed (see pages 109, 110–11, 112, 113, 114, 118 and 121–2);

❖ given the wide variety between dioceses in counselling services provided for clergy, their spouses and dependent children, standards should be established which ensure that at least basic provision is available in every diocese (see pages 118 and 119);

287

❖ courses of training for lay and ordained ministries should include an introduction to the ministry of spiritual direction, and individuals who develop a special gift for this ministry should be encouraged and helped in further studies and practice (see pages 110, 113, 119, 121 and 123–4);

❖ courses of training for lay and ordained ministry should include an introduction to the ministry of reconciliation (hearing confessions), and that priests should be helped to develop this ministry through appropriate supervision and guidance in their continuing ministerial education (see page 121).

Chapter 7: The Impact of Limitation and Illness

We recommend that:

❖ churches should remove barriers to people with disability, when appropriate, enabling and empowering them for ministry (see pages 128, 131 and 255);

❖ local churches or 'Churches Together' could helpfully offer a network of people who are trained in offering pastoral support to those who are mentally unwell (see pages 133 and 134);

❖ people with persisting illness and disability need protection from insensitive ministry; hence the importance of training in this area for ordinands and of including it in continuing ministerial education (see page 144).

❖ the Church of England should continue to support specialist ministries to those with disabilities (for example, chaplaincy to the deaf) and encourage initiatives to study the relationship between physical and mental disabilities and Christian faith (see page 142).

Chapter 8: Healing for Those Who Are Dying or Bereaved

We recommend that:

❖ theological colleges, courses and schemes should make provision for ordinands to be exposed to the needs of dying people and their families. Ordinands could helpfully be involved in experiential and interactive sessions in palliative care as a powerful tool for learning (see pages 153–4);

❖ the needs of the sick person are best met when the different professions involved seek permission from the individual concerned to share together, whilst respecting their individual professional codes of confidentiality (see page 156);

❖ in-service training for clergy should help to develop an understanding of the grief journey (see page 159).

Chapter 9: Deliverance from Evil

We offer the following recommendations:

❖ we endorse the normal practice of suitable people having episcopal authorization for deliverance ministry and the widespread appointment of diocesan teams (see page 168);

❖ we endorse the guidelines issued by the House of Bishops in 1975 (see pages 168 and 180–81);

❖ we commend the practice of keeping careful and confidential records, within the constraints of the Data Protection Act 1998 (see pages 180–81);

❖ clergy and lay people involved in this ministry should have appropriate training and supervision (see page 180);

❖ a multidisciplinary approach is to be desired and we recommend that those authorized for this ministry should have access to consult and work with other clergy and with doctors, psychologists and psychiatrists (see pages 168 and 180);

❖ services involving deliverance ministry should be simple and use appropriate pastoral and sacramental ministry whilst always ensuring that the welfare of the person being ministered to is of paramount concern (see page 180).

Chapter 10: Complementary Medicine and Alternative Approaches to Healing and Good Health

We recommend that:

❖ the Church of England, working with our ecumenical partners, should establish a Review Group, with agreed terms of reference and criteria, to assess in the longer term the compatibility with Christian teaching of widely used forms of complementary medicine and alternative therapies, taking into account interfaith issues (see pages 47, 83–4, 183, 184, 192, 196 and 198);

❖ the Church of England should provide ecumenically agreed guidance for Christians who are considering or using these approaches, including the kind of questions that might be asked about these approaches to healing, health and wholeness (see pages 74, 183, 192–3, 196 and 199–200);

❖ the relationship between the healing ministry and those forms of complementary and alternative approaches to healing which are becoming integrated with conventional health care should be reviewed, in cooperation with the HCC and health care professionals within the NHS (see pages 60, 190, 194 and 201);

❖ training for ministry, particularly for hospital and prison chaplains, should include an appreciation of the range of complementary and alternative approaches to healing and the issues which surround them (see pages 41–2, 55, 184, 192–3, 197, 201, 203 and 204–5);

❖ the relationship between spiritual guidance/direction and health care provision should be reviewed and recommendations made for the increased availability of spiritual direction as part of total health care (see pages 185, 192, 203 and 205);

❖ local churches should be encouraged to communicate effectively information about the healing ministry, to raise awareness particularly amongst non-church-attenders; for example, putting notices in surgeries and providing leaflets (see pages 186, 196, 203, 204 and 206).

Chapter 13:   Healing Services in the Church of England

We recommend that:

❖ a wider range of worship resources for services of prayer for healing, appropriate for use in parishes, hospitals and prisons, should be developed; flexibility, for use in different contexts, is essential and ecumenical cooperation desirable (see pages 243 and 254–5);

❖ better communications should be established with other Anglican Provinces and other denominations to facilitate awareness of different material available in the ministry of healing (see page 251);

❖ services of penance/reconciliation which acknowledge the healing potential of forgiveness should be promoted (see pages 246–7).

Chapter 14:   Developing the Healing Ministry in the Parish

We recommend that:

❖ the healing ministry should be clearly defined as part of the Church's mission and ministry, effectively led, overseen, resourced and supported through diocesan structures (see pages 258–9, 261–2, 268, 269 and 274–5);

❖ the Church of England should adopt and promote nationally and within parishes the guidelines for good practice in the healing ministry as incorporated in this report (see pages 268, 269, 271, 272, 275 and 279);

❖ bishops should review the work of diocesan advisors on the healing ministry and, noting the additional workload involved in carrying out the recommendations in this report, consider the future needs within dioceses and the required number and quality of advisors (see pages 264–5, 268, 269, 272, 273, 274 and 275);

❖ each diocese should conduct a survey, in cooperation with the Ministry Division and central support of the healing ministry, to evaluate the current state of this ministry in parishes (see pages 259–60, 266 and 276);

❖ deanery synods and chapters should be encouraged to review the current state of the healing ministry in their area, develop and support proposals for increased effectiveness, including ecumenical cooperation (see pages 262, 266–7, 270 and 274–5);

❖ each parish should evaluate ways in which the healing ministry is being carried out as part of mission, and make proposals for improved effectiveness, noting local needs and challenges and expressions of this ministry in ecumenical partnerships (see pages 259–60, 262–3, 264, 265, 266–7, 270, 271, 273–4, 275–9 and 280).

Conclusion

The challenge now is to ensure that this report and its recommendations are used constructively, within the Church of England, in cooperation with the chaplaincies and the health care professions, with our ecumenical partners, and within the Anglican Communion, to bring wide awareness of the central place of this ministry within the life and mission of the Church and our society, at every level.

The introductory paragraphs of this final chapter highlight the need for a coherent approach, which depends to a large extent on effective communication, to increase awareness and encourage interest in this ministry. In January 2000, we invited the House of Bishops to consider in draft form this report, its implications and recommendations. We are grateful to the House for its agreement to the publication of this report in time for Pentecost 2000, encouraging discussion in the dioceses and parishes, leading towards a renewed commitment to the healing ministry at the beginning of the third Christian millennium.

Appendix 1

Good Practice
in the Healing Ministry

Introduction

As we begin the third millennium, the healing ministry within the Church of England is increasingly becoming part of normal everyday life, expressed in many ways – publicly and privately, ecumenically and in cooperation with the caring professions. These detailed guidelines have been produced in response to requests from people and organizations involved in the ministries of healing and deliverance, taking into account their concerns. To some extent they reflect the guidelines and codes of conduct and ethics already established for the medical and caring professions and material produced by certain dioceses and healing organizations.

The Incarnation and the ministry of Jesus inaugurated God's reign and the establishing of the kingdom of God. Jesus proclaimed his kingdom in his sayings, in his parables, in prayer and through the healing miracles. He commands his followers to continue to pray for the coming of the kingdom (Matthew 6.10) and to heal the sick (Luke 9.1-6; 10.9). In obedience to this command and after the example of Jesus, the disciples healed the sick, healings took place in the early Church and this ministry has continued to this day. It witnesses to the compassion of Jesus, who wants us to be whole, and to the establishing of God's kingdom among us.

The healing ministry is carried out in our society which reflects continually changing values and attitudes to health and healing. The Church of England's response is to ensure that the ways in which the healing ministry is carried out are theologically sound, responsible, loving and leading people to a closer relationship with God. The way in which we minister to people in need is one of the most important ways in which we spread the message of the gospel.

Key terms used in these guidelines are defined as:

❖ **health** – a dynamic state of well-being of the individual and society, of physical, mental, spiritual, economic, political and social well-being – of being in harmony with each other, with the material environment and with God (the World Council of Churches' definition in the report of its Christian Medical Commission);

❖ **healing** – progress towards health and wholeness;

❖ **disease** – a failure in ease, whether physical, mental or spiritual in location of pathology or disorder;

❖ **deliverance** – release from evil spiritual influences which oppress a person or hinder the individual's response to God's saving grace;

❖ **clergy** – all persons ordained by the bishop as priest or deacon for service in the Church of England;

❖ **licensed lay ministers** – all lay persons licensed by the bishop to a ministry, e.g. readers;

❖ **lay team members of** a healing team – persons who have the approval of the local church congregation and parish priest to be involved in the healing ministry;

❖ **parishioner** – the person to whom the clergy have a responsibility in the Church or community; the parishioner may not necessarily be resident in the parish within which he or she receives the healing ministry.

The purpose of the guidelines

We need recognizable and acceptable standards of conduct for all those involved in the Church of England's healing ministry. A common understanding of what constitutes good practice will encourage everyone involved to maintain these standards. Guidelines for good practice are also a means of encouraging and retaining the confidence of parishioners and those ministering to them, affirming good practice where it already exists in many places.

The guidelines are a broad framework and relevant to everyone involved in the healing ministry, including those involved in the deliverance ministry, where additional care and safeguards are necessary. They are not intended to be overprescriptive, but to meet concerns about boundaries, provide good models of practice and point out key issues which need leadership and oversight. No framework, however, can cover every possibility or prescribe action and non-action for every situation which may arise.

Clergy, licensed lay ministers and team members must determine which parts apply to particular settings and use them sensitively. It is recommended that everyone involved in the ministries of healing and deliverance should be fully aware of these guidelines.

The context

The healing ministry is part of the broad mission of the Church, expressed in the following ways:

❖ **publicly** as part of services:

  – at healing services, including the Eucharist, baptism and confirmation;

  – in institutions such as hospitals, hospices, nursing homes, residential homes for elderly and disabled people, prisons, etc.;

  – at healing centres and related conferences;

  – at Christian holiday venues, such as Spring Harvest and New Wine, which are often ecumenical.

❖ **privately** within the home, hospitals and hospices, discreetly in church side chapels, etc;

❖ **ecumenically** across the denominations, including local services, the hospital and prison chaplaincies;

❖ **in cooperation with the medical and caring professions.**

The most common forms of healing ministry take place in the settings described above.

Public and private prayers of intercession

Christian worship has always included prayers of intercession customarily addressed to the Father through the Son and in the power of the Holy Spirit and in union through the Son who 'indeed intercedes for us' (Romans 8.34). Intercessory prayer, in which we pray individually and corporately for those who are suffering, combines our love with God's love and our will with his will, so as to cooperate with him in building his kingdom.

The laying on of hands

This action whereby a person or people lay hands on the head of someone has its origins in the Old and New Testaments and is associated with blessing, commissioning and healing. It takes place at confirmation and ordination and is included in modern liturgies for the ministry to the sick. Actions can often 'speak louder than words' and touch conveys a message of love and assurance as well as being a link with Christ's apostolic command to heal the sick. This form of touch can make a sick person feel less fearful or alone in their suffering. Hands are usually placed gently on or side by side of a person's head, or on his or her shoulders, and accompanying prayers said quietly and reverently. The laying on of hands often takes place in silence (or where there are prayers, followed by silence).

Anointing

Anointing affirms our relationship with Christ who is 'the anointed one', and like water, bread and wine, oil is a natural resource which is blessed and used sacramentally in the ministry of the Church. We pray that as we are outwardly anointed with oil, we shall be inwardly anointed with the Holy Spirit. A sick person should be prepared for anointing and told what will take place. It is customary to anoint a person with thumb or forefinger, making the sign of the cross, with a small amount of oil on the forehead and sometimes the palms of the hands. Anointing is often accompanied by the laying on of hands and sometimes Holy Communion and reconciliation.

Reconciliation and absolution

Confession is increasingly seen as an act of reconciliation which begins with God calling us back to himself. The Anglican tradition values the use of a general confession as a communal act in the liturgy and makes provision for private confession to a priest. Private confession may be made in a formal or less formal setting and may include spiritual advice and counsel as well as absolution. Pronouncing God's love and forgiveness is a gift from God to the Church and its place in the 1662 *Book of Common Prayer* service of the 'Visitation of the Sick' indicates its significance in the ministry of healing.

Healing the family tree

The exploration of a person's family tree can enable some people to have a sense of belonging. The study of family trees can also be a useful means of discovering a possible explanation of broken relationships, lost or unmourned relatives, traumatic events and family traits. Pastoral counselling centred around a family tree may later be focused in a service of Holy Communion where members of an earthly family are remembered and brought into the healing love which is found in the Holy Trinity.

Healing of memories

Healing of memories is a term in common currency to describe a situation in which an individual is unhappily influenced by things which – though not necessarily consciously remembered – continue to affect their attitudes and behaviour. In the healing of memories, the memory is not wiped out but its effect is no longer painful and debilitating. Professional counselling, prayer, the laying on of hands, anointing, confession and Holy Communion are among the appropriate means of bringing about the healing of memories.

Ministry to the sick

The Church has a distinctive role to play in ministry to the sick because it has always linked the proclamation of the good news with healing. Modern health care and healing recognize the need to minister to the spiritual and religious needs of patients, as well as their physical needs. Christian ministry has a distinctive quality of love as well as a distinctive gospel message. This ministry of healing is therefore offered in love by the Church explicitly by prayer, religious rites and chaplaincy, and implicitly by Christians engaged in many areas of ministry to the sick as doctors, nurses, carers and visitors. Christians minister to the sick in the name of Jesus and also to Jesus himself (Matthew 25.31f.).

Ministry to the dying

For Christians, death is not the end but a beginning and the process of dying is often filled both with sadness and with hope for a fuller life with God. Hospice care in Britain has been pioneered by Christians, and modern medicine with its advances in pain control can enable people to die with dignity and to prepare them and their loved ones for their death. People facing death are often concerned about dying with broken relationships, unfinished business or a fear of what lies ahead. Here the Church can offer a ministry of reconciliation and the assurance that 'neither death nor life . . . nor anything else in all creation will be able to separate us from the love of God, in Christ Jesus our Lord' (Romans 8.38,39).

Deliverance

It is a tradition for Christians to pray for deliverance from evil; the petition in the Lord's Prayer is an obvious example of this. Praying with people for their needs and protection is often an appropriate way of ministering to them. There are, however, some situations where a pastor is ministering to a disturbed person who appears or claims to be afflicted by a power of evil or evil spirit. Inappropriate ministry may make matters much worse and the House of Bishops' guidelines should be observed. (See the specific guidelines below on p. 308)

The wider implications

God's gifts of healing are occasionally experienced instantly or rapidly, but in most cases healing is a gradual process, taking time to bring deep restoration to health at more than one level. This ministry should not exist in isolation either; it relates in varying ways to other areas of Church activity including:

❖ pastoral care;

❖ spiritual development;

❖ the boundaries and overlap with the medical and caring professions, social services, etc;

❖ ecumenical cooperation, particularly at local level and through the chaplaincies;

❖ community issues, justice and equality issues and ethical matters, international issues;

❖ the whole mission of the Church, which could be described as healing in its broadest and deepest sense.

Directory of specific guidelines

The healing ministry is Jesus' ministry entrusted to us, always to be exercised with reverence, love and compassion. As a sound guideline, recognize the presence of God in those receiving this ministry and honour his presence in them.

It is important that the healing ministry is seen to be an example of best practice for others to look to and that it does not fall behind the best practice of secular institutions. Good practice is an issue for everyone involved in this ministry. *These guidelines are set out alphabetically for ease of reference and so that they can be understood and adopted as a whole framework.*

Accountability

Within the Anglican context, clergy and licensed lay ministers are accountable to their bishop. Lay team members should be accountable to their parish priest. Ultimately, all involved in the healing ministry are accountable to God for their actions and omissions. No one should work independently, believing that he or she is accountable only to God.

Clergy, licensed lay ministers, team leaders and members involved in this ministry need to be clear about the lines of accountability and who holds relevant authority within their local church. Clergy in certain institutions have to work within a dual accountability both to their bishop and the institution which employs them.

Boundaries (see also *Personal conduct)*

It is important that each person involved in the healing ministry knows and acknowledges his or her limits of expertise and training and the limits of other team members; if limits are overreached, the risks increase. Everyone should be willing to seek advice and when necessary, to refer individuals to specialists, for example for professional counselling, medical expertise and the deliverance ministry. Good referral networks and their contact details should be developed and readily available. Any diocesan pastoral regulations relating to the ministries of healing and deliverance should also be observed by those ministering.

Clergy and lay healing team members need to develop an awareness of the personal boundaries which should be observed when dealing with troubled individuals. Hidden motives in the relationships between those ministering and parishioners need to be acknowledged sensitively.

Everyone involved in the healing ministry should develop an awareness of the psychological and emotional boundaries which must be respected. It is important to be able to identify and own when this situation is the result of personal needs or when it arises from the needs or projections of the person being ministered to. There is most risk when the situation is a powerful combination of the needs of both parties.

Child protection

Children are vulnerable; they must always be respected and ministered to with care. For clarification of responsibilities see the House of Bishops' Policy on Child Protection. Awareness of legal constraints and of their full implications is essential. Follow the specific guidelines laid down in the Children Act 1989 for all activities on church premises and when ministering to children elsewhere.

Christian Listening

Healing services rarely provide an ideal setting for listening in detail to an individual's situation and needs, so it is important to have appropriate facilities and structures outside the context of healing services and as part of pastoral care offered within the local church. Training in Christian Listening is strongly recommended for those who are interested in this form of ministry.

Collaboration

The healing ministry should be carried out in a collaborative and co-operative manner with health care professions and others involved in providing care, whose particular contributions to the care of parishioners deserve to be recognized and respected. Clergy and lay team members need to be aware that other people involved in providing care are bound by codes of ethics and good practice. The concepts of good practice in these areas tend to have an educative effect on the public and can influence parishioners' expectations of accountability and good practice on the part of ministers.

Consideration should be shown when requesting help from professionals involved in health care provision who live in the parish. They may already feel pressurized by the emotionally demanding nature of their day-to-day work, without the added complications and stresses of a church-referred clinical burden. It is also possible that parishioners may be unaware of the professional codes by which professionals are bound and may have unreasonable expectations. If health care professionals are willing to be involved in the healing ministry in the parish, set clear guidelines and boundaries to ensure that they are not overburdened.

Collusion

Collusion should be avoided with people who attempt either deliberately or unconsciously to manipulate those who minister to them, either in counselling or prayer, with any diagnosis that is believed to be false, particularly in relation to the deliverance ministry.

Competence

Every person involved in the healing ministry needs to ensure, and continue to monitor, that he or she (and other members of the healing team) are properly prepared and fit to be involved in this ministry. This involves being willing to consider seriously any concerns expressed about the competence of any member, including oneself. If one's personal fitness or that of another team member is in doubt or compromised, it is important to recognize when the individual affected should withdraw because of, for example, personal/emotional difficulties, illness, substance abuse, exhaustion or conflicts of interest.

Complaints

The complaints procedure is in itself straightforward, provided that it is clear against whom it is that a complaint is being made. Complaints about a member of the clergy (ordained person; this does not cover readers or lay pastoral workers for example) are currently covered by the complaints procedure in the Ecclesiastical Jurisdiction Measure 1963. Complaints about any clergy should be made to the bishop who has disciplinary power over them. Complaints about a lay person are not covered by Church of England legislation, so only if the complaint verges on areas of criminal activity would the Church ask the police to investigate it.

The substance of what complaints can be made about and the standards against which complaints can be compared are difficult areas because of lack of written or authoritative norms against which appropriate behaviour can be assessed. Where guidelines for good practice are established, these may reasonably be used as a benchmark against which behaviour and related complaints could be measured. Recognition and implementation of the House of Bishops' draft guidelines (on pp. 325-7) provide a framework for objective assessment of complaints and help to discourage the kind of behaviour from which they could arise.

If members of a local healing team are operating under the control of the clergy and have been trained or prepared by them for this ministry, then a complaint could be made to or against the clergy if team members behave in an abusive or unacceptable way. If, however, laity become too exuberant or overintense and/or carry out the healing ministry independent of the clergy, it would be unreasonable to discipline the clergy for a situation beyond his or her control.

Certain types of behaviour are liable to result in complaints. Within the ministries of healing and deliverance, there is scope for unwitting or even deliberate abuse and ministers who are self-aware will know of the temptations and dangers which can arise. For example, certain forms of humour, innuendo, flirting and touch can be interpreted as sexual harassment.

More serious forms of abusive physical contact can amount to a criminal offence. The victim may feel unable to complain because of fears of not being believed or even be misled into thinking that the abuse may bring some benefit, spiritually or psychologically. Complaints of such behaviour should be taken seriously and treated sympathetically and sensitively.

Anyone who suspects misconduct by another person involved in the ministries of healing and deliverance, which cannot be resolved or remedied after discussion with the person concerned, should implement the complaints procedure, doing so without breaches of confidentiality other than those necessary for investigating the complaint.

Allegations of sexual abuse, including that of children, may be made or become known. The House of Bishops' Policy on Child Protection provides guidelines for cases of alleged abuse of children. Furthermore, each social service department has a local code of practice for child protection and investigation. In the case of adults with learning disability, sexual abuse of them is a criminal offence. Allegations by other adults of abuse may be appropriately investigated by the police and lawyers.

The insurer should be given immediate notice of any incident that might lead to a claim under the insurance policy. Failure to comply with this requirement may prejudice any cover provided. Clergy should also be aware of the provisions of Canon Law as set out in Canon B 29 of the Ministry of Absolution and the Proviso to Canon 113 of the Code of 1603.

In the first instance, complaints about a lay healing team member should be referred to the priest in charge of the healing ministry team. If the complainant is not satisfied with the outcome of this referral, the complaint should be referred on to the archdeacon. Where lay healing team members are found to have behaved in an unacceptable way, they should be removed from the team and not involved further in this ministry.

Confidentiality

People's privacy and dignity should be respected and protected; most people do not want to discuss their problems publicly or to be overheard by strangers. Parishioners are entitled to expect that the information they give to ministers in the context of the ministries of healing and deliverance will remain confidential and not be misused in any way. Everyone involved in these ministries should be sensitive to the issue of confidentiality, which is a means of providing people with safety and privacy. Betrayal of confidential material destroys trust. Those involved need to be told of any limitations to confidentiality which may arise.

Care must be taken not to pass on personally identifiable information through overlapping networks of confidential relationships. Confidential information should not be shared or made available to others, including members of the family, friends or marriage partner, either of the parishioner or the person entrusted with confidential information, except where agreed upon with the parishioner.

The right of the parishioner if he or she so wishes to share personal information with one member of the healing ministry team and not with another should be safeguarded. On the other hand, team members should also be aware of the danger of being manipulated and split by the parishioner sharing personal information with more than one member of the team.

Disclosure of confidential details in public and semi-public intercessory prayer, on prayer boards, in prayer lists, etc. should be avoided. Confidential details must not be used in the production of video and audiotape recordings for training or publications, reports or conferences, etc. except with the express permission of everyone involved.

It is important not to promise confidentiality without some qualifications; for example, if what is 'confided' involves criminal activity, abuse of children or similar harm to others. Exceptional circumstances may arise which give good grounds for believing that serious harm may occur to a person being ministered to and/or other people involved. In such circumstances, after careful consideration and before disclosing any confidential information, the consent of the person concerned should be sought whenever possible unless there are also good grounds for believing that they are no longer willing or able to take responsibility for their own actions. In such cases, those ministering should if possible consult with someone in a position senior to themselves before taking action which may well take the case out of their hands. The parishioner involved should be informed that such disclosure has taken or will take place.

Any disclosure of confidential information should be restricted to relevant information, conveyed only to appropriate people and for appropriate reasons likely to alleviate the exceptional circumstances. The ethical considerations include achieving a balance between acting in the best interests of the parishioner and the minister's responsibilities to the wider community.

Conflicts of interest

No one involved in the healing ministry should use his or her position within the ministries of healing and deliverance to establish or continue any improper personal relationship, with the purpose of receiving any personal advantage or gain, whether monetary, emotional, sexual or material. Clergy and lay team members should beware of any gift, money, favour or hospitality which might be interpreted as seeking or exerting undue influence or leave opportunities for accusations of charging for the healing ministry.

It is important that those ministering are aware of the needs of the parishioner and act with compassion, whilst keeping a proper emotional and psychological distance. Each person involved in this ministry must be aware of his or her personal emotional needs and beware of the possibility of exploiting vulnerable people for his or her own needs.

Particular risks exist for the abuse of power and conflicts of interests in dual relationships, such as those between team members. At all times, the well-being of the parishioner is paramount and the boundaries of the relationship should be made clear, without rejecting the other person. If the boundaries are unacceptable, it may be advisable to end the pastoral relationship in the best interests of both parties.

Consent

It is important to ensure that every person knows and understands how they are going to be ministered to and that they consent, before they receive healing or deliverance ministry. For this reason, it is necessary to include a brief but clear description of the ways in which the ministry will be carried out before or at the beginning of a service, for example, for the benefit of newcomers. Please note that there is only proof of consent if this is provided in writing by the parishioner, although in many instances this is not practical.

People of full age (18 years and over) and of ordinary mental capacity should be allowed to consent. The issue of consent should be revisited if the purpose or nature of the healing ministry approach alters; for example, healing ministry leading to deliverance ministry. People should be encouraged to ask questions whenever they are in doubt.

Consent should not be taken for granted; no one should be ministered to against their will. The right of people to decline the healing and deliverance ministries must be respected. It is easy, for example, to assume that those sitting in wheelchairs in a healing service are there for the laying on of hands; those ministering should not just assume that they want prayer for their mobility.

Sensitivity is essential in relation to issues of power and control, particularly in institutional and high-dependency settings and those involving children and families. Care should be taken in those situations where a parishioner's ability to make informed choices may be impaired; for example because of learning disabilities, serious illness, severe pain and emotional distress or heavy medication.

It may be necessary for those involved in the ministries of healing and deliverance to make a judgement about the competence of a person over 18 years of age, to make an informed decision involving his or her consent. If someone is not capable of informed consent, consent should be obtained from the person who has the legal authority to give it on the parishioner's behalf. Even if the person with legal consent has given it, there may be circumstances when the parishioner (child or adult) has expressed a strong view that he or she does not want to be ministered to, in which case the parishioner's view should be respected.

The feelings and wishes of children being ministered to should be taken sensitively into consideration; for example, children should not be ministered to against their will. Ensure that adequate safeguards are taken to prevent exploitation, neglect and physical, sexual or psychological abuse.

The consent of the parishioner must be gained before sharing his or her confidential details with other parties such as professional workers, medical doctors or psychiatrists.

Cooperation

People need to find a closer, deeper relationship with God as far as is possible and to be active partners in their healing. The parishioner's needs should be discussed with him or her in order that the healing ministry can proceed with caution and with informed consent.

Counselling

Pastoral care, which has great value and is one of the ways in which we carry out the mission of the Church, should not be confused with the work of professional counsellors and psychotherapists who will have their own guidelines and indemnity. While all clergy are pastors, not all clergy are counsellors.

Clergy and laity who are trained in counselling should make clear to parishioners what they consider to be appropriate *and must make clear whether* they are offering pastoral care or professional counselling. Consideration needs to be given to the issue of how the relationship between the minister and the parishioner may be affected in other contexts. Professional counsellors should adhere to the codes of ethics and practice of their regulatory organizations and observe the need for professional insurance cover.

Debriefing (see also Confidentiality)

Team members or partners working together in the healing ministry need to meet regularly to debrief each other and, when appropriate, pray together. Care should be taken, however, not to breach confidentiality.

Deliverance

This is an area of ministry where particular caution needs to be exercised, especially when ministering to someone who is in a disturbed state. The House of Bishops' guidelines on the deliverance ministry should be followed and cases referred to the diocesan advisors when necessary; the advisors' special expertise should be used in order to help as effectively as possible those who think they need this ministry.

The House of Bishops' guidelines (1975) on the deliverance ministry state that the following factors should be borne in mind:

1. It should be done in collaboration with the resources of medicine.

2. It should be done in the context of prayer and sacrament.

3. It should be done with the minimum of publicity.

4. It should be done by experienced persons authorized by the diocesan bishop.

5. It should be followed up by continuing pastoral care.

Diagnosis and discernment

Superficial and hasty judgements are to be avoided; time should be taken, as far as is practical, to listen carefully and make a thorough assessment of the parishioner's needs, as part of an initial diagnosis to make an informed decision about the most appropriate form of healing ministry for that person.

There is an important distinction between diagnosis and discernment. Diagnosis is done intellectually and involves clear distinctions between types of conditions. Discernment is a spiritual gift and is the prayerful choice between different courses of action where there are no clear signs or definitions of condition or need.

It usually takes time for the healing ministry to be effective at different levels in each individual. Further needs may emerge and it is important not to be overhasty. Through prayer, the ways in which God is healing the parishioner and how he or she can best be helped may be discerned.

Ecumenical and interfaith issues

Sensitivity and general awareness are necessary. The healing ministry is the point at which people mix most readily across the denominations and can be a time when they are very vulnerable. The healing ministry may be carried out in cooperation, where appropriate, with clergy and representatives of other denominations. The development of the ecumenical expression of the healing ministry needs to be encouraged, wherever possible.

Sometimes people of other faiths also attend healing services and may need particularly sensitive assistance, taking into account their world-view.

Emergencies

Even in extreme cases, it is rarely necessary to act immediately; it is very helpful primarily to establish an atmosphere of calm. No one involved in the healing ministry should allow themselves to be pushed into actions through other people's expectations and insistence. If something quite unexpected happens, it may be necessary to reconsider the approach and, if necessary, stop ministering.

Those ministering need to be attentive towards the person for whom they are praying. If someone becomes very distressed or noisy, assistance should be sought (if it is available) to help the individual to be taken to another place if possible and then to calm the situation down.

Ethical issues (see also *Accountability and Supervision*)

Clergy and laity may find themselves caught between conflicting ethical principles, which could involve issues of public interest or private conscience. In these circumstances, it is advisable to consider the particular situation in detail and, if necessary, the issues should be discussed with the diocesan advisor and/or someone who is senior to the people involved. Even after conscientious and prayerful consideration of the ethical issues involved, some dilemmas cannot be resolved easily or wholly satisfactorily. Supervision can be helpful in providing a source of objective advice on ethical issues.

Expectations

There should be:

❖ an expectation and belief that God is, as ever, at work in society and in individuals, communities and the whole creation;

❖ an openness to the unexpected, unusual and even the embarrassing;

❖ and, equally, a thankfulness for the 'ordinary' everyday miracles and signs of God's healing touch, which are too easily taken for granted.

Gifts of the Spirit (see also *Discernment*)

Certain individuals, groups or communities are used by God in ministering powerfully in various areas of the healing ministry. These charisms are often related to natural gifts (e.g. in the medical and nursing professions), but sometimes they are manifested without any connection with human abilities. Such gifts of the Spirit should be received with thanksgiving and yet with wisdom and discernment (see 1 Corinthians 12.1–11).

Those who exercise these gifts need to be helped to minister humbly, with the support of their congregation and under its leadership. Spiritual gifts can often become more effective if those who exercise them learn from others and accept further training; but in some cases, a charism of healing may be manifested only once in a person's experience.

Hospital chaplains

The special ministry of hospital chaplains should be recognized and respected, and the usual courtesies observed when informing them of the admission of patients. Chaplains should be encouraged to be members of a local church for mutual support and benefit.

Influences

Everyone involved in the healing ministry needs to have a sound grasp of the theology on which it is based. This is the responsibility of everyone involved but particularly the clergy and other team leaders.

The healing ministry is non-judgemental: those involved in it are encouraged to consider and address their own prejudices and stereotyping to avoid projection of their personal internal codes of behaviour, which could lead to unreasonable expectations being placed upon other people. People involved in this ministry should not be easily shocked, should the emotions of those receiving ministry be released.

The introduction of concepts or imagery which are more commonly associated with New Age approaches to healing, such as crystals and pendulums, should be avoided.

Information (see also *Confidentiality* and *Public statements)*

Informed consent: people have a right to know what is being provided and to have some idea of how they will be ministered to, in order to trust, to feel at ease and to cooperate. Information must be in a readily accessible form which people, including the unchurched, can understand; for example, pew leaflets written with clarity and without jargon can be very helpful. People involved in the healing ministry should be prepared to provide information for those with learning disabilities, language problems or sensory impairment, older people and those with mental health problems.

A sensitive balance is needed between strengthening faith in God and avoiding statements which are likely to lead to misunderstandings and unrealistic expectations. Avoid overemphasis on physical expressions of healing; it is preferable to encourage a deeper understanding of healing of the whole person, through Christ. The healing ministry provides opportunities for further reflection and a deeper understanding of the Church's mission, which embodies healing in the broadest sense.

Insurance (see also *Child protection*)

Public liability insurance is usually provided as part of a package of cover for parishes. The following comments relate to cover provided by Ecclesiastical Insurance Group (EIG) under their Parishguard policy; please refer to the wording of the policy cover for other Church organizations, or if cover is provided by another insurer. In simple terms, Parishguard covers healing ministry activities of the clergy and others authorized by the PCC (being anticipated as a normal function of ministry with the awareness of the rural dean or archdeacon). Indemnity is provided for legal liability arising from accidental bodily injury or damage to property. There are special cover extensions for 'administrative errors or omissions' and 'pastoral care'. An optional extension is available for professional counselling. Alternative arrangements for insurance cover for professional counsellors may also be available through an individual's professional regulatory body.

The Church of England has recognised the various complex issues surrounding the deliverance ministry. It has sought to centralize its expertise and maintain a measure of control via a specialized diocesan appointment. Extensions of insurance cover are available for a range of professional diocesan roles such as the authorized diocesan deliverance team. Deliverance ministry is not regarded by EIG as a general parish activity; an individual parish should consult its insurers on any liability risk which might reasonably be seen as a special activity or function.

All reasonable steps should be taken by those involved in the healing ministry to ensure awareness of current law as it applies to this ministry, e.g. some approaches might be misconstrued as assault if carried out without clear ongoing consent. The insurance does not cover the perpetrator of a criminal act, e.g. abuse or assault, although a measure of insurance exists for legal expenses in certain situations. With an increasingly litigious society and expectations of higher professional standards, insurers regularly review the cover provided by their policies and must pursue a 'risk management' approach to prevent claims. It is imperative that those involved in the healing ministry operate within authorized codes, with appropriate supervision, and adhere to current best practice.

Introducing healing services

It is important to safeguard the proper representation of lay people in the decision-making processes related to healing services. The PCC and congregation need to understand and support the concept and those involved, before healing services are introduced. If a regular liturgical healing service is to be held in a parish church, the PCC should approve its use by resolution.

The cooperation of those in the congregation with medical and nursing training is highly desirable at an early stage. Where appropriate local medical centres and surgeries should be informed of the ministry being offered in the parish church.

Language

The language used should be inclusive and sensitive to the situation, understandable and acceptable to those receiving the healing ministry. Excessive noise levels are not conducive to an atmosphere of peace, love and patient hope.

Networks for advice, support and referrals

The telephone numbers of relevant contacts should be available for emergencies. It is helpful to develop networks for advice, support, resources and referrals, including people in the caring professions and social services and other secular networks, if appropriate. The contact details for the diocesan advisor on the deliverance ministry should also be readily available for clergy and healing ministry team leaders, but not passed to those seeking help in this area, as a general rule.

Non-discrimination

The healing ministry is available for everyone; there is no place for discrimination of any kind. The common humanity and uniqueness of each individual must be respected and valued.

Non-exploitation

The healing ministry is non-exploitative. Clergy and team members must not exploit emotionally, sexually or financially those receiving the healing ministry. Emotions are sometimes released during this ministry, which can leave the person feeling vulnerable. No one who receives the healing ministry should be put under emotional pressure or manipulated, particularly through guilt or fear. Furthermore, no pressure should be put on people to give premature testimony of healing.

Clergy in particular, because of their role as pastors, spiritual guides and representatives of the faith, need to be aware of the issue of power and their position of comparative strength. Authority explicitly derived from God is particularly awesome and yet can be misused, consciously or unconsciously. Those ministering are encouraged to seek in all humility and love to keep in touch with the vulnerability and weakness which the parishioner may be feeling.

Clergy and lay team members should also seek to recognize their own emotional needs and ensure that these are met outside involvement in the healing ministry. Care and sensitivity are needed to ensure that this ministry is not used to make parishioners dependent on those ministering to them.

Personal conduct

General manner and appearance: the way in which clergy and lay team members behave with courtesy and consideration is part of the message of the gospel. First impressions count. It is considerate to dress appropriately and be conscientious about personal hygiene. The distinction between informality and intimacy is important. Informality can put people at ease; intimacy can lead to overfamiliarity and unnecessary risks.

When two or more people meet, messages can be conveyed verbally and also non-verbally through body language; for example, stance, posture, repeated movements and facial expressions. All such methods of communication can be used to make the most of healing opportunities, or knowledge of their use can be abused and lead to domination, manipulation, exploitation or misunderstanding of motive and lack of trust.

The ways in which people communicate non-verbally give out powerful signals, which may be different from those consciously intended. Touch should be used with care and forethought. Used in the right context, it can be an important element in conveying comfort and healing. Used carelessly, touch can be dangerously ambiguous.

Any form of sexual advance or contact between those ministering and the parishioner in the context of the ministries of healing and deliverance is unacceptable, harmful and grounds for allegations of misconduct.

Prayer

Since the healing ministry is based on prayer in the name of Jesus Christ, those ministering should be helped to grow in their personal spirituality. To minister sensitively to others, they should be guided in the use of both formal and spontaneous prayer.

Intercessory prayers are best when succinct and accompanied by periods of silence so as to focus on God. When praying for people by name in public, it is pastorally desirable to ask for their permission to do so. Some may not wish their illness to be known for personal, work or family reasons. Sensitivity also needs to be exercised in giving details of people's illnesses. Prayer may need to be informed but the purpose of intercession is to hold people before God and not to provide information, spread gossip, give clinical diagnoses and reports of personal opinions of someone's condition.

Prayer support

Prayerful support for everyone involved in the healing ministry, caring professions and the wider Church, including hospital and prison chaplains, is important and to be encouraged. Those involved in the deliverance ministry particularly need daily prayer support from friends and colleagues and their local community.

Proof of healing

People should be encouraged to recognize God's healing power in everyday and ordinary events, improved relationships with others, and particularly in their deepening relationship with God, rather than depending exclusively on 'signs and wonders'. Phenomena that can accompany this ministry, for example being 'slain in the Spirit', can sometimes be a genuine expression of release and acceptance of God's healing touch, but they are not always a measure of true healing and should not be sought for their own sake.

Proper preparation

The daily prayer-life of clergy and lay team members is an essential factor in the way in which they can be used in the healing ministry, and its quality is reflected in the way in which they minister and relate to other people. Before carrying out this ministry, it is important to make time for prayer, personal and corporate, and if possible reflection, receiving Holy Communion and fasting in certain circumstances for example. Plans for any follow-up ministry which may be necessary and for the unexpected should be in place. All team members need to be properly aware of these plans in advance.

Proxy healing

The practice of intercessory prayer has always included the provision for worshippers to intercede for other people for whom they are concerned. Although sometimes people wish to receive laying on of hands for others, opinions differ as to the appropriateness and use of the practice of proxy healing. This issue is worth discussion within the PCC and healing teams, to form a local view on the acceptability of proxy healing.

It should be borne in mind that proxy healing should not in any way breach confidentiality or betray trust, through intermediaries requesting prayers for others not present. Those ministering to individuals requesting proxy healing on behalf of others should be alert to the potential harm which could be done when confidential details are passed on, as part of requests for prayer ministry, particularly in public and semi-public settings.

Public statements (see also Confidentiality, Information and Representation)

Good relations with the media are vital, for we rely on journalists to communicate Church affairs to the wider public through the press, radio and TV. Interest in the ministries of healing and deliverance in these circles is considerable, and there have been some interesting and informative articles and programmes on these topics in the past. Certain sections of the secular media can exploit those who make public statements about their healing: it is helpful to consider how to deal with these issues effectively, before they arise. Many dioceses run courses on how to respond to the media.

All public statements and advertising should be accurate as far as possible. No one should be pressurized into making public statements until they are ready and willing. It is important to avoid making false or exaggerated claims or statements which cannot be adequately supported and which could exploit people's vulnerability or lack of knowledge. Nothing should be offered which cannot be guaranteed. No one should be led to believe they are being offered something, for example, a guarantee of cure, which is in fact not being offered. Clergy and lay team members need to be aware of legal decisions involving the Advertising Standards Authority etc. and it is advisable to keep a record of conversations or interviews with the media.

Personal statements which may be construed as the official view of the Church should be avoided. Clergy and lay team members should be aware of, and use if necessary, the Church structures, e.g. diocesan communications officer, Archbishops' Council spokespersons, House of

Bishops' appointed spokespersons and so on. Where information is recorded, it will almost inevitably be edited and therefore potentially subject to misrepresentation. It is advisable to insist on seeing the edited version prior to transmission, if at all possible.

Reconciliation

The Anglican attitude towards confession has sometimes been described as 'all may, none must, but some should'. The Church pronouncing God's love and forgiveness is a gift from God and its place in the service of the 1662 *Book of Common Prayer*'s service 'Visitation of the Sick' indicates its significance in the ministry of healing.

Canon B 29, concerned with the ministry of absolution, makes reference to the unrepealed proviso to Canon 113 of the Code of 1603 concerning what is commonly called the 'seal of the confessional', by which a priest hearing a confession is 'charged and admonished' not to reveal anything committed to his or her trust and secrecy under 'pain of irregularity'. It is widely and generally accepted therefore, that whatever is said to a priest by a penitent during a private confession is accorded total confidentiality. When in doubt, however, a priest may go to his or her bishop or another priest with what happens in the confessional for supervision, maintaining of course the anonymity of the person making the confession.

Records (see also *Confidentiality*)

Where appropriate, and with the individual's permission, it is helpful to keep adequate records, including relevant details of appointments and meetings involving the ministries of healing and deliverance, always taking into account the need for confidentiality. Comparison of notes taken on different occasions may reveal issues not openly expressed, which may help to find the most appropriate form of healing. Parishioners need to be assured of the utmost confidentiality. Records should include only such information concerning parishioners and others involved as is strictly necessary, and exclude superfluous information, particularly that which could be potentially embarrassing or damaging.

It is the responsibility of clergy and lay team members to be aware of any changes to legislation and regulations concerning rights of access to records. To ensure confidentiality, written and other portable forms of records must be kept in a secure place such as a locked filing cabinet. Stored information including computer-based records is subject to statutory regulations such as the Data Protection Act. All those who keep such records should be aware of the necessity to register under the Act. When records are no longer needed, arrangement should be made for their safe disposal.

The records kept need to contain accurate relevant information to assist those ministering and caring for the person, as it may be advisable, after gaining the parishioner's permission, to share notes/records with other professions (such as medical practitioners and psychiatrists in relation to the deliverance ministry).

Accusations and incidents of wrongful acts may only come to light after a long period of time, perhaps many years. Whilst it is difficult to be prescriptive, special thought should be given to safeguarding records on an indefinite basis, particularly if an individual case is complex in nature or involves children under 18 years of age. An analogy can be drawn with current employment practices which require the retention of records for a minimum period of 40 years. Case law continues to revise the boundaries of the Limitation Acts. Where records are clearly no longer needed arrangement should be made for their secure disposal.

Representation

Clergy and lay team members should always set an example of good practice and not behave or allow others involved to behave in ways which would undermine confidence in the Church or the ministries of healing and deliverance. Behaviour should be such as to embody the communication of the gospel and to uphold and enhance the good standing of the Church as a body concerned with the pastoral care and well-being of everyone.

Reviews

Regular reviews should be undertaken of the way in which the healing ministry is carried out locally, with those involved. For example, support for local healing services can vary and a regular review may highlight the issues to be addressed before they present serious problems.

Responsibility for 'follow-up'

Those carrying out the healing ministry need to make adequate provision for follow-up as part of normal pastoral care. For example, bereavement counselling, home visits for the housebound to receive this ministry, prayer support through healing prayer groups and intercessions in public services. In particular, continuing support and care for those who have received the deliverance ministry is an important factor in their healing and strengthening.

Safety (see also *Situations to avoid*)

All reasonable steps should be taken to promote and ensure the safety of everyone involved, including team members, the congregation and particularly those receiving the healing ministry. If anyone finds themselves in a situation which makes them uneasy, they should try to identify whether the fears are rooted in reality and take sensible and calm action to avoid placing anyone at risk.

When individuals who are standing receive the laying on of hands, there is the possibility that the person will fall to the floor. In some circles this phenomenon is described as 'being slain' or 'resting in the Spirit'. Although discernment is needed in these circumstances, it is usually better to continue ministering to others and leave the individual to 'rest in the Spirit'. Ministering in a carpeted area is advisable.

It is important that people who have received the healing ministry do not stop taking prescribed medication without first consulting their doctors.

Settings for ministry

As far as possible the environment should be suitable, for example safe, clean, well lit, suitably heated and ventilated, with comfortable seating provided and access and facilities available for elderly and disabled people. A quiet, peaceful and reverent atmosphere is conducive to the healing ministry.

It is helpful to distinguish between and adapt to the different kinds of places in which the healing ministry is offered, for example, healing services in church, ministry to the sick in hospital and at home, healing ministry at conferences and healing centres. If ministering to someone in the home setting, care should be taken to avoid informality slipping into, or appearing to become, inappropriate intimacy.

Situations to avoid

These include avoiding, in the context of the healing ministry, interviewing or ministering to persons of the opposite sex, children and adolescents on one's own. It is advisable to avoid having two or more men ministering to a woman alone; whenever possible someone should be involved who is the same gender as the person receiving this ministry.

Clergy and others involved in the healing ministry should take sensible steps to protect themselves from possible physical risk or scandalous accusations when visiting members of the local community, particularly those not already known or those known to have behavioural problems. It is also preferable to avoid late night visits from people not already known, if no one else is around to assist/witness in case of unexpected behaviour.

Where practical, it is advisable for clergy and licensed lay ministers who are single or working alone to ensure that details (name, address, date, etc.) of pastoral visits are known to others, within the boundaries of confidentiality.

Social and cultural contexts

Clergy and lay team members need to be aware of the context in which the healing ministry is being carried out and sensitive to the world-view of the parishioner. The social and cultural backgrounds of some people predispose them to beliefs in, for example, superstitions and curses. They may have dabbled in the occult or New Age practices and they may have confused Christian teaching with that of other religions. Social and cultural backgrounds may also influence or mask family tensions. It is important to be aware of the possibility of people's behaviour being affected by substance abuse.

Spiritual dangers

These include:

❖ concentration on self – wanting to be a 'healer' rather than a channel for healing;

❖ residual doubt about the authority of God;

❖ uncritical use of the gift of discernment, and lack of discernment concerning those who claim to have this gift;

❖ enthroning, through overemphasis, the powers of evil rather than Christ;

❖ personality cults; it is advisable to work in pairs and/or teams and change partners when appropriate.

Supervision

Clergy and lay team members should be aware of the need for and benefits of supervision in some related areas of activity, e.g. the provision of counselling, spiritual direction, deliverance ministry and bereavement counselling.

Support networks

The healing ministry can be stressful and the particular strains it places on those involved in it need to be acknowledged. Those involved have a responsibility to seek adequate support for their own needs and should make sure that they know what facilities are available for them to receive counselling if necessary and that they have adequate rest, quiet days, retreats and spiritual direction.

Teams (see also *Confidentiality* and *Records*)

Sound leadership and good communication are essential for effective teamwork. Team leaders have a responsibility to show reasonableness and consideration towards members and trainees. They have responsibility for ensuring that members have proper training and that relevant gifts within the healing ministry are developed without any sense of competition.

Team members, who should have the respect and trust of their congregation, PCC and parish priest, have joint responsibility for their actions and omissions. Clergy and team leaders should ensure that everyone involved in this ministry is fully aware of and accepts these guidelines. Those who prove to be unsuitable should cease to be involved. The onus should not be on the unsuitable to do the proving; it is the responsibility of the leader to remove such persons from the team if they are not willing to step down voluntarily.

Testimonies (see also *Confidentiality*)

Testimonies can be of considerable valuable in the context of a healing service. Those who give testimonies, however, should always bear in mind that they will be addressing some who have not received the healing they had hoped for through the Church's healing ministry. Sensitivity, humility and encouragement are more appropriate and helpful than triumphant speeches. It is wise to allow at least a month after experiencing God's healing touch before inviting someone to testify to this.

Thanksgiving

Praise and thanks should be offered to God, in every time of ministry, for the healing received and prayers, too, that the healing given will continue. The Eucharist is the highest liturgical celebration of thanksgiving for healing.

Timing

Reasonable time limits on healing sessions and services should be set. It is important to avoid protracted sessions which overtire those ministering and those receiving; prayer for individuals in a healing service should not become an opportunity for counselling. Knowing when to stop is just as important as knowing when to start. Some people in the congregation may be ill and an hour-long service, for example, may be too long. Provision and permission for them to come and go can be helpful.

Traditions

Respect for the traditions and spiritual experience of other Christians will help to show that different approaches are complementary, rather than mutually exclusive. God works in different ways in different circumstances, responding to infinite varieties of need.

Training, teaching and preaching about the healing ministry

All those involved in the healing ministry should accept the need for preparatory and continuous training and supervision. Ministers and leaders of healing teams should also accept personal responsibility for keeping up to date with the contemporary healing scene and ensure that they are trained in the wider healing ministry, both initially and for continuous training of themselves and others.

No one should act in isolation; all should be trained as part of being 'under authority'. Personal appraisal should include an assessment of training resources and opportunities to develop awareness and appreciation of other approaches and resources needed. A church congregation involved in this ministry needs to be encouraged to give thought to its own need to be prepared and trained beforehand and to appraise its progress.

Because there are many misunderstandings about the healing ministry, any suitable opportunities which arise to preach and teach soundly about it should be taken up. The public need help to become more aware of this ministry, to develop their understanding of it and where and how it can be found locally.

Working with other people involved in caring and healing

The healing ministry is never isolated from the wider setting of the Church and society. Other people are usually involved, including:

- ❖ professionals involved in medicine and provision of health care, social and community workers;
- ❖ family and friends, neighbours and work colleagues;
- ❖ where possible, members of the medical and caring professions in the congregation;
- ❖ the wider Church structures.

Collaboration and cooperation, based on recognition and respect between ministers and these groups, are important factors in helping parishioners towards healing and wholeness.

House of Bishops' draft guidelines for good practice in the healing ministry

The healing ministry is Jesus' ministry entrusted to us, always to be exercised with reverence, love and compassion. The guiding principle is to recognize the presence of God in those receiving this ministry and honour his presence in them.

1. **Prayer and preparation.** The healing ministry is based on prayer in the name of Jesus Christ; those involved in this ministry should be prayerful, regularly practising Christians who acknowledge his healing love and are willing to pray and listen for guidance in order to minister appropriately to others.

2. **Safety.** All reasonable steps should be taken to ensure the safety of the person receiving this ministry. People have a right to know what is being provided and how they will be ministered to.

3. **Accountability and diocesan regulations.** Everyone involved in the healing ministry needs clear lines of accountability to recognize who holds relevant authority within their local church. All reasonable steps should be taken by those involved to ensure their awareness of current law as it applies to this ministry, e.g. data protection; informed consent. Legal liability issues must be considered from an insurance viewpoint. Existing diocesan regulations should also be followed.

4. **Training.** Individuals should receive appropriate training in this ministry and be kept up to date with developments and its ecumenical expression. Healing team leaders must ensure that members have opportunities for training and a common understanding of good practice.

5. **Competence and boundaries.** Every person in this ministry should be aware of his or her personal limitations and ensure that he/she is properly prepared and fit to be involved. If a person's fitness is doubtful or compromised or there is a conflict of interest, he/she should withdraw from ministering to others. Professional boundaries with health care and chaplaincies should be observed.

6. **Personal conduct.** The healing ministry is part of the message of the gospel; the personal conduct of everyone involved should encourage confidence in this ministry and not undermine it. Language, personal hygiene, general appearance, body language and touch used by those ministering should be appropriate, considerate and courteous towards those receiving it. No one should be ministered to against their will.

7. **Confidentiality and public statements.** People's privacy and dignity should be respected and protected. Any limitations to confidentiality should be explained in advance and any disclosure should be restricted to relevant information and not misused in any way, conveyed only to appropriate people, and normally with the parishioner's consent.

8. **Counselling and psychotherapy.** These specific treatments, as distinct from pastoral care and listening, should only be provided by accredited counsellors and therapists who adhere to the codes of ethics and practice of their regulatory organizations and have professional insurance cover.

9. **Deliverance.** The House of Bishops' guidelines (1975) should be followed and diocesan advisors consulted when necessary.

10. **Partnership.** The healing ministry should be carried out in co-operation, where appropriate, with chaplains and representatives of our ecumenical partners, and those involved in professional and voluntary health care, whilst recognizing that they may be bound by other codes of conduct.

Appendix 2

Detailed Recommendations to the House of Bishops and the Church of England

A summary of the main recommendations

The aim of the following proposals is to move from the current situation, where the healing ministry is not coordinated, overseen, supported or promoted nationally within the Church of England, to a situation where it is an effective and integrated part of normal daily life in every parish, supported and coordinated at diocesan and national levels.

The improved effectiveness of the healing ministry needs to be addressed simultaneously at each level within the Church and also ecumenically. The necessary changes in approach cannot be achieved simply by a hierarchical drive down or out from the central structures, a grass-roots-led revival or an individual diocesan scheme. Furthermore, to develop this ministry within the Church of England in isolation from the ways in which it is carried out ecumenically is to waste precious opportunities and to fail to respond to the call to unity. The success of the recommendations depends on a coordinated approach for momentum, clear communication and cooperation.

The main recommendations are set out in Chapter 15. Further recommendations based on research and in particular the surveys of advisors and chaplains are set out in this appendix, grouped under the main recommendations and marked with an asterisk✶. The purpose is to provide a more detailed overview of the potential development and support of the healing ministry over several years. *It is not envisaged that all of the detailed recommendations could or should be put into place in the immediate future,* because of the current lack of allocated resources and because the Review Group's main recommendations invite the Archbishops' Council to consider the wider implications. Rather, it is hoped that this agenda will be followed item by item over the next five to ten years. Future initiatives will need to be linked to continual monitoring of this ministry, in order to ensure their sound base on a broad and accurate overview of its current state, including training and cooperation with our ecumenical partners and health care organizations.

Healing in the Scriptures and Tradition

We acknowledge the importance of the bishops' role as teachers and guardians of the faith. Inherent in the episcopal office is a duty and opportunity to commend the ministry of healing to the Church and to promote it within each diocese. We recommend and encourage bishops to teach the scriptural importance of this ministry and its significance in furthering the kingdom of God.

✽ We also recommend that:

❖ bishops, clergy and readers in the Church of England should use suitable opportunities to communicate through preaching and teaching, good example and practice, the theology of the healing ministry to members of the Church and our wider society in order to promote its better understanding particularly amongst those who most need this ministry. (Chapter 2 sets out the theology of this ministry in terms which are readily accessible to laity and clergy and which give it fresh impetus for the new millennium. Chapter 9 also sets out the theology underpinning the deliverance ministry);

❖ this theology should be communicated in ways which are accessible to all age groups, all social and cultural backgrounds and to people with learning difficulties and other disabilities: the vocabulary used should take into account the diverse use of related words and phrases in our society, which sometimes leads to confusion and ambiguity;

❖ the theology of the healing ministry should be given greater prominence in training for ordinands, as part of continuing ministerial education (CME), particularly years one to four and training for readers

329

and for licensed lay workers in areas related to pastoral care and health care. In all other theological education, students need to be encouraged to develop a balanced understanding of this ministry; training should relate to the evangelistic potential of healing and wholeness as part of the Church's missiology;

❖ the House of Bishops should provide effectively communicated guidance on issues which are related to health care which are of concern to many people in our society, such as euthanasia, force-feeding, abortion and genetic engineering;

❖ consideration should be given to the possibility of developing with our ecumenical partners an understanding of the theology of this ministry which the main denominations can jointly own;

❖ research and study of the theology and spirituality which form the basis of each of the most widely used complementary and alternative healing approaches available in our society should be carried out, to enable guidance to be provided on these approaches to members of the Church;

❖ the Board of Education and the National Society should consider how to ensure that the theology, history and current wide expression of the healing ministry are taught in appropriate ways in schools, so that children and young people are aware early in life of its implications, expression and availability;

❖ the Archbishops' Council should consider those aspects of the Church of England at each level which need healing, including its relationships with the other denominations, to enable us to be a 'Church being healed' as well as a 'healing Church'.

The Healing Ministry in the Church of England Today

We recommend that:

❖ the Archbishops' Council should be asked to address through the Ministry Division the clearly identified need for improved training for the healing ministry and the strong call for its central support and coordination (see pages 41, 47, 51, 54, 55, 56, 59 and 62);

❖ the healing ministry should be given the weight appropriate to its importance as a gospel imperative, in the recruitment, selection and training of ordinands, in continuing ministerial education, in provision for lay training and related areas within the Church of England (see pages 38, 40, 44, 46, 47, 52, 54, 55, 56, 59 and 62);

❖ the Archbishops' Council should consider the resourcing for this ministry through an existing allocation within the national budget (see pages 43 and 47);

❖ a formal national network should be established of diocesan advisors appointed by the bishops, enabling them to be acknowledged and affirmed within the Church of England and supported through the central structures. We envisage that the Ministry Division could play a coordinating role, acting in particular as a central reference point for a network of diocesan advisors. The resourcing of this network could, judging by the example of other networks (such as that for Bishops' Visitors), be relatively modest (see pages 41, 43, 44, 46, 47 and 51);

❖ the Church of England should cooperate with the Churches and Provinces of the Anglican Communion in the support and encouragement of the healing ministry worldwide (see pages 84–5).

✣ We also recommend that:

❖ the improved effectiveness of the healing ministry partly depends on its clear presence within the central structures of the Church of England and the ways in which it relates to the substructure of the Archbishops' Council. Awareness of the whole of the Church's mission in its broadest sense, as an expression of the healing between God and every human being, needs to be emphasized, through:

   – social responsibility;

   – education;

   – hospital chaplaincies;

   – prison chaplaincies;

   – ministry, particularly training;

   – finance and resource allocation;

–   ecumenical relationships;
–   the Anglican Communion.

(NB. The human factor which determines more than any other whether the healing ministry has a high profile in a parish is the interest and commitment to this ministry of the parish priest. On many occasions during research for this report, the point has been made that there is no coherent approach across the Church of England to training clergy in the healing ministry. All too often, this ministry is seen as an option or at best a minor area of interest, instead of one of the gospel imperatives. The link between training in this ministry and the wide range of ways in which it can be expressed in the parishes as part of everyday life also needs to be strong and effectively supported.)

✻ We also recommend that the new advisory and coordinating body, set up within the Ministry Division of the Archbishops' Council, should have its terms of reference developed taking into account the following possible areas of activity:

❖   to monitor the healing ministry as it is carried out within the dioceses and parishes; to keep the whole spectrum of activity within the ministries of healing and deliverance across the denominations and their ecumenical expression in focus and to provide a database to enable the effective support of these ministries;

❖   to develop appropriate policies for this ministry on which to base and propose an annual budget and account for its expenditure, to coordinate, promote, aid and further support this ministry at national level;

❖   to liaise with other relevant parts of the substructure of the Archbishops' Council to ensure that the healing ministry is taken into account in the development of policies, discussions and decision-making in related areas;

❖   to inform and encourage effective and pastorally sound training for this ministry for ordinands and as part of Post-Ordination Training (POT) and Continuing Ministerial Education (CME), the appropriate points in stages of training should be determined for the different aspects of this ministry and to develop and provide a range of sound models for good practice at parish level;

❖ to inform, encourage and, where appropriate, provide sound training for those involved in training others in the healing ministry. We recommend that the coordinating body set up with the Ministry Division should develop and produce training material, including written resources and videos, to help establish a common understanding of the good practice of this ministry in parishes and deaneries, taking into account its range of expression across the traditions and across the denominations;

❖ to encourage the adoption throughout the Church of England of the House of Bishops' draft guidelines for good practice in the healing ministry and to review these guidelines in the light of developing trends; to encourage the following of the House of Bishops' guidelines on the deliverance ministry (1975) and assess the need for further or amended guidelines from time to time; where appropriate, to seek advice on the issue of insurance cover for those involved in these ministries;

❖ a Church-wide policy should be agreed and communicated on confidentiality and openness of records; this policy should be developed in cooperation with other institutions and professional bodies involved in health care;

❖ procedures should be developed for responding to and investigating complaints related to the ministries of healing and deliverance. Clergy and laity need a clear understanding of boundaries within these ministries and guidance to avoid giving grounds for complaints;

❖ to consider the legal implications of complaints against laity who are involved in the healing and deliverance ministry, particularly where they are involved in local healing teams under the guidance of clergy; to make recommendations for appropriate procedures and safeguards for all concerned;

❖ the pastoral care implications for those affected by bad practice need careful consideration and recommendations should be made for their future care;

❖ a national policy should be developed and agreed on the title and job description for advisors, to avoid the wide variations around the

333

dioceses, to encourage wider awareness of their role and how they can assist the parishes, and to provide them with a framework within which they are effectively supported;

❖ the diocesan advisors appointed by the bishops should be supported through the provision of an annual national conference organized by the Ministry Division, to provide a forum for discussion, communication of new insights and developments in the healing ministry, support and fellowship;

❖ to organize regular regional conferences, to encourage more local cooperation, ongoing training, exchange of ideas and insights, information and support, including to hospital and prison chaplains. These regional conferences should also be open, where appropriate, to advisors in the other main denominations in the ministries of healing and deliverance;

❖ to coordinate initiatives and conferences and produce regular bulletins for those already involved in the healing ministry in the dioceses and parishes; to communicate information on key events and training courses, review books and research material and generally raise awareness of current issues in this ministry;

❖ to explore the viability of establishing and supporting a joint network between the prison and hospital chaplains and the diocesan advisors, to assist the coordination and support of the healing and deliverance ministries through the prison and hospital chaplaincies;

❖ to provide general information to public enquirers and the media about the healing ministry and agreed related areas, seeking opportunities to promote the healing ministry within our society; to provide information for the national network of healing advisors and other healing organizations; to run a web site to provide up-to-date information to promote this ministry to the unchurched and an on-line news-sheet and resource directory for those involved in the healing ministry; to encourage the adoption of healthy lifestyles and preventative medicine amongst clergy and laity. The web site should be relevant to the other denominations and to the Churches and Provinces in the Anglican Communion;

❖ to liaise with the voluntary and independent organizations involved in the healing ministry, to inform and encourage good communication and promotion of this ministry; to encourage the adoption of the House of Bishops' draft guidelines for good practice by these organizations. Many of the trusts and organizations involved in the healing ministry provide valuable independent specialist resources but are not accountable to the central structures of the Church, which allows them freedom to adapt and develop at their discretion. It is important that they are aware of these guidelines on the healing ministry and the House of Bishops' guidelines on the deliverance ministry (1975). We recommend that the Church of England develops and maintains links with the voluntary organizations and trusts involved in the healing ministry, to ensure that they are aware of wider developments within this ministry and to support effective communication in both directions;

❖ to work with the Board of Social Responsibility to raise greater awareness in our society of the needs of chronically sick, mentally ill, disabled and dying people; to help overcome forms of brokenness in this world, such as prejudice and fear of mental illness, AIDS and substance addiction, while we wait for the coming of the kingdom;

❖ to encourage the relationship between the healing ministry and medicine, based on the theology of this ministry; to develop a vocabulary for this ministry which is clearly understood and shared between clergy, laity and health care professionals;

❖ to encourage greater awareness, within the general public, of the ways in which God works through the medical professions, health care and social services, prison service and legislative and justice system;

❖ to maintain a national advisory network of consultants and specialists in healing- and health care-related areas, such as psychiatry, palliative care, hospice care, professional counselling, who understand and support the Church's healing ministry;

❖ to assist in a constructive breaking down of barriers of confidentiality between the different professional disciplines involved in health care within our society; to develop a common code of confidentiality to enable closer working relationships between chaplains and health care professionals, in order better to care for parishioners;

❖ to evaluate and encourage the ecumenical expression of the healing ministry, through close cooperation with the healing organizations in the main denominations, in particular seeking practical ways of working together and sharing of resources and information at national, regional and local levels;

❖ to research and evaluate with representatives of our ecumenical partners the range of complementary medicine and alternative therapies available in our society and their effects on spirituality; to research the possibility of a link between the rise in popularity of these approaches to healing and the fall in church membership; to assist the House of Bishops in developing guidelines for church members on the appropriateness of these approaches to health and healing;

❖ to increase awareness of this ministry in health care agencies and social services; to raise awareness in the Church of England of the issues and challenges facing the hospital chaplaincies in the NHS;

❖ to work with the Anglican Communion office and to provide information on the ministries of healing and deliverance to those Churches and Provinces in the Anglican Communion who would like assistance to encourage these ministries in their areas; to share where possible training material and other resources to assist the Church in developing countries to develop these ministries; to encourage adoption of the guidelines for good practice; to circulate a newsletter or bulletin providing current information and encouraging wider awareness of the ways in which the healing ministry is being carried out across the Anglican Communion, and to support and encourage the ecumenical expression of the healing ministry throughout the Anglican Communion.

❖ In order to provide adequate resources for the central co-ordination and support for the healing ministry within the Ministry Division, we recommend that:

❖ the national budget should make provision for the central co-ordination and support of the healing ministry in future; as this ministry becomes more effective and more widely carried out, the need for adequate financial provision will increase;

❖ the General Synod should receive an annual report reviewing the healing ministry, including its ecumenical expression and proposals for its continuing support and promotion;

❖ this report should be made available for discussion in the dioceses, and to ecumenical partners in the healing ministry, to encourage better understanding of this ministry's place within the Church's mission;

❖ the healing ministry of the Church should be effectively represented in relation to the other key bodies influencing health and healing in our society, and to encourage wider and more accurate understanding of its place within the life and mission of the Church in the world;

❖ there should be a clear overlap in membership and communications between the new body coordinating the healing ministry within the Church of England's central structures and the other key bodies influencing health and healing in our society;

❖ a small number of reliable key personnel should develop close links between the various interest groups and national bodies, to ensure that the Church is aware of what is happening and able to help shape events related to this ministry, within the Church of England, ecumenically and within society, for example the Government, the NHS and the media.

The issue of training for the healing ministry has been highlighted as an area of particular concern. Many older clergy have received no formal training in the ministries of healing and deliverance. Currently the provision of specific training in these areas is limited to an average of a few hours over a three-year course. Few courses provide significant amounts of practical training in the healing ministry and there does not appear to be any consensus about what kind of training should be provided in these areas, at what stage and by whom. It is also unclear whether current training in these ministries is taught by people who are themselves trained, experienced and fully aware of the diversity of practical expression across the traditions and denominations. Furthermore, there are ecumenical opportunities to develop training for clergy and laity in the healing ministry, in order to encourage a common understanding and greater awareness of the ways in which it can be expressed ecumenically at local level.

✻ We further recommend that:

❖ the particular qualities needed for the healing ministry should be incorporated into the recruitment and selection criteria and given the weight appropriate to its importance as a gospel imperative; diocesan directors of ordinands, bishops' vocation advisors, Ministry Division selectors and others involved in the recruitment and selection of candidates should be made fully aware of the healing ministry and encouraged to be supportive of it; they should also be aware of the need to find suitable candidates for training who regard this ministry as a central part of mission in the parishes;

❖ a detailed review should be carried out, following the initial survey done for this report of the theological and practical training provided for these ministries in colleges, on regional courses and on Ordained Local Ministry (OLM) courses and the practical experience and guidance available as part of parish placements, placements in hospitals, hospices and prisons, etc. and the ways in which these are overseen and assessed;

❖ the healing ministry should be taught as a practical subject, underpinned by a sound understanding of the theology of healing and wholeness. National guidelines need to be developed and adopted for teaching this ministry to a minimum standard, as part of training for ministry and through placements, to ensure that it is adequately taught, including its practical expression, the guidelines for good practice and extemporaneous prayer, in order for newly ordained clergy to exercise this ministry effectively and confidently in the parishes;

❖ all ordinands should be provided with opportunities for placements in parishes where their understanding of this ministry will be developed under the guidance of parish priests with a sound, broad and practical experience in this area and who support the ministry and the principles embodied in the guidelines for good practice; parish placements should provide ordinands with an appropriate range of opportunities to experience and share in this ministry according to different circumstances;

❖ ordinands should be made aware of the importance of cooperation between clergy and the health care professions, hospital and prison chaplaincies; provision should be made for those in training to experience effectively the hospital, hospice and prison environments, where there may be opportunities to be involved in interactive sessions. Ordinands should also be made aware of the boundaries between the professions, between clergy and these professions and the kind of codes of conduct which affect these cooperative working relationships;

❖ ordinands should be aware of the ways in which the prison chaplains carry out the healing ministry and the particular dynamics which relate to this, within prisons; also of the wider implications of custodial sentences and the need to address the issues which affect prisoners and their families, during and after the term of imprisonment, as part of their healing;

❖ training for ministry should include modules (or similar) on the types of counselling and spiritual direction and the ministry of reconciliation, and ordinands need to be trained to hear confessions as part of reconciliation. Ordinands should also be aware of the boundaries between, and the appropriate use of, the different kinds of counselling and spiritual direction;

❖ training should cover the ecumenical expression of the healing ministry and the ways in which it is carried out within the different traditions of the Church. As far as is practical, ordinands should be provided with opportunities to hear directly from advisors from the other denominations and to attend services with prayers for healing held by and organized in cooperation with our ecumenical partners. Ordinands also need to be aware and have experience of the different expressions of the healing ministry within the traditions, which tend to span the denominations and which have much in common;

❖ training should cover care for people suffering from chronic illness, permanent limitations and disabilities, mental illness, or who are terminally ill and dying; care for the carers and coping with burn-out; care of the bereaved, including children and people with learning disabilities; the issues relating to our ageing society such as senile dementia, Alzheimer's disease, loss of mobility and loneliness;

❖ training should cover self-care, including the need for retreats, spiritual direction and supervision in certain types of ministry;

❖ training should include an appreciation of complementary medicine, alternative therapies and other world-views which influence our society and the wide search for health and wholeness;

❖ a thorough review should be carried out of the current provision of training in the ministries of healing and deliverance as part of CME, particularly years one to four;

❖ national guidelines should be developed and adopted for the teaching of the healing ministry as part of CME, particularly to those clergy who are recently ordained or who have not received any formal training in this ministry. The Church of England needs to decide what should be taught as part of training for ministry before ordination and what would be more effectively taught as part of CME;

❖ CME on the healing ministry should be developed, with particular regard to its relationship with pastoral care and mission, expressed practically as part of everyday life in the parishes. Such training should be kept up to date and set within the broad context of this ministry as it is carried out in the Church of England, taking into account the different traditions and forms of expression;

❖ clergy should be encouraged as part of CME to develop their awareness of how the other denominations carry out this ministry and the opportunities for its ecumenical expression, particularly within local communities;

❖ clergy should be trained to recruit and select suitable team members, in order to carry out this ministry as part of normal everyday life in their parishes and to organize appropriate training for them;

❖ clergy should be encouraged after ordination to develop their skills in counselling through further training such as a certificate or diploma course or through training with an organization such as Relate;

❖ opportunities should be provided for clergy to gain a deeper understanding and appreciation of the work of hospital and hospice chaplains and how this relates to the care of parishioners, in and out of the hospital or hospice;

❖ clergy should be provided with opportunities to learn about the ways in which prison chaplains are involved in the healing ministry and how this relates to prisoners and their families, during and after custodial sentences. Clergy need to be aware of the ways in which their church communities can welcome and support ex-offenders, while protecting vulnerable people.

❖ training should be provided and kept up to date in the other approaches to health and healing which are available in our society, including complementary and alternative medicine. Guidance should be given on the key issues and questions to be considered. This training needs to be based on objective research and cooperation with our ecumenical partners, to provide sound and well-informed advice to Christians;

❖ training in the deliverance ministry needs to be reviewed in the light of current practice in the parishes and recommendations made for the level of awareness/training needed for clergy in the future, how this should be carried out safely and effectively and at what stage, that is, during training for ministry, as part of CME or strictly as a specialist activity;

❖ the deliverance ministry should be covered in CME, to encourage widespread awareness and acceptance of the House of Bishops' guidelines and the reasons why these are necessary. Clergy should be aware of the contact details of diocesan advisors on the deliverance ministry and the ways in which they can help with advice and referrals;

❖ people involved in teaching the healing ministry should be encouraged to adopt a minimum standard and common understanding of the ways in which it needs to be carried out according to the guidelines for good practice. In order to do this, some of those involved in teaching may need further training themselves in order to be aware of current developments and the ways in which this ministry is carried out in the wider Church. This issue should be considered in more detail following further research into training for ministry. Such training should be carried out ecumenically where possible, to agreed ecumenical standards;

❖ the Ministry Division should develop and provide national training resources to help ensure an appropriate standard of training for laity involved in the healing ministry and a common understanding of good practice;

❖ the Ministry Division should develop and provide national guidelines on the selection criteria, minimum acceptable training requirements and, where necessary, the accreditation of laity for healing ministry teams;

❖ the current resourcing for training for laity in the healing ministry should be reviewed by each diocese and adequate provision made in future for the resources needed to train and set up local healing teams and to increase awareness of the healing ministry in the parishes.

❖ the Hospital Chaplaincies Council should develop further its training provision and practical support for the healing ministry throughout the chaplaincies, explore the issue of formal links with the prison chaplaincies and encourage closer links between chaplains and parishes, diocesan and national structures of the Church of England;

❖ minimum standards for training in the healing ministry should be agreed between the HCC and the College of Health Care Chaplains, in cooperation with the Free Churches' Council Health Care Chaplaincy Board, and that Health Care Chaplaincy degree and vocational courses should cover this ministry in close relation to its expression in hospitals and hospices, etc;

❖ training should include study of the ways in which ecumenical chaplaincies work, the opportunities and the challenges which they face and the range of expression of this ministry across the traditions and denominations; opportunities should be found for hospital, hospice and community placements in order for chaplains in training to gain useful practical experience. It is also important that hospital chaplains are aware of the ways in which the healing ministry is expressed as part of everyday life in the parishes, and the value of close links with the local church and those involved in caring for the sick in the parishes;

❖ further training courses should be available to hospital chaplains to keep them up to date, to develop greater awareness of issues such as mental health, counselling and listening skills, psychology and psychotherapy. (Training has also been requested on management skills to help chaplains work more effectively with the hospital structures);

❖ the financial implications of increased levels of training provision should be considered and recommendations made for appropriate levels of funding in future budget;

❖ the issues of access for chaplains to records of patients and a code of confidentiality between hospital and prison chaplains and professional health care organizations including the NHS should be considered;

❖ support and advisory networks should be developed to help chaplains needing advice and support in dealing with difficult situations and decisions, ethical dilemmas, etc;

❖ up-to-date information, training and guidance should be available on the wide range of complementary medicine and alternative therapies available in our society and the effects these have on people's lifestyles, world-views, health and spirituality;

❖ consideration should be given to the organization of regional conferences for hospital chaplains, to raise general awareness of the wider expression of the healing ministry. These regional conferences could be held jointly where appropriate with the prison chaplaincies in the same regions;

❖ the Hospital Chaplaincies Council should be involved in the future development of new liturgy for the healing ministry, particularly for services in specialized circumstances; for example, funerals for new-born babies, services of 'regret' following abortions, services of remembrance for families, funeral services 'in absence' for those whose partners are too ill to attend, rites of reconciliation as increasingly requested in hospitals, particularly when marriages have broken down;

❖ hospital chaplains should be kept well informed about events in their dioceses, deanery chapters and local parishes. Dioceses and parishes should be encouraged to become more aware of the work of hospital chaplains and the ways in which they can be supportive, particularly through prayer;

❖ hospital chaplains should seek opportunities to increase greater awareness in the Church of England and within our society of their role in health and healing, for example through addressing diocesan and deanery synods, chapters and PCCs.

❖ prison chaplains should be more effectively supported and encouraged in their expression of the healing ministry. Formal and ecumenical links should be established with diocesan advisors and hospital chaplains across the denominations and closer links made with local parishes and communities to assist prisoners, ex-offenders and their families, and that prison chaplains should be involved in training for ministry;

❖ prison chaplains should be trained in the healing and deliverance ministries and that the Church of England should continue to develop a better understanding of the theology of healing and wholeness, taking into account the need for particular sensitivity in the ways this theology is expressed to certain groups within our society (such as victims of abuse);

❖ prison chaplains should follow the guidelines for good practice for both ministries, and an ecumenically acceptable code of conduct should be discussed between the prison and hospital chaplaincies to underpin future initiatives to work together more closely, including an agreement on confidentiality;

❖ prison chaplains should have regular opportunities to meet with diocesan advisors on the ministries of healing and deliverance to share expertise etc. and to provide a network for advice and support; prison chaplains should have opportunities to work with the diocesan advisors to help the advisors develop a better awareness of these ministries as they are carried out in the prison service;

❖ prison chaplains should be involved in the development of liturgy for the healing ministry, in particular liturgy for special circumstances such as liturgy for funerals in absence, healing the family tree and liturgy which allows prisoners to express their own feelings and hand over their pain to God as part of their healing;

❖ prison chaplains should be encouraged to train further in listening skills, counselling and particularly for loss and bereavement, which are key issues in caring for prisoners and their families;

❖ prison chaplains should be encouraged to work with local clergy in order to develop helpful links with parishes, increase awareness of the role of the local church in the healing of offenders and enable the better integration of the released prisoners into the local community while protecting vulnerable people;

❖ the prayerful and practical support of the prison chaplaincies by the diocese and the parishes should be encouraged;

❖ prison chaplains should be given opportunities to contribute to training for ministry (POT and CME) by sharing their experience and expertise in the healing ministry and issues of social justice, etc., and by providing opportunities for placements in prison chaplaincies as part of a national training curriculum;

❖ the Church of England should seek ways to ensure that the prison chaplaincies are seen to be part of the main body of the Church and not just sector ministries. Prison chaplains should seek and be provided with appropriate opportunities to contribute to the life of the diocese through involvement in the diocesan boards and committees, etc. Bishops should visit prisons regularly to support and encourage prison chaplains, to show prisoners and society that the Church values prisoners as much as non-offenders;

❖ there should be regular reviews of the ways in which the healing ministry is carried out in the prison service and that this should be part of the national overview of this ministry, in order that it should be supported effectively and coordinated with related areas such as the hospital chaplaincies and the work of youth officers.

The response to the questionnaire sent to all the Churches and Provinces in the Anglican Communion has been greatly appreciated. Because of constraints due to time limits and varying standards in communications systems, the replies have been slow to arrive and continue to come in even during the editorial stage of this report. On the basis of the information received at this stage, the overall impression is that the healing ministry is still an under-resourced or neglected area in many, but not all, of the Provinces and Churches. This report is regarded by some of the respondents as an opportunity to learn from the Church of England and to improve the effectiveness of the healing ministry within the Anglican Communion.

✢ We recommend that:

❖ the healing ministry should be an integral part of theological education to enable its fulfilment as a gospel imperative, taking into account the range of churchmanship; the theology of this ministry as set out in this report should be offered for sharing across the Anglican Communion;

❖ the healing ministry should be properly resourced and supported, depending on local circumstances, in each diocese within the Communion; practical resources such as training material, research and general information should be shared, particularly with the Churches and Provinces in the Third World and developing countries;

❖ there should be a network and forum under the sponsorship of the archbishops and bishops and with their approval, supported through the Ministry Division and working in cooperation with the Anglican Communion office, linking advisors in the healing ministry across the Communion;

❖ this network should exist primarily for the exchange of information, to provide support where appropriate and to monitor the development of this ministry. It should encourage a better understanding and raise awareness of and confidence in the healing ministry amongst clergy and laity. General information including addresses, papers and draft and approved liturgical and training resources for local use in this ministry should be made available for sharing across the Anglican Communion, through an international newsletter, a web site and, when practical from time to time, an international conference;

❖ training material should be developed for clergy and laity involved in the healing ministry, including written material, tapes and in particular videos on training and good practice, taking into account the different approaches to this ministry according to churchmanship and limited practical resources in parts of the Anglican Communion. Where and when possible, people able to train others in the healing ministry should be resourced and provided with opportunities to travel to those parts of the Communion who would like assistance in establishing this ministry and improving its effectiveness;

❖ the ecumenical expression of the healing ministry should be encouraged across the Anglican Communion, taking into account the relative strength of presence of the denominations in each geographical area and key local factors which may affect opportunities for ecumenical cooperation; for example, in the development of ecumenical liturgy, training material and guidelines for good practice;

❖ the increasing incidence of occult involvement, including in advanced countries, should be acknowledged and people trained effectively in the deliverance ministry, taking into account the regional and local cultures and other related factors;

❖ guidelines for good practice should be shared across the Anglican Communion;

❖ a copy of the report on the healing ministry should be sent to each of the primates and bishops in the Anglican Communion and, where known, to their advisors on the healing ministry.

The Ecumenical Expression of the Healing Ministry

We recommend that:

❖ the Church of England should work with our ecumenical partners and health care organizations to develop and establish a new ecumenical Churches' Healing Ministry Group (CHMG). This group would coordinate, support and promote this ministry, at national and regional levels (see pages 48, 61, 77, 79, 83, 84, 85-6 and 88);

❖ the Church of England and our ecumenical partners should develop and agree a basis for future initiatives and ecumenical cooperation within the healing ministry (see pages 77, 78, 79-80, 83, 85-6 and 89);

❖ the Churches' Healing Ministry Group should be a springboard for interchurch initiatives and ecumenical cooperation between the Church and the health care organizations (see pages 77, 82, 83, 85-6, 88, 89 and 155);

❖ non-eucharistic liturgy for services of prayers for healing should be developed by the Churches' Healing Ministry Group drawing upon experience in the healing ministry as currently practised within the main denominations (see pages 48, 69, 78 and 89);

❖ liturgy for special circumstances, particularly for use in prisons and hospitals, should be developed in cooperation with the hospital and prison chaplaincies, including rites for penance and reconciliation which emphasize the healing potential of the assurance of forgiveness, and for children and people with learning difficulties (see pages 84, 85-6, 89, 135, 259 and 260);

❖ the guidelines for good practice which are included in this report are offered to our ecumenical partners for discussion and adaption if necessary by individual denominations, leading towards an ecumenically agreed understanding of good practice in the healing ministry (see pages 59, 85-6 and 89);

❖ training for the healing ministry for ordained and lay people should be developed, supported and coordinated ecumenically where appropriate (see pages 48, 55, 79-80, 85-6 and 89);

❖ the valuable work of hospital chaplains and prison chaplains in this ministry should be affirmed and a review considered of the relevant Church of England and ecumenical committee structures and communication networks (see pages 51, 62, 63, 80, 82, 83 and 85-6).

The following proposals have been drafted for discussion with the main denominations, particularly the Methodist Church, the United Reformed Church, the Baptist Union and the Roman Catholic Church.

* We recommend that:

❖ a new Churches' Healing Ministy Group (CHMG) should be set up, for the ecumenical coordination, support and promotion of the healing ministry of Jesus Christ. The CHMG must be of a manageable size and meet sufficiently often to be a proactive body. It would be a focused working group with clear terms of reference, rather than a representative forum;

❖ the criteria for membership should be based on a strong, practical commitment to the healing ministry, expressed through an agreed theology, shared resources, shared financial support and agreed guidelines for good practice, taking into account current legislation and the guidelines for related professions. The terms of reference would also acknowledge the diversity of expression of this ministry across the traditions which span the main denominations, and take into account the related diversity of support needed;

❖ membership of this group initially would be the Church of England (from which representations should overlap with the central support with the Ministry Division), the Methodist Church, the United Reformed Church, the Baptist Union and the Roman Catholic Church, up to a total of fourteen members with the option for the denominations to send a substitute member if the normal representative is unable to attend a particular meeting. The Hospital Chaplaincies and Prison Chaplaincies should also be represented;

❖ the terms of reference of the CHMG and its general effectiveness should be reviewed regularly (perhaps every three years) in order to ensure that it continues to support the healing ministry and to respond to the wider issues and changes in society;

❖ consideration should be given to the joint appointment of staff and funding for a small central office. This ecumenical organization could be notionally based at Church House, Westminster even if much of its work is done at a base established outside London. The benefit of a location in Church House would be to ensure strong links and good communication between the CHMG, the Ministry Division and other relevant parts of the Church of England's internal structures;

❖ the two or three people from each denomination on the CHMG should be sufficiently influential in their own denomination to be able 'to argue the case' for implementing the Group's recommendations. One-way representation would not be enough; the representation needs to be accurate and active both ways. The appointment of 'observers only' is not recommended, as it would allow for input and influence without commitment;

❖ the people appointed should be people broadly representative of their denomination, whose personal integrity is recognized, who are known to be objective and reliable, well aware and appreciative of the variety of practice in this ministry within their own denomination;

❖ the CHMG would organize, in cooperation with the Ministry Division, an annual meeting of diocesan/district/circuit healing ministry advisors, hospital chaplains and prison chaplains (and possibly other groups) as part of its remit to act as a forum and to build ecumenical links at all levels. Regional meetings could be held once or twice a year. Local ecumenical healing groups should be encouraged, to meet regularly to support the ecumenical expression of the healing ministry at parish/diocesan/district level and to share local training and other resources when and where appropriate;

❖ the CHMG would also help to shape training across the denominations for ordinands, laity, hospital and prison chaplains and others involved in the healing ministry, at national, regional as well as local level, to ensure a minimum level of training and a common understanding of its theology and good practice, and to provide further training and resources for those who need them. A sound understanding of the range of expressions of this ministry and the other approaches to healing in society should be included in training to help future priests, ministers and chaplains to work together more effectively and sensitively;

❖ a directory of resources which the denominations could commend jointly should be considered. The CHMG would be an appropriate body to consider the development of acceptable criteria for inclusion and oversee the necessary checks on organizations wishing to be included. Further consideration could be given to a CHMG mark of accreditation, to indicate resources, training and publications which were acceptable, helping to build public confidence in the healing ministry;

❖ the CHMG, in cooperation with the Ministry Division, should issue a newsletter or bulletin quarterly to all advisors and other interested parties, covering advance news of forthcoming events, book reviews, leading articles, key issues in society affecting the healing ministry and links with the NHS and abroad. The group would encourage and contribute to the well-informed promotion of this ministry through the media as well as church newspapers, healing and health magazines and professional journals;

❖ the CHMG would carry out research for the denominations on issues such as assessing why this ministry often flourishes in churches outside traditional structures and which factors in their theology and ecclesiology are relevant. A professional survey is needed to assess how the majority of the population in this country perceive the Church's healing ministry. This research could lead on to a joint report on this ministry, as a step toward healing between the denominations;

❖ the CHMG would also help to develop an accurately informed and defensible position for the churches in response to issues related to complementary medicine, alternative therapies, New Age spiritualities and teaching on Christian lifestyle and values, based on a common understanding of the theology, spirituality and world-view of each of the well-known approaches to healing and wholeness in our society. (This is an area where the denominations have much in common and through working ecumenically, they would be more able to provide Christians with coherent guidance by taking a common official line.);

❖ the funding of the CHMG would need to be established to ensure that it could fulfil its task properly, perhaps supported by a combination of joint funding plus subsidized charges for conferences, training and news-sheets;

❖ the denominations would continue to develop their own approaches to the ministries of healing and deliverance and to make their own policies, better informed in the light of shared experience, yet also working ecumenically wherever it makes good sense;

❖ consideration should be given to the need for the development of a national ecumenical network for prison chaplains and hospital chaplains, established for the exchange of information and expertise, support and inspiration. The network would also enable better pastoral care of prisoners who move around the prison network and who are also often in and out of hospital, as prisoners and as ex-prisoners. Regional ecumenical meetings of prison and hospital chaplains should be organized where and when it would be helpful, to enable prison chaplains to form links with hospital chaplains at local levels as part of this network;

❖ liturgy should be developed ecumenically, with a particular awareness of its expression across the traditions, since this ministry is the
area where people from the denominations mix most readily. There
is, for example, a clear need for an adaptable non-eucharistic healing
service for use in a variety of parish situations and for ecumenical use
at local level which the main denominations would be prepared to
commend jointly. This kind of service should be developed by an ecumenical group which is expert at producing liturgy and also understands the need to embrace the wide range of traditions and different
ways in which the main denominations carry out the healing
ministry;

❖ although it could be developed by diocesan liturgical committees, it
would be preferable to have liturgy for the healing ministry for particular circumstances agreed at national level as rubrics for use in
hospitals and prisons. The involvement of hospital and prison chaplains in the development of specialized liturgy for this ministry is
important as they are the most experienced people in these areas and
aware of the kind of liturgy needed urgently;

❖ the issue of multi-faith prison chaplaincies and the implications of
these should be considered by the Church of England in cooperation
with our ecumenical partners;

❖ the concept of community chaplains, based on the Canadian model,
should be considered, taking into account the ecumenical implications of setting up community chaplaincies and the main denominations should discuss and develop ecumenically, if practical, the
opportunities in this area.

The Healing Ministry in Professional Health Care Settings

We recommend that:

❖ the relationship between the healing ministry and medicine should be
encouraged on the basis of a working theology of this ministry, and
that a vocabulary for this ministry needs to be developed which is
clearly understood and shared between clergy, laity and health care
professionals (see pages 94, 95, 99, 100, 102 and 103);

❖ in order to help the medical and theological disciplines work together on healing, support should be given to making provision for
medical and theological students to be trained together in pastoral
aspects of collaborative health care and ethics (see pages 94, 98, 101,
103-4, 106-7 and 108);

❖ mutual supervision should be considered (doctors being supervised
by clergy on spiritual aspects of medical care and clergy by doctors
on medical aspects of spiritual care) to work towards a holistic
approach to healing (see pages 97, 98, 101, 104 and 105).

The Healing Ministry and Professional Care Provision in the Parishes

We recommend that:

❖ clergy and other church representatives should be encouraged to initiate and maintain links between themselves and others working in
the community, such as doctors, police and the social and voluntary
services; for example, through occasional lunches or seminars. In the
light of the Government's expressed desire for partnerships between
the statutory and the voluntary sectors, this recommendation may
suggest creative use of church premises (with appropriate funding) in
wider health care provision for the community (see pages 107–8).

❖ all those using counselling skills in pastoral care should receive
adequate training and supervision (see pages 110, 112, 113, 114,
115 and 122–3);

❖ those offering formal counselling should receive adequate training
and supervision, work with a recognized code of ethics and practice
and be accredited by or working towards accreditation by a reputable body (see pages 110, 114, 117 and 122–3);

❖ boundaries between counselling and other forms of pastoral care and
between people in dual and multiple roles (that is, simultaneously in
more than one relationship with one another) are monitored and regularly reviewed (see pages 109, 110–11, 112, 113, 114, 118 and
121–2);

❖ given the wide variety between dioceses in counselling services provided for clergy, their spouses and dependent children, standards should be established which ensure that at least basic provision is available in every diocese (see pages 118–19);

❖ courses of training for lay and ordained ministries should include an introduction to the ministry of spiritual direction, and that individuals who develop a special gift for this ministry should be encouraged and helped in further studies and practice (see pages 110, 113, 119, 121 and 123–4);

❖ courses of training for lay and ordained ministry should include an introduction to the ministry of reconciliation (hearing confessions), and priests should be helped to develop this ministry through appropriate supervision and guidance in their continuing ministerial education (see page 121).

The Impact of Limitation and Illness

We recommend that:

❖ churches should remove barriers to people with disability, when appropriate, enabling and empowering them for ministry (see pages 128, 131 and 155);

❖ local churches or Churches Together could helpfully offer a network of people who are trained in offering pastoral support to those who are mentally unwell (see pages 133 and 134);

❖ people with persisting illness and disability need protection from insensitive ministry, hence the importance of training in this area for ordinands and of including it in continuing ministerial education (see page 144);

❖ the Church of England should continue to support specialist ministries to those with disabilities (e.g. chaplaincy to the deaf) and encourage initiatives to study the relationship between physical and mental disabilities and Christian faith (see page 142).

Healing for Those Who Are Dying or Bereaved

We recommend that:

❖ theological colleges, courses and schemes should make provision for ordinands to be exposed to the needs of dying people and their families. Ordinands could helpfully be involved in experiential and interactive sessions in palliative care as a powerful tool for learning (see pages 153–4);

❖ the needs of the sick person are best met when the different professions involved seek permission from the individual concerned to share together, whilst respecting their individual professional codes of confidentiality (see page 156);

❖ in-service training for clergy should help to develop an understanding of the grief journey (see page 159).

Deliverance from Evil

We offer the following recommendations:

❖ we endorse the normal practice of suitable people having episcopal authorization for deliverance ministry and the widespread appointment of diocesan teams (see page 168);

❖ we endorse the guidelines issued by the House of Bishops in 1975 (see pages 168 and 180–81);

❖ we commend the practice of keeping careful and confidential records, within the constraints of the Data Protection Act (see pages 180–81);

❖ clergy and lay people involved in this ministry should have appropriate training and supervision (see page 180);

❖ a multidisciplinary approach is to be desired and we recommend that those authorized for this ministry should have access to consult and work with other clergy and with doctors, psychologists and psychiatrists (see pages 168 and 180);

❖ services involving deliverance ministry should be simple and use appropriate pastoral and sacramental ministry, whilst always ensuring that the welfare of the person being ministered to is of paramount concern (see page 180).

❖ We also recommend that:

❖ existing diocesan guidelines for ministerial practice should be followed;

❖ clergy should avoid colluding with urgent and sometimes dramatic requests for deliverance ministry, so as to be able to make a considered judgement of the situation;

❖ clergy involved in the deliverance ministry should be encouraged to be well-informed about mental health issues;

❖ the decision for a priest to perform a service of exorcism should only be taken after all other avenues have been explored and the risks assessed, and with the authority of the bishop; as far as possible the service should not be emotionally charged;

❖ counselling should form an important part of the process and clergy should receive supervision and work closely with medical and other health care professionals; there must be provision for pastoral care and counselling following the service. We recommend that the Christian Deliverance Study Group (CDSG) produce detailed guidelines for the provision of appropriate aftercare for those who have received the deliverance ministry;

❖ the Ministry Division and the CDSG should work together with other relevant organizations to monitor and provide up-to-date information on cults, New Age spiritualities and the occult;

❖ the contact details of diocesan advisors on the deliverance ministry should be made available to clergy in every diocese, so that they know whom to contact for advice, in an emergency;

❖ diocesan advisors on the deliverance ministry should have regular opportunities to meet with prison chaplaincies and chaplains working in mental health care;

❖ diocesan advisors in the deliverance ministry should have contact with advisors in this area in the other main denominations;

❖ because of the stressful nature of this ministry at times, provision should be made for a support and counselling network for clergy and laity involved in it.

Complementary Medicine and Alternative Approaches to Healing and Good Health

We recommend that:

❖ the Church of England, working with our ecumenical partners, should establish a Review Group, with agreed terms of reference and criteria, to assess in the longer term the compatibility with Christian teaching of widely used forms of complementary medicine and alternative therapies, taking into account interfaith issues (see pages 47–8, 83–4, 183, 184, 192, 196 and 198);

❖ the Church of England should provide ecumenically agreed guidance for Christians who are considering or using these approaches, including the kind of questions that might be asked about these approaches to healing, health and wholeness (see pages 74, 183, 192–3, 196 and 199–200);

❖ the relationship between the healing ministry and those forms of complementary and alternative approaches to healing which are becoming integrated with conventional health care should be reviewed, in cooperation with the HCC and health care professionals within the NHS (see pages 60, 190, 194 and 201);

❖ training for ministry, particularly for hospital and prison chaplains, includes an appreciation of the range of complementary and alternative approaches to healing and the issues which surround them (see pages 41–2, 55, 184, 192–3, 197, 201, 203 and 204–5);

❖ the relationship between spiritual guidance/direction and health care provision should be reviewed and recommendations made for the increased availability of spiritual direction as part of total health care (see pages 185, 192, 203 and 205);

❖ local churches should be encouraged to communicate effectively information about the healing ministry, to raise awareness particularly amongst non-church attenders; for example, putting notices in surgeries and providing leaflets (see pages 186, 196, 203, 204 and 206).

Healing Services in the Church of England

We recommend that:

❖ a wider range of worship resources for services of prayer for healing, appropriate for use in parishes, hospitals and prisons, should be developed; flexibility, for use in different contexts, is essential and ecumenical cooperation desirable (see pages 243 and 254–5);

❖ better communication should be established with other Anglican Provinces and other denominations to facilitate awareness of different material available in the ministry of healing (see page 251);

❖ services of penance/reconciliation which acknowledge the healing potential of forgiveness should be promoted (see pages 246–7).

✽ We also recommend that:

❖ the House of Bishops should consider the issue of anointing and how its use could be explored further, developed and encouraged among the laity; the healing ministry is a wonderful way of sharing ministry between clergy and laity. When licensed lay workers, such as pastoral assistants, lay chaplains in hospitals and members of healing teams are visiting the sick, prayers for healing should be encouraged;

❖ prayers for healing for use with children and people with learning difficulties should be developed and that the Boards of Education and Mission and the National Society should explore the possibilities of involving children in services for prayer for healing;

❖ educational material should be developed to help those with learning difficulties to understand and appreciate the healing ministry, including the practical experience of this ministry;

❖ the liturgical material already available for this ministry in the authorized services of other denominations and other Provinces of the Anglican Communion, should be taken into account.

Developing the Healing Ministry in the Parish

We recommend that:

❖ the healing ministry should be clearly defined as part of the Church's mission and ministry, effectively led, overseen, resourced and supported through diocesan structures (see pages 258–9, 261–2, 268, 269 and 274–5);

❖ the Church of England should adopt and promote nationally and within parishes the guidelines for good practice in the healing ministry as incorporated in this report (see pages 268, 269, 271, 272, 275 and 279);

❖ bishops should review the work of diocesan advisors on the healing ministry and, noting the additional workload involved in carrying out the recommendations in this report, consider the future needs within dioceses and the required number and quality of advisors (see pages 264–5, 268, 269, 272, 273, 274 and 275);

❖ each diocese should conduct a survey, in cooperation with the Ministry Division and central support of the healing ministry, to evaluate the current state of this ministry in parishes (see pages 259–60, 266 and 276);

❖ deanery synods and chapters should be encouraged to review the current state of the healing ministry in their area and develop and support proposals for increased effectiveness, including ecumenical cooperation (see pages 262, 266–7, 270 and 274–5);

❖ each parish should evaluate ways in which the healing ministry is being carried out as part of mission, and make proposals for improved effectiveness, noting local needs and challenges and expressions of this ministry in ecumenical partnerships (see pages 259–60, 262–3, 264, 265, 266–7, 270, 271, 273–4, 275–9 and 280).

✷ We also recommend that:

❖ the draft guidelines for good practice in the healing ministry should be 'owned' by the Church of England and, in particular, approved and supported by the House of Bishops;

❖ the House of Bishops' guidelines on the deliverance ministry (1975) should be actively promoted by bishops, their advisors and diocesan training officers amongst the clergy and local healing teams;

❖ awareness and acceptance of the guidelines by the widest possible range of people involved in the healing ministry within the Church of England should be encouraged, to help ensure that the ministries of healing and deliverance are carried out safely and effectively;

❖ the public commitment to and involvement in this ministry of the bishops and senior staff in each diocese are essential to show that with preaching and teaching, healing is at the heart of the Church's mission. Guidance is needed to build confidence and encourage clergy and laity involved in the healing ministry to include a proper balance of prayer, sacramental ministry and pastoral care. Clergy need to be reminded that Jesus commissions us to preach, teach and heal the sick – the healing ministry is not just an optional extra for those clergy and parishes with a particular interest in it;

❖ bishops, clergy and readers should preach and teach about this ministry to raise general awareness of it as a gospel imperative and encourage the better understanding by clergy and laity of the theology of this ministry in parishes and deaneries;

❖ bishops should be seen to be actively involved in the healing ministry, including taking part in services with prayer for healing in parishes, cathedrals and other Christian centres of worship;

❖ the ministries of healing and deliverance should be overseen carefully to ensure that they are carried out soundly and safely and, if problems occur, they should be addressed effectively;

❖ because the healing ministry is increasingly becoming part of everyday life in the parishes, a greater awareness of its place in the mission of the Church should be encouraged throughout the diocesan structures: that is, its potential as a form of sensitive evangelism;

❖ this ministry should be clearly linked within the diocesan boards and committees along the lines of the links within the Archbishops' Council's substructure e.g. the Ministry Division, the Boards of Mission, Social Responsibility and Education, the Councils for Evangelism, and those responsible for ecumenism;

❖ an annual report on the healing ministry and the work of the diocesan advisors should be made to each diocesan synod, similar to those prepared for the main diocesan boards. This would increase awareness and encourage debate about the kind of resources needed for the future; annual reports on the work of hospital chaplains, prison chaplains and other areas related to health care and healing, such as ministry to the deaf, are also recommended;

❖ diocesan boards of finance should make adequate provision for the healing ministry to support its improved effectiveness in future budgets, commensurate with its priority as a gospel imperative;

❖ training groups and officers for POT, CME and lay training should be trained in the ministries of healing and deliverance and resourced to train clergy and approved laity in the diocese;

❖ in those dioceses which have their human resources grouped in this way, diocesan staff should be made aware and kept informed of developments in the healing ministry, and encouraged to support it in the parishes; for example, diocesan youth officers should be encouraged to liaise with prison chaplains to help young ex-offenders who have received this ministry in prison to have follow-up pastoral care when they return or move to a parish;

❖ in those dioceses which have pastoral assistants or similar licensed lay workers, their role in the healing ministry as part of pastoral care in the parishes should be considered and developed where appropriate;

❖ diocesan communication officers should be trained and supportive of this ministry, to encourage its best presentation in the press and to help with media interest in particular cases; we also recommend that diocesan magazines, bulletins and web sites should include a section on the healing ministry and those places where it is frequently available;

❖ members of diocesan liturgical committees should be encouraged to read this report and work with those already involved in this ministry in their dioceses, to produce liturgy according to clearly defined local needs;

❖ hospital and prison chaplains should liaise more closely with parish priests, taking into account confidentiality, to help the continuation of pastoral care of parishioners who have received the healing ministry in hospital, hospice, residential homes or prisons, etc;

❖ hospital and prison chaplains should be encouraged to develop links with parishes to share experience, to help set up and support local healing teams and to encourage members of the congregation to become involved in lay visiting schemes in local hospitals;

❖ hospital chaplains should develop, where appropriate, links with GP practices, healing homes, hospices, voluntary care organizations and pastoral care teams in local churches;

❖ resources and contacts for the healing ministry and related areas, for example contacts for referral for counselling, healing organizations and local healing homes, should be listed in the diocesan directory;

❖ where healing organizations and homes, etc., exist in certain dioceses, it would be helpful to have formal links with the diocese, to support those involved full-time in the healing ministry in these places through prayer and also to be aware of what they can offer to parishes and individuals;

❖ each diocese should develop a network of spiritual directors to link with the diocesan advisors on the healing ministry, chaplaincies and NHS;

❖ diocesan libraries should be encouraged and financed to provide a helpful and adequate range of reference books and related material for study and research on these ministries;

❖ an annual diocesan celebration of the healing ministry should be held, including a Eucharist with prayers for healing and the laying on of hands, to which those people in the diocese who are involved in the ministries of healing and deliverance should be invited to take part to demonstrate publicly its central place in the life of the diocese; such an event could be organized and shared ecumenically.

As the healing ministry becomes a part of normal parish ministry in every parish, the demands on part-time or retired priests acting as diocesan advisors will increase considerably. As the issues of oversight, training provision and wider awareness of practice across the churches become more high profile, the appointment by bishops of suitable people as advisors will become more necessary.

✤ We recommend that:

- ❖ bishops should review the work of their advisors on the healing ministry and, taking into account the additional workload involved in carrying out the recommendations in this report, consider the future needs of their diocese and the necessary number and quality of advisors. In particular, we recommend a review of the appropriateness of appointing advisors who already have full-time commitments to their parishes or other roles and suggest that the appointment of part-time and full-time advisors is more realistic in future;

- ❖ teams should be set up where appropriate, rather than relying on individuals working alone, to enable the sharing of expertise, training, insights, workload and support; the effectiveness and membership of the teams should be reviewed regularly; we also recommend that the diocesan advisors in both ministries meet together regularly;

- ❖ those appointed as diocesan advisors in both ministries should be properly trained, up to date and appreciative of the wider practice of the healing ministry across the traditions and its ecumenical expression; diocesan advisors should be aware of and support the House of Bishops' draft guidelines for good practice in the healing ministry and the House of Bishops' guidelines on the deliverance ministry (1975);

- ❖ diocesan advisors on the ministries of healing and deliverance should be given a job description based on an agreed national 'template', with clear lines of accountability, guidance from their bishops, and regular reviews of their work as advisors;

- ❖ diocesan advisors in the healing ministry should be involved in CME, particularly years one to four, to train clergy and to ensure that they are kept up to date and aware of the guidelines for good practice and related issues;

- ❖ diocesan advisors in the deliverance ministry should be involved in CME, particularly years one to four, to ensure that newly ordained clergy understand the need for and follow the House of Bishops' guidelines on this ministry;

❖ diocesan advisors should be involved in the setting up of parish/benefice/deanery healing teams involving laity, to help ensure that they are suitable, trained to a minimum standard and aware of the guidelines for good practice, and to assist in the drafting of pew leaflets and other information on the healing ministry for use at local level;

❖ diocesan advisors should be provided with adequate practical resources to carry out their role, including appropriate financial provision for promoting this ministry in the parishes, training clergy and laity and producing resource booklets on the healing ministry for use in the diocese, and book and study grants for further research into the healing ministry;

❖ a diocesan health and healing forum should be established for regular meetings of diocesan advisors and others involved in the provision of conventional health care, including GPs, psychiatrists, psychotherapists, professional counsellors, hospital and prison chaplains and representatives of local healing homes and organizations, for discussion and sharing of information on the wider issues related to healing and health care, and for support, advice and fellowship;

❖ diocesan advisors should have regular opportunities to meet with prison and hospital chaplains within the diocese to exchange information, advice and support;

❖ diocesan advisors and others involved in the healing ministry should be provided with reliable information on complementary medicine and alternative therapies, in order to provide others with guidance and advice;

❖ diocesan advisors should be encouraged to work collaboratively with the advisors on this ministry in the other denominations; and that wherever appropriate, opportunities should be taken to express the healing ministry ecumenically, to help bring about healing between the denominations at local and regional levels; we also recommend that diocesan advisors seek opportunities to pool resources and work ecumenically in areas such as training for lay people;

❖ diocesan advisors should be supported through prayer in their diocese and spiritual guidance should be available for those who find it helpful;

❖ each diocese should carry out a careful survey, with the same questions asked in every diocese, to evaluate the current state of the healing ministry in its parishes. For objectivity and overview, this survey ought to be done by an experienced team, including diocesan advisors, to ensure that the summary does not over- or understate the case;

❖ the summary from each diocesan survey should be sent in confidence to the Ministry Division to collate the results for a national view of this ministry, in order to provide a sound basis for determining the level and type of resourcing needed at national and diocesan level and appropriate financial provision needed for its future support and increased effectiveness.

✱ We also recommend that:

❖ rural deans and joint lay chairmen should invite diocesan advisors on the healing ministry to make presentations on how to develop this ministry at deanery and parish levels;

❖ rural deans should invite diocesan advisors on the ministries of healing and deliverance to address chapter meetings and encourage the clergy to follow the House of Bishops' guidelines for the deliverance ministry and the House of Bishops' draft guidelines for good practice in the healing ministry;

❖ hospital chaplains and prison chaplains should be invited to address clergy chapters and deanery synods to increase awareness of their work, and encouraged to be a valuable resource for the healing ministry in the deaneries;

❖ the healing ministry should be included in the development of deanery pastoral teams, particularly in rural and other areas where it is difficult to maintain teams at parish or benefice level;

❖ deanery synods should appoint a person to be the contact for healing and health issues amongst the parishes, to assist locally the diocesan advisors, to communicate effectively information about healing services and training days and encourage greater awareness of the healing ministry in those parishes where it is not part of everyday life and mission.

In Chapter 14 we have made recommendations for the establishment and improved effectiveness of the healing ministry in the parishes. The parish church should be seen as a healing presence, through which God works to bring healing and wholeness to individuals, families, friends, the local community and, ultimately, to the whole of creation.

✣ We recommend that:

❖ parishes should be encouraged to regard the healing ministry as an important expression of the Church's broad mission, but particularly to those suffering disease and distress in the wider community; the local church needs to be able to minister to all kinds of brokenness, at all levels, as part of everyday life;

❖ parishes should ensure that the healing ministry is a part of normal everyday life, integrated into the wide range of activities already carried out, particularly pastoral care, and that it is made readily available to everyone, including the unchurched;

❖ parishes should be encouraged to review regularly the ways in which they carry out the healing ministry and to seek ways to carry it out ecumenically;

❖ in parishes where the healing ministry is not well established or clearly visible, the diocesan advisor should be invited to address the PCC and the congregation to explain its place in the mission of the Church and how it can be developed effectively in the parish, including advice on setting up services with prayers for healing, how this ministry relates to pastoral care; the value of prayer support and healing teams which include lay people; and training and resources available in the diocese;

❖ since it is recognized that lay people are members of the priesthood of all believers, and that being healed and helping others to be healed is part of our discipleship, the gifts of the laity should be encouraged and developed in the parishes, under the guidance of the clergy, and suitable training provided;

❖ to attract people to this ministry and the services where it is offered, issues related to the provision of an appropriate physical environment should be addressed, including safety, suitable heating and lighting, fresh air and cleanliness, comfortable seating, and access and facilities for people with disabilities;

❖ clergy and healing teams should be aware of and follow the approved guidelines for good practice for the healing and deliverance ministries and the relevant diocesan guidelines for ministerial practice;

❖ clergy and healing teams should develop sound networks of contacts for referral, advice and support; support structures for clergy, pastoral care workers and home carers are provided locally or within the diocese;

❖ congregations and communities should develop and express practically a good understanding of the usual responses to loss and bereavement, building bridges between prayer and ministry teams and the parishioner requesting help, and providing support and practical help where appropriate;

❖ parishes should be aware and supportive, through corporate and individual prayer, of diocesan advisors in the healing ministry, hospital, hospice and prison chaplains, local hospitals and residential homes for elderly and disabled people, health care professionals and those involved in voluntary care for the sick and disabled people in the parish;

❖ the possibilities for collaboration between the parish church, the other denominations and the local community should be explored to find ways to provide key facilities: for example, homes for the homeless, new crematoria, reconciliation facilities on church premises;

❖ parishes should develop their contacts with hospital chaplains to draw on their expertise and experience and to help the building up of lay visiting schemes in local hospitals;

❖ where counselling is offered as part of the healing ministry in parishes, those involved should make it quite clear what kind of counselling is being offered and that the relevant guidelines must be followed. It is not recommended that clergy offer formal counselling to members of their own congregation, but reciprocal arrangements with ministers of other churches (including other denominations) could be a very fruitful means of broadening the Church's ministry;

❖ in situations involving people with personality disorders, the issues of safeguards and supervision should be addressed and close professional liaison encouraged because of the impact on other individuals and groups, which may be considerable; people with persisting illness and disability may need protection from inappropriate evangelism and prayers for miraculous cures. We recommend that congregations show the Lord's love and compassion in practical ways rather than waiting expectantly for a cure.

Summary

This report, the first of its kind, offers an overview of the healing ministry, its expression within the Church of England and the other main denominations in England, its place within our society and the other forms of health care and healing which are available, and the wider view across the Anglican Communion. It is based on extensive research involving bishops, clergy and laity who are actively involved in and committed to this ministry. The information was gathered between the autumn of 1998 and the summer of 1999. It was reviewed and incorporated in this report by the autumn of 1999, to ensure that as far as possible, the overview which it provides is up-to-date, balanced and accurate.

The introductory paragraphs of this appendix highlight the need for a coherent approach, which depends to a large extent on effective communication, to increase awareness and encourage interest in this ministry. The challenge now is to ensure that this report and its recommendations are used constructively, within the Church of England, in cooperation with the chaplaincies and health care professions, with our ecumenical partners and within the Anglican Communion, to bring wide awareness of the central place of this ministry within the life and mission of the Church and our society.

Appendix 3

Promoting the Healing Ministry

In order to help the promotion of good practice within the healing ministry, suggestions are included in this appendix for:

❖ basic guidelines for criteria for selection of healing team members;

❖ a pew leaflet to explain in readily accessible language this ministry to inform enquirers.

Developing the healing team

The detailed guidelines for good practice set out in Appendix 1 provide a framework within which healing teams are encouraged to minister, including references to the introduction of services with prayers for healing. These suggested criteria assume that the PCC and congregation support the healing ministry within their parish. The criteria also assume that the parish priest has a sound understanding and some experience in this ministry. These guidelines may need to be modified according to the nature of particular congregations, or when they are used to recruit members for deanery healing teams, but the basic requirements need to be kept in view. The factors which need consideration in determining an individual's suitability to join a healing team are grouped as follows.

Prayer and discernment

The basis on which a prayer ministry team exercises this ministry is that it is a group of Christians who pray together with faith, hope and love, seeking God's will.

❖ Individuals who feel called to be involved in healing teams should be willing to pray and listen, in order to discern where God is leading them in this aspect of the Church's mission and ministry; they need to be willing to grow in spiritual maturity.

❖ People involved in the healing ministry should be sufficiently self-aware to recognize their own spiritual, mental, emotional and physical needs for healing. A prayer life which acknowledges and is open to the healing love of Jesus Christ is essential, as is a willingness to recognize and seek healing for oneself, in order to be available as a channel of his grace. Sometimes people who feel drawn to be involved in a healing team are initially more concerned about seeking healing for themselves, which is why prayerful and patient discernment is such a valuable process before becoming part of a healing team. Nevertheless, the Church has always valued the role of the 'wounded healer' and individuals who have experienced some healing themselves can often be sensitive and valuable members of the team.

❖ Individuals seeking to be involved in this ministry need the support of others, through prayer and Christian fellowship, and willingness to support prayerfully the other team members. They also need to be willing to try and love and serve them in Christ's name.

Personal qualities needed

The following personal qualities are needed in those wishing to join a healing team:

❖ patience, with themselves, other team members and those seeking healing; maturity and self-awareness to help absorb the disappointments and hurts which can sometimes result through endeavouring to help others;

❖ humility; acknowledgement that healing comes from Jesus Christ, not the individual;

❖ acceptance of one's personal limitations and willingness to refer those in need for specialist help, when necessary;

❖ compassion and empathy, in order to help discern the needs of others and the most appropriate and helpful way of ministering to them;

❖ the ability to listen, or learn how to listen, for listening is a great part of this ministry – listening to God and to other members of the team as well as to the one who is seeking help;

❖ reliability and trustworthiness; a willingness to work collaboratively in order to fulfil God's will.

In addition, individuals seeking to join the healing team need to be well-known and regularly practising members of the local church, enjoying the trust and confidence of the clergy and PCC.

New members of the congregation expressing interest in joining the team should be able and willing to provide references, which need to be checked even if the person claims to have previous experience in this ministry.

It is helpful to have both men and women on the team, ordained and lay, and a range of ages (including young people) and outlook in order to affirm that the healing ministry is for everyone and not limited to a particular group in the local community. The size of the team needs to be kept to manageable levels, allowing for changes in pairing, vacations and other absences.

Guidelines for good practice

In order to develop a common understanding of good practice, everyone involved in this ministry should be aware of and abide by the House of Bishops' draft guidelines for good practice in the healing ministry. People interested in joining healing teams should be provided with an opportunity to familiarize themselves with the guidelines and express their willingness to work within them, before being accepted into a team.

Confidentiality

It is essential that those who wish to be involved in healing teams understand the issues surrounding confidentiality (particularly in the local context) and accept the need for great care in the exchange and dissemination of information relating to those receiving this ministry and their close contacts. Individuals need to be realistic and fair about possible conflicts of interests and the potential difficulties of relationships in more than one capacity with other people in the local community.

Accountability, leadership and appraisal

A willingness to be accountable and work under the leadership of the parish priest or chaplain is a key issue, as is the willingness to be appraised from time to time and, if necessary, be prepared to stand down from the healing team if circumstances indicate that this is advisable. Acceptance of the limitations of the kind of ministry which can be exercised by the healing team is also necessary.

Recognizing personal limits

❖ Whilst mental and physical illness in general terms should not preclude people from consideration for membership of a healing team, a realistic and adequately informed assessment of an individual's physical and mental health and his or her personal circumstances should be carried out, to ensure that those to whom he or she might minister would not be placed at risk in any way.

❖ Similarly, the personal behaviour of the individual should be such that he or she encourages public confidence in this ministry and does not put people off through inappropriate behaviour or lack of self-awareness and personal care.

Training and continual learning

❖ Individuals who are interested in joining healing teams should be able and willing to undergo training as advised by the parish priest, including training to keep up to date with developments in this ministry. They should also be committed to reading widely about this ministry and related areas.

❖ Specialist skills and professional qualifications are not necessary but may be useful; however, those with specialist knowledge, particularly in health care, still need to work within the team under the guidance of the priest and according to the guidelines for good practice, when ministering as part of the healing team.

Cautions

❖ 'Wanting to be a "healer"'– involvement of people who think they have special powers or 'have tingling hands' – will need careful discernment. The source of healing in the Church's ministry of healing comes from Jesus Christ and this should be faithfully acknowledged by everyone involved.

❖ Individuals who tell their priest that they are convinced that they have a gift of healing and that God is calling them to exercise that gift more widely need to be treated circumspectly, especially if they have recently transferred themselves from another church. Difficulties can occur unless they are willing to submit to the pastoral leadership of a congregation.

❖ 'Spiritual bullying'– whilst the healing ministry is a central part of the Church's mission, it is particularly relevant to the vulnerable and frail who need to be protected from overenthusiasm, insensitive evangelism, inappropriate ministry or potential abuse.

❖ Because the healing ministry is for everyone, including children and those with learning difficulties, care should be taken not to involve people who have a criminal record of abusing, exploiting or harming others.

Suggested text for a pew leaflet

The following pages contain a suggested pew leaflet, designed to explain the healing ministry in readily accessible language to inform enquirers. This may be photocopied.

The Church's ministry is a continuation of the ministry of Jesus Christ. We seek to fulfil it in the power of the same Holy Spirit who anointed Jesus at his baptism in the Jordan. Jesus' ministry was totally faithful and obedient to his Father. The gospel of the kingdom of God is the good news of healing which Jesus proclaimed. 'Go and preach the gospel. . . . Go and heal the sick' summarizes the commission Christ gave to his Church. So Christians have always been called to have a special concern for those sick in mind, body and spirit. The Church's ministry can be described as one of healing - the healing of ourselves, and of our relationships with God, with one another and with our environment.

The Healing Ministry is:

VISIONARY . . . because it beckons us towards the future and a glimpse of the kingdom, and the hope of the whole of creation renewed.

PROPHETIC . . . because it calls us to reconsider our relationships with God, each other and the world and to seek forgiveness and a new start in our lives.

DYNAMIC . . . because Jesus Christ is with us to the end of time: when we pray for his help, he comforts, strengthens and heals us, responding to our deepest needs.

What can we hope for through this ministry?

We believe that God loves us and wills the very best for us. But we also know that suffering of all kinds and ultimately death are conditions from which we cannot escape. But God is not distant. In Jesus Christ he shared in this life's suffering and death on the cross, and he can draw close to us in times such as these. However, his resurrection in the power of the Holy Spirit gives us hope that we might have a foretaste of his kingdom here and now and that through the Church's ministry we shall receive his love, strength and healing touch. What form that healing will take we cannot tell:

It may be:

❖ help to carry us through a prolonged illness or disability;

❖ a recovery more rapid than expected;

❖ experiencing our fear of death being driven out by God's love;

❖ a healing which is so unexpected that we immediately want to thank God.

The Church of England has recently published a detailed report called *A Time to Heal* (Church House Publishing) which contains a great deal of information and guidance on the healing ministry and has also produced new services for healing and wholeness.

The healing ministry is for everyone; we all need healing in some way. Through the healing ministry, Jesus Christ meets us at our point of need.

What are the most common forms of healing ministry?

Public and private prayers of intercession. Christian worship has always included prayers of intercession customarily addressed to the Father through the Son and in the power of the Holy Spirit. Intercessory prayer, in which we pray individually and corporately, for those who are suffering, combines our love with God's love and our will with his will, so as to cooperate with him in fostering his kingdom.

The laying on of hands. Actions can often 'speak louder than words' and touch conveys a message of love and assurance as well as being a link with Christ's apostolic command to heal the sick. Hands are usually placed gently on or side by side of a person's head, or on his or her shoulders, and accompanying prayers said quietly and reverently. This form of touch can make a sick person feel less fearful or alone in their suffering.

Anointing. We pray that as we are outwardly anointed with oil, we shall be inwardly anointed with the Holy Spirit. It is customary for a priest to anoint a person with thumb or forefinger, making the sign of the cross, with a small amount of oil on the forehead and sometimes the palms of the hands. Anointing is often accompanied by the laying on of hands and sometimes Holy Communion and reconciliation.

Reconciliation and Absolution. Confession is increasingly seen as an act of reconciliation which begins with God calling us back to himself. The Anglican tradition values the use of a general confession as a communal act in the liturgy and makes provision for private confession to a priest. Private confession may be made in a formal or less formal setting and may include spiritual advice and counsel as well as absolution.

Friendship, forgiveness, listening, acceptance and affirmation can also have a healing grace. So in different ways we are all able to take part in the Church's healing ministry, looking forward in faith to the kind of healing he wills for those for whom we are praying.

The healing ministry is available in the following ways:

❖ **publicly** as part of services:

❖ **at healing services,** including the Eucharist, in institutions such as hospitals, hospices, nursing homes, residential homes for elderly and disabled people, prisons, etc., and at healing centres and related conferences;

❖ **privately** within the home, hospitals and hospices, and discreetly in church side chapels etc;

❖ **ecumenically** across the denominations, including local services, the hospital and prison chaplaincies;

❖ **in cooperation with the medical and caring professions.**

Appendix 4

A Glossary for the Healing Ministry

Alternative medicine/therapy: 'instead of conventional medicine'; many people, however, use alternative therapies in addition to conventional medicine. Treatments for cure other than those used in conventional medicine.

Christian Listening: the ministry of a Christian trained to listen to another in formal or semi-formal circumstances, sometimes including prayer but without counselling.

The Church: used in this report to denote the worldwide Christian community; denominations are given their full name.

Clergy: all persons ordained as bishop, priest or deacon for service in the Church of God.

Complementary medicine/therapy: 'in support of conventional medicine'; the term embraces a wide diversity of therapies and diagnostic methods and there are no sharp dividing lines between conventional and complementary medicine/therapies. A common factor in complementary medicine/therapies is the emphasis on encouraging the self-healing capacities of the body.

Confession: see 'Reconciliation, Ministry of'.

Conventional/orthodox medicine: modern scientific diagnostic and therapeutic principles and techniques used in health care; a common factor in conventional medicine is the emphasis on pathology; some forms of complementary medicine are increasingly regarded as conventional.

Counselling: a therapeutic ministry offered by an accredited person under agreed conditions of time, attention, respect and confidentiality. This specific treatment, as distinct from pastoral care and listening, should only be provided by accredited counsellors and therapists who adhere to the codes of ethics and practice of their regulatory organizations and have professional insurance cover.

Deliverance: release from spiritual evil which oppresses people or places or which hinders the individual's response to God's saving grace. Prayer by an individual or a group of Christians for a person who, it is believed, is being troubled by evil.

Diocesan advisor: a qualified person, ordained or lay, appointed by the bishop to help parishes, communities and groups to engage more effectively in the healing ministry in its widest sense.

Disease: a specific malfunction of the body, mind or spirit, either acquired or inherited, which causes distress or unease to an individual. A state of *illness* exists when that specific disease takes over the whole well-being and function of the person. Not all diseases are illnesses.

Healing: progress towards health and wholeness. The process through which an individual develops a physical, mental, spiritual, economic, political and social state of well-being, in harmony with God, with others and with the environment.

Health: a dynamic state of well-being of the individual and society, of physical, mental, spiritual, economic, political and social well-being – of being in harmony with each other, with the material environment and with God (the World Council of Churches' definition in the report of its Christian Medical Commission). Normal working of the body as a living, physical organism with respiratory, motor, digestive and other functions, but the word is etymologically connected with wholeness (hence holistic approach to health).

Health care chaplain: the name given to ordained men and women who exercise their ministry attached to hospitals and other institutions or communities who care for those who are physically or mentally ill.

Holy oil (unction): oil has many biblical, practical and symbolic uses and there are three oils used in the ministry of the Church. The oil used in the ministry of healing is olive oil which has been blessed by a bishop or priest, and following the example of the apostles (Mark 6.13) and the teaching of St James (James 5.14,15) the sick are anointed by a priest, usually on the forehead and sometimes also the hands. The anointing is accompanied by prayer. The term 'extreme unction' is sometimes used when the sick person is about to die.

Hospital chaplain: see 'Health care chaplain'.

Holistic medicine: a system of health care, involving conventional and complementary medicine and alternative therapies, which emphasizes personal responsibility and cooperative relationships between those involved, and which aims to treat the whole person, body, mind and spirit, leading to optimum overall health. It is concerned with the long-term development of the individual rather than just a response to a particular instance of disease, and takes into account the individual's environment and lifestyle.

Integration: the dynamic process towards wholeness in which the diverse elements of perception are being drawn together.

Laying on of hands: this action whereby a person or people lay hands on the head of someone has its origins in the Old and New Testaments and is associated with blessing, commissioning and healing. It takes place at confirmation and ordination and is included in modern liturgies for the ministry to the sick. Actions can often 'speak louder than words' and touch conveys a message of love and assurance as well as being a link with Christ's apostolic command to heal the sick.

Lay team member (of a healing team): a person who has the approval of the local church congregation and parish priest, to be involved in the healing ministry.

Licensed lay minister: a lay person licensed by the bishop to a ministry, for example a reader.

Minister: (1) a Christian exercising a ministry as described below; (2) an ordained member of a denomination which normally refers to him or her as 'the minister' (especially in the Free Churches).

Ministry: the exercise by a Christian of spiritual gifts and natural abilities given by God for the building up of the Church and for the common good. All Christians are engaged in ministry. In particular ministries there may be a structure of authorization and accountability in place.

New Age: a blanket term used to refer to a movement which seeks self-improvement and personal wholeness through a variety of means including non-conventional and alternative health care, therapies including the use of crystals, astrology, techniques designed to heighten awareness and spiritual teachings from a variety of faith traditions. It is eclectic in style and looks towards a new age of enlightenment and harmony.

New Churches: formerly known as 'House Churches'. Networks of non-denominational congregations which were initiated in the 1960s and 1970s, generally as a result of the charismatic movement.

Occult: the word means 'hidden' and its practitioners believe that there are within ourselves and our world hidden powers and forces which can be harnessed and be used for good or evil. Occultism is sometimes criticized as being an attempt at spiritual manipulation and oppression, in contrast to the Christian view that spiritual gifts are given by God in response to the relationship he has with us.

Reconciliation, Ministry of: the formal pronouncement of the forgiveness of sins (absolution) by a bishop or a priest in the name of Jesus after hearing an individual's confession.

Service of prayer for healing/healing service: an act of worship in which prayer is offered for the healing of individuals, usually with the laying on of hands and sometimes with anointing and Holy Communion.

Spiritual direction: guidance in the development of an individual's Christian life and prayer by someone (usually called a director) with a wide and perceptive knowledge of spiritual paths of various traditions. In the Western Church it has often been associated with the ministry of reconciliation, but this is not necessarily the case today, especially as some able directors are to be found among laymen and -women.

Spiritual: (1) relating to the work of the Holy Spirit; (2) super-sensible experiences.

Spiritual(ist) healing: forms of therapy which claim to use spiritual forces in the cause of healing. Spiritualist churches are not considered by mainstream churches to be orthodox in doctrine or practice.

Spirituality: studies, attitudes, beliefs and practices which animate people's lives and help them to reach out towards super-sensible realities.

Therapy: a particular treatment which enables the healing process.

Wholeness: a growing awareness of harmony between oneself, one's neighbours, one's environment and God.

Appendix 5

Recommended Reading

David Aldridge, *One Body: A Healing Ministry in your Church*, SPCK, 1987.

Robina Coker, *Alternative Medicine: Helpful or Harmful?* Monarch Publications, 1995.

Ian Cowie, *Prayers and Ideas for Healing Services*, Wild Goose Publications, 1995.

Martin Dudley (ed.), *A Manual for Ministry to the Sick*, SPCK, 1997.

Martin Dudley and Geoffrey Rowell (eds), *Confession and Absolution*, SPCK, 1990.

Martin Dudley and Geoffrey Rowell (eds), *The Oil of Gladness: Anointing in the Christian Tradition*, SPCK, 1993.

Professor Abigail Rian Evans, *Redeeming Market Place Medicine: A Theology of Health Care*, The Pilgrim Press, 1999.

Margaret Guenther, *Holy Listening: The Art of Spiritual Direction*, Darton, Longman & Todd, 1992.

John Gunstone, *Prayers for Healing*, Highland, 1992.

George W. Gusmer, *The Ministry of Healing in the Church of England: An Ecumenical-Liturgical Study*, Alcuin Club Collections no.56: Mayhew-McCrimmon, 1974.

George Hacker, *The Healing Stream: Catholic Insights into the Ministry of Healing*, Darton, Longman & Todd, 1998.

Gerard Hughes, *God of Compassion*, Hodder & Stoughton, 1998.

Morton Kelsey, *Healing and Christianity*, Harper & Row, 1976.

Roy Lawrence, *The Practice of Christian Healing*, Triangle, 1998.

Kenneth Leech, *Soul Friend: Spiritual Direction in the Modern World*, Darton, Longman & Todd, 1994.

Matthew Linn, Sheila Fabricant Linn and Dennis Linn, *Simple Ways to Pray for Healing*, Paulist Press, 1998.

Anne Long, *Listening*, Darton, Longman & Todd, 1990.

Jim McManus, *Healing in the Spirit: Inner Healing and Deliverance in Today's Church*, Darton, Longman & Todd, 1994.

Francis MacNutt, *Deliverance from Evil Spirits*, Baker Book House, 1995.

Francis MacNutt, *Healing*, Hodder & Stoughton, 1996.

Morris Maddocks, *The Christian Healing Ministry*, SPCK, 1990.

Morris Maddocks, *Twenty Questions about Healing*, SPCK, 1992.

The Mental Health Foundation, *The Courage to Bare Our Souls*, 1999.

Michael Mitton and Russ Parker, *Requiem Healing*, Darton, Longman & Todd, 1991.

Russ Parker, *Forgiveness Is Healing*, Daybreak, 1993.

Althea Pearson, *Growing Through Loss and Grief*, Marshall Pickering, 1998.

Mark Pearson, *Christian Healing: A Practical and Comprehensive Guide*, Hodder & Stoughton, 1996.

John Penton, *Widening the Eye of the Needle: Access to Church Buildings for People with Disabilities*, Church House Publishing, 1999.

Michael Perry, *Gods Within: A Critical Guide to the New Age*, SPCK, 1992.

Michael Perry, *Deliverance*, SPCK, 1996.

John Richards, *But Deliver Us from Evil*, Darton, Longman & Todd, 1974.

John Richards, *The Question of Healing Services*, Darton, Longman & Todd, 1989.

Barbara Shlemon Ryan, Dennis Linn and Matthew Linn, *To Heal as Jesus Healed*, Resurrection Press, 1997.

Margaret Spufford, *Celebration*, Fount, 1989.

Averil Stedeford, *Facing Death*, Heinemann Medical, 1988.

Harold Taylor, *Sent to Heal: A Handbook on Christian Healing*, The Order of St Luke the Physician, Ringwood, Victoria 3134, Australia.

Gareth Tuckwell and David Flagg, *A Question of Healing*, Fount, 1995.

Graham Twelftree, *Christ Triumphant*, Hodder & Stoughton, 1985.

Robert Twycross (ed.), *Mud and Stars: Report of a Working Party*, Sobell, 1991.

Jean Vanier, *Becoming Human*, Darton, Longman & Todd, 1999.

Dominic Walker, *The Ministry of Deliverance*, Darton, Longman & Todd, 1997.

John Wilkinson, *The Bible and Healing: A Medical and Theological Commentary*, Handsel/Eerdmans, 1998.

John Woolmer, *Healing and Deliverance*, Monarch, 1999.

Appendix 6

Research Carried Out for the Report

In order to develop an overview of the current state of the healing ministry, research was carried out in the following areas.

The Church of England

❖ **Diocesan bishops.** All 44 bishops were invited to reply to a strictly confidential questionnaire, covering issues including their personal involvement in this ministry, an overview of its expression, its current state and how it relates to other areas of ministry within their own dioceses and the bishops' key concerns. Thirty-five diocesan bishops replied with very helpful information.

❖ **Diocesan advisors on the healing and deliverance ministries.** Sixty-seven advisors appointed by their diocesan bishops were invited to reply to a strictly confidential questionnaire, covering similar issues to those included in the bishops' survey, and additional questions on the role and work of advisors and the key opportunities and challenges which they face. Training, communications, support and resources needed and the ecumenical expression of the healing ministry in their dioceses were also surveyed. A summary of the draft outline for the report was provided to allow the diocesan advisors the opportunity to comment and provide relevant information. Over several months, 52 of the 67 advisors returned extensive replies and the response to the survey was excellent. Many advisors provided valuable insights and resource material; far more information has been provided than could be incorporated into this report.

❖ **Hospital chaplains.** A survey was carried out, inviting a cross-section of 20 chaplains selected by the HCC to reply providing details of their work and the ways in which the healing ministry is expressed in the NHS. Questions related to resources available, including training, communications and support networks, relationships between hospital chaplains and the diocesan structures, exploring ideas for promoting the healing ministry and its ecumenical expression, the key issues and challenges for hospital chaplains working within the NHS and views on guidelines for good practice. Fourteen of the chaplains provided full and helpful replies.

❖ **Prison chaplains.** Ten chaplains were interviewed and involved in extensive group discussion, to develop an overview of the ways in which the healing and deliverance ministries are expressed within HM Prison Service. The chaplains were selected by the Prison Chaplaincy and represented a broad cross-section of experience and expertise, within the prison chaplaincy and parishes.

❖ **Training provision within the Church of England.** The 40 theological colleges, regional courses and OLM schemes recognized by the House of Bishops were invited to reply to a questionnaire to assess the current state of training in the healing and deliverance ministries. The key questions covered:

– How much interest in the Church's ministry of healing is there amongst the ordinands?

– What teaching is given on the healing ministry, at what stage in the pastoral training and how much time is given to this?

– What teaching is given on the deliverance ministry, at what stage in the pastoral training and how much time is given to this?

– What outside resources and personnel are used in teaching these ministries?

– Requests for the supply of available course material related to the teaching of these ministries, including lecture notes, guidelines, reading lists and liturgy used.

Twenty-six replies were received in time to be used in the preparation of this report.

The ecumenical expression of the healing ministry

Advisors and key individuals involved in the healing ministry were interviewed from:

* ❖ the Roman Catholic Church in England;
* ❖ the Methodist Church;
* ❖ the United Reformed Church;
* ❖ the Baptist Union;
* ❖ the Russian Orthodox Church and the Greek Orthodox Church;
* ❖ the New Churches (formerly known as House Churches).

The research covered the organization, oversight and resourcing of the healing ministry; its practical expression and the extent to which this is ecumenical; training and guidelines for good practice; approach to evidence; and the key concerns and challenges faced by each denomination in this ministry.

As part of the research for this report several meetings of the Joint Methodist and United Reformed Church Health and Healing Development Group were attended, which have provided valuable insights into the collaborative expression of the healing ministry between these dominations. This group also includes representation from the Free Churches' Council and the Baptist Union.

NB. Hospital and prison chaplains were also surveyed on the ecumenical nature of the chaplaincies.

The Anglican Communion

With the help of the office of the Anglican Communion and its Secretary General, the Reverend Canon John Peterson, 40 questionnaires were sent to the primates of the Anglican Communion, inviting them to provide information on the ways in which the healing and deliverance ministries are carried out within the Provinces. Issues covered included the ways in which these ministries are overseen, coordinated and resourced and any guidelines for good practice; the local expression and any ecumenical initiatives involving the healing ministry; training; specially developed liturgical material; key concerns and regional challenges. Information provided in response to the survey was limited but it has provided useful insights into the common problems and challenges being faced by other parts of the Anglican Communion in the expression of these ministries.

Independent organizations involved in the healing and deliverance ministries

Although some research was carried out and visits made to learn about the work of some of these organizations, no formal survey was undertaken, partly because it was felt that this was not specifically within the terms of reference of the Review Group for this report and partly because of the considerable investment of time and resources which would be required to carry out a thorough survey. Most of these organizations are independent and are not accountable to or overseen by the Church of England. Their approaches to the healing and deliverance ministries vary and there are no agreed criteria at this stage against which to assess their work and effectiveness. Further research is recommended as a follow-up to this report and in order to consider the development of a resources directory for people involved in or seeking the healing and deliverance ministries.

Codes of conduct and guidelines for good practice

Nineteen sources of information were used to research the understanding of good practice within the health care professions and existing health and healing organizations related to the healing ministry. These sources are listed.

Complementary medicine and alternative therapies

Research was carried out including a survey of complementary medicine and alternative therapies. A questionnaire was sent to 92 of the regulatory and other national organizations which promote and oversee the increasing range of approaches to health and healing. The overall response was returned in such a variety of forms that comparison across the range was impractical. Much of the information was provided in general leaflets and brochures rather than in direct replies to specific questions in the survey. The Review Group appreciated the considerable amount of information provided by these organizations and their representatives. Because of the great diversity of information provided, a greater awareness emerged of the scale of the task involved in assessing the range and effects of these approaches to health and healing.

After careful consideration, the Review Group concluded that such a detailed assessment and comparison of individual approaches was not within the Group's terms of reference or practicable given the time available. It was decided, however, that the information provided valuable insights into the issues and questions which need to be addressed by the Church in order to provide guidance to Christians. Furthermore, these issues are of interest and concern to the chaplaincies and our ecumenical partners. It is suggested that the denominations work together to develop guidelines and advice using the helpful information provided as part of this initial research.

Other areas of research

Within the time and resources available, other organizations and individuals involved in the healing and deliverance ministries were researched, mainly on a confidential basis, and the findings have to a large extent been incorporated into this report whilst safeguarding the identities of those who have been interviewed.

The Review Group would like to express its appreciation to all those who took part in the research and surveys, for the interest, time and care which have been so generously given.

Notes

Introduction

1. *The Church's Ministry of Healing: Report of the Archbishops' Commission*, Church Information Board, 1958.

2. John Richards (ed.), *The Church's Ministry of Healing: The Report of the 1958 Archbishops' Commission*, Marshall Pickering, 1986, p. 4.

3. *Healing and Wholeness*, WCC, 1990, p. 6.

4. Morris Maddocks, *Twenty Questions about Healing*, SPCK, 1981, p. 7.

Chapter 1: The Church's Ministry of Healing

1. Quoted in George Hacker, *The Healing Stream: Catholic Insights into the Ministry of Healing*, Darton, Longman & Todd, 1998, p. 44, from Francis MacNutt, *Healing*, 1974 edn, p. 333.

2. On this revival see the essay by Geoffrey Rowell, 'The sacramental use of oil in Anglicanism and the churches of the Reformation', in *The Oil of Gladness*, Martin Dudley and Geoffrey Rowell (eds), SPCK, 1993, pp. 134–153.

3. Questions about the practice of restricting anointing to the dying began to be raised in Roman Catholic circles long before the Second Vatican Council (1962–5). This prepared for the gradual opening up of this sacramental sign to wider use in the *Constitution on the Sacred Liturgy*, which directed:

> 'Extreme Unction' which may more fittingly be called 'Anointing of the Sick', is not a sacrament intended only for those who are at the point of death. Hence, it is certain that as soon as any of

the faithful begins to be in danger of death from sickness or old age, this is a suitable time for them to receive this sacrament'. (chapter 3, para. 73)

When the *Rite of Anointing and Pastoral Care of the Sick* was published in 1972 it went further, and said the recipient should be one 'whose health is seriously impaired by sickness or old age' and made provision for the anointing to be repeated '(a) when a sick person recovers after being anointed and, at a later time, becomes sick again; (b) when during the same illness the condition of the sick person becomes more serious' (no. 109). See Joseph Marteos, *Doors to the Sacred. A Historical Introduction to Sacraments in the Christian Church*, SCM Press, 1981, pp. 389ff. and Charles W. Gusmer, *And You Visited Me: Sacramental Ministry to the Sick and Dying*, Pueblo Publishing Company, 1984, pp. 82–86.

4. See, for example, his paper on 'Salvation' in the *Report of the 1923 Anglo-Catholic Congress*, Society of SS Peter & Paul, 1923, pp. 143–50.

5. G.C. Rawlinson, *An Anglo-Catholic's Thoughts on Religion*, Green and Co., 1924, pp. 151–8.

6. Kenneth E. Kirk, *The Vision of God*, Longmans, Green and Co., pp. 233, 289, 445.

7. Charles W. Gusmer, *The Ministry of Healing in the Church of England: An Ecumenical-Liturgical Study*, Alcuin Club Collections no. 56, Mayhew-McCrimmon, 1974.

8. Morris Maddocks, *The Vision of Dorothy Kerin*, Hodder & Stoughton, 1991, p. 177.

9. Peter Hocken, *Streams of Renewal*, Paternoster Press, 1997, p. 50.

10. George Bennett, *Commissioned to Heal*, Arthur James, 1979, p. 30.

11. Gusmer, *The Ministry of Healing*, traces the development of this ministry by studying the various official and unofficial liturgical texts published by Anglicans.

12. F. A. lremonger, *William Temple*, Oxford University Press, 1948, pp. 612–13. When the law of the Church of England was revised, Canon B 37 directed that the parish priest is to care for the sick and take the sacrament to him or her at home; then

If any such person so desires, the priest may lay hands upon him and may anoint him with oil on the forehead with the sign of the Cross using the form of service sanctioned by lawful authority and using pure olive oil consecrated by the bishop of the diocese or otherwise by the priest himself in accordance with such form of service.

(*The Canons of the Church of England promulgated by the Convocations of Canterbury and York 1964 and 1969*, SPCK, 1969)

13. *Promoting Mental Health: The Role of Faith Communities – Jewish and Christian Perspectives*, Health Education Authority, 1999.

14. *The Courage to Bare Our Souls*, The Mental Health Foundation, 1999.

Chapter 2:   Healing in the Scriptures and Tradition

1. John Richards (ed.), *The Church's Ministry of Healing: The Report of the 1958 Archbishop's Commission*, Marshall Pickering, 1986, p.15.

2. Ibid, p.16.

3. See note 1, p.17.

4. On the Church's healing ministry in the early centuries see Paul F. Palmer, *Sources of Christian Theology, vol. 2, Sacraments and Forgiveness*, Darton, Longman & Todd, 1959, pp. 274–87; Morton T. Kelsey, *Healing and Christianity*, Harper & Row, 1973, pp. 157–99; Martin Dudley and Geoffrey Rowell, *The Oil of Gladness: Anointing in the Christian Tradition*, SPCK, 1993, pp. 77–91.

5. Lucien Deiss, *Early Sources of the Liturgy*, Geoffrey Chapman, 1967, p. 132.

6. Ibid, p.15.

Chapter 4:   The Ecumenical Expression of the Healing Ministry

Peter Brierley and Heather Wraight (eds), *UK Christian Research Handbook Silver Jubilee Edition 1998/99*, Paternoster Publishing, 1997.

Annual Report 1998 Hospital Chaplaincies Council, GS Misc 556, The General Synod of the Church of England.

Revd Bob Payne, *A Paper on Community Chaplaincy, for HM Prison Service*, June 1999.

Chapter 5: The Healing Ministry in Professional Health Care Settings

1. Quoted in Charles Gusmer, *And You Visited Me: Sacramental Ministry to the Sick and Dying*, Pueblo, 1984, p. 155.

2. Chris Bryant, *Possible Dreams: A Personal History of the British Christian Socialists*, Hodder & Stoughton, 1996, p. 49.

3. Peter Hennessy, *Never Again: Britain 1945–1951*, Vintage, 1993, p. 121.

4. In *Christian Socialism: Scott Holland to Tony Blair*, SPCK, 1998, Alan Wilkinson discusses Roman Catholic suspicion of the welfare state and state health provision. We are grateful to Canon Wilkinson for advice on these paragraphs. He points out that even in the 1940s there was considerable resistance to the formation of the NHS within the medical profession, and that opposition also came from municipal authorities who were reluctant to see their local hospitals slip out of their control.

5. Those who served in the NHS in its early years inform us that in most hospitals the responsibility of certain nurses for individual patients was accepted as a normal feature on most wards.

6. Viktor Frankl, *Man's Search for Meaning*, Pocket Books, 1983.

7. Robin Skynner, *Institutions and How to Survive Them*, Methuen, 1989.

8. Kamaldeep Bhui, Scot Welch and Keith Lloyd, *Pocket Psychiatry*, Saunders, 1997.

9. See Roy Oswald and Otto Kroeger, *Personality Type and Religious Leadership*, Alban Institute, New York, 1988; Thomas E. Clarke, 'Jungian types and forms of prayer' in *Teach Us To Pray*, and *From Image to Likeness*, Paulist Press, 1985.

Chapter 6: The Healing Ministry and Professional Care Provision in the Parishes

1. *Standards of Practice in Pastoral Care*, Working Party of the Biennial Consultation of Diocesan Advisors on Pastoral Care and Counselling, revised edition, 1995.

2. British Association for Counselling 1986 Information Sheet, *Definition of Terms in Use with Expansion and Rationale*.

3. Margaret Gill, *Free to Love: Sexuality and Pastoral Care*, HarperCollins, 1994, p. 221.

4. Peter Sanders, *First Steps in Counselling*, PCCS Books, 1994, p. 8.

5. BAC, *Code of Ethics and Practice*, 1999.

6. Peter J. Van de Kasteele, *Clinical Theology Newsletter*, no. 64, 1994.

7. Kenneth Leech, *Soul Friend: Spiritual Direction in the Modern World*, Darton, Longman & Todd, revised edition 1994, p. 85.

Chapter 7: The Impact of Limitation and Illness

1. Robert Twycross (ed.), *Mud and Stars*, Sobell, 1991.

2. Ibid.

3. Margaret Spufford, *Celebration*, Fount, 1989.

4. Ken McGreavy, *Address at Pilgrim Hall*, 1988.

5. Roy McCloughry, *Address at Acorn Christian Trust Conference*, 1999.

6. A. C. Oommen, *Address to Canterbury Diocese Chaplains*, 1975.

7. Bishop David Jenkins, *Address to CCHH*, Swanwick, 1981, and Bishop Morris Maddocks, quoted by Bishop Stephen Neill in *The Christian Healing Ministry*, SPCK, 1990.

8. Michael Fulljames, 'Concepts in Mental Health', Canterbury Council for Health and Healings, 1988.

9. Geoffrey Lay, *Seeking Signs and Missing Wonders*, Monarch, 1998.

10. Jürgen Moltmann, *The Crucified God*, SCM Press, 1974.

11. Thérése Vanier, *Address at Burrswood*, 1983.

12. See note 10.

13. Frances Young, 'A Catalyst for Transformation', *Chrism*, 1998, vol. 35, no. 2.

14. Norman Autton, *The Pastoral Care of the Mentally Ill*, SPCK, 1963.

15. See note 13.

16. N. Eiesland, *The Disabled God: Towards a Liberation Theology of Disability*, Abingdon Press, 1994.

17. Dorothy Kerin, *Burrswood Healing Service*, 1962.

18. See note 13.

19. Elizabeth Kubler-Ross, *On Death and Dying*, Macmillan, 1969.

20. See note 1.

21. D. Daniels, 'Sickle Cell Anaemia: A Patient's Tale', *British Medical Journal*, (1990) 301:673.

22. Joni Eareckson, *Joni*, Pickering and Inglis, 1978.

23. Marie De Hennezel, *Intimate Death*, Little, Brown & Co. 1997.

24. See note 21.

25. See note 1.

26. See note 1.

27. Jean-Dominique Bauby, *The Diving Bell and the Butterfly*, Fourth Estate, 1997.

28. J. Van Henkelem, 'Weep With Those Who Weep', *Christian Counsellor's Journal* (1980) 1(4):2.

29. Viktor Frankl, *Man's Search for Meaning*, Pocket Books, 1983.

30. David Storter, *Spiritual Aspects of Healthcare*, Mosby, 1995.

31. See note 1.

32. Helen Keller, quoted in *Healing and Wholeness*, (1991) 1:40.

33. Frances Makower, *Faith or Folly*, Darton, Longman & Todd, 1988.

34. See note 3 .

35. See note 1.

36. Norman Autton, *Touch,* Darton, Longman & Todd, 1989.

37. Jean Vanier, *The Broken Body,* Darton, Longman & Todd, 1988.

38. See note 1.

39. Paul Tournier, *Escape from Loneliness*, SCM Press, London, 1962.

40. Gareth Tuckwell, 'Christian Healing', *Catholic Medical Quarterly'* (1991) vol. 42, no.2.

41. Ibid.

42. Ibid.

43. See note 11.

44. A. A. Milne, *Winnie the Pooh*, Methuen, 1926.

45. See note 37.

46. C. S. Lewis, *The Four Loves*, Fount, 1960.

47. R. Sabath, 'Burn Out,' *Sojourners Fellowship Journal,* quoted in a personal communication, 1989.

48. Gordon Macdonald, *Ordering Your Private World*, Highland, 1987.

49. David Flagg, personal communication, 1993.

50. See note 47.

51. See note 37.

52. See note 1.

Sheila Cassidy, *Sharing the Darkness: The Spirituality of Caring*, Darton, Longman & Todd, 1988.

The ICD-10 Classification of Mental and Behavioural Disorders, World Health Organization, 1992.

Chapter 8: Healing for Those Who Are Dying or Bereaved

1. Robert Twycross (ed.), *Mud and Stars*, Sobell, 1991.

2. Gareth Tuckwell, 'Healing the dying', *Chrism*, 1997, vol. 34, no. 3.

3. Robert Twycross, personal communication, 1999.

4. See note 1.

5. See note 1.

6. H. Holman, letter quoted in *Chrism*, vol. 26, no. 10.

7. See note 2.

8. Quoted in Sheila Cassidy, *Sharing the Darkness*, Darton, Longman & Todd, 1988.

9. Maggie Callanan and Patricia Kelley, *Final Gifts*, Hodder & Stoughton, 1992.

10. M. Quoist, *The Breath of Love*, Gill & Macmillan, 1986.

11. See note 2.

12. See note 9.

13. Laurence Freeman, from a tape entitled 'Death and Dying' quoted in Basset, *Beyond the Blue Mountain*, Medic Media, 1999.

14. Spoken by Jean Vanier at Agape Canterbury Retreat, 1990.

15. David Flagg, 'The Grief Journey', *Burrswood Herald*, Summer 1989.

16. Russ Parker and Michael Mitton, *Requiem Healing*, Darton Longman & Todd, 1991.

17. Michael Fulljames, personal communication, 1999.

Sheila Cassidy, *Light from the Dark Valley*, Darton, Longman & Todd, 1994.

Averil Stedeford, *Facing Death*, Heinemann Medical, 1988.

Jenny Gateau, *Mike's Story*, Triangle, 1997.

Althea Pearson, *Growing through Loss and Grief*, Marshall Pickering, 1998.

Chapter 9: Deliverance from Evil

1. General Synod, *Report of Proceedings,* vol. 6, no. 2, July 1975.

2. Adolf Harnack, *Die Mission und Ausbreitung des Christentums in den ersten drei Jahrhunderten,* 3rd edn., revised and augmented, Leipzig, 1915, vol. 1, p. 141.

3. Graham Twelftree, *Christ Triumphant,* Hodder & Stoughton, 1985, p. 107.

4. Belief in the presence of the demonic in a pagan's life is illustrated by this quotation from a sixth-century commentator:

> There cannot be any doubt that before a man is reborn in Christ he is held close in the power of the devil: and unless he is extricated from the devil's toils, renouncing him among the first beginnings of faith with a true confession, he cannot approach the grace of the saving laver (John the Deacon (c.AD 500), E. C. Whitaker, *Documents of the Baptismal Liturgy,* SPCK, 1960, p. 145).

5. Michael Wilson, 'Exorcism: a clinical/pastoral practice which raised serious questions', in *The Expository Times,* vol. 86, July 1975, pp. 292f.

6. Harvey Cox, *Fire from Heaven,* Cassell, 1996, pp. 285–6

7. *The Catechism of the Catholic Church,* 1994, makes the distinction this way:

> In a simple form, exorcism is performed at the celebration of baptism. The solemn exorcism, called 'a major exorcism', can be performed only by a priest and with the permission of the bishop. The priest must proceed with prudence, strictly observing the rules established by the Church (n. 1673).

On 26 January 1999 the Congregation for Divine Worship and the Discipline of the Sacraments published a new rite of exorcism in the Roman Ritual. The Latin text is 80 pages long and English translation is not expected for some time.

8. Compare with the New Code of Canon Law of the Roman Catholic Church: 'No one may lawfully exorcise the possessed without the special

permission of the local Ordinary. This permission is to be granted by the local Ordinary only to a priest who is endowed with piety, knowledge, prudence and integrity of life' (Canon 1172).

9. Jim McManus, Provincial of the Redemptorists in the UK, says that he prays with individuals for deliverance in silence in *Healing in the Spirit: Inner Healing and Deliverance in Today's Church,* Darton, Longman & Todd, 1994, pp. 113–15.

The ICD – 10 Classification of Mental and Behavioural Disorders, World Health Organization, 1992.

Chapter 10: Complementary Medicine and Alternative Approaches to Healing and Good Health

1. *The Church's Ministry of Healing: Report of the Archbishops' Commission,* Church Information Board, 1958, p. 80.

2. Ibid, p. 84

3. RCCM, *Public Usage of Complementary Medicine: An Overview,* Research Council for Complementary Medicine Information Service, London, 1997.

4. Thomas et al., *National Survey of Access to Complementary Health Care via General Practice,* University of Sheffield, August, 1995.

5. The Foundation for Integrated Medicine, *Integrated Healthcare: A Way Forward for the Next Five Years,* The Foundation for Integrated Medicine on behalf of the Steering Committee for The Prince of Wales's Initiative on Integrated Medicine, 1997.

6. See note 3.

7. See note 5.

8. International Self-Realization Healing Association, *Code of Conduct for Healers,* provided with reply to the survey, 1999.

9. Dr Philippe Pien, 'Integrated Chronotherapy Method', *Journal of Natural Medicine,* vol.3, Issue 1, Spring 1999.

Wilfred Barlow, *The Alexander Principle*, Victor Gollancz, 1991.

British Medical Association, *Complementary Medicine: New Approaches to Good Practice*, Oxford Medical Publications, 1993.

Philip M. Chancellor, *The Illustrated Handbook of the Bach Flower Remedies*, The C. W. Daniel Company, 1991.

Dr Robina Coker, *Alternative Medicine: Helpful or Harmful?*, Monarch, 1995.

Stephen Fulder, *The Handbook of Alternative and Complementary Medicine*, Oxford University Press, 1996.

Dr Christopher Hammond, *How To Use Homeopathy*, Element Books, 1991.

Marc S. Micozzi (ed.), *Fundamentals of Complementary and Alternative Medicine*, Churchill Livingstone, 1996.

The Mission Theological Advisory Group, *The Search for Faith and the Witness of the Church,* Church House Publishing, 1996.

John P. Newport, *The New Age Movement and the Biblical Worldview*, Eerdmans, 1998.

Penelope Ody, *The Herb Society's Complete Medicinal Herbal*, Dorling Kindersley, 1993.

Michael Perry, *Gods Within: A Critical Guide to the New Age*, SPCK, 1992.

The Radionic Association, *Radionic Journal*, Winter 1998.

Wanda Sellar, *The Directory of Essential Oils*, The C. W. Daniel Company, 1992.

Peter Spink, *A Christian in the New Age*, Darton, Longman & Todd, 1991.

Robert Tisserand, *The Art of Aromatherapy*, The C. W. Daniel Company, 1992.

Charles Vincent and Adrian Furnham, *Complementary Medicine: A Research Perspective*, John Wiley & Sons, 1997.

Charles Vincent and Adrian Furham, 'Complementary medicine: state of the evidence', *Journal of the Royal Society of Medicine*, vol. 92, April 1999.

James Watt (ed.), *The Church, Medicine and The New Age*, Churches' Council for Health and Healing, 1995.

Linda Wilson, *Working in Complementary Therapies*, How To Books, 1998.

Chapter 11: Evidence for Healing

1. Morris Maddocks, *A Healing House of Prayer*, Eagle, 1998, p. 8.

2. Wayne Gruden, *Systematic Theology: An Introduction to Biblical Doctrine*, Inter-Varsity Press, 1994, p. 368.

3. Eamon Duffy, *Saints and Sinners: A History of the Popes*, Yale University Press, 1997, p. 191. In passing we note that questions have been asked about how far these conditions have been kept for the many canonizations authorized by Pope John Paul II in recent years.

4. The Medical Bureau at Lourdes: tel: (33) 5 62 42 79 08; fax: (33) 5 62 42 79 77; email: bmedical@lourdes-france.com. The Catholic Media Office, 39 Ecclestone Square, London SW1V IBX; tel: 020 7828 8709; fax: 020 7931 7678; email: cathmedia@easynet.co.uk. There is nothing in the new Code of Canon Law or the Catechism of the Catholic Church relating to a formal declaration of a miracle.

5. Ibid.

6. *The Church's Ministry of Healing: Report of the Archbishops' Commission*, Church Information Board, 1958, p. 28.

7. Ibid.

8. Jack Dominian, the Roman Catholic psychiatrist, has used psychological methods and models to discuss the humanity of Jesus in *One Like Us*, Darton, Longman & Todd, 1998. Although his use of Scripture is devotional rather than academic, his reflections are thought-provoking.

9. Quoted by Tom Smail in a lecture reported in *Wholeness*, no. 34, March–April 1998.

Chapter 12: Questions People Ask about the Healing Ministry

1. See the discussion of the meaning of these biblical words in John Wilkinson, *Health and Healing,* Handsel Press, 1980.

Chapter 13: Healing Services in the Church of England

1. *The Church's Ministry of Healing: Report of the Archbishops' Commission,* Church Information Board, 1958, p. 49.

2. Ibid, p. 54

3. *Report of the Lambeth Conference of 1958,* SPCK, 1958, paragraph 2.92.

Church of England official orders

Ministry to the Sick, Joint Publishers of the ASB, 1983.

Ministry at the Time of Death, Church House Publishing, 1991.

Patterns for Worship, Church House Publishing, 1995.

Common Worship: Pastoral Services (Church House Publishing, forthcoming) (also available as *Wholeness and Healing,* GS1152E, General Synod, 1999).

Other Anglican Provinces and other denominations

An Anglican Prayer Book 1989 (Church of the Province of Southern Africa), Collins Liturgical Publications, 1989.

A Pocket Ritual (excerpts from The Roman Ritual), Mayhew-McCrimmon, 1977.

Church Service Book (United Reformed), OUP, 1989.

Patterns and Prayers for Christian Worship (Baptist Union), OUP, 1991.

Book of Common Order of the Church of Scotland, St Andrew Press, 1994.

The Methodist Worship Book, Methodist Publishing House, 1999.

Other sources

Iona Community Worship Book, Wild Goose Publications, 1991.

Ian Cowie, *Prayers and Ideas for Healing Services,* Wild Goose Publications, 1995.

John Gunstone, *Prayers for Healing*, Highland Books, 1987.

Stuart Thomas, *To Minister His Grace*, Kevin Mayhew, 1995.

Individual services of prayer for healing from:

- ❖ York Minster
- ❖ Westminster Abbey
- ❖ The Church of Christ the Healer, Burrswood
- ❖ Divine Healing Mission, Crowhurst
- ❖ Diocese of Bath and Wells.

Chapter 14: Developing the Healing Ministry in the Parish

1. Sean McDonagh, *To Care for the Earth: A Call to a New Theology,* Geoffrey Chapman, 1986.

2. *Meeting the Challenge: How Churches Should Respond to Sex Offenders*, Board of Social Responsibility Occasional Paper 1, July 1999.

3. Part of a prayer attributed to St Teresa of Avila.

4. *General Synod July Group of Sessions 1998 Report of Proceedings*, vol. 29, no. 2, debate on 'The Misuse of Drugs: Report by the Board for Social Responsibility'.

David Aldridge, *One Body: A Healing Ministry in your Church*, SPCK, 1987.

Andrew Boyd, *Dangerous Obsessions: Teenagers and the Occult*, Marshall Pickering, 1996.

Ian Cowie, *Prayers and Ideas for Healing Services*, Wild Goose Publications, 1995.

Stephen Fulder, *The Handbook of Alternative and Complementary Medicine*, Oxford Medical Publications, 1996.

Richard Giles, *Re-pitching the Tent*, Canterbury Press, 1999.

John Gunstone, *Prayers for Healing*, Highland Books, 1987.

George Hacker, *The Healing Stream*, Darton, Longman & Todd, 1998.

Gerard W. Hughes, *God of Compassion*, Hodder & Stoughton, 1998.

Neville A. Kirkwood, *A Hospital Handbook on Multiculturalism and Religion*, Morehouse Publishing, 1993.

Roy Lawrence, *Make Me a Channel*, Scripture Union, 1996.

Roy Lawrence, *The Practice of Christian Healing*, Inter-Varsity Press, 1996.

Kenneth Leech, *Drugs and Pastoral Care*, Darton, Longman & Todd, 1998.

Giles Legood (ed.), *Chaplaincy: The Church's Sector Ministries*, Cassell, 1999.

Matthew Linn, Sheila Fabricant Linn, Dennis Linn, *Healing the Eight Stages of Life*, Paulist Press, 1988.

Matthew Linn, Sheila Fabricant Linn, Dennis Linn, *Healing Religious Addiction*, Darton, Longman & Todd, 1995.

Andrew Linzey, *Animal Rites,* SCM Press, 1999.

Andrew Linzey, *Animal Theology,* SCM Press, 1994.

Anne Long, *Listening*, Darton, Longman & Todd, 1990.

Dr Kenneth McAll, *Healing the Family Tree,* Sheldon Press, 1994.

Marc S. Micozzi (ed.), *Fundamentals of Complementary and Alternative Medicine,* Churchill Livingstone, 1996.

Henri J. M. Nouwen, *Wounded Prophet,* Darton, Longman & Todd, 1999.

John Penton, *Widening the Eye of the Needle: Access to Church Buildings for People with Disabilities*, Church House Publishing, 1999.

Michael Perry, *Gods Within: A Critical Guide to the New Age,* SPCK, 1992.

Ronald Rolheiser, *Seeking Spirituality*, Hodder & Stoughton, 1998.

Barbara Shlemon Ryan, Dennis Linn and Matthew Linn, *To Heal as Jesus Healed*, Resurrection Press, 1997.

Jean Vanier, *Becoming Human*, Darton, Longman & Todd, 1999.

James Woodward (ed.), *Embracing the Chaos: Theological Responses to AIDS*, SPCK, 1990.

Appendix 1: Good Practice in the Healing Ministry

Resources considered and used in the preparation of the appendix and the House of Bishop's draft guidelines include the following:

The Association of Christian Counsellors, *Code of Ethics*.

The Bishop of Liverpool's Panel for the Ministry of Healing, *Wholeness and Healing: Some Basic Guidelines*, 2nd. edn, 1997.

British Association for Counselling, *Code of Ethics and Practice for Counsellors*, January 1998; *Code of Ethics and Practice for Supervisors of Counsellors*, January 1996; *Code of Ethics and Practice for Trainers*, January 1997.

British Psychological Society, *Code of Conduct: Ethical Principles and Guidelines*, July 1998.

Churches' Council for Health and Healing (CCHH), *Guidelines for Good Practice*, Methodist Publishing House, October 1997.

College of Health Care Chaplains, *Code of Professional Conduct*.

Diocese of Norwich, *Tend My Flock: Good Practice in Pastoral Care*.

Diocese of Oxford, *Code of Ministerial Practice*, Pentecost 1996.

Division of Clinical Psychology of the British Psychological Society, *Professional Practice Guidelines*, 1995.

The House of Bishops' Policy on Child Protection, Church House Publishing, 1999.

The House of Bishops' Guidelines on the Deliverance Ministry (1975).

General Medical Council, *Good Medical Practice*, July 1998; *Maintaining Good Medical Practice*, July 1998.

Methodist Church, *Some Elements of Pastoral Practice: A Discussion Document*, Methodist Publishing House.

Network of Christians in Psychology, *Guidelines on the Involvement of Christian Psychologists in the Provision of Psychotherapy and Counselling to Local Church Communities,* Working Paper, 1995.

The United Kingdom Central Council for Nursing, Midwifery and Health Visiting, *Code of Professional Conduct for the Nurse, Midwife and Health Visitor.*

Working Party of the Biennial Consultation of Diocesan Advisors in Pastoral Care and Counselling, *Standards of Practice in Pastoral Care,* February 1995.

Index